WDSC: Step by Step

WDSC
Step by Step

A Practical Guide to Becoming Proficient in WebSphere Development Studio Client

Joe Pluta

MC PRESS

First Edition

Second Printing—March 2005

© 2004 MC Press Online, LP
ISBN: 1-58347-051-4

Corporate Offices
125 N. Woodland Trail
Lewisville, TX 75077 USA

Sales and Customer Service
P.O. Box 4300
Big Sandy, TX 75755-4300 USA

www.mcpressonline.com

This book is dedicated to my baby boy, Anthony. Before you came into my life, I had never seen an angel, and now I get to hold one every day.

Acknowledgements

As I write books, I learn more and more. My last book, *Eclipse: Step by Step*, was the first in the MC Press *Step by Step* series. It was well-received, but at the same time, people did ask for some changes to the approach. In this book, I kept true to the *Step by Step* philosophy: I took nothing for granted and walked you through each step in the process. But I also did some things a bit differently in response to what you, my readers, asked for. So the moral of the story is that you should ask for what you want; you just might get it!

Eclipse, because of its fast-paced evolution, was a challenging topic. WDSC is another challenging subject, for the same reasons. WDSC continues to evolve, and some of the features explained in this book are so new that there is no public documentation anywhere else on the planet. Kudos to IBM's George Farr and Phil Coulthard for this wonderful product. Also, ongoing thanks to each of the teams that contribute to the technological underpinnings of WDSC. Without the Eclipse and WebSphere Studio development teams, there would be nothing to build WDSC on top of. You're all incredible folks putting out an insanely powerful product.

I have to thank my family, but particularly my wife, Lisa, and my incomparable stepdaughter, Kelly: Without their support, this book wouldn't have made it to press. Baby Anthony gets acknowledged just because he's the baby and he's beautiful!

And as always, I need to thank Merrikay Lee of MC Press for allowing me this opportunity yet again. I always say this is my last, but somehow, somewhere along the line, she and I decide that I'll do another one. So here's to another one…

Contents

Foreword

By Jon Paris

WDSC is probably the best thing to ever happen to iSeries programmers—well at least since the introduction of RPG IV anyway! But WDSC is a big thing to get your arms around. It is the Swiss Army knife of development tools, encompassing everything from tools for maintaining your old green-screen applications to tools for developing the latest and greatest in Java and XML-powered Web applications.

Together with my partner Susan Gantner, I have been educating developers on the iSeries workstation development tools for many years, going back to the early days of the original OS/2-based CODE/400 product, in fact. So when WDSC came along, it was a natural to add to our education offerings. We soon found, though, that not only was there an enormous amount to learn, but there was very little in the way of printed information. We found lots of online documents, but it was difficult to navigate through them *and* perform the tasks at the same time. It was easier to learn by trial and error and believe me there have been many of those along the way!

But even after using the product for two years, there were still areas of the tool that I wanted to know more about but had not had a chance to fully explore. And the opportunity to learn about those was the reason I was foolhardy enough to volunteer to tech edit this book for Joe. While the two of us have had many heated discussions on iSeries development topics over the years, we definitely agree on one thing: The future of iSeries development depends on integrating the best of the traditional methods with the best of the new. Throwing the "RPG baby" out with the bathwater makes no sense. Blending RPG IV with Java and JSPs is a potent mixture that is tough to beat and makes far more sense. WDSC gives you the tools to make this vision a reality.

So if you are setting out to discover the joys of WDSC, where do you start? The answer is right here in your hands. Joe has produced an excellent step-by-step guide that will lead you through the major tool components needed to design and maintain tomorrow's iSeries applications. In his own inimitable style, Joe manages to highlight WDSC's strengths while also informing the reader of its weaknesses and foibles. He has also succeeded admirably in the most difficult task of all: making the process both educational and entertaining!

I not only thoroughly enjoyed reading this book, I also learned a lot, and I'm sure you will, too.

Foreword

Welcome to the third book in the MC Press *Step by Step* series, *WDSC: Step by Step*.

If you are an iSeries programmer looking to learn how to take advantage of the incredible set of tools that make up WebSphere Development Studio Client for iSeries (WDSC), then this is the one book you need. This is not a reference book; it is a tutorial. This book uses the features of WDSC as they would be used in the course of developing a real-world application. In fact, even if you're a Web application designer who has no plans to touch the iSeries, this book can still provide essential insight into portions of WDSC you might not know existed, such as the template language used to generate navigation bars.

But it is green-screen programmers who will find this book invaluable. *WDSC: Step by Step* is designed to entirely demystify WDSC in one fast-paced, easy-to-follow tutorial. By the end of this book, you will have used over a dozen different tools and techniques to design, develop, and deploy a fully functioning client/server Web application.

The book is backed by forums and an online demonstration of the program you will be building. You can look at the online extensions of the book here:

 http://forums.plutabrothers.com/books

The Web application uses RPG for its business logic. My philosophy is not that green-screen programmers need to *replace* their skills, but instead that they need to *enhance* their skills, and *WDSC: Step by Step* is designed to do exactly that. You start with an empty workbench, build a simple Web site, apply a standard look and feel, and eventually call an RPG program to load your Web site with dynamic content.

You do not need to know Java, you do not need to know HTML, and you do not need to know Eclipse. Knowledge in any of these areas will make the corresponding steps go more quickly, but this book was designed with traditional iSeries programmers as the primary audience. All source is provided on the accompanying CD-ROM, along with in-depth code reviews that you can refer to in your own time.

Because WDSC is so flexible, most of the chapters in the book (we call them "Steps") can be completed without any connection to the host. That means you can actually do most of the steps of this book on a laptop or on a home computer with no iSeries connection. Only the final steps that actually connect the Web portion of the application to the RPG back-end will require a connection to the host.

Another unique feature of this book is "checkpointing." A checkpointed step is one that you can start at any time. Let's say you really wanted to learn about how templates work. Step 4 is the place to start. You can copy the appropriate workspace off of disk and start right at that Step. Or perhaps after finishing the book, you decide you want to come back and review the section on JSP Model II in-depth. You could restart from Chapter 9. Or three months from now, you want to review how the Cascading Style Sheet (CSS) editor works. Just bring up the checkpoint for Chapter 5.

So why did I write this book? Well, I received lots of feedback from *Eclipse: Step by Step*, with the majority of it asking for more books like it—particularly one on WDSC. Well, this is that book. The same painstaking care that went into the original *Step by Step* book was poured into these pages. Programs work, images on the page match what you see on your screen, source compiles, pages display, and buttons function. Rather than provide a few unrelated examples that don't apply to the business of software development, *WDSC: Step by Step* shows you in a real-world environment what steps you need to take to create a working client/server application.

As in *Eclipse: Step by Step*, each step in this book has a checklist of tasks to perform, and each task is documented with screen shots and my editorial comments. Nothing is assumed, nothing left to your imagination. There is no magic in programming, except maybe knowing where to start, and that's where *Step by Step* comes in. The idea of a *Step by Step* book is that once you've finished it, you will understand the subjects well enough to continue learning more on your own. *WDSC: Step by Step* is no exception.

Green-screen programmers of the world unite! You have nothing to lose but SEU!

Joe Pluta
Pluta Brothers Design, Inc.
September 2004

Step 1

Welcome to WDSC!

And welcome to *WDSC: Step by Step*.

About the time this book goes to editing, the next version of WebSphere Development Studio Client for iSeries (WDSC) will be getting ready for release. The biggest additions to Version 5.1.2 are new support for JavaServer Faces and the integration of Enterprise Generation Language (EGL), a feature borrowed from WebSphere Studio Enterprise Developer. You'll also see enhancements to the various Web-enablement tools, such as WebFacing and HATS. I consider most of these to be "advanced" features, dealing specifically with the integration of Web applications and legacy systems. As with any other release, there are minor changes to the UI as well. Wherever changes have been made to the tool, I'll address them in the text. I have also included a complete addendum on the CD-ROM that includes screen shots for areas that have changed. SideStep 5 of the book addresses this addendum in detail.

But WDSC is much more than that. WDSC is like an amalgam of all the tools required to build a great application, from Web site design to application deployment. Combine FrontPage and Dreamweaver, mix in VisualAge for Java, and add a dash of Paint Shop Pro, and you begin to get an idea of the capabilities that WDSC brings to the table. Include on top of that the unique capabilities of the built-in CSS and XML editors, the ability to syntax check Java code within a JavaServer Page (JSP), and the flexibility of the template language, and you've got more than a Web site designer; you've got a Web application development environment that allows you to build all of your pieces in one coherent environment.

If that weren't enough already, you then add the unique testing and deployment capabilities of WDSC—from integrated JUnit testing to the WebSphere Test Environment, from hot deployment to WAR/EAR creation—and now you've got an unsurpassed Web development environment.

But that's only what WDSC brings to the table itself. WDSC is built on the Eclipse platform, so it's also able to include all of the great Eclipse plug-ins currently available—things ranging from high-end UML editors to SQL tools to editors for other languages.

So how can one book possibly teach you all of that? Well, it can't. What a book can do, though, is guide you through every step needed to create a dynamic, data-oriented Web site and make you comfortable and productive using the tool. For green-screen programmers especially, that means being able to use WDSC in place of the old green-screen and being introduced to the brave new world of GUIs and browsers.

Prerequisites

In order to do all this, there are a few prerequisites. Most importantly, you need to have WDSC installed on your machine. During the installation, you must also install the WebSphere Test Environment. So the machine needs to be a good-sized machine. These are the minimum requirements to run a full-blown WDSC session (including the WebSphere Test Environment):

1. A CPU of 2GHz or better

2. 1GB of RAM

3. 2GB of disk space

4. 1024×768 screen resolution *highly* recommended

5. Windows 2000 or better for Windows machines

That might look like a hefty machine, but if you plan to do development using today's generation of tools, that's a minimum (technically, you may squeak by on half the RAM and a slightly slower CPU, but you'll occasionally be dissatisfied with response times). Personally, I find that 1280×1024 is necessary if I plan to use the tools on a daily basis, but the specs I posted above are enough to get started.

With some judicious shopping on the Internet, you can find a machine with those specifications for under $1,000 US. It could be a little more if you go with a flat-screen monitor, which I find indispensable, but I write for a living.

As I said, you'll need to have WDSC installed on your machine, including the WebSphere Test Environment. That's where the 2GB of disk space goes. Not only that, you need to have everything up-to-date. As of this writing, the latest version of WDSC is Version 5.1.0.3. If you aren't quite sure how to upgrade WDSC, don't worry about it; I was confused, too. However, SideStep 1 provides documentation on the upgrade process.

For the client/server development, you'll need the following:

1. An iSeries at V5R1M0 or later

2. A value in your HOSTS file that points to the machine (the book assumes a name of WDSCHOST)

3. A user profile on the iSeries (the book assumes a name of WDSCUSER with a password of WDSCUSER) that is authorized to

    a. CRTLIB

    b. STRSRVJOB, ENDSRVJOB, STRDBG, ENDDBG

    c. The program Q5BATTACH in QSYS

Please note that these requirements are only necessary for the client/server portions of the book, starting at Step 11. Prior to that step, you don't even need to be connected to an iSeries; you can do all your development and testing right on your workstation.

Since a prerequisite is that you have already installed WDSC, I am going to assume that you have tried to load it. When you do load it, you get the following dialog:

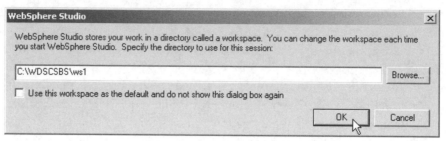

Figure 1-1: This is the startup dialog for WDSC.

I highly recommend the above setting. It will create a folder in your hard drive root called WDSCSBS, and then it will create a workspace called "ws1" within that folder (a workspace is just a hierarchy of folders). I suggest this because if you choose to use Checkpoints later, you want to know exactly where to copy those Checkpoints to, and if you follow the suggestion, you will always copy them to C:\WDSCSBS. (If you don't have enough room on your C: drive, substitute another drive letter, but still add WDSCSBS to the root.)

> **Warning:** Do *not* check the "Use this workspace as the default..." box. If you do, you'll have a hard time using different workspaces, and the ability to use different workspaces is one of the key productivity features of WDSC. It's also a requirement for the Checkpoint capabilities of this book.

> **Note:** If you do *not* get the above dialog, that means you've already started WDSC at some point in the past and checked the box "Use this workspace as the default...". Because of this, WDSC will not show the workspace prompt again. In order to re-enable this prompt, you must change the Windows Registry. This is not a simple process, nor is it recommended for those who are not Windows experts. However, without this change, it is difficult to use different workspaces, which I believe is a key to using WDSC. So, I highly recommend that you get the key changed; either do it yourself or have someone knowledgeable in Windows help you out. This is the key to change: HKEY_CURRENT_USER\Software\IBM\Websphere Studio\Workspace. In that key, you should see several values. One will be named wdsc510_status or wdscadv510_status, depending on whether you have WDSC Standard Edition or WDSC Advanced Edition installed. The data for this key will be Disable. If you change this value to Enable, the next time you start WDSC, you will see the prompt in Figure 1-1.

How It Works

The *Step by Step* books are very simple in format. The entire book is broken down into a series of sequential steps that are meant to be followed in order. Each Step will have a checklist. The checklist will look something like this:

❑ **1.1(a) Place toothpaste on the toothbrush.**

❑ **1.1(b) Brush teeth vigorously for two minutes.**

The number on the left refers to the Step (1.1, 1.2, 2.1…) and the task within that step (a, b, c…). The number on the right refers to the page where that particular task can be found.

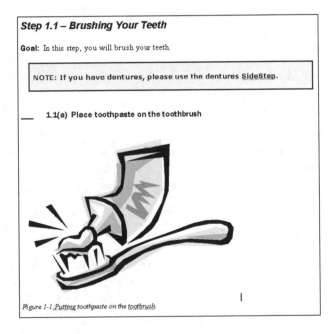

Each Step will start on a new page and will have a heading and a goal statement. There may be a paragraph or two of additional information as well. Each task will have detailed instructions and one or more associated illustrations (occasionally, several tasks will refer to the same image—for example, when you're being instructed how to fill out the fields of a dialog box).

Some of the steps may seem very simple, especially if you already have some experience in a given area, but I wanted to be sure not to leave anything out. If you follow all the Steps to the letter, by the time you finish the book, you will have completed the goal of creating a complete client/server Web application using WDSC.

SideSteps and InSteps

SideSteps are the *Step by Step* equivalent of appendices. These chapters are found at the end of the book, and they outline various procedures that are somewhat peripheral to the actual topic: upgrading WDSC, for example, or deploying an EAR file to WebSphere Express. InSteps, on the other hand, are detailed explanations of topics—explanations that aren't crucial to your finishing the book but provide additional insight to the topic.

What I'll Cover

In keeping with the spirit of the *Step by Step* series, *WDSC: Step by Step* will walk you through all of the areas of WDSC you would use to build a real, working application. Everything from basic Web site design to client/server programming will be covered. And it will all be done within the context of what you would encounter in your daily programming endeavors. By the end of the book, you will have created a working application that provides a Web interface to an RPG back-end on the iSeries, completely designed, written, and tested within the WDSC environment.

Web Site Development

Any good Web application development platform will provide the ability to create pages, manage them, and publish them. Web page development has become very complex, and a number of techniques are available, from ColdFusion to Perl. However, IBM's direction (and that of a good segment of the Web application world) is Sun's J2EE development paradigm, which centers on servlets and JSPs.

In addition, to create professional Web sites, you need to know how to create graphics, how to implement style sheets, and how to create a standard look and feel for your entire site. WDSC has tools for these areas, and you'll be introduced to all of them.

In the first section of the book you will:

1. Create a Web project for your Web site

2. Add Web pages

3. Organize your Web site

4. Apply a template

5. Create a logo

6. Modify your style sheets

7. Customize your navigation links

All of these steps will be done within the WDSC workbench, and by the time you're done, you'll have all the pieces for a working Web site.

Web Site Testing

Next, you'll be briefly introduced to one of the most powerful features of WDSC, the WebSphere Test Environment (or WTE). The WTE allows you to actually test your Web site right on your desktop *as if you had published it to a production Web application server.* This is a crucial productivity enhancement because it means you can actually test your entire Web site without having to go through the time-consuming process of deploying your application to a server. Not only that, but you can then debug the application right there on your desktop, setting breakpoints in the various pieces of your application. While you will only get a short initiation into the WTE, you'll be using it throughout the book, so rest assured that you'll become acquainted with it in as much detail as you need.

The productivity gains of the WTE alone are worth more than the cost of the tool, much less this book. By the way, I feel the need to mention that WDSC sells for about $2,400 US for a single-user license, but iSeries developers get it for free. It's *good* to be an iSeries developer!

Dynamic Web Sites

The next section of the book will cover dynamic Web site design. As I mentioned earlier, there are a number of designs, but I will introduce you to perhaps the most powerful design technique, JSP Model II.

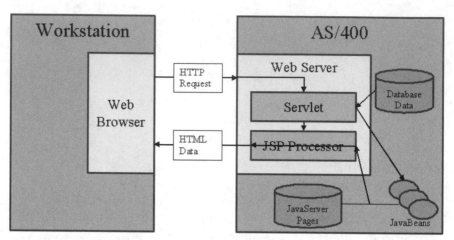

Figure 1-2: The JSP Model II architecture is very powerful.

In JSP Model II development, the servlet receives a request, reads database data to build Beans, and then passes the Beans to a JSP to render the data for the user. Sound familiar? It should, because it's basically the same thing we've been doing with green-screens since the early days of the midrange. You get a request from the user, you read data from the database and stick it into screen variables, and then you output a display file record to the user.

And while there are many ways to build Web sites, with lots of third-party and open-source tools and template engines to help you, in this book you'll do it all from the ground up, using the basic J2EE technology and WDSC. I'll explain each piece of the architecture so that you not only know how something works, but why it works the way it does. I'll also spend some time discussing the architecture so that you have a firm understanding of the pros and cons of the JSP Model II approach.

In addition, you'll be introduced to another facet of the WTE: the debugging mode. This is where the WTE becomes invaluable. You can set breakpoints in either the servlet or the JSP, and you can then do all the things you're used to doing in debugging: inspect variables, set watch points, even change variables on the fly. This is a far cry from the days of logging problems to "stdout" and digging through server execution dumps to try to find an error.

The iSeries Extensions

What really sets WDSC apart from its various ancestors is its rich set of extensions specific to the iSeries. Integration with various iSeries functions—from editing to compiling to debugging—continues to improve with each release. At this time, you can pretty much develop an entire application without having to ever sign on to a green-screen. There are some shortcomings—spooled file and native database viewers would be nice features to have—but WDSC is a formidable successor to the green-screen development tools we've come to love.

In *WDSC: Step by Step*, you'll run through the paces of editing, verifying, compiling, and debugging a simple program in order to get you familiar with these extensions. And after all of this, you're just getting started!

Multi-Language Development

One of the problems with tutorials is that they tend to be simple in nature and not very business-oriented. By the time you get around to applying this knowledge to a business application, you've forgotten what you learned. But the iSeries is all about business, and thus, so is WDSC. And the crowning achievement of this book is to take all the introductory material that you learned in the previous steps and *immediately* use it to create a real (albeit simple) business application. But unlike other tutorials, where the examples are somewhat standalone, in *WDSC: Step by Step* the object of the entire book is to have a single, cohesive Web site that has both static and dynamic information connected to an RPG back-end for business logic. You can then build from this foundation to make your own Web site, without having to worry about how you will integrate the various pieces. I've done all the integration for you!

Deployment

And finally, while I don't spend a lot of time on this particular subject, I do go through the basics of deploying a Web site like the one you'll build. The reason I don't spend a lot of time on this topic is because many different factors come into play when you are deploying Web applications. So rather than try to address every possible occurrence, I simply provide the basics. However, even though it's impossible to guess what your network configuration will be, I have included a couple of SideSteps that walk you through deployment on the server you are most likely to use: WebSphere Express on the iSeries. But please note that the rest of the book is entirely independent of what Web application server you use.

A Different Look

The MC Press *Step by Step* book series employs a technique of walking the reader through each step of a process visually via screen shots. But in *WDSC: Step by Step*, we've added something called "InSteps," which provide additional detail on a specific topic. If you're following the book's lessons step by step, you can just skip these InSteps. Then, at your leisure, you can read them to get more information on the topic or a detailed look at the actual code.

In order to fit everything I've mentioned into one book, I must assume a certain degree of Integrated Development Environment (IDE) knowledge. For example, I'm going to assume you're relatively familiar with Windows and a mouse. While previous IDE experience is unnecessary, I'm also going to assume that you understand how pop-up menus work and what a right-click is. If these terms are foreign to you, you might want to pick up a copy of *Eclipse: Step by Step*. The first book in this series, *Eclipse: Step by Step* leaves *nothing* to the imagination and is a perfect introduction to the WDSC/Eclipse environment.

Additional Materials

WDSC: Step by Step includes a CD-ROM that contains hundreds of megabytes of supplementary materials.

Checkpoints

First are the Checkpoints. Please take the time to review SideStep 2 prior to beginning the book. In it, I explain the Checkpoint concept. But in a nutshell, Checkpoints are places where you can "restart" the book. That is, even if you haven't done all the preceding steps, by loading the appropriate Checkpoint data from the CD-ROM, you can start the book at (nearly) any arbitrary point.

There are two sets of Checkpoint data: workspaces, which are located in the folder Workspaces, and save files, which are located in the folder Savefiles.

Imports

These are the various source files in text form that you can copy and paste into your workbench at various points in the process. I suggest that you open the file in the text editor of your choice and then simply copy and paste the data into the appropriate source member as directed in the book.

Movies

These are short MPEG movie clips for some of the more involved procedures. This is a new and unique concept, and we're really looking for feedback from you, the readers.

jtopen_4_1_3

This folder contains the complete unzipped release of the latest JTOpen software at the time this book went to print. The JTOpen project is one that I am proud to be affiliated with. For more information, please stop by the Web site:

http://www-124.ibm.com/developerworks/oss/jt400/

We hope you enjoy *WDSC: Step by Step*! It's been a labor of love to write, and I only hope it's as productive to read as it was challenging to write.

Step 1.1—What Is WDSC?

Before I jump into the working of the product, I'd like to get one task out of the way, which is to get the product family straight. Dozens of products out there bear the WebSphere moniker, but the only ones that relate to this discussion are the WebSphere Studio tools. All are built on Eclipse, and all are related.

WebSphere Studio Site Developer (WSSD): This product provides a wide assortment of Web development tools, ranging from the Site Designer to the Image Designer. It turns Eclipse into a true Web application development environment.

WebSphere Studio Application Developer (WSAD): WSAD is essentially WSSD with EJB support added.

WebSphere Development Studio Client for iSeries (WDSC): WDSC is a free tool that all iSeries developers get, provided they have the WebSphere Development Studio product (currently 5722WDS) on the host box. This is WSSD plus the iSeries Extensions.

WDSC Advanced Edition (WDSC/AE): WDSC/AE is basically WDSC plus EJB support, although there are a few extras thrown in, such as enhanced WebFacing functionality.

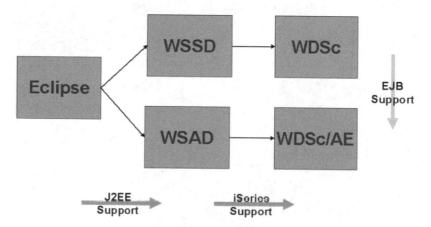

Figure 1-3: This shows the relationships between the various WebSphere Studio products.

Note that there is also a product on your iSeries called 5722WDS, which contains all the host-side pieces of the software. This replaced the individual compilers a few releases ago, and it contains all of the compilers as well as the host servers that support WDSC.

Step 2

The Web Site Designer

When you first start WDSC, you're brought to a page that looks like the one in Figure 2-1. Here, you set up all of your host connection information.

Release Note: The screenshots throughout the book assume Version 5.1.0.3. Minor differences can be expected for other releases. For example, what actually appears in the Welcome page depends on your release.

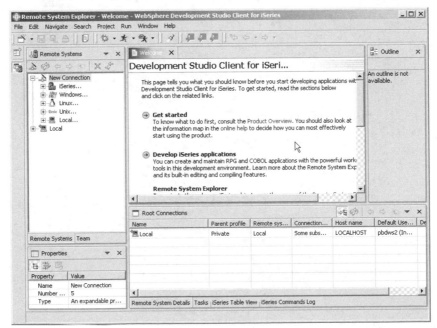

Figure 2-1: This is the initial screen you'll see after installing WDSC.

That's a good place to start for some situations, especially when you're using WDSC primarily as a replacement for SEU. But in this book, I'm going to cover the entire Web development process, from a basic Web site all the way up to a complete Web-based business application. And to do that, you'll need to start in the Web perspective.

This is the longest chapter in the book because it covers all of the basics of creating a Web site and adding pages. It also includes a number of InSteps that provide additional information on the topic. For example, InStep 2.1.a goes into some detail about the various views that make up the Web perspective.

Step 2.1—Open the Web perspective

> ## GOAL
>
> In this step, you will open the Web
> perspective using Eclipse's main menu bar.

There are three standard ways to switch perspectives. The first is to use the Window menu from the main menu bar. The second is to open a project of a type associated with a specific perspective. For example, if you attempt to create a dynamic Web project and you are not in the Web perspective, WDSC will ask if you'd like to switch to that perspective (this behavior can be turned off). A third method is to use the perspective icons. When you open a perspective, the icon for that perspective will appear in the icon list along the left side of the workbench. You can quickly select any open perspective by simply clicking on the appropriate icon.

Release Note: Menus frequently change between releases. For example, in V5.1.2, the Open Perspective submenu has two additional options, iSeries Projects and WebFacing. For this and other release-specific information, refer to SideStep 5.

In this step, you will use the first method.

❑ **2.1(a) From the main menu bar, select Window/Open Perspective/Other....**

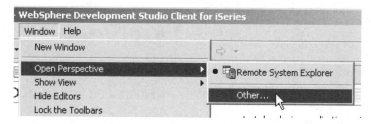

Figure 2-2: The Window menu on the main menu bar is a typical WDSC menu.

❑ **2.1(b) Roll down and select the Web perspective; then click OK.**

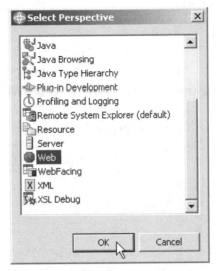

*Figure 2-3: The Select Perspective
wizard is one of dozens of wizards
in WDSC.*

The Web perspective will appear, as shown below.

Release Note: This perspective sometimes changes between releases, even between minor releases. Version 5.1.2 added a whole new pane on the left side for a couple of views called Page Data and Client Data. Refer to SideStep 5 for more information.

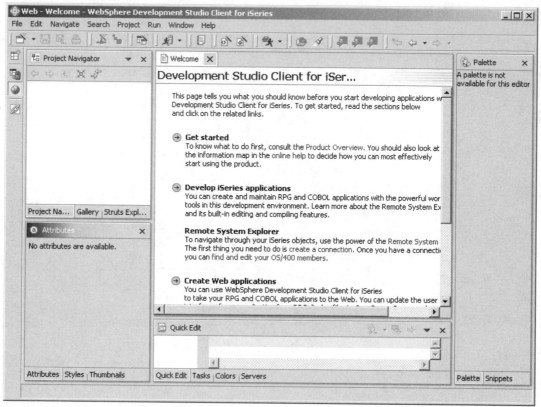

Figure 2-4: This is the Web perspective, where you'll do your initial development work.

For more information on the Web perspective, read InStep 2.1.a. Otherwise, continue to Step 2.2 to create your project and get started developing a Web site.

InStep 2.1.a—The Web perspective

The primary goal of a *Step by Step* book is to get you to a specific result as quickly as possible. However, some readers desire more in-depth information about the current topic than is required to proceed.

InSteps (a combination of In-Depth Step and Inline Step) present material that is optional; you need to read it only if you want more knowledge of the topic at hand. If you're not interested, you can simply skip ahead to the next step (in this case, Step 2.2).

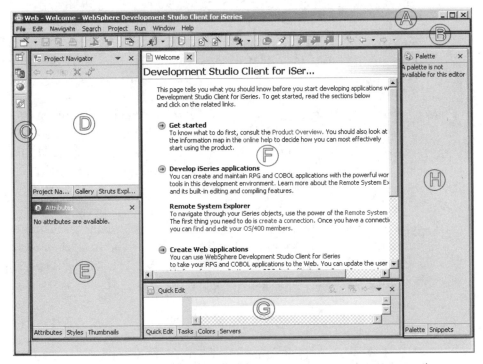

Figure 2-5: The Web perspective has features common to other perspectives as well as its own unique features.

If you're still with me, then you want more information on the Web perspective. Figure 2-5 shows the Web perspective with the various functional areas labeled. There are really two groups of these: The primary areas A, B, and C are common to just about every perspective, while the other areas are usually perspective-specific.

> **Note:** As I remarked in Step 2.1, Version 5.1.2 added a whole new pane on the left side between panes D and E. Refer to SideStep 5 for more information.

First, the common areas:

A: This is the main menu bar. The top-level items (File, Edit, and so on) rarely change, though the options within each menu may change based on the perspective. The Help option in particular provides lots of great options for learning the product.

B: This is the tool bar. Its icons change quite a bit. The icons on the far left represent standard options such as New, Save, Save As, and Print and tend to be present in every perspective, but after that, the icons are specific to the perspective. That isn't to say that some icons aren't shared between perspectives; it's just that, unlike the main menu bar, the tool bar may be almost entirely different from one perspective to the next.

C: This is the perspective bar. There are three segments to the perspective bar. The top segment contains a single icon. This icon is the tool for opening a new perspective. The next segment contains a list of open perspectives. In Figure 2-5, you can see two icons in this segment; these are the icons for the two perspectives currently open in the workbench: the Remote Systems Explorer (which came up by default) and the Web perspective (which you just opened). The bottom segment contains "Fast Views." These views are not visible in any panes in the workbench, but you can bring them up quickly by clicking on the Fast View icon. How many Fast Views there are depends on the perspective. In a later chapter, I'll show you how to create your own perspective and define your own Fast Views.

Next, the areas specific to the Web perspective:

D: This pane by default contains the Project Navigator view. Currently empty, this view will eventually allow you to navigate through all the components of all your

Web projects. Different perspectives have different navigators, each tuned specifically to that perspective's particular role. Also note that there are other views in this pane: the Gallery and the Struts Explorer. The Gallery allows you to search through a variety of images, while the Struts Explorer will help you build a Struts-based application using a graphical editor.

E: This is the Attributes view. Typically, it shows the attributes of the object currently selected in the editing pane. It usually is only active with HTML or JSP elements. There are other views as well. The Styles view is used when editing Cascading Style Sheet (CSS) files, while the Thumbnails view is used in conjunction with the Gallery view of the D pane. The Thumbnails view shows thumbnail representations of the objects in the folder selected in the Gallery view.

F: This is the primary editor pane. All editors show up in this pane. You can further subdivide this pane, stacking editors side by side or top and bottom. This allows you to edit multiple members simultaneously or easily cut and paste between them.

G: This is typically the status pane. You'll see console output down here, as well as the standard Tasks view, which contains a list of errors to fix and other things to do. The Quick Edit view is a way of quickly entering in small chunks of code, sort of like a macro. I don't use it that much. You'll also note the Servers tab; you can use this to check the status of your servers. The Colors tab provides a palette of standard colors that you can click on in order to get the corresponding hexadecimal notation to use with HTML and CSS source code.

H: The Palette pane usually contains a selection of several items: the Palette, the Outline, and Snippets. The Outline view is usually available when you're editing something; it shows the overall outline of it, as you might guess. It's very useful for Java and quite useful but a little quirky with HLL languages. The Snippets view is another macro view, and like Quick Edit, I don't use it often. On the other hand, I use the Palette all the time, at least when I'm editing HTML/JSP pages. This allows me to drag and drop widgets onto my page. Very powerful.

Step 2.2—Add a Web project

GOAL

In this step, you will create a new
Web project.

There are three types of Web projects in WDSC: static projects, dynamic projects, and template application projects. For the purposes of this step, it's only important to know that dynamic projects allow JSPs, which are the core of our entire architecture.

❑ **2.2(a) From the main menu bar, select File/New/Dynamic Web Project.**

*Figure 2-6: Select File/New/Dynamic Web Project
from the main menu bar.*

The Dynamic Web Project wizard appears, as shown in Figure 2-7. There are many advanced configuration options available when you create a dynamic Web project. You can either accept the default values or configure them yourself by selecting the "Configure advanced options" checkbox. In this step, however, you don't need to address those issues, so you can leave the box unselected. Click Finish, and the wizard will create your project. Once the wizard is done, you'll see a new Web project, as shown in Figure 2-8.

❑ **2.2(b) In the Project name field, enter 'MySite.'**

❑ **2.2(c) Leave Configure advanced options unchecked.**

❑ **2.2(d) Click the Finish button.**

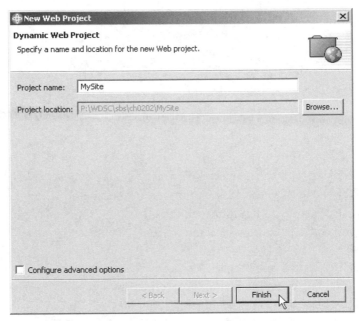

Figure 2-7: This is the Dynamic Web Project wizard.

This Web project will have been created with a number of default values, from the context root to the JSP version (MySite and 1.3, respectively). You might also notice that something else got created: DefaultEAR. This is not a Web project; it's an Enterprise Application Project. Enterprise Application Projects are exported as EAR files and are used to deploy applications to Web servers.

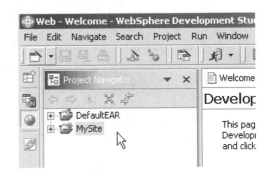

Figure 2-8: The MySite project has been created, along with something called DefaultEAR.

Note: Sometimes the default view is changed to the Struts Explorer, in which case you'll only see MySite, not DefaultEar. To get back in sync with the book, just click on the Project Navigator tab at the bottom of the pane.

Step 2.3—Open the Web Site Designer

The Web Site Designer is the primary editing tool for Web sites. If you've used Web site design tools like Microsoft FrontPage or Macromedia Dreamweaver, you will probably be familiar with the interface. But even if you haven't, don't worry; Web Site Designer is very intuitive.

To get started, expand the MySite project. In a tree view such as the one used in the Project Navigator, objects are either expanded or contracted. If an object is expanded, the object's children are displayed in the tree view as well, and the object will have a small minus sign (-) to the left of it. If an object is contracted, its children are not shown, and it has a plus sign (+) to the left. You can expand any contracted object by clicking on the plus sign for that object.

When the project MySite was created, it was created in contracted mode. In order to do more work, you'll have to expand it to get at its children. Click on its plus sign, as shown in Figure 2-9. You'll then see the view shown in Figure 2-10.

❑ **2.3(a) Expand the MySite project.**

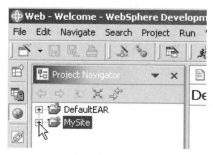

Figure 2-9: Expand the MySite project.

Once you've expanded a Web project, there are several ways to bring up the Web Site Designer. One way is to highlight the Web Site Configuration object, select option Open or Open With, and then choose Web Site Designer. The fastest way, though, is to simply double-click on the Web Site Configuration object. Most objects in WDSC have a default option that is invoked by double-clicking; for the Web Site Configuration object, this default action is to open it with Web Site Designer.

> **Release Note:** In V5.1.2, the name Web Site Configuration was changed to Web Site Navigation.

❑ **2.3(b) Double-click on the Web Site Configuration.**

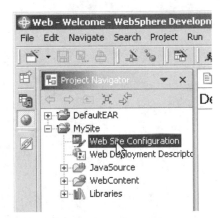

Figure 2-10: Double-click on the Web Site Configuration object to open the Web Site Designer.

Whichever method you choose, the next screen will be the one shown in Figure 2-11. The central editor view will now have a new tab called MySite, which is the Web Site Designer page for the MySite project. It's empty right now, but you'll fix that in the next step.

> **Release Note:** In V5.1.2, the new tab is called "Navigation - My Site," and the editor has a hint page designed to help you get started. Also, the palette on the right is not empty; it has a drawer named "Site" with a number of tools for configuring your site. Also, the JavaSource folder is renamed Java Resources, and the Libraries folder moves into that folder.

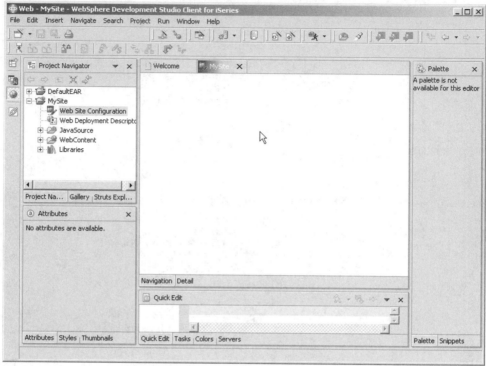

Figure 2-11: A new tab labeled MySite appears in the editor view; this is the Web Site Designer.

In Figure 2-11, you'll see that a new toolbar has been added (you can see an expanded version in Figure 2-12). This toolbar contains all the pertinent tools for Web Site Designer, from adding pages to changing the layout of the screen. You can do most options three ways: by using the toolbar, by right-clicking on the Web Site Designer view, or by using one of the main menu options (either Edit or Insert, depending on what you are trying to do). I still use the right-click approach, although the toolbar is probably just as easy. I just prefer keeping my mouse in the editing view as much as possible.

> **Release Note:** Like menus, toolbars frequently change between releases. Please check SideStep 5 for more information if you are on a release later than 5.1.0.3.

Figure 2-12: The Web Site Designer toolbar contains the standard Web Site Designer options.

Step 2.4—Add an HTML page

> ## GOAL
> In this step, you will add an HTML page to your Web site.

First, you need to add a top page. This is the root of your Web site, usually your home page. You can do that using the leftmost icon on the toolbar shown in Figure 2-12, or you can right-click inside the Web Site Designer view to bring up a context menu and select Add New Page/As Top. The second method is shown in Figure 2-13.

❏ **2.4(a) Right-click on the Web Site Designer view for MySite.**

❏ **2.4(b) Select Add New Page/As Top.**

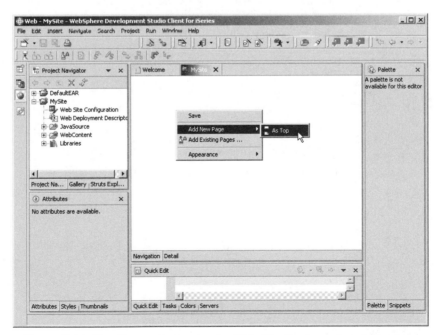

Figure 2-13: Use the context menu for Web Site Designer to add the top page.

You could also have used the main menu (Insert/Add Page/As Top), but I like the context menus because they keep me in the view I'm working on. You'll find context menus throughout WDSC, and they usually have most of the features you need, especially during editing. At other times, you'll want to have views up that make navigation easier, especially for opening source members. In Step 11, you will learn how to create your own perspective; this will allow you to create a customized interface containing only those views that you use most often.

Whichever method you choose, you will see the display shown in Figure 2-14. The new page appears with its navigation label highlighted so that you can rename it. This is the name used when creating navigation links, so give it a little thought. Also, the page appears inside a box made up of dashed lines. That's because you haven't actually added it yet; you've simply identified that a page belongs here.

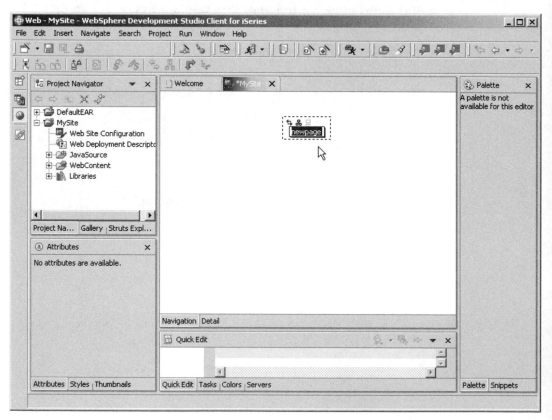

Figure 2-14: The newly added page appears, ready to edit.

Rename the page by typing in a name and pressing Enter. You will see the screen as shown in Figure 2-15.

❑ **2.4(c) Type "Index" and press Enter.**

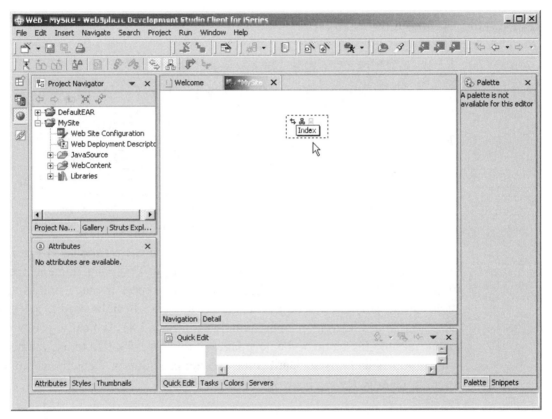

Figure 2-15: The page is now renamed for navigation purposes, but it still has not been created.

At this point, you've renamed the page so that it will appear correctly in the various navigation links (which I'll cover in a little more detail in Step 2.8). But the box is still dashed because you haven't yet created the page. To do that, simply double-click inside the dashed box. You'll see the pop-up shown in Figure 2-16, prompting you to enter the type of the page, either HTML or JSP. Select HTML and press OK to create an HTML (rather than JSP) page.

Release Note: V5.1.2 adds a new type, Faces JSP, but you still select HTML.

❑ **2.4(d) Double-click on the new Index page to bring up the Create a Page wizard.**

❑ **2.4(e) Select HTML and click OK.**

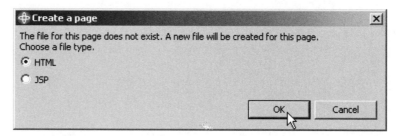

Figure 2-16: This pop-up prompts you for the type of the new page: HTML or JSP.

The next thing you see will be the New HTML File wizard shown in Figure 2-17, which allows you to quickly create an HTML page. This panel contains the required fields, and of those fields, the Folder, Markup Language, and Model fields are usually left at their defaults (the Model field can be used to select a template, but you'll learn more about templates in Step 2.8). Typically, you would enter only the file name of the new page. In this case, I'd like to use the name index.html. This fairly standard name is often used during Web application deployment to identify the top page of a Web site.

Release Note: The model field is not available in V5.1.2; instead, a checkbox labeled "Create from page template" appears. Leave that box unchecked.

❏ **2.4(f) Enter index.html into File Name, leave other fields, and click Finish.**

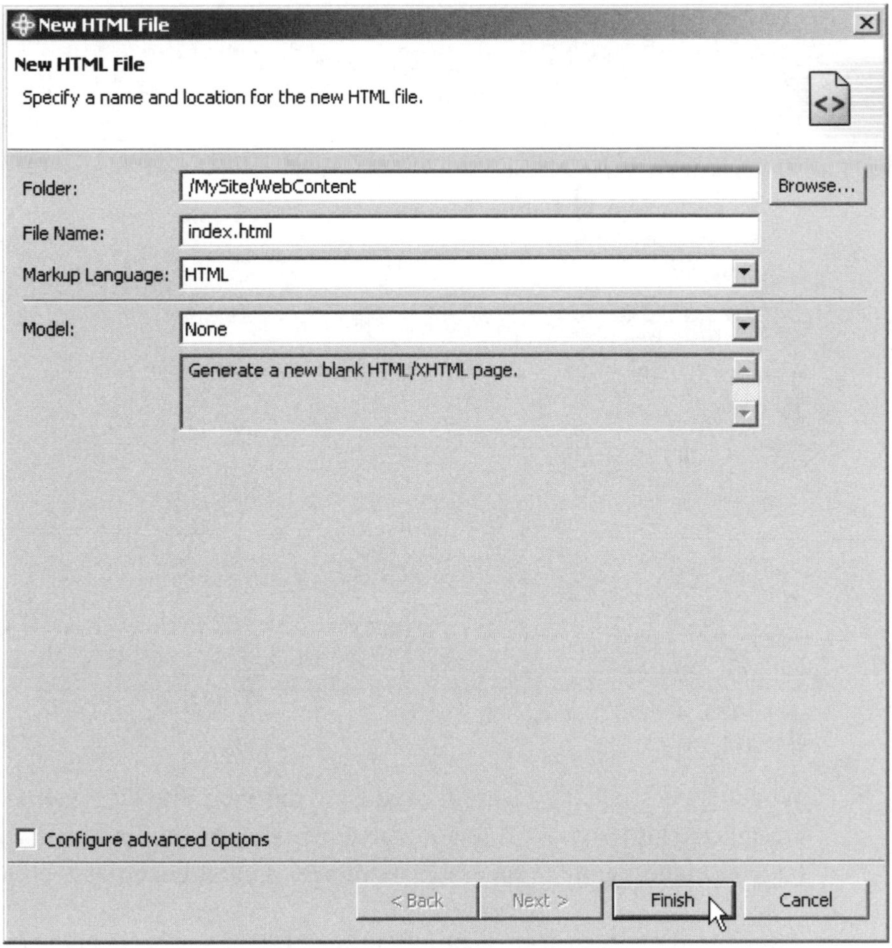

Figure 2-17: Enter index.html as the file name and click Finish.

This is going to cause the workbench to change dramatically to the screen you see in Figure 2-18.

Release Note: Like menus and toolbars, palettes are also subject to change between releases. Please refer to SideStep 5 for more information on releases later than V5.1.0.3.

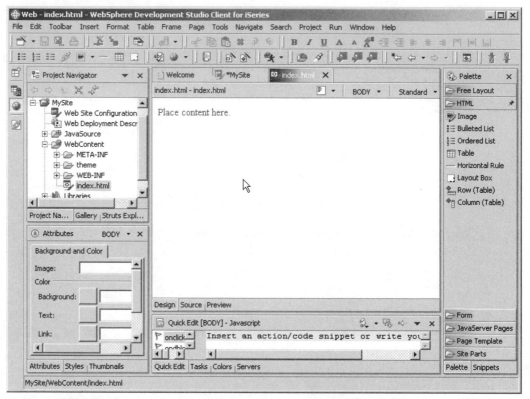

Figure 2-18: Adding a new page switches you from the Web Site Designer to the Page Designer.

What happens is that you are moved from the Web Site Designer to the Page Designer. This may take a few moments, especially the first time you do it, since Page Designer requires several parts of WDSC that have not been used until now.

Although the screen seems entirely different, that's not exactly true. But since many of the views are context-sensitive, they change. For example, the Attributes view in the lower left pane changes to the attributes of the current tag. Since we aren't in a specific tag, it shows the attributes of the BODY tag for the entire HTML document. You could now change the color or the background image simply by modifying the appropriate field in the Attributes view.

Similarly, the Quick Edit view changes to allow you to interact with the BODY tag. The Palette view also changes to allow you to add new widgets directly to the newly created page. An entire book could be written on the functionality of the Page Designer, but this book's focus is a working JSP application, so we need to move ahead. I'll show you quickly how to modify the page, and then you'll save and move on.

On the bottom of the editor panel, you'll see three tabs: Design, Source, and Preview. These indicate the current mode of the Page Designer. In Design mode, which is what you see in Figure 2-18, the editor panel acts as a WYSIWYG design tool, allowing you to directly manipulate and change the HTML widgets on the screen. By clicking on the Source tab, you get to Source mode (Figure 2-19), where the editor allows you to directly edit the source of the HTML page. Finally, clicking on Preview mode changes the editor panel into an IE-compatible browser window that you can use to test the look and feel of your new page, as in Figure 2-20. Be warned that the Preview mode is only meant as a preview of the current page; it tends to not navigate well to other pages, and it cannot help you test JSP pages. That is done via the WebSphere Test Environment, which is covered starting in Step 6.

❑ **2.4(g) Click on the Source tab at the bottom of the editor.**

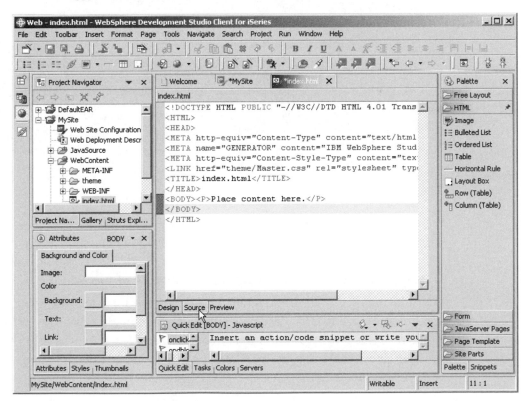

Figure 2-19: This is Source mode.

❑ **2.4(h) Click on the Preview tab at the bottom of the editor.**

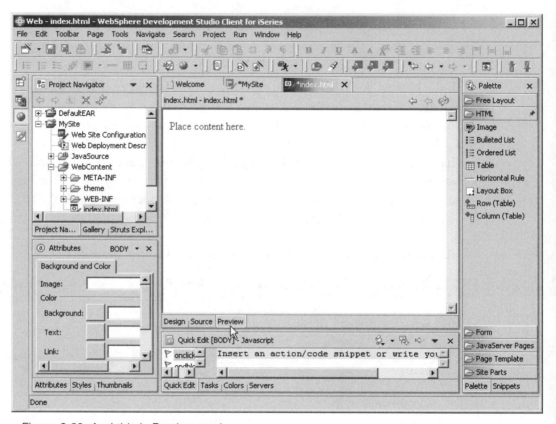

Figure 2-20: And this is Preview mode.

You cannot edit this screen. To edit the screen, you need to be in Source or Design mode. Click on the Design tab to re-open the WYSIWYG editor.

❑ **2.4(i) Click on the Design tab at the bottom of the editor.**

You'll be returned to the same screen you saw in Figure 2-18. Now, you can edit the screen. Notice that the designers left a nice little marker that says "Place content here." This is where your primary content goes. It's somewhat obvious in this situation, but when you use a template, it's nice to know where the non-template body information starts.

To edit the content, simply highlight it using standard mouse controls. You can double-click and drag or use shift-click to highlight blocks of information. In this case, highlight the phrase "Place content here" as shown in Figure 2-21.

❑ **2.4(j) Select the phrase "Place content here."**

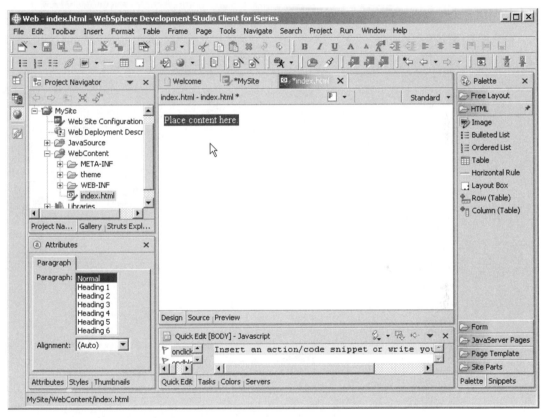

Figure 2-21: Highlight the phrase "Place content here."

Notice that the Attributes view in the lower left pane changes as well. Since you have highlighted text, the Attributes view allows you to specify paragraph tags, such as H1 (Heading 1), and also allows you to specify the alignment. When you change a different kind of tag, the Attributes view shows the appropriate fields for that tag.

Changing the contents of text is especially easy. Simply type the new text. In this case, type "This is the index page." As you type, a box will appear around the paragraph. Click outside the paragraph box to exit it. Your screen will change as shown in Figure 2-22.

❑ **2.4(k) Type "This is the index page" and click outside the paragraph.**

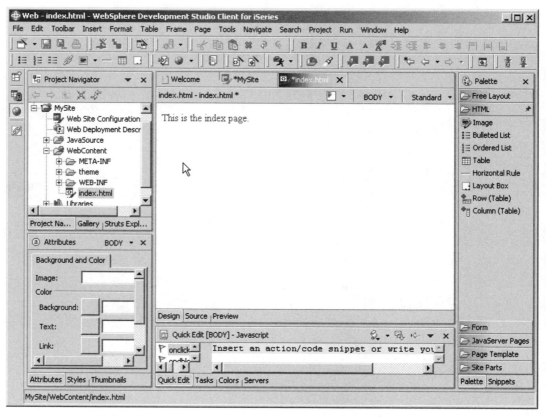

Figure 2-22: The workbench looks like this after you've changed the text.

Now that the page has been added, you can get back to your general Web design by using the MySite tab in the Editor view. Click on that tab, and your workbench will look like Figure 2-23.

□ **2.4(l) Click on the MySite tab.**

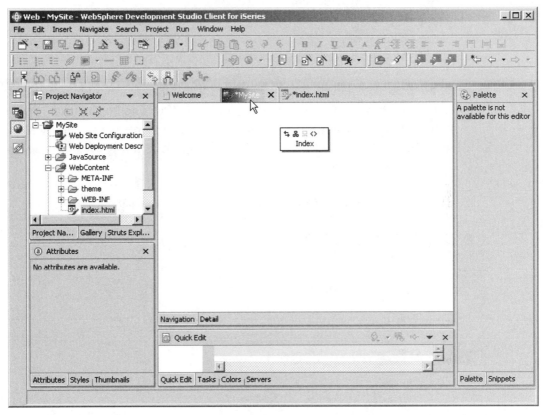

Figure 2-23: This is the Web Designer after you've successfully added the index.html page.

The box around Index (your index.html page) is no longer dashed. This indicates that the page has actually been added. However, one important point to remember is that WDSC does a lot of "temporary" changes. Since making things permanent can require a lot of resources, WDSC often does the minimum amount necessary to identify your changes and then allows you to actually execute those changes at your discretion. It's sort of like commitment control; the changes aren't actually applied to the database until you explicitly apply them. Occasionally, this can cause a problem, especially if your workstation locks up for some reason, so I suggest that you save your changes as often as is practical.

Since this is an important issue, it's nice that WDSC provides an easy way to identify whether changes are pending. You'll notice that the names in some of the tabs in the Editor view are preceded by an asterisk (*). See Figure 2-24.

Figure 2-24: Asterisks preceding the names indicate objects with pending changes.

These asterisks indicate objects that need to be changed. In our case, both the index.html page and the entire Web site MySite need to be changed. Since there's more than one, the easiest way is to use the main menu and select File/Save all, as in Figure 2-25. You'll see the asterisks disappear, as in Figure 2-26, and it will then be time to move to Step 2.5.

❑ **2.4(m) From the Main Menu, select File/Save All.**

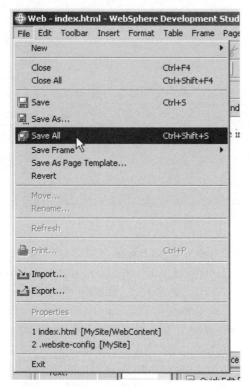

Figure 2-25: Use the main menu's File/Save All command to apply all pending changes.

Figure 2-26: And you're done!

Step 2.5—Add a JSP page

Adding a JSP page is very much the same as adding an HTML page, especially if you don't use the advanced features on the Add JSP Page wizard. In this step, you'll add a JSP called (with a marked lack of creativity) JSP1.jsp. JSP1 will also be its navigation label for now. Remember when I said you should be careful entering your navigation labels? Well, that still holds, but we're going to relax the rule a little bit. Later, I'll show you how to rename the pages, and you'll see how that affects your site design. For now, though, you'll just use a nice placeholder name.

❑ **2.5(a) Select Index by left-clicking on it.**

This will get you to Figure 2-27.

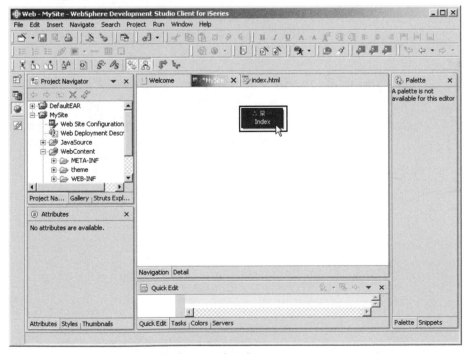

Figure 2-27: Left-click on Index to select it.

This time, I'll show you how to use the toolbar to add a page. If you move your cursor to the farthest left icon in the Web Site Designer toolbar, a caption will pop up reading "Add New Page as Child," as shown in Figure 2-28.

Release Note: Remember that toolbars and positions change from release to release. You can also reposition them yourself, so don't be alarmed if the toolbar does not appear exactly as depicted here.

Caution: Be *sure* it says Add New Page as Child. If you did not correctly select the Index page in 2.5(a), this tool will instead be captioned "Add new page to top level" and will not add the page as a child of Index.

Figure 2-28: Use the toolbar to add a child.

❑ **2.5(b) Click on the tool captioned 'Add New Page as Child.'**

This will add a new page directly below Index, as shown in Figure 2-29.

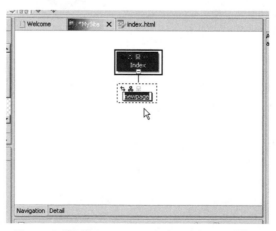

Figure 2-29: Your new page has been added.

And just like it did when you added the first page, the Web Site Designer again selects the navigation label to allow you to change it immediately. To do that, just type in the new name (in this case, JSP1) and press Enter.

❑ **2.5(c) Type "JSP1" and press Enter.**

Your new page will be renamed as shown in Figure 2-30.

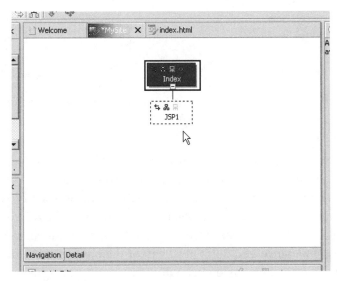

Figure 2-30: The name has been changed to JSP1.

Although you have added a new page, you still haven't told the Web Site Designer what kind of page it is, which is indicated by the fact that the box around JSP1 is made of dashed lines. Following the same procedure you took in Step 2.4, double-click on the newly added JSP1 to bring up the Create a Page wizard. Then, select type JSP and click OK.

❏ **2.5(d) Double-click on the JSP1 page to bring up the Create a Page wizard.**

❏ **2.5(e) Select JSP and click OK.**

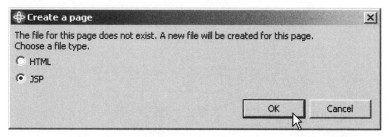

Figure 2-31: Select JSP this time, so that you add a JSP rather than a static HTML page.

Now, you will see the New JSP File wizard. This first page of the wizard is very similar to the New HTML File wizard from Step 2.4.f, with a couple of extra checkboxes. As with the HTML Wizard, you can specify advanced configuration options that, in addition to the advanced features of HTML, also include the ability to specify tag libraries, special methods, and additional deployment information. However, since you don't need any of the advanced features, you simply need to enter the file name and click OK.

Release Note: Like the New HTML File wizard, later versions of the New JSP File wizard add a checkbox called "Create from page template." Leave it unchecked.

❑ **2.5(f) Enter JSP1.jsp into File Name, leave other fields, and click OK.**

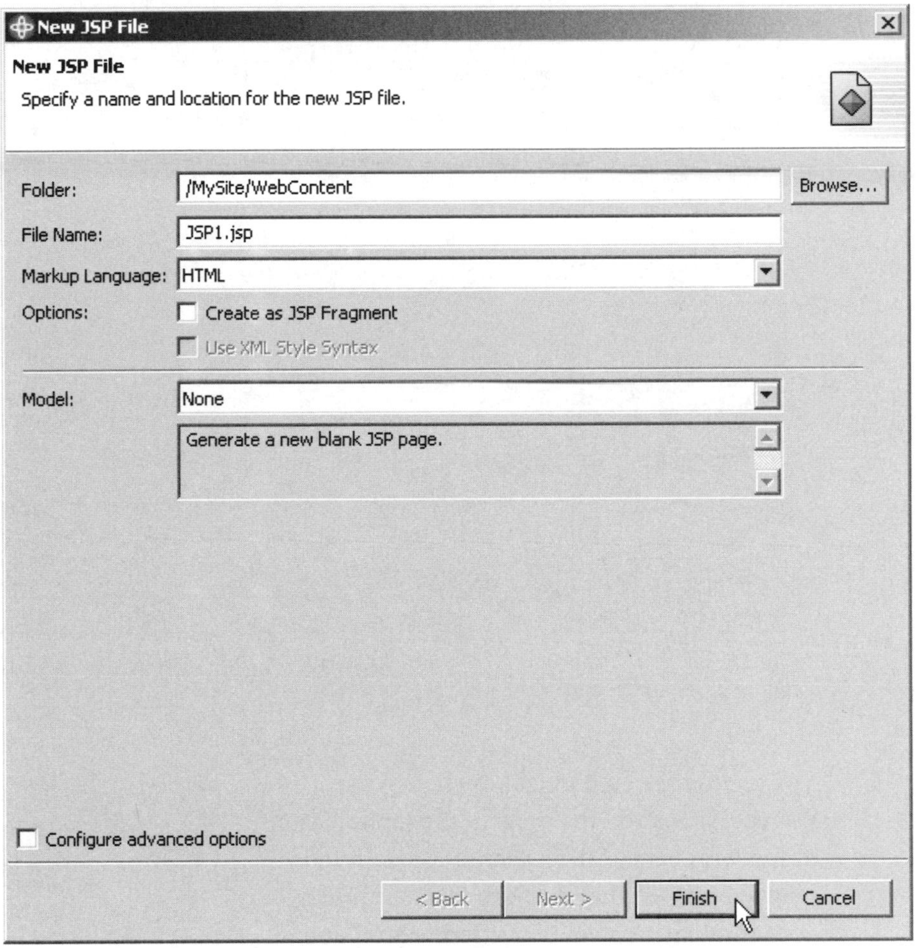

Figure 2-32: The only thing not defaulted correctly is the file name. Enter JSP1.jsp.

This will invoke the Page Designer, and you will get a screen like the one in Figure 2-33, which looks almost identical to the one you saw in Figure 2-18 after Step 2.4.f. That's because the Page Designer works on both HTML and JSP pages.

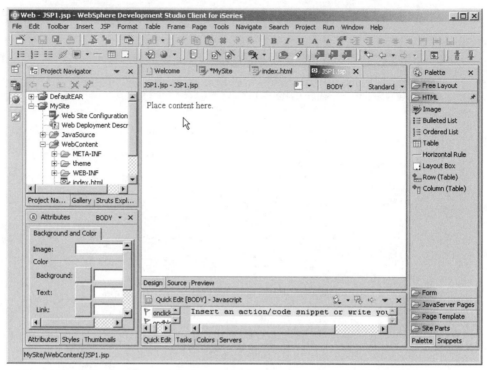

Figure 2-33: Since JSP and HTML are quite similar, the WYSIWYG screen is also relatively unchanged.

You should take a moment to check your Project Navigator, the view in the top left pane of the workbench. If you scroll down in that view, you'll see that the Web Content folder now contains two new files: index.html and JSP1.jsp.

Right now, the files index.html and JSP1.jsp are at the "root" of your application context. If your application becomes too complex for such a simple structure, you can use Project Navigator to create folders and segregate your pages. Using Project Navigator allows WDSC to update the links, thus allowing your application to continue to navigate properly.

Figure 2-34: Find JSP1.jsp in the Project Navigator.

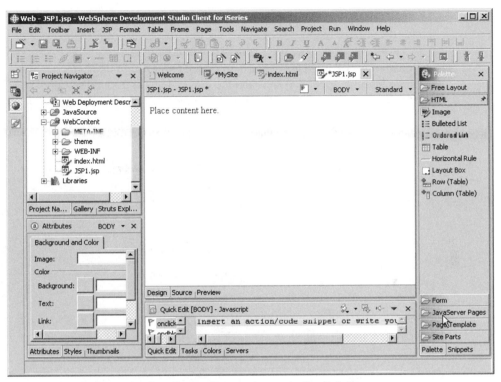

Figure 2-35: Open the JavaServer Pages drawer in the Palette.

The rest of this step is going to be a mini-tutorial on how to create a JSP using the Palette. If you're not interested in this aspect of WDSC, you can skip ahead to Step 2.6, where you will learn how to rearrange the pages in your Web site. (Remember to unzip the workspace for Ch0206 prior to getting started.) However, if you haven't used WDSC much, I'd suggest you stick with the next few pages, because the methods used here are the same for whatever types of widgets you eventually add to your Web pages.

To start with, you'll need to open up the tool drawer for JavaServer Pages. Figure 2-35 shows the cursor in the lower right of the workbench, ready to click on the JavaServer Pages drawer of the Palette. Do that, and you'll see that drawer open as shown in Figure 2-36.

Release Note: The addition of the EGL and JavaServer Faces support in V5.1.2 caused many views to become considerably more complex. IBM chose to increase the minimum screen resolution rather than rearrange the screens, so from V5.1.2 on, many views are difficult to read in 800x600 mode. The Palette view is one of these. With the addition of the Data drawer and the reduction in width of the view, the JavaServer Pages drawer (now called JSP Tags) is more difficult to use. In fact, if at all possible, you will have to increase your resolution in order to use any version of the tool after V5.1.0.3.

❑ **2.5(g) Click on the JavaServer Pages drawer of the Palette.**

Figure 2-36: Clicking on the JavaServer Pages drawer opens it up to show the JSP widgets.

Now, before placing new widgets, you should get rid of the default "Place content here" message. Highlight it as in Figure 2-37, and then delete it to get Figure 2-38.

Note: Be sure you are in the Design mode, not the Preview mode!

❑ **2.5(h) Highlight the default text.**

❑ **2.5(i) Delete the default text.**

Figure 2-37: Highlight the default text, and then delete it.

Figure 2-38: The page is now empty and ready for widgets.

At this point, you can begin to use the Palette. As you've seen, the palette has a number of drawers, and each drawer contains a number of widgets. To place a widget on your display, first select it in its drawer by left-clicking on it (a selected widget will have a slightly lighter background than the unselected widgets around it). In this case, I'd like you to select the Scriptlet widget, which will allow you to actually add some Java code to the JSP.

❑ **2.5(j) Left-click on the Scriptlet widget to select it.**

Figure 2-39: Click on the Scriptlet tool to start dragging it.

Once you've selected your widget, move your cursor back to the editing pane. Note that the cursor has now changed to a standard "add object" cursor. In Windows, that is an arrow with a small box attached to it and a plus sign, as shown in Figure 2-40.

Figure 2-40: Drop it in the upper left corner of the display.

Position the cursor near the top left of the page and left-click. This will cause a number of changes in your workbench, as shown in Figure 2-41.

❑ **2.5(k) Position your cursor in the editor pane.**

❑ **2.5(l) Left-click near the top-left corner of the edit pane.**

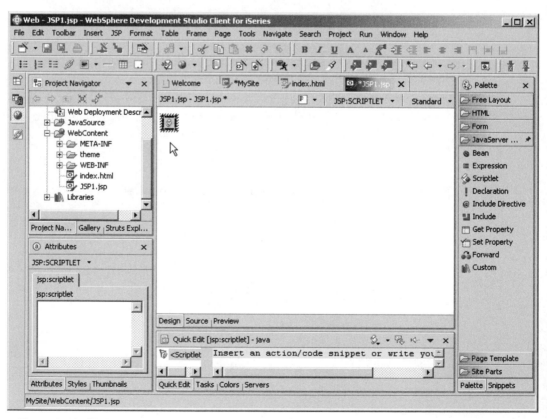

Figure 2-41: Click near the top left corner of the editor panel to drop the scriptlet widget.

Three things happen when you "drop" a widget onto the editor panel. First, you'll see a graphical representation of the widget in the editor. This icon should be similar to the one on the same widget in its drawer. In this case, the icon is a small scroll, meant to represent JavaScript code. The next change is that the Attributes box will change to the appropriate attributes for the dropped widget. For a scriptlet, that means a small box where you can enter the code for the scriptlet. This box will be available whenever the widget is selected in the editor panel. Finally, you'll notice that the widget is no longer selected in the drawer. That is the default action. You can only add one copy of a widget; to add more than one, you must go back to the drawer and reselect the widget.

OK, on to the actual code. For this example, I want you to create a small loop that will execute three times. Each iteration of the loop will print out "Hello World!" followed by the iteration counter. If you're unfamiliar with Java, the syntax will be unusual, but you'll need to learn it if you plan to do any JSP programming, so now is as good a time to start learning as any!

❑ **2.5(m) Enter the code as shown.**

Type in the following code:

```
for (int i = 0; i < 3; i++) {
```

This is the standard Java syntax for making the value i count from zero to two. Java is a zero-based language, meaning that the first entry in an array is zero, so you'll often see looping constructs like this that start at zero (rather than one, as in most RPG programs).

The opening brace ({) marks the beginning of the code controlled by the loop. Thus, anything from this point on until the closing brace (}) will be executed three times. That includes any normal HTML in the JSP page, as well as any other expressions or scriptlets.

Figure 2-42: Create a scriptlet that loops from zero to two.

❑ **2.5(n) Left-click anywhere in the editor to see the results.**

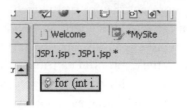

Figure 2-43: Now the editor shows the beginning of the code.

I like the fact that even in the "WYSIWYG" Design mode, the editor attempts within reason to show you the contents of the scriptlet. This is really a lot more helpful than some IDEs, which just show you an icon that says, "There is a scriptlet here." Often, just the beginning of the scriptlet is enough to remind you as a programmer of what the scriptlet is attempting to do.

Next, I want you to add information that will be repeated within the loop (three times, based on the loop code). I indicated earlier that this information could be normal HTML like in any Web page, or it could include Java scriptlets or expressions. The difference between a scriptlet and an expression is that a scriptlet is executed and usually does not write data to the page, while an expression is evaluated and the result of that evaluation is written to the page. Thus, an expression always outputs HTML, but a scriptlet usually doesn't.

❑ **2.5(o) Type "Hello World!" in the editor.**

By typing in "Hello World!" you are ordering the JSP to output that text directly to the browser. It's inside the scriptlet loop, so it will be executed three times, and it will output the same text each time. You could include HTML tags here as well.

Figure 2-44: Type in the text "Hello World!"

Next, I want you to add an Expression widget from the JSP drawer. This widget will evaluate whatever valid Java expression you write and then output the results of that evaluation to the browser.

❑ **2.5(p) Left-click on the Expression widget to select it.**

Figure 2-45: Go back to the JSP drawer to get the Expression widget.

❑ **2.5(q) Left-click in the editor after the exclamation point.**

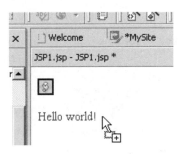

Figure 2-46: Add the expression after the "Hello World!" text.

Figure 2-47: You see the icon for the expression.

I want you to output the contents of the variable "i"; that's the loop counter, and it should roll from zero to one to two as the loop executes.

❏ **2.5(r) Type the expression "i" in the Attributes view.**

Figure 2-48: Use the Attributes view to write the expression to be displayed.

❏ **2.5(s) Left-click anywhere in the editor to see the results.**

And now that you've identified what will repeat (the words "Hello World!" and a counter), you need to close the loop. You do this by adding a scriptlet that contains nothing but a closing brace.

❏ **2.5(t) Left-click on the Scriptlet widget to select it.**

Figure 2-49: And now, like the scriptlet, the editor shows the contents of the expression.

❏ **2.5(u) Left-click in the editor after the expression.**

Figure 2-50: Use the same technique as before to add a scriptlet.

❑ **2.5(v) Type the closing brace (}) in the Attributes view.**

*Figure 2-51: In the
Attributes view, add the
code, which is simply a
closing brace.*

❑ **2.5(w) Left-click anywhere in the editor to see the results.**

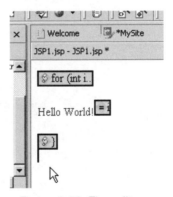

*Figure 2-52: The editor
again shows the contents
of the code.*

That's it! You've added a working loop to your JSP. It's not particularly sophisticated, but it shows how you can add code using nothing but the Design mode of
the editor. You could have done it all in Source mode. Let's take a glance at what
the generated source code looks like.

☐ **2.5(x) Click on the Source tab at the bottom of the editor to see the source code.**

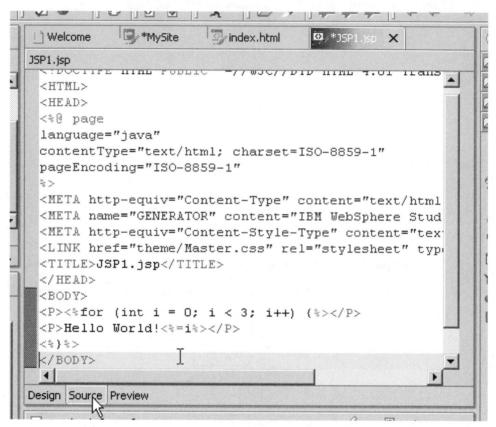

Figure 2-53: Finally, click on the Source tab to see the generated source code for the JSP.

The part that was generated by all your hard work is between the <BODY> and </BODY> tags:

```
<%for (int i = 0; i < 3; i++) {%></P>
<P>Hello World!<%=i%></P>
<%}%>
```

It's not a lot, but it's pretty much what you would expect: the loop at the top, the end of the loop at the bottom, and the "Hello World!" and the counter sandwiched in between.

Unfortunately, since this is a JSP, you can't really "preview" it, since executing the Java code requires an application server. You get to it a little later (in Steps 6 and 7). But first, I'd like to show you a few more features of the product.

Before I can do that, I need you to save your workspace. In the list of tabs at the top of the editor view, you should see that both JSP1.jsp and MySite have the asterisks preceding their names, indicating that they have changes that need to be saved. Please execute the main menu option File/Save All to save everything as you did in Step 2.4(m).

❑ **2.5(y) From the Main Menu, select File/Save All.**

That's it for this step.

Step 2.6—Rearrange your Web site

GOAL

In this step, you will use Web Site Designer to rearrange your Web pages.

Why would you need to rearrange your Web site? The answer is that the feature of WDSC that creates navigation widgets relies on the layout of the site. Pages will be shown in the navigation widgets in the sequence in which they appear in the Web Site Designer. To change the order of a navigation widget, you must rearrange the Web site.

The current Web site, with only two pages, is just a little too simplistic to demonstrate this process, so I'm going to have you add another page. This will be an HTML page called About Us, and it will represent the standard corporate information page.

At the end of the last step, you were in the Page Designer. I need you to get back to the Web Site Designer. To do that, click the MySite tab at the top of the editor view. Your workbench will look like Figure 2-54.

❑ **2.6(a) Click the MySite tab.**

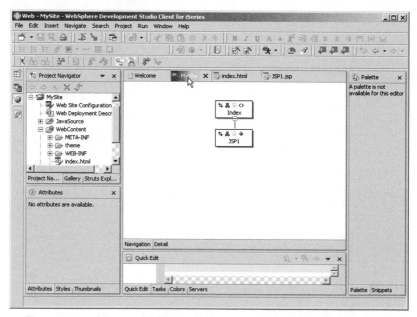

Figure 2-54: Click on MySite to return to the Web Site Designer.

Now that you've successfully returned to the Web Site Designer, you can add a new page. This time, use the pop-up menu. Right-click on the Index page, then select Add New Page/As Child, as shown in Figure 2-55.

> **Release Note:** You probably won't be surprised to learn that the menu changes considerably in release V5.1.2. It's not a problem, though; the option you need is still there.

❑ **2.6(b) Right-click on the Index page.**

❑ **2.6(c) Select Add New Page/As Child.**

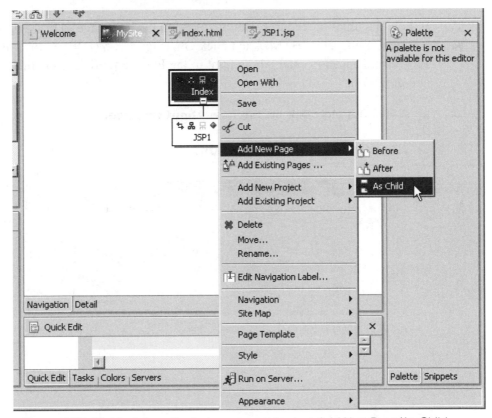

Figure 2-55: Right-click on the Index page and select Add New Page/As Child.

A box will be added to the right of page JSP1. The navigation label will be highlighted as is usual on a new page. Type in "About Us" and press Enter. Your editor should look like Figure 2-56.

❏ **2.6(d) Type in "About Us" and press Enter.**

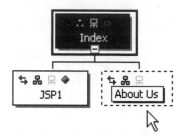

Figure 2-56: Enter "About Us" as the navigation label for the new page.

Follow the usual procedures. Double-click on the new page to bring up the Create a Page wizard, select HTML, and click OK (Figure 2-57). When the New HTML File wizard appears, enter About.html in the File Name field and click Finish (Figure 2-58).

❏ **2.6(e) Double-click on the new About Us page.**

❏ **2.6(f) Select HTML and click OK.**

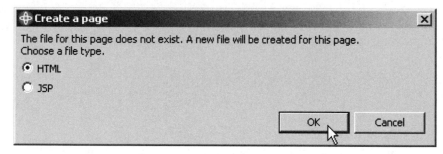

Figure 2-57: Select HTML and click OK.

❏ **2.6(g) Enter 'About.html' in the File Name field and press Finish.**

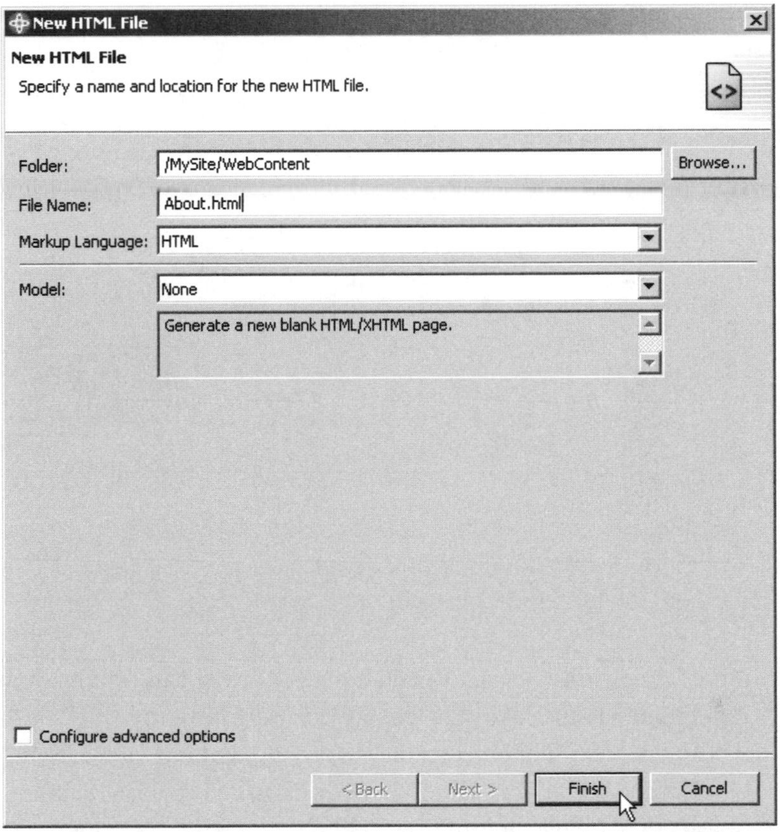

![New HTML File dialog box. Title bar reads "New HTML File". Heading "New HTML File" with subtitle "Specify a name and location for the new HTML file." Folder field: /MySite/WebContent with a Browse... button. File Name field: About.html. Markup Language dropdown: HTML. Model dropdown: None. Description box: "Generate a new blank HTML/XHTML page." A "Configure advanced options" checkbox is unchecked. Buttons: < Back, Next >, Finish, Cancel.]

Figure 2-58: Enter About.html as the File Name and click Finish.

This will bring you to the Page Designer again, looking like Figure 2-59.

The page might come up in Preview or Source mode as well, but no matter. You can click on the Design mode tab to get to Design mode. Change the text to "The About page" (refer to Steps 2.4(j) and 2.4(k) on how to change the text). Don't save the changes. Instead, go back to the Web Site Designer. Do this by again clicking on the MySite tab in the editor view to get the view shown in Figure 2-60.

Figure 2-59: The new HTML page looks like any other new page.

❑ **2.6(h) Change the text to 'the About Us page.'**

❑ **2.6(i) Click the MySite tab.**

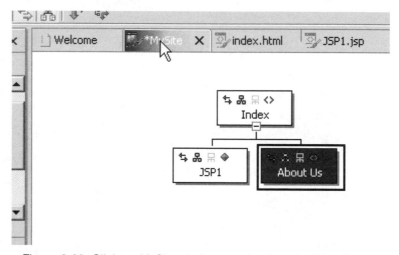

Figure 2-60: Click on MySite again to get back to the Web Site Designer.

All of this work was just to add a page. Now, I can finally show you just how easy it is to change the layout of your Web site. Currently, JSP1 is "in front of" the About Us page. That means that in any navigation view, JSP1 will be before About Us. Let's say that you want those positions reversed; you want About Us to appear before JSP1. Well, in order to do that you need to change their positions. This is as easy as 1, 2, 3.

1. Click the About Us page.

2. Drag it to the left of the JSP1 page.

3. Drop the About Us page.

The following paragraphs will walk you through it.

First, click the About Us page and, holding down the mouse button, start to drag it to the right. The cursor will turn into an arrow inside of a light-colored rectangle with a dashed border. If you look closely, you'll also notice a heavy black bar directly to the left of the About Us page, as shown in Figure 2-61. This is the insert position, and it indicates where the page will be inserted if it is dropped.

❏ **2.6(j) Left-click the About Us page and begin dragging it left.**

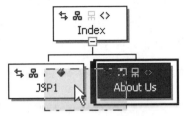

Figure 2-61: Click the About Us page and start dragging to the left.

Continue dragging the cursor left until the heavy black bar moves to the left of the JSP1 page as illustrated in Figure 2-62. Now "drop" the page by releasing the mouse button. This will cause the two pages to switch positions, as shown in Figure 2-63. Feel free to practice moving the pages around some more to get used to the procedure.

❏ **2.6(k) Continue dragging the cursor to the left.**

❏ **2.6(l) Once the heavy bar moves left of JSP1, release the mouse button.**

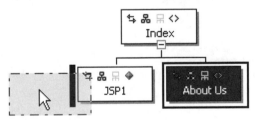

Figure 2-62: After the cursor bar (the heavy black bar) appears on the left of JSP1, drop the page by releasing the mouse button.

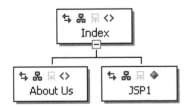

Figure 2-63: The pages will then switch positions.

While the tree view shown in Figure 2-63 is fine for simple Web sites, it can quickly become unwieldy. I prefer the alternate view, known as the "hanging" style. You can switch between the two views very easily using either a menu or the toolbar.

To use the toolbar, look for the two-headed arrow near the right of the Web design toolbar, as shown in Figure 2-64. Click on it, and the view will change from the top-down graphic to a left-to-right presentation as displayed in Figure 2-65. As Web sites get more complex, this view is often easier to read.

❑ **2.6(m) Click on the Change Layout Orientation tool.**

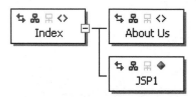

Figure 2-64: Click on the Change Layout Orientation tool.

That's the end of this step. Once again, you should notice that the MySite tab indicates changes pending. So does the About.html tab, which might make you choose the Save All option as we usually do. However, I'm going to show you a slightly different way to save all of your pages. In this case, simply right-click on the editor view and select Save as shown in Figure 2-66.

Figure 2-65: This is the alternate layout for a Web site, which I prefer.

❑ **2.6(n) Right-click in the editor view and select Save.**

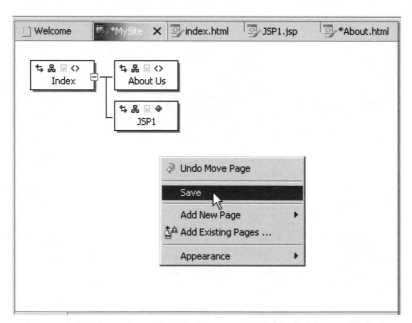

Figure 2-66: As with most editors, you can right click in the Web Site Designer and select Save to save your work.

A wizard may pop up, showing you any other resources that have pending changes that need to be saved. Leave them all selected and click OK to save everything.

Caution: If you uncheck any boxes prior to clicking OK, those files that were unchecked will *not* have their changes saved. This being the case, I still like to save using the Save All command from the menu.

❑ **2.6(o) Leave the box for About.html checked and click OK.**

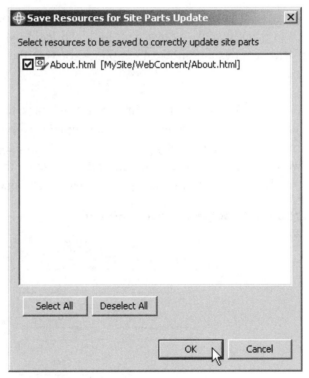

Figure 2-67: Leave About.html checked and click OK to apply its changes.

Step 2.7—Applying a template

One of the most powerful features of WDSC is its use of templates. Templates can be used to quickly apply a consistent look and feel to your entire Web site. And while IBM supplies a number of templates for you, they are designed to be customized.

Now that your Web site is up to three pages, it's time to make it a little prettier. In order to do that, you're going to apply a template. To see why that's important, let's first take a look at what you've got so far. Figure 2-68 shows the layout of your Web site, while Figures 2-69 through 2-71 show the various pages you've created. Click on the tab for each page to get the associated display.

❑ **2.7(a) Click on the tab for each page.**

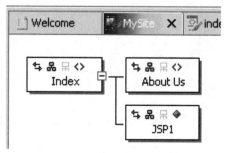

Figure 2-68: Here is the Web site layout.

Figure 2-69: Click on the index.html tab to see the index page.

Figure 2-70: Click on JSP1.jsp to see the JSP.

Figure 2-71: Click on About.html to see the About Us page.

You'll notice that, among other things, pages are initially created with no navigation capabilities. You cannot move from one page to another. This is the sort of thing that a Web site design tool ought to be able to handle, and in fact WDSC does a superb job of it using a special sort of Web design object known as a template.

I'll go into a lot more detail about templates in Steps 4.1 through 4.3, but for now I just want to show you how applying a template can quickly and easily provide a cohesive, professional look and feel for your entire site. The following pages will walk you through the process, and there's also a movie on the accompanying CD. Look for CH0207.mpg in the folder /movies.

The first thing you need to do is click on the MySite tab to get back to the Web Site Designer. Your screen will once again look like it does in Figure 2-68.

❑ 2.7(b) Click the MySite tab.

You can apply a template to one page at a time or to all the pages in your Web site at once. I'll show you how to do the latter procedure, but doing pages one at a time is the same process. It's very helpful to be able to visually select which pages you want to apply a template to, since you may have a different template for different levels of your Web site.

One minor annoyance with Web Site Designer (and I do mean minor) is that there is no "Select All" capability as there is in many other parts of WDSC. Instead, you have to manually select all the pages. The easiest way to do that is to use the "lasso" method: Draw a rectangle around all the pages in your site to select them all. This sort of lassoing technique is fairly standard in many graphical applications.

> **Release Note:** V5.1.2 adds the Select All option, which is available from the Edit menu or via the shortcut key Ctrl+A.

Lassoing a group of pages is a three-step process, similar to the one you used to reposition pages in the previous step. In this case, you start by positioning your cursor above and to the left of the group of objects you wish to lasso, as shown in Figure 2-72.

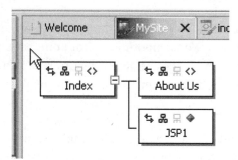

Figure 2-72: Place the cursor above and to the left of the pages.

❏ **2.7(c) Position your cursor above and left of the group of objects.**

The three-step process is as follows:

1. Click the mouse button.

2. While holding down the button, move the mouse down and to the right.

3. When the entire group is "lassoed," release the mouse button.

The following figures show the steps in detail.

❑ **2.7(d) Click the mouse button.**

Clicking the mouse button will change the cursor to a crosshair, as depicted in Figure 2-73. You can now start dragging the mouse down and to the right, keeping the mouse button depressed.

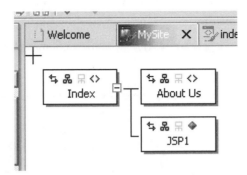

Figure 2-73: When you click the mouse button, the cursor changes to a crosshair.

❑ **2.7(e) Drag down and to the right.**

As you drag the mouse, you'll see a dashed box that grows along with the position of the mouse. Continue to drag the mouse until the box includes all the pages in your Web site, as shown in Figure 2-74.

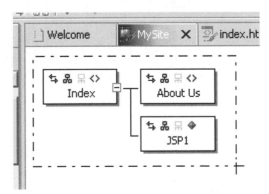

Figure 2-74: When you begin dragging the cursor, a dashed box appears.

Once the box completely surrounds all the pages, you can let go of the mouse, which will cause all the pages within the box to be selected. Your screen will look like the one in Figure 2-75. There have been reports that the lasso method does not work properly on some versions of WDSC. In those cases, after lassoing pages, the Template option was unavailable. If that happens to you, you will have to select multiple pages the "old-fashioned" way: Click on one to select it; then, holding the Ctrl key down, click on another to select it also. Do this until all three pages are selected.

❑   **2.7(f) When all the pages are lassoed, release the mouse button.**

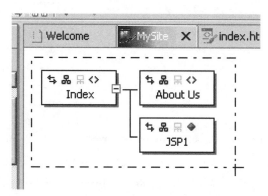

Figure 2-75: After releasing the mouse button, the lassoed pages will be selected.

Now that all the pages are selected, you can apply a template to all of them at once. Right-click on one of the selected pages and then select Page Template/Apply Template, as shown in Figure 2-76.

❑ **2.7(g) Right-click a page and select Page Template/Apply Template.**

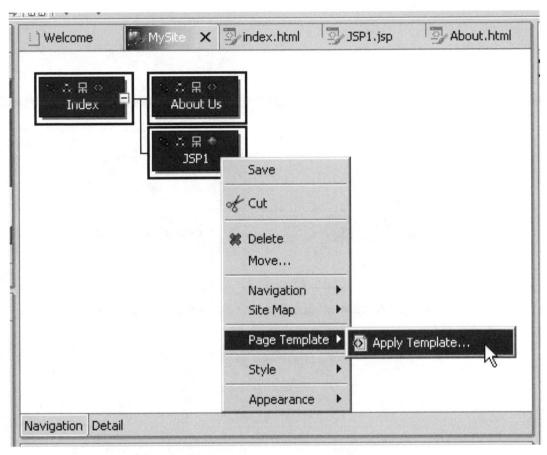

Figure 2-76: Right-click one of the pages and select Page Template/Apply Template.

This will begin the process of applying the template. The first thing you will see is the Apply Page Template wizard, as shown in Figure 2-77.

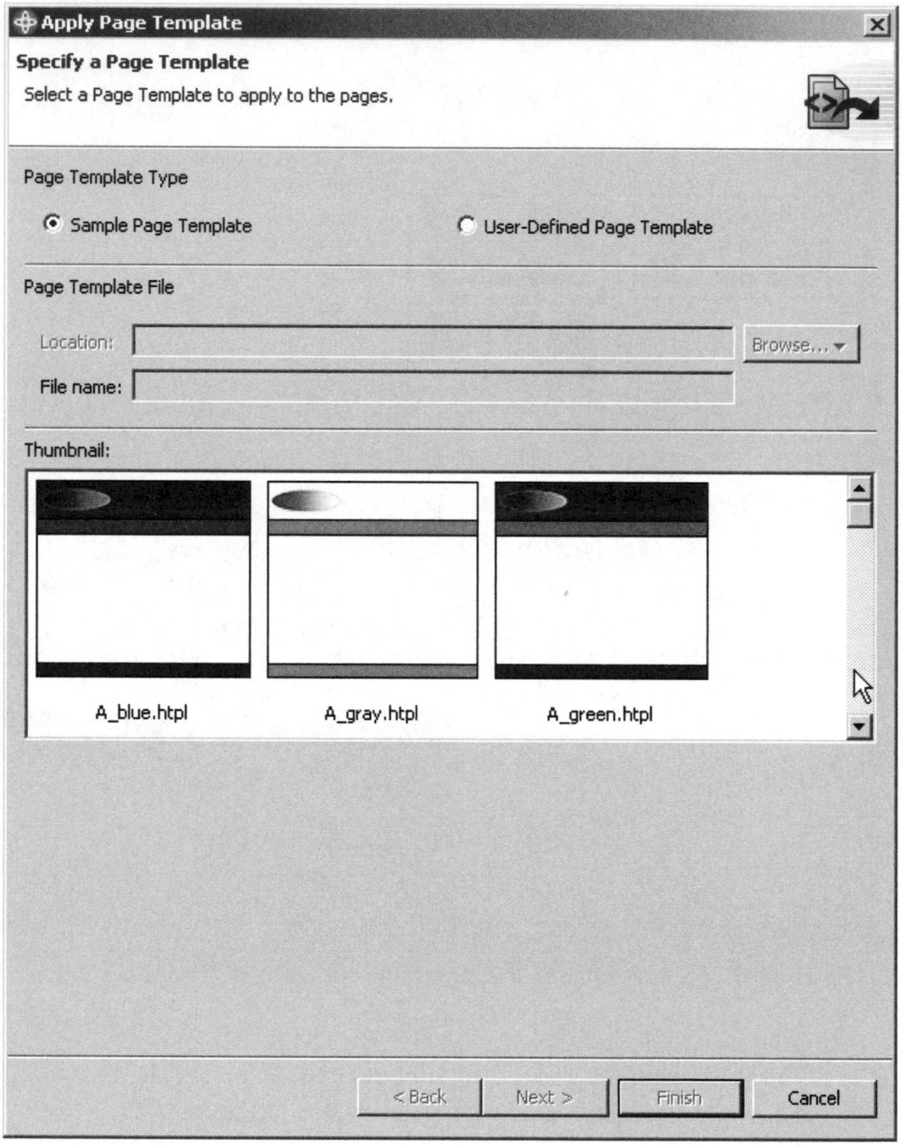

Figure 2-77: Scroll through the sample templates until you find B-01_green.htpl.

This wizard has a number of options, starting with the radio button option that allows you to select between the supplied Sample Page Templates and your own User-Defined Page Templates. Since you haven't had an opportunity to create your own templates yet, you should leave this option as it is and concentrate on the various sample templates available.

The listbox in the center of the wizard shows a quick preview of the available templates. There are quite a few variations of left and top navigation as well as a choice of three color palettes. You can use the scroll bars to page through the various templates to find one that suits your needs. For this step, please scroll until you see the one labeled B-01_green.htpl. This is the one you will be using.

❑ **2.7(h) Scroll until B-01.green.htpl is visible.**

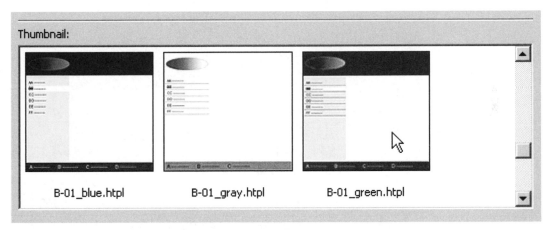

Thumbnail:		
B-01_blue.htpl	B-01_gray.htpl	B-01_green.htpl

Figure 2-78: Left-click on the B-01_green.htpl template.

❑ **2.7(i) Select it by clicking on it; then click Next.**

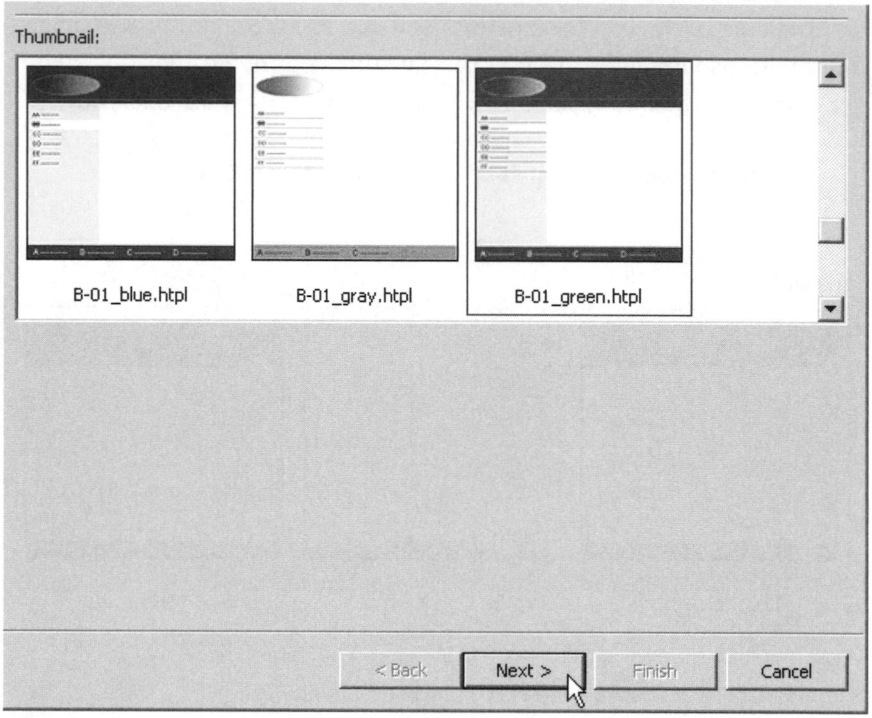

Figure 2-79: Click the Next button.

Now that you've selected the template, you have to assign parts of the template to your pages. I don't want to spend too much time on this now; I'll cover templates in more detail later in the book. So, for now, just think of the template as a form with fill-in-the-blanks sections. Each section has a name. You then assign sections from your HTML pages to those names through a mapping process.

> **Release Note:** The mapping process is a bit different in V5.1.2. There is an additional screen that allows you to select a "typical" page, and then the mapping page is a actually easier to use (it attempts to create a default map and seems to do a good job). In this case, steps 2.7(j) through 2.7(m) can be replaced by simply clicking the Next button twice. Once you've done that, proceed from step 2.7(n).

In the standard scenario, there are only two places where you would plug information into a template: the meta-data section at the top, where you define things like the title of the page, and the content section, where the actual HTML for the page goes. Thus, a template typically has two sections: head and body. These are generally mapped to the HEAD and BODY sections of your page. The following paragraphs will show you how to do exactly that. The tool allows you to create more complex templates in which you can define other mappings, but this standard mapping will be sufficient for just about any page you are likely to need in a normal Web site.

When you're using a standard IBM template, the Insert Contents page of the Apply Page Template wizard usually comes up with two content areas (head and body) on the left, and the HEAD and BODY regions of your page are listed on the right. The head content area is pre-selected, and all you need to do is assign the HEAD region of your page to it. Do that by selecting (clicking on) the HEAD region in the right listbox.

❑ **2.7(j) Select the HEAD region in the right listbox.**

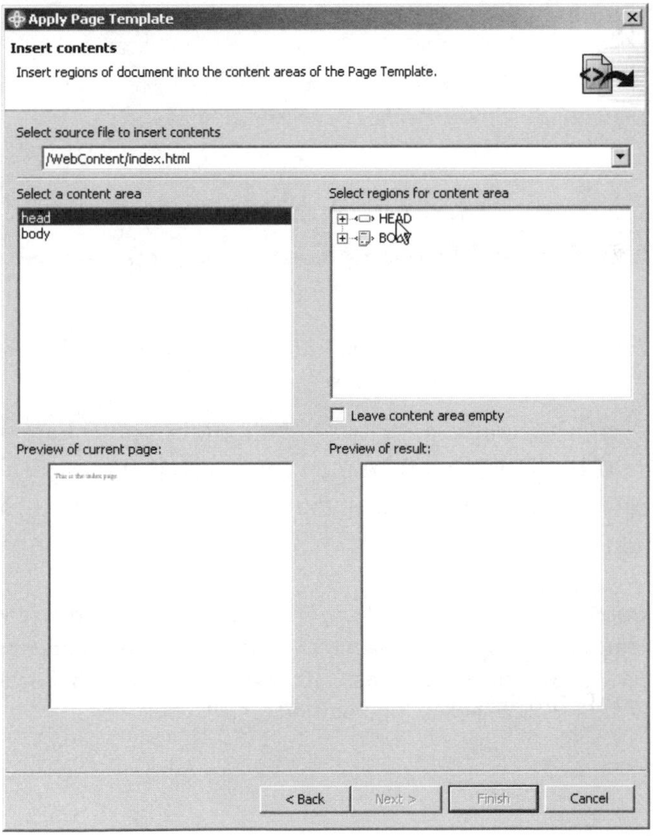

Figure 2-80: Select (left-click) the HEAD region to assign it to the head content area.

This assigns the HEAD region of your page to the head content area of the template. However, the body content area is still unassigned, so you'll see an error as shown in Figure 2-81. To remove this error, assign the BODY region of your page to the body content area.

❑ **2.7(k) Select the body content area in the left listbox.**

❑ **2.7(l) Select the BODY region in the right listbox.**

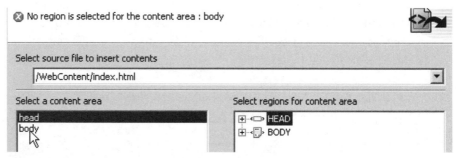

Figure 2-81: Select the body content area.

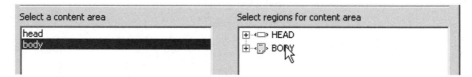

Figure 2-82: Assign the BODY region to the body content area.

Once you've assigned regions to both of the content areas, the Apply Page Template will process for a moment or two and then display a preview of the selected page as viewed with the template. Figure 2-83 shows how the wizard will look.

> **Caution:** Although it is unlikely that you will have problems with the standard templates, please be certain that all your pages have the appropriate regions prior to assigning templates. If, for example, one of your selected pages did *not* have a BODY section, unpredicted results could occur.

❑ 2.7(m) Press the Next button.

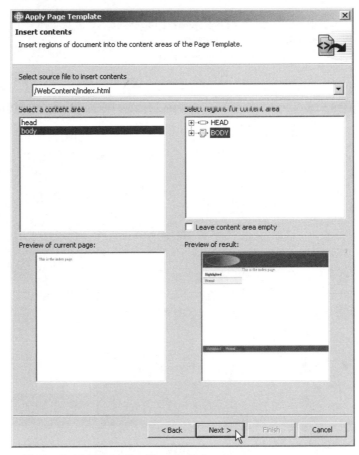

Figure 2-83: Press the Next button.

At this point, the template can be applied to the pages. Click on the Next button to begin the process. The wizard will now present the Select Pages prompt, which shows a list of all the pages to which this template will be applied. In your case, it should have three pages listed: index.html, JSP1.jsp, and About.html, as shown in Figure 2-84. If this is correct, press the Finish button to continue with processing.

Release Note: The Select Pages dialog in Figure 2-84 is slightly different in V5.1.2, and the verification dialog shown in Figure 2-85 does not appear.

❑ **2.7(n) Press the Finish button.**

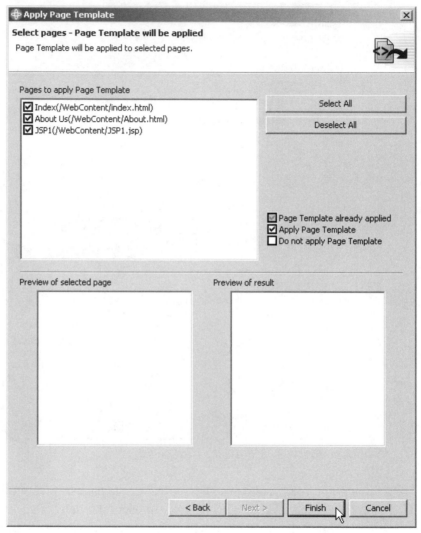

Figure 2-84: Verify that the list of pages is correct; then press the Finish button.

There is one last verification step. Since a large Web site could take a long time to process, WDSC prompts you to be sure you really want to do this. Click Yes and the template will be applied.

❏ **2.7(o) Click Yes.**

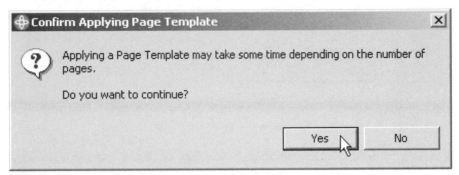

Figure 2-85: WDSC prompts you to make sure you really want to do this.

Once you click the Yes button, you will be returned to the workbench. You'll see that the pages are still selected, as in Figure 2-86.

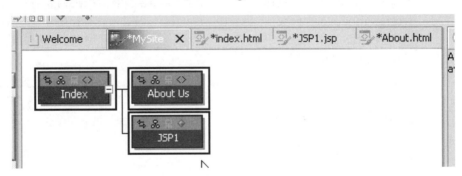

Figure 2-86: Save this using the right-click and Save technique.

At this point, you can save the Web site. Right-click and save like you did in Steps 2.6(n) and 2.6(o).

❏ **2.7(p) Right-click in the editor and select Save.**

❏ **2.7(q) Leave all boxes checked and press OK.**

When done, click on an empty spot in the editor screen to see a screen like the one in Figure 2-87. Everything is saved, and though you can't tell from the figure in the book, each page has a light-blue top border that indicates that the page has a template applied.

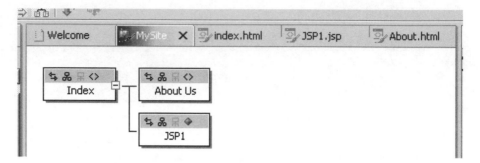

Figure 2-87: With templates in place, the updated Web site looks like this.

That's all it takes to apply a template. But what does it do? You can see that for yourself by going through and clicking on each of the pages in the editor. Because of a quirk in the way WDSC works, the changes may not be visible immediately. You might still see a screen like that in Figure 2-88. If that happens, click on the Design mode tab at the bottom of the view and then back to the Preview mode to see the effect of the changes. If you do this, you should see pages like the one shown in Figure 2-89.

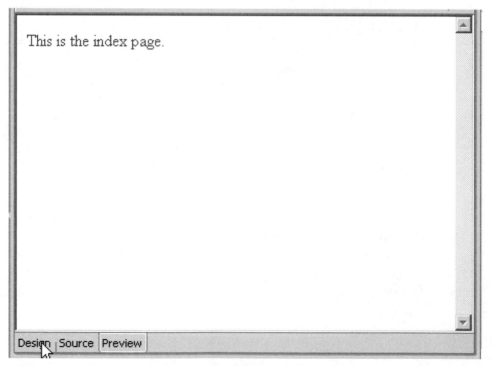

Figure 2-88: Click Design and then Preview to refresh the image.

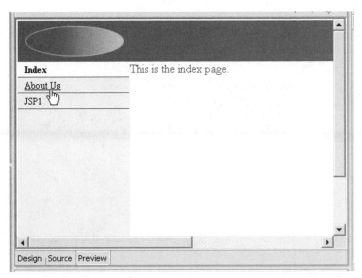

Figure 2-89: This is the index page after the template is applied.

Figure 2-89 shows the actual changes. Note that the original content area is still preserved, but the template adds a banner/logo area at the top of the screen as well as clickable navigation links on the left side.

The changes also affect the other pages. Click on the JSP1.jsp tab to see the changes there (Figure 2-90). In this figure and the next one, I moved the cursor over the "About Us" link to show you that it is indeed a hyperlink.

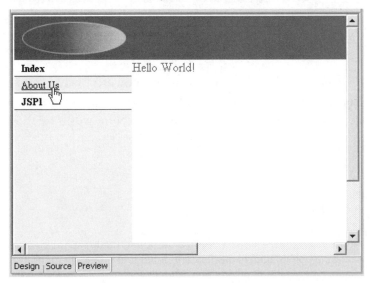

Figure 2-90: JSP1.jsp was also changed (as was About.html).

If you were to expand this view by double-clicking on the JPS1.jsp tab, you would also see a navigation bar at the bottom of the page, as shown in Figure 2-91.

Figure 2-91: If you maximize the view, you can see the bottom navigation bar as well.

It's clear that applying a template is a powerful way to add a consistent look and feel to your application, as well as a way to manage the navigation. In the next step, you'll see how the template architecture works to allow you to make changes to your Web site quickly and efficiently.

Step 2.8—Navigation and naming

In this final introductory step, you will rename one of your pages and then rearrange your Web site. Once that's accomplished, you'll see how the templates are automatically reapplied to regenerate your Web site.

If you haven't done so already, return to the Web Site Designer by clicking on the MySite tab in the editor view.

❑ **2.8(a) Click the MySite tab.**

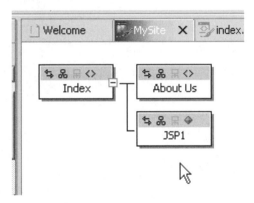

Figure 2-92: The existing Web site looks like this.

Remember, the name that you see in this view, the navigation label, is the name used on the various navigation widgets. And in fact, if you look back at Figure 2-91, you'll see that the navigation widgets show About Us followed by JSP1. Well, let's say you want to change that. First, you want to rename JSP1 to something else. Eventually, this is going to be a customer list, so call it Customers. Second, you want to rearrange the pages so that the newly renamed Customers panel is before the About Us panel.

You can do all of that from the Web Site Designer view. To change the navigation label for the JSP1 page, simply right-click on the page and select Edit Navigation Label as illustrated in Figure 2-93. This will cause the navigation label to become editable. Enter the new name (Customers) as shown in Figure 2-94 and press Enter.

❑ **2.8(b) Right-click on the JSP1 page and select Edit Navigation Label....**

❑ **2.8(c) Type "Customers" and press Enter.**

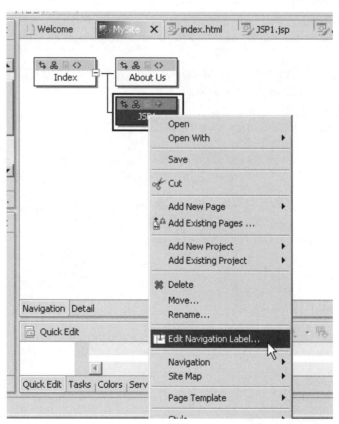

Figure 2-93: Right-click on the JSP1 page and select Edit Navigation Label.

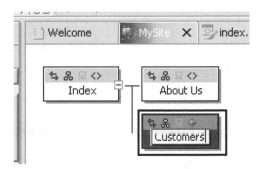

*Figure 2-94: Type in the new navigation
label Customers and press Enter.*

Next, you want to rearrange the pages. Do this using the same drag-and-drop technique you used in Step 2.6. The only difference is that, because you changed the layout orientation, you'll be dragging the page down, rather than left and right. Click on the About Us page and drag it down so that the heavy black cursor bar appears below the Customers page, as shown in Figure 2-95, and then release the mouse button to rearrange the pages.

❑ **2.8(d) Click the About Us page and drag it down past Customers.**

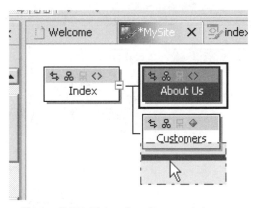

*Figure 2-95: Using the drag-and-drop
technique, drag the About Us page
underneath the Customers page.*

Once you've done that, you'll see that the About Us page is now positioned underneath the Customers page. However, if you were to go into the individual pages, you wouldn't see the changes yet. This is because they haven't yet been applied (as indicated by the asterisk in the MySite tab). To actually commit these changes, you need to save the Web site configuration.

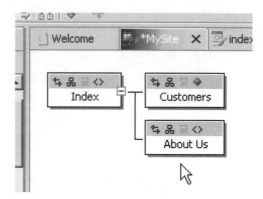

Figure 2-96: The pages are rearranged and renamed.

To save the configuration, right-click anywhere in the editor view and select Save, as shown in Figure 2-97.

❑ **2.8(e) Right-click in the editor view and select Save.**

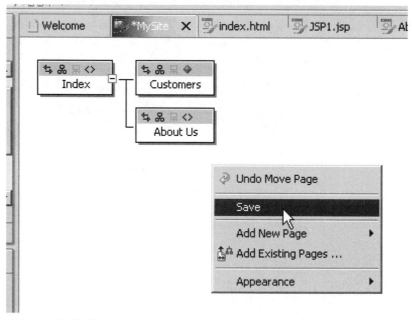

Figure 2-97: Right-click in the editor view and select Save.

As your Web site gets bigger, this sort of operation can take longer and longer. You can monitor the progress of the operation by watching the status bar at the bottom of the workbench, as shown in Figure 2-98.

Setting contents: /MySite/.website-config. JSP Validation: Checking for Java compilation errors.

Figure 2-98: The status bar at the bottom of the workbench indicates the progress of the operation.

After it's done, go take a look at one of the Web pages (remember that you may need to click on the Design tab and then Preview). For example, the index page already reflects the changes to both the page name and its repositioning. This sort of change is tedious, time-consuming, and error-prone, especially in a large, complicated Web site. With WDSC's Web Site Designer and the judicious use of templates, it's as easy as point-and-click.

❑ **2.8(f) Click the index.html tab to see the results.**

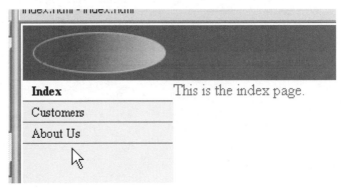

Figure 2-99: And that's how easy it is to change your Web site layout.

And that does it for your introduction to the Web Site Designer and the Web Page Designer. It's far from an exhaustive reference, but it has shown you all of the basic features required to create Web pages, arrange them, and apply templates for navigation and look and feel.

In subsequent steps, I'll show you more about the Image Designer, which you can use to create graphics. I'll also delve a little more deeply into the uses of templates and CSS. Once you've become familiar with those pieces, you can start testing a live Web site.

Step 3

The Image Designer

At the end of Step 2.8, you were looking at the index page of your Web site. You had applied a template, but the template was quite simple. The logo is little more than a simple oval. I think it's time we fixed that, don't you?

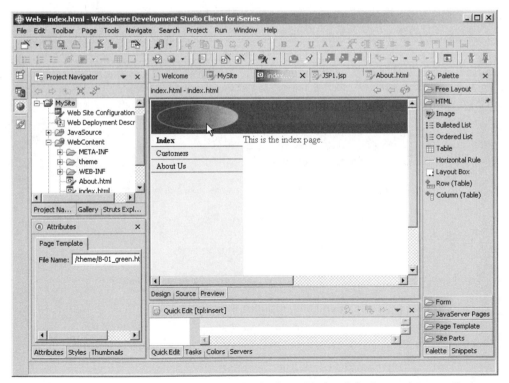

Figure 3-1: This is what your index page looks like with the default template applied.

In this step, you'll be introduced to many of the features of the WebArt Designer, a powerful standalone utility that allows you to create and maintain both static and animated images and to export them in various formats.

Step 3.1—Open the WebArt Designer

There are two ways to invoke the WebArt Designer. One way is to selects Tools/WebArt Designer from the main menu. This will open the WebArt Designer with a new, empty canvas to work on. The second method is to edit an image in your workspace. The default option for most image types is to invoke the WebArt Designer, so simply double-clicking on an image will automatically open up the Designer.

Since the plan is for you to update your logo, I'd like you to start WebArt Designer by editing the logo graphic. You could have figured out where your logo is by reviewing the source code for one of the pages, but for expediency's sake, I'll cheat a little bit and tell you where the logo is.

The logo got installed in your project when you applied the template. If you take a look in the folder called "theme," you'll find a number of new objects.

❑ **3.1(a) Expand the theme folder.**

Figure 3-2: Expand the theme folder.

In the theme folder, there are a number of objects, as shown in Figure 3-3. You will see a file containing the template source (B-01_green.htpl) as well as the style sheet for the template (green.css). But what's most important for our immediate purpose is the GIF file named logo_green.gif, which is the green oval logo. Double-click on that logo.

❑ **3.1(b) Double-click on the file logo_green.gif.**

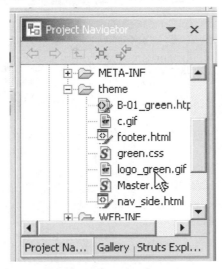

Figure 3-3: Double-click on logo_green.gif to open up the WebArt Designer.

WebArt Designer is not completely integrated into the workbench, and so a new window will appear. It will look like the window shown in Figure 3-4. This is the WebArt Designer.

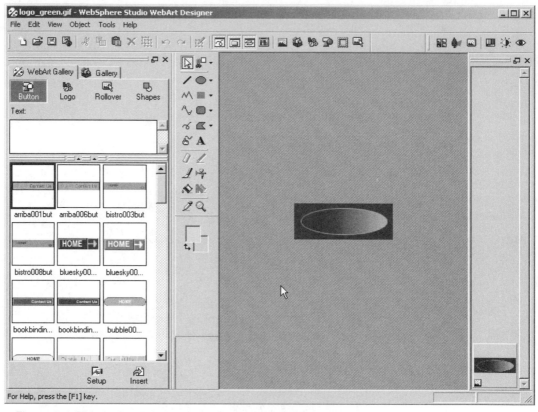

Figure 3-4: This is the default screen for the WebArt Designer.

The left side of the WebArt Designer is a tabbed palette. This palette contains two separate galleries with hundreds of images. The Gallery tab contains simple icons, some animated, that you can include in your Web pages. The WebArt Gallery is a more interactive environment, where you enter text and transform it into a button or a rollover as needed.

The right side of the Designer contains a canvas with a toolbar along the left side and an object list on the right. The bottom half of the toolbar changes with the tool selected, while the object list contains a list of all the objects you've used to create the current image. If you're familiar with any drawing tools, you'll feel at home working with the WebArt Designer, but if not, I'll give you a quick introduction in the next few sections.

Step 3.2—Add text to the logo

In this step, you'll use just the toolbar to modify the logo graphic to contain some text. This will require only a couple of the tools in the toolbar, but once you see how one tool works, you can transfer that knowledge to the other tools.

The logo as it comes in is a little small, so I'd like you to expand the logo in order to better work on it. This is easy enough to do by first clicking on the magnifying glass tool and then selecting the appropriate magnification level.

❑ **3.2(a) Select the magnifying glass.**

Figure 3-5: Select the magnification tool to change the zoom level.

This will cause the screen to change to something like the one shown in Figure 3-5. The bottom half of the toolbar will now show a scale of magnification levels, from 1/4 to 4. Please select 2; this will show the image twice its normal size, as shown in Figure 3-6. Also, the cursor will have changed to a magnifying glass with a plus sign (+) inside it, and if you left-click in the editor pane, it will magnify the image to the next level (right-click will shrink the image).

❑ **3.2(b) Click on magnification level 2.**

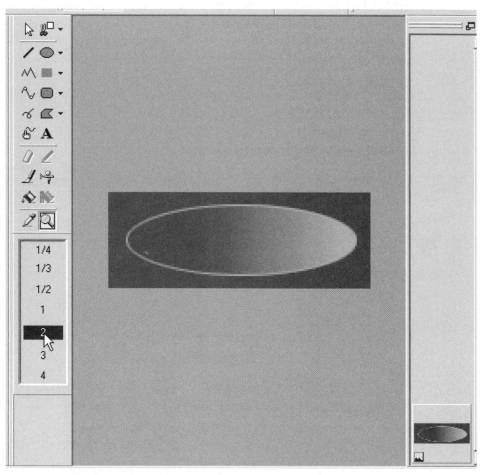

Figure 3-6: Set the zoom level to 2.

Now the canvas is large enough that you can easily work within it. Select the text tool to identify the text to use. The toolbar will change as shown in Figure 3-7.

❑ **3.2(c) Click on the text tool.**

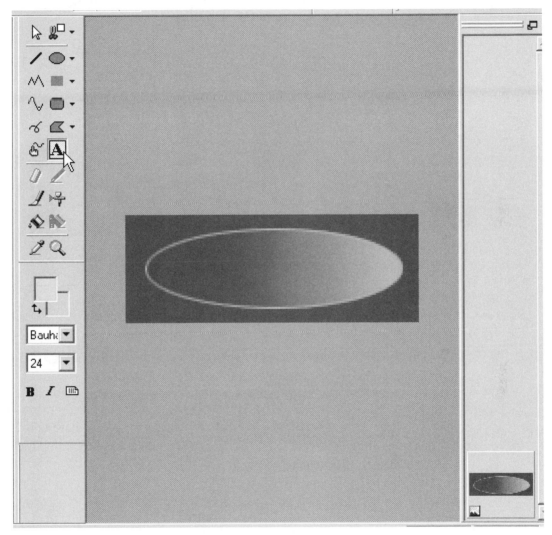

Figure 3-7: Now select the text tool.

The fonts and sizes available will depend on your system. For this step, choose the Verdana font and the 18 point size. The color will default to whatever color was last used. Don't worry about that; you can change it later.

❑ **3.2(d) Select Verdana from the font drop-down.**

❑ **3.2(e) Select 18 from the point size drop-down.**

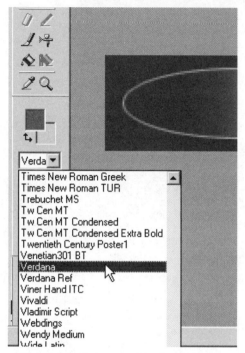

Figure 3-8: Select the Verdana font.

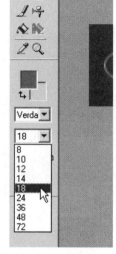

Figure 3-9: Select point size 18.

Now you can add text to your logo. Position your cursor somewhere in the upper left quadrant of the logo and left-click. This will open a text box into which you can enter the appropriate text.

❑ **3.2(f) Left-click somewhere in the upper left of the oval.**

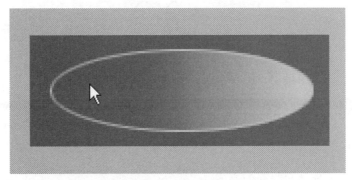

Figure 3-10: Click on the oval to get a text box.

Enter the text "MyComp" and then click outside of the text tool area.

❑ **3.2(g) Enter the text "MyComp" and click outside the text rectangle.**

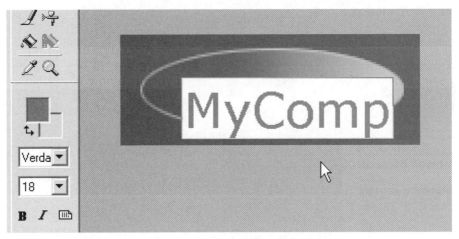

Figure 3-11: Enter the text "MyComp" and click outside the text rectangle.

Use the cursor to drag and drop the text to the appropriate location.

❑ **3.2(h) Position the text by dragging it with the cursor.**

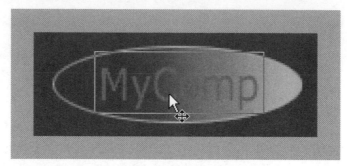

Figure 3-12: Use the cursor to drag the text to the correct location.

If you don't like the color of the text, it's quite easy to change. Simply double-click on the letters (alternatively, you can click on the text object in the object list on the far right of the Designer). You'll get a pop-up properties dialog like the one in Figure 3-13.

❑ **3.2(i) Double-click on the text to change its properties.**

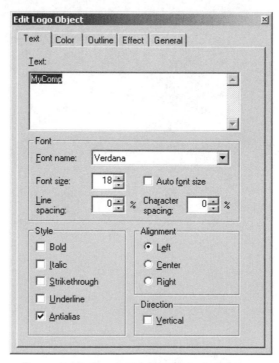

Figure 3-13: The Edit Logo Object dialog offers lots of options for customizing your logo.

This dialog allows you to change a great many properties of the text in the logo, from the color to the effects used. Click on the tabs at the top of the dialog to navigate through the choices. The Color tab brings up a standard color chooser, shown in Figure 3-14.

❑ **3.2(j) Select light blue.**

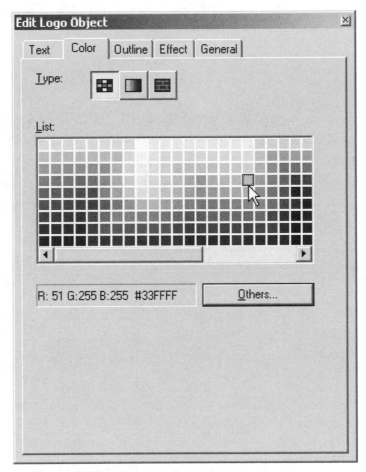

Figure 3-14: The colors offered are pretty standard.

The color chooser uses the standard RGB color definitions. You can also add a gradient (the color's hue varies from one side of the text to the other) or a texture. The other tabs have other effects, including transparency, which I particularly like. In any event, while the picture in the book doesn't do it justice, I chose a light blue color for the text, which will offset it nicely against the green of the oval. Notice that the changes take place as soon as you change the property in the dialog. For example, as soon as I click on the light blue square, the text in the WebArt Designer changes to light blue. There is no Save button; instead, simply close the dialog when you're done.

❑ **3.2(k) Close the dialog.**

The finished product is shown in Figure 3-15.

Figure 3-15: Here's the new MyComp logo.

Just to make the point, please take a glance at the object list in the far right column. Note that it now shows two objects: the green oval that came from the original GIF file, and the MyComp text. It's important to recognize that the images you create in the WebArt Designer are really made up of objects that can be individually edited. Whether you need that capability will determine how you save the file. I'll review that in more detail in the next step.

Step 3.3—Save the logo

Now that you've added text to your logo, you need to save it back to your project. While it's relatively easy to do, it's not entirely seamless. Since the WebArt Designer is invoked as a separate program, there is a little bit of quirkiness involved in actually saving something. You may also need to save things twice (in order to be able to edit the graphic later), so it helps to have the steps laid out for you.

First, you can attempt to save the object. This part of the product is actually done well; the Designer warns you that you may be losing information if you save the file.

❑ **3.3(a) Select File/Save Canvas from the main menu.**

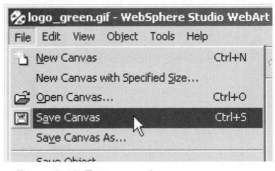

Figure 3-16: Try to save the canvas.

You'll immediately see the warning message shown in Figure 3-17.

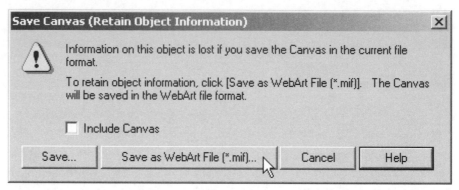

Figure 3-17: If you plan to make any changes to the image, be sure to save in WebArt format.

And what does this error mean? Well, it has to do with the format of the saved file. Back in Step 3.2, I pointed out that the image is actually made up of a number of separate objects. In this case, the objects include the original green oval GIF file that you started with and the light blue text that you added during Step 3.2. Together, these create an oval with text. However, the only way to save that information is to save it as a special file type, called a WebArt file, with the extension .mif. However, browsers aren't smart enough to display .mif files (and .mif files are quite a bit bigger than other graphics formats), so you'll also need to save the file as a conventional graphics file.

How do you decide which format to save the file in? Well, in this case, if you think you might need to go back sometime and change the font or color of the text, then it's a good idea to save the file in WebArt format so that you can easily go in and change the objects. Although it's a little bit of a hassle to save a file in WebArt format, (as I'll illustrate in a moment), unless you're absolutely sure this is the final version of the image, you should save your files in Web Art format.

❑ 3.3(b) Click Save as WebArt File (*.mif).

Now, why do I say it's a hassle? Primarily because the WebArt Designer is not fully integrated into WDSC. As a specific point, when you want to save a .mif file, you will get a Save Canvas As box (Figure 3-18), which requires you to navigate your way to your project. Personally, I think the WebArt Designer should default to the current project, but even so, it's a fairly minor quirk, especially since in subsequent uses of the Designer, the Save As will remember where you last saved an image.

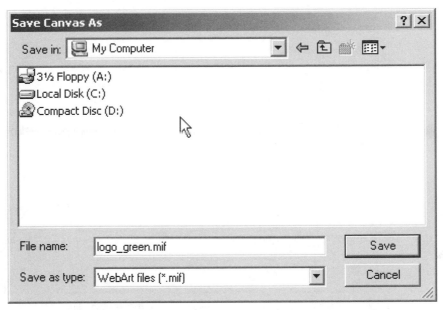

Figure 3-18: Save Canvas As requires you to navigate to your project.

Start by finding your workspace. You specified the location of the workspace when you started WDSC. If you're using the default workspace I recommended, it will be at C:\WDSCSBS\ws1.

❑ 3.3(c) Navigate to your workspace.

Once you navigate to your workspace, you will see a panel similar to the one in Figure 3-19. These are the current contents of your workspace. Note the DefaultEAR and MySite folders clearly present.

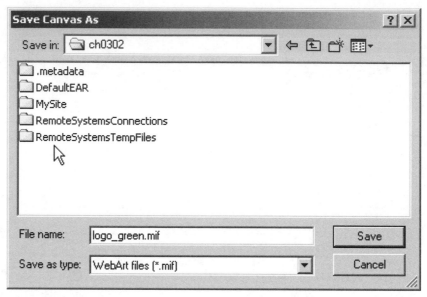

Figure 3-19: This is what your workspace should look like.

Having gotten there, drill a couple levels further down—into MySite, into Web Content, and finally into theme.

❑ **3.3(d) Drill down to MySite/Web Content/theme.**

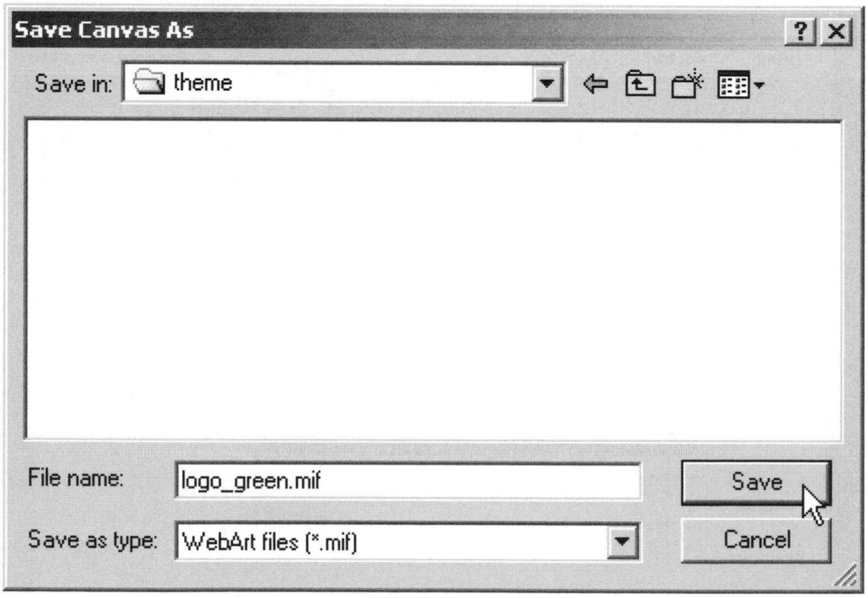

Figure 3-20: Drill down to the theme folder.

Save the file in WebArt format here as logo_green.mif. This will allow you to modify the graphic later as a WebArt file, not just as a GIF.

❑ 3.3(e) Save the file as logo_green.mif.

However, you still have to save the file in a conventional graphic format in order for it to be used in your Web site. The original graphic was a GIF, so that's the format you should save it as. Since you just got done saving in WebArt format, you'll have to use Save Canvas As in order to switch to GIF format. However, the WebArt Designer will at least remember where you last saved, so you don't have to go through drilling down all over again.

❑ 3.3(f) Select File/Save Canvas As... from the main menu.

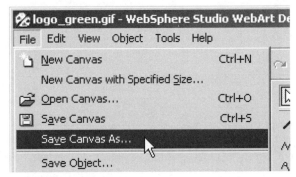

Figure 3-21: Save Canvas As... will allow you to now save the file in GIF format.

In the Save As... box, select GIF in the Save as type box. You are already in the right folder, so click Save. You'll be prompted to overwrite the existing file. Say Yes.

❑ **3.3(g) Select GIF in the Save as type field.**

❑ **3.3(h) Click Save.**

❑ **3.3(i) Click Yes when asked to overwrite the existing file.**

❑ **3.3(j) Click Yes when warned that information will be lost.**

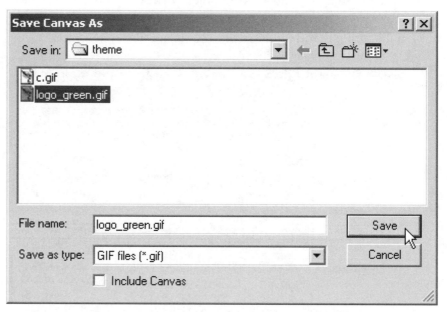

Figure 3-22: Select type GIF and click Save. When prompted to overwrite, click Yes.

At this point, the GIF attribute settings box will appear. Typically, I just use the default settings.

❑ **3.3(k) Leave the defaults and click OK.**

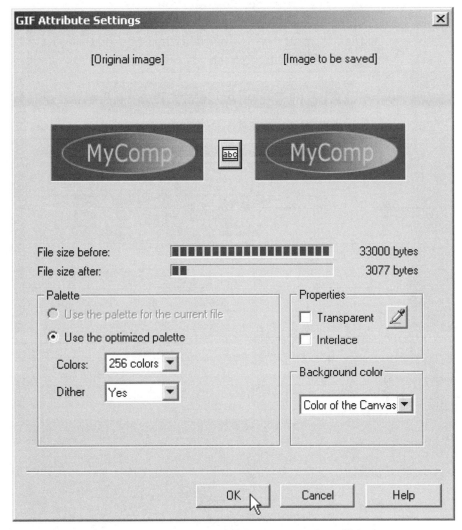

Figure 3-23: The default settings for GIF files are usually sufficient.

Close the WebArt Designer (you can use File/Exit from the main menu) and return to WDSC. If you click on the Index.html tab, you may find that the logo hasn't changed yet, as shown in Figure 3-24. Remember that sometimes you have to go out of Preview mode and back in to see the effects of changes. Click on the Design mode tab at the bottom of the editor, and then click on Preview mode again, and you should see your new logo, as illustrated in Figure 3-25.

It's worth noting that the other views, such as the Project Navigator, will not automatically show files added this way. You'll see logo_green.gif because it already existed, but you won't see logo_green.mif. The easiest way to make new files appear is to refresh the view by right-clicking on the project in the Project Navigator and selecting Refresh.

❑ **3.3(l) Click on Design mode and then on Preview mode.**

Figure 3-24: Click on Design and then back on Preview to refresh the view.

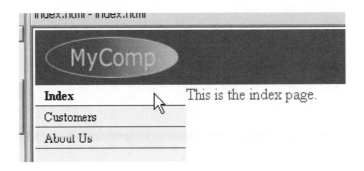

Figure 3-25: Now your index page shows your custom-designed logo.

This is just scratching the surface of the capabilities of the WebArt Designer. I encourage you to spend some time playing with the various properties and with the galleries. I think you'll be pleasantly surprised by the depth of function of this little-known tool.

Step 4

Templates

Perhaps the most powerful tool IBM provides in the Web design portion of WDSC is the ability to apply templates to pages. You use these templates to generate pages. Then, later, you can modify the templates, and those changes are automatically propagated to your pages. You can even build your own templates from scratch.

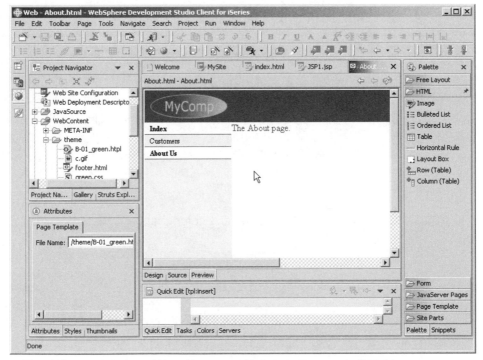

Figure 4-1: Here's your About Us page with its new corporate logo.

When you last left the workbench, it looked like Figure 4-1. You had actually modified your entire Web site's look and feel by changing the logo graphic. This is a rather slick maneuver, but making other site-wide changes is rarely so easy. For example, changing the banner text on every page or using a different navigation style can be a tedious, time-consuming task. Templates give you the ability to make those sorts of changes quickly and easily.

Step 4.1—What is a template?

> ## GOAL
> In this step, you will learn what a template consists of.

A template can be thought of as a framework for your Web pages. In it, you store common information that is used throughout your Web site. For example, if you have a common logo and banner for your site, you can store it in the template, and it will automatically be included in every page that uses that template.

The standard IBM templates include not only the HTML that makes up the template itself, but also the associated objects, including GIF files, style sheets, and navigation site parts.

I mentioned navigation site parts…. IBM provides a powerful (but undocumented) programming language for creating navigation code based on the layout of your Web site. As a page is generated from the template, the Page Designer can query the Web Site Designer to get the layout of the Web site and then generate navigation buttons accordingly. The code that performs this generation is called a "site part," and page templates generally include one or more of these, depending on the type of navigation that is required.

Finally, IBM has modified the Page Designer to be template-aware. Whenever a page has a template applied, special comments are embedded in the source code for that page. The Page Designer recognizes these codes and changes the way it interacts with the page. Those sections that are generated by the template cannot be modified by the user. That way, if the template is modified, the modifications can be applied to all pages generated from that template.

Step 4.2—What happens when you apply a template?

GOAL

In this step, you will learn at a high level what really happens when a template is applied to a Web page.

The most important thing to realize is that when a template is applied, a copy is actually made in your workspace and you really use that copy, not the original. As shipped, the IBM templates are stored in a special folder located deep in the directory structure of WebSphere Studio:

{WDSC_ROOT}\wstools\eclipse\plugins\com.ibm.etools.Webedit.sample_5.1.0

I covered the concept of WDSC_ROOT at the beginning of the book in the introduction step, but in case you forgot, it's relatively simple to find. If you installed WDSC onto C: using the defaults, you'll have a folder something like this on your C: drive:

C:\Program Files\IBM\WebSphere Studio\Site Developer\v5.1

Site Developer might be Application Developer, depending on whether you've installed the standard or advanced edition of WDSC. The v5.1 may change, depending on which version of the tool you've installed. Also, you could have installed it in an alternate location. However, once you've located the correct root folder, the rest of the folder structure is constant.

Within that folder are a number of subfolders for various parts of the Web design process, including the gallery for the WebArt Designer, which I introduced you to in the previous step. The templates are located here (with national language-specific templates located in com.ibm.etools.webedit.sample.nl1_5.1.0). However, when you apply a template, objects get copied from these folders into your workspace. These objects include, among other things, a CSS file, some GIFs, some navigation site parts, and the template itself. I'll cover each in a little more detail, but for now, it's enough to know that they get copied from the folder above (or more specifically, from subfolders of that folder) into your workspace in a folder named "theme." And once copied into your workspace, they are then yours to modify as you see fit.

Because of this, any changes you make to your template are not globally available to other projects, workspaces, or users. Instead, you'd have to export that template in order for others to use them. WebSphere offers capabilities to save templates into another project in an effort to make them accessible to other users. These then become User-Defined Templates, which can be accessed by others. You can then go into another project and import the template from the external folder. But the capabilities of User-Defined Templates are limited; I have found no way to automatically include GIF files and navigation site parts in the same way that the standard templates do. Therefore, if you want to import a template, you also have to manually import all of the associated files that it uses. This is not particularly difficult, but it's not documented anywhere.

Instead, I typically use the standard templates and then modify them for my own use. They're local to the project, but I'm comfortable with all of the pieces.

Be aware that lots of pieces get imported into your theme folder when you use one of the standard templates. Not only that, but the pieces can have name collisions. For example, most of the templates use the name "footer.html" for the footer navigation site part. If you use two different templates for your pages, this could conceivably cause a naming conflict when importing the second template into your folder. Because of this, WDSC will rename pieces that could have conflicts. WDSC does this by placing an underscore at the end of the name, so you could see a name like "footer_.html" in your theme folder.

Step 4.3—Deconstructing a template

> ## GOAL
> **In this step, you will get a close look at the inner workings of a template.**

In previous steps, you used the B-01_green template for your work, so let's take a look at that template in more detail. First, let's look at the generated page. Since you're going to need all the real estate you can get, I'm going to have you maximize the view. You'll use a standard Eclipse technique by which you can cause a single view to take over most of the workbench. This allows you to temporarily get a larger view of a single view.

To maximize the About Us page, double-click on its tab (About.html) at the top of the editor view. The About Us page will expand to fill the workbench, as shown in Figure 4-2.

❑ **4.3(a) Double-click on the About.html tab to maximize it.**

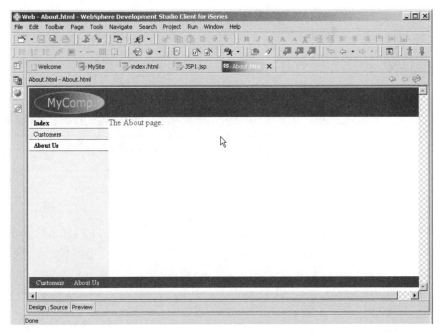

Figure 4-2: The About Us page is now maximized, taking up most of the workbench.

When you originally created this page, you only entered the words "The About page." So that must mean that all the rest of the code is generated. And in fact, if you click on the Design tab at the bottom to go into design mode, that will be graphically displayed.

❑ **4.3(b) Click on the Design mode tab.**

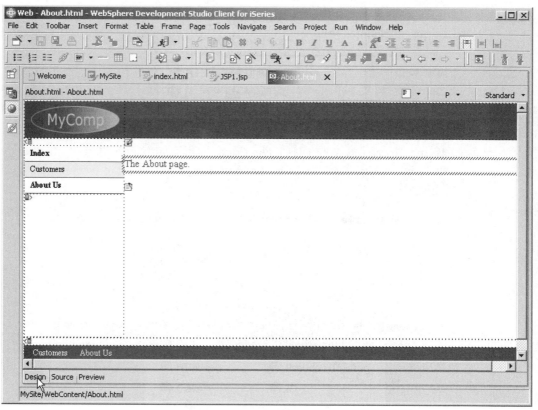

Figure 4-3: Here's the About Us page in design mode.

At this point, the cursor will be in the area that can be edited, specifically the paragraph you entered that says "The About page." But try to click anywhere else on the page. For example, click underneath the left navigation bar, as shown in Figure 4-4. The Page Designer uses crosshatching to indicate the areas of the page that cannot be edited.

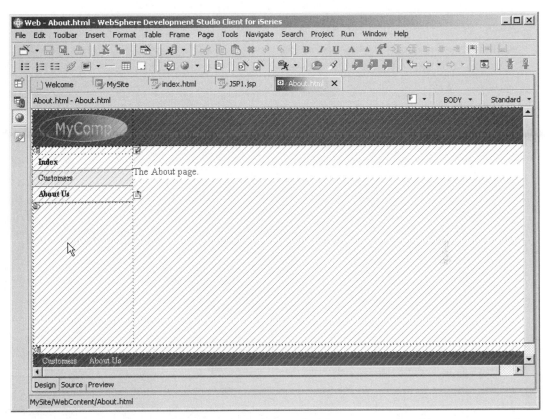

Figure 4-4: If your cursor is placed outside of the editable area, crosshatching appears on the page.

The cross-hatched part of the screen cannot be changed in Design mode. The WDSC team has gone further: You cannot edit the code in Source mode, either. If you switch to Source mode by clicking on the Source mode tab at the bottom of the edit view, you'll see mostly gray text, indicating areas that cannot be edited, as shown in Figure 4-5.

❑ **4.3(c) Click on the Source mode tab.**

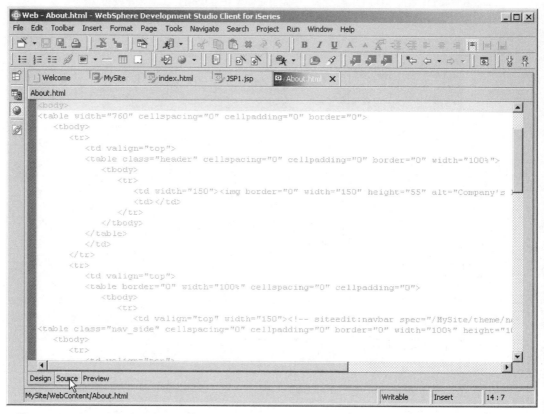

Figure 4-5: Non-editable portions of the template are shown in gray text.

The sections of the HTML code that came from the template (and thus cannot be edited) are shown in gray text. The editor will not allow you to change the contents of those areas.

Areas that are editable are shown in their normal coloring. Roll up to the top of the source to see an example of this. Figure 4-6 shows the top of this particular source file, with a number of editable META tags in the header.

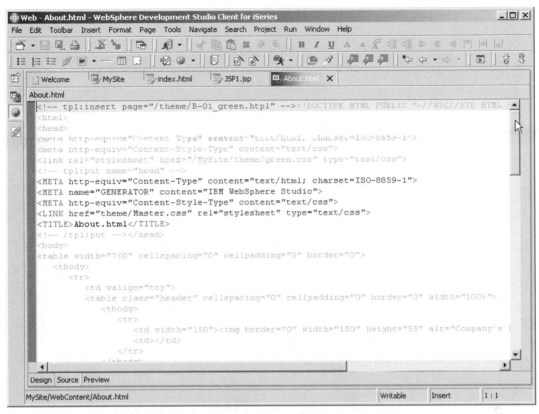

Figure 4-6: At the top of the About Us page are a number of editable tags.

How does the editor determine what is editable and what is not? That's done by actually analyzing the HTML and looking for special comments embedded in the source code. In the following section, I'll walk you through the generated source for this particular page.

First, take a look at the initial lines of the template and the generated HTML. (If you want to see the code for the template in the editor, you can bring it up by double-clicking on the B-01_green.htpl file in the theme folder and then clicking on the Source mode tab.)

Listing 4-1: These are the first two lines of the B-01_green template.

```
<!DOCTYPE HTML PUBLIC "-//W3C//DTD HTML 4.01 Transitional//EN">
<html>
```

Listing 4-2: These are the first three lines of a page generated from the template.

```
<!- tpl:insert page="/theme/B-01_green.htpl" ->
<!DOCTYPE HTML PUBLIC "-//W3C//DTD HTML 4.01 Transitional//EN">
<html>
```

The only difference is the additional first line in the generated code, which indicates what template this page is based on. It is used to later regenerate the page if the template changes. The tpl: syntax indicates that this tag is part of the template language used in WDSC.

Next, take a look at the header portion of the code.

Listing 4-3: Here's the HEAD section of the template.

```
<head>
<meta http-equiv="Content-Type" content="text/html; charset=ISO-8859-1">
<meta http-equiv="Content-Style-Type" content="text/css">
<link rel="stylesheet" href="/MySite/theme/green.css" type="text/css">
<!- tpl:insert attribute="head" ->
<title>B-01_green</title>
<!- /tpl:insert -></head>>
```

Listing 4-4: Here's the HEAD section of the generated code.

```
<head>
<meta http-equiv="Content-Type" content="text/html; charset=ISO-8859-1">
<meta http-equiv="Content-Style-Type" content="text/css">
<link rel="stylesheet" href="/MySite/theme/green.css" type="text/css">
<!- tpl:put name="head" ->
<META http-equiv="Content-Type" content="text/html; charset=ISO-8859-1">
<META name="GENERATOR" content="IBM WebSphere Studio">
<META http-equiv="Content-Style-Type" content="text/css">
<LINK href="theme/Master.css" rel="stylesheet" type="text/css">
<TITLE>About.html</TITLE>
<!- /tpl:put -></head>
```

Most HTML documents have a HEAD section much like this one. It starts with a HEAD tag and ends with a /HEAD tag. In between are typically a TITLE tag, a number of META tags, and maybe a couple of LINK tags for CSS references. This HEAD section is no different, with one exception: There are two TPL tags.

In the template, you'll notice a pair of tags: tpl:insert and /tpl:insert. These identify an editable area in the template, also called a content area. In this case, the name of the content area is "head." You may recall this name from when you actually applied the template back in Step 2.7. You mapped this to the HEAD region of your pages. What happened when the template was applied to the page was that the appropriate tags from the HEAD region of the page were included within this section of the template. The tags are changed to tpl:put and /tpl:put, and the code between those tags can be edited.

The next section is the BODY section, which is similarly constructed: In the template, there are tpl:insert and /tpl:insert tags, which are then replaced by tpl:put and /tpl:put tags in the generated code. And in between those latter two tags is the original HTML you added: <P>The About page.</P>

This is the only code you can actually modify. The rest of the code is protected. However, if you look closely at the code, you will notice a couple of other tpl: tags, and these tags are extremely important. These are the siteedit: tags, and they are used to generate the navigation widgets. An example of a siteedit: tag and the code it generates are shown in Listing 4-5.

Listing 4-5: The code between siteedit: tags generates the navigation widgets.

```
<!- siteedit:navbar spec="/MySite/theme/nav_side.html" targetlevel="1-3"->
<table class="nav_side" cellspacing="0" cellpadding="0" border="0"
width="100%" height="100%">
    <tbody>
        <tr>
            <td valign="top">
            <table border="0" width="100%" cellspacing="0" cellpadding="2">
                <tbody>
                    <tr>
                        <td class="nav-s-highlighted"><a href=
                            "/MySite/index.html">Index</a></td>
                    </tr>
                    <tr>
                        <td class="nav-s-normal"><a href=
                            "/MySite/JSP1.jsp">Customers</a></td>
                    </tr>
```

```
            <tr>
                <td class="nav-s-highlighted">About Us</td>
            </tr>
          </tbody>
        </table>
        </td>
      </tr>
   </tbody>
 </table>
 <!- /siteedit:navbar ->
```

I will return to this particular piece of code later. For now, it is sufficient to note that the code between the siteedit:navbar and /siteedit:navbar tags is generated based on the current layout of the Web site and is regenerated whenever the site is rearranged in Web Site Designer. This is the secret to always having up-to-date navigation widgets.

Step 4.4—Modifying a template

Right now, your template at least has a little customization because you've changed the logo to contain MyComp as the company name. That was fairly easy to do: You simply changed the GIF file, which in turn automatically changed all the pages. In this step, you're going to continue the customization, only this time you will do it by changing the template itself.

To do that, you need to edit the template. Since you currently have the About Us page maximized, you can't see the other views. Restore the About Us page to its normal size by once again double-clicking on the About.html tab.

❑ **4.4(a) Double-click on the About.html tab to restore the page to normal size.**

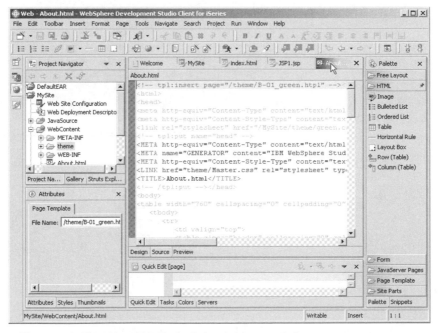

Figure 4-7: The About Us page is back to normal size.

Now that the About Us page is restored, you can use the Project Navigator view to edit the template. First, you'll need to expand the theme folder if it's not already expanded, as illustrated in Figure 4-8, and then double-click on the B-01_green.htpl template as shown in Figure 4-9.

❑ **4.4(b) Expand the theme folder.**

❑ **4.4(c) Double-click on the B-01_green.htpl template to open it.**

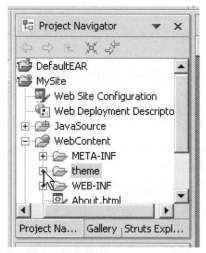

Figure 4-8: Expand the theme folder.

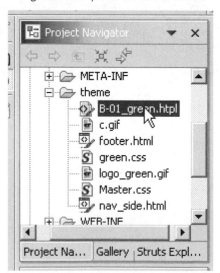

Figure 4-9: Open the template (B-01_green.htpl) by double-clicking on it.

At this point, the template should come up in the editor view in Design mode, as depicted in Figure 4-10.

> **Note:** If the template comes up in a mode other than Design mode, simply click on the Design mode tab to switch the view to the one you see in Figure 4-10.

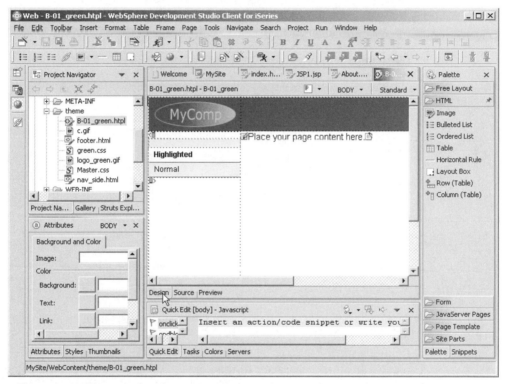

Figure 4-10: The template is open now.

Now that the template is open, you can modify it.

Position your cursor just to the right of the company logo and type in a corporate motto. In Figure 4-11, the phrase "The Best Company in the World!" has been entered immediately to the right of the MyComp logo (this may be hard to see in the book).

> **Release Note:** Due to a bug in the Design mode of V5.1.2, in order to execute this step, you must scroll the view all the way to the right. You will see a very narrow cell at the extreme right of the screen. Click inside this cell and start typing. When you type the first letter, the cell will expand. If you scroll back to the left, the screen will now look like the one shown in Figure 4-11.

❑ **4.4(d) Type in a motto to the right of the logo.**

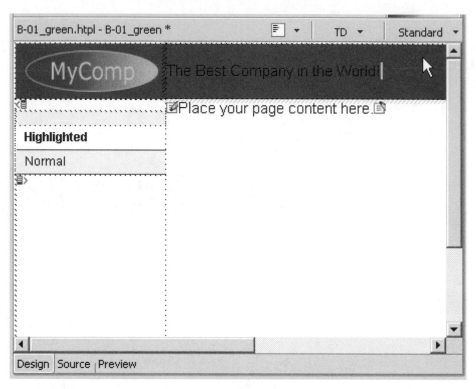

Figure 4-11: Position your cursor to the right of the logo and type in "The Best Company in the World!"

You can add a little character to the phrase. Select the entire phrase and then click the Increase Font Size tool, as shown in Figure 4-12. The Increase Font Size tool is part of the Format toolbar; if the Increase Font Size tool is not visible, use the main menu option Toolbar to show the Format toolbar. Because of a bug, the Format toolbar may not be visible even if Format is checked in the Toolbar menu, and vice versa. You may have to uncheck and recheck the Format option in the Toolbar menu to get the Increase Font Size tool to appear.

❏ **4.4(e) Select the entire motto and press the Increase Font Size tool.**

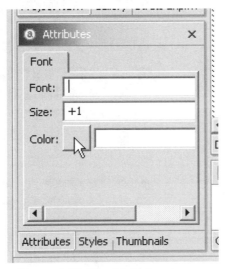

Figure 4-12: Select the motto and then click the Increase Font Size tool.

At this point, you'll notice that the Attributes view in the lower left will change to a dialog for paragraphs. This is because, under the covers, the Page Designer has added a paragraph tag around your text in order to increase the font size. That's handy, because you can use the dialog to also change the color. Click on the color button as shown in Figure 4-13. A color selector like the one in Figure 4-14 will appear. Select the color white and click OK as depicted in Figure 4-15.

❏ **4.4(f) Click the color selector button.**

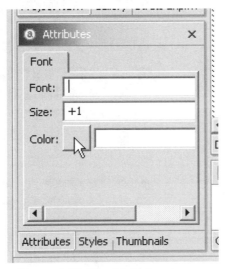

Figure 4-13: The Attributes view now has the paragraph dialog; click the color selector button.

❏ **4.4(g) Select the color white.**

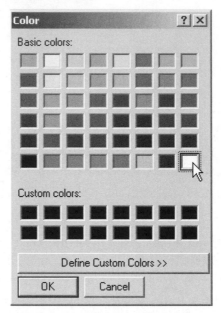

Figure 4-14: Select white.

❏ **4.4(h) Press OK to apply the color change.**

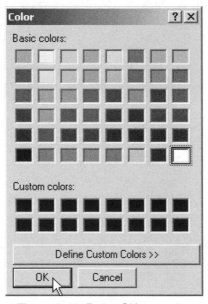

Figure 4-15: Press OK to apply the change.

Click somewhere in the editor (to de-select the banner text). You will now see a nice white banner phrase like the one in Figure 4-16.

Figure 4-16: You've now updated the template.

You've changed the template. Now you have to propagate that change throughout your Web site. This is the part that is really about as close to magic as you'll get in a Web tool. All you have to do is save the template, and all the rest of the work will be done for you.

❑ **4.4(i) Right-click in the editor view and select Save.**

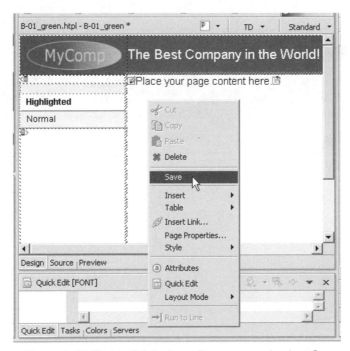

Figure 4-17: Right-click in the editor pane and select Save to save the template changes.

The cursor changes to the infamous hourglass, and the changes begin. Page Designer will save the template. Then, it will find all pages that currently use that template and regenerate them. You don't have to do a thing, except watch the status bar.

Setting contents: /MySite/WebContent/theme/B-01_green.h...JSP Validation: Validating /MySite/WebContent/JSP1.jsp

Figure 4-18: The status bar will indicate the progress as the change is propagated throughout the Web site.

Once everything is done, the cursor will no longer be an hourglass, and you can then click on one of your pages to see the results. Click on the About.html tab, and then click on the Preview tab to see the change. (If you are already in Preview mode, you'll need to click on a different mode and then back to Preview mode to refresh the view.)

❑ **4.4(j) Click on the About.html tab.**

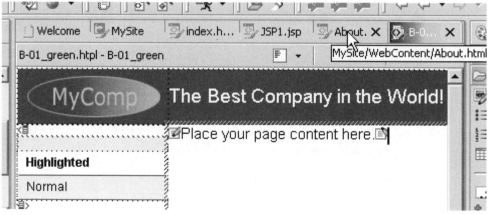

Figure 4-19: Click on the About.html tag to bring up the About Us page.

❏ **4.4(k) Click on the Preview mode tab if you're not already in Preview mode.**

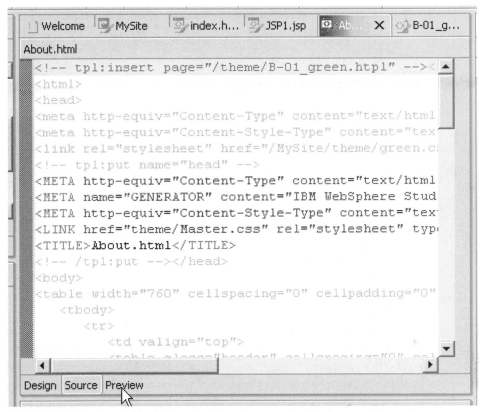

Figure 4-20: If the About Us page is in Source or Design mode, click on Preview mode.

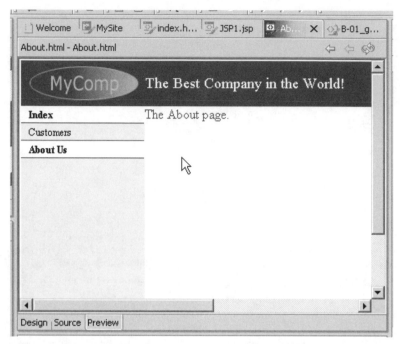

Figure 4-21: And here is your page, with the changes implemented.

There are a couple of points to be made here. First, the motto is not editable when you are editing individual pages. If you were to try to select the motto in Design mode, the "protected mode" cross-hatching would appear. In Source mode, you simply wouldn't be able to change the source. The only way to change the motto is to go back to the template and change it there.

The other thing you may have noticed is that the font for the motto is different when looking at the About Us page than it is when looking at the template. That has to do with the style sheets associated with the pages. The template references only the green.css style sheet, while the page itself also includes the Master.css style sheet a little later in the HEAD section. Both contain definitions for the BODY style, but in green.css, the font family is Arial, while in Master.css, it is Times New Roman. When looking at the template, there is no Master.css, so the font for the banner is Arial. Since the reference to the Master.css style sheet appears later in the page, its definition takes precedence and thus the font used is Times New Roman.

I'll discuss style sheets in more detail in Step 5, but one way to avoid this problem is to make sure all style sheet references are in the template.

Step 4.5—Navigation site parts

GOAL

In this step, you will be introduced to the concept of site parts, which are used to generate navigation widgets.

Note: The rest of Step 4 is dedicated to modifying site parts. Learning this technique will allow you to change how your navigation widgets look. It's not a simple task; you'll learn a completely new syntax, much of which is not intuitive. WDSC supplies a number of preconfigured widgets, and if you're comfortable with how they look, you don't have to learn the syntax. If you find this particular topic a little overwhelming, you can skip this chapter and the InStep, and just follow the instructions in Step 4.6. You can come back to these steps another time and read about the site part language.

Navigation site parts are small documents that look a little bit like HTML but are really macros for generating code. They have their own tag language, which looks a little bit like the Java Standard Tag Library (JSTL). Some people have mentioned that the language looks a bit like XSLT. I haven't been able to find any documentation on the language, but I have done enough empirical study to learn how much of it works and even to be able to modify the navigation site parts as needed.

Navigation site parts are designed to allow you to easily add a dynamic widget to your page that will change as your Web site changes. Navigation site parts process a set of pages through a macro. The flexible nature of defining the pages to be processed allows this process to be used for navigation, breadcrumbs, even site maps.

Navigation site parts can be added to any page by selecting the Site Parts drawer from the Palette, but they're really most powerful when used in a template; that way, your entire Web site can get updated automatically in response to changes.

As I said, there's not much information on this language out there. As far as I know, this book contains the only published documentation available anywhere—another exclusive for *Step by Step* readers! Not that you'll get an exhaustive reference here, either. All I can do is relate to you what I've found while playing with the tool.

I'd like to start by taking a look at an example of a working navigation bar, one that has been implemented in a page and is working properly. In fact, let's just use the navigation bars supplied with the B-01_green template, since that's the template we've been using throughout the book. I like this particular template because it's a nice middle ground between simple and complex; it has two navigation bars, one on the left side and one on the bottom of the page. I like the fact that the page has a footer; I think having most if not all of the pages share a common size lends a certain consistency to the Web site.

There are actually two parts to the use of any navigation site part. There is the site part itself as well as the line of code in the template that activates the site part. Both are critically important, and unfortunately both are completely undocumented. But that's part of the fun!

Let's pull out all the activation lines in the template. In this particular template, there are two:

Listing 4-6: This is the code in the B-01_green template that invokes the side navigation bar.

```
<!- siteedit:navbar spec="/MySite/theme/nav_side.html" targetlevel="1-3"->
(...)
<!- /siteedit:navbar ->
```

Listing 4-7: This code creates the footer navigation bar.

```
<!- siteedit:navbar spec="/MySite/theme/footer.html" target="sibling"->
(...)
<!- /siteedit:navbar ->
```

Notice that both have similar, though not completely identical, syntaxes:

spec	"/MySite/theme/nav_side.html"	"/MySite/theme/footer.html"
targetlevel	"1-3"	
target		"sibling"

Each identifies a "spec," or specification. This is the name of the HTML file that contains the navigation site part. And while the left navigation bar uses the keyword targetlevel, the footer simply specifies target. The difference semantically has to do with whether you are processing all pages in the Web site or just pages directly related to the current page.

In the case of the left navigation bar, you want a complete list of all pages in the Web site, or at least those in the first three levels of the hierarchy. For the footer, you are generating links only to this page's siblings. This high-level selection of pages to process is done in the page that invokes the site part. If you insert a navigation site part using the supplied wizards, you will be prompted for all of these fields.

If you do insert a site part, one or more files will be copied into your workspace. If the site part is brought in via a template, it will be stored in your theme folder, but if you manually add a site part to a page, any imported files will show up in the same folder as the page. More than one file may be imported if the navigation site part you select uses graphics; for example, the horizontal tab navigation site part uses small graphics to create a "tabbed" look and feel.

Now let's examine how the site parts actually work. I've described them as macros and alluded to the fact that they use a syntax similar to JSTL. By that, I mean that there are certain tags that act as controllers and others that output expressions. Unlike a JSP scriptlet approach, where you would code your loop using pure Java, this is more like the tagged approach favored by JSTL and Struts. For example, there is a tag known as forEach, which will iterate through a set of objects. There is also a set of conditional tags—choose, when, and otherwise—which together are used to create a standard case structure.

This language is used on the set of pages that you specified in the siteedit tag. For example, if you specified siblings as your target, the forEach tag would be used to cycle through each of the siblings. This is an object-oriented approach, where each page is an object that has attributes. You can test these attributes to further refine your processing.

The following is an example of an IBM-supplied navigation site part. Specifically, this is the document nav_side.html, which is used to create a navigation bar on the side of your Web page. I'll review the various sections of the document.

```
<!DOCTYPE HTML PUBLIC "-//W3C//DTD HTML 4.01 Transitional//EN">
<html>
```

These first two lines contain standard HTML header code. The idea is that the document is supposed to look like any standard HTML document, only with lots of embedded siteedit tags to control the generation of the code.

```
<head>
<title>nav_side.html</title>
</head>
```

This is the HEAD region of the document. It basically just contains the name of the document.

```
<body>
<table class="nav_side" cellspacing="0" cellpadding="0" border="0"
width="100%" height="100%">
    <tbody>
        <tr>
            <td valign="top">
            <table border="0" width="100%" cellspacing="0" cellpadding="2">
                <tbody>
```

The BODY region begins the actual code for the widget. In this case, the code is a table with a specific class. That table has a row, which has a cell, which has another table. While this specific example is a little bit of overkill, you can make your own navigation site part with little or no trouble.

```
<!-siteedit:forEach var="item" items="${sitenav.items}"->
```

This is a standard forEach loop. Since it's working on sitenav.items, I know that the invocation tag used the target attribute to specify a set of Web pages. InStep 4.5.a has more information on the details of the way this functions.

```
<!--siteedit:choose-->
```

This statement starts a standard case construct.

```
<!-siteedit:when test="${item.self}"->
        <tr>
            <td class="nav-s-highlighted">${item.label}</td>
        </tr>
<!-/siteedit:when->
```

This is an example of one condition. In this case, if the Web page is the one we're currently on, we don't need to have a link, and thus you don't see an anchor tag. This actually is the heart of the entire navigation site part concept: being able to specify which pages to present in the navigation widget and to then present each page differently, whether it is the current page, or an ancestor, or whatever. This is what allows you to write a single navigation site part to handle most or all of your Web site (rather than writing a different one for each page).

```
<!-siteedit:when test="${item.ancestor}"->
        <tr>
            <td class="nav-s-highlighted">
                <a href="${item.href}">${item.label}</a>
            </td>
        </tr>
<!-/siteedit:when->
<!-siteedit:otherwise->
        <tr>
            <td class="nav-s-normal">
                <a href="${item.href}">${item.label}</a>
            </td>
        </tr>
<!-/siteedit:otherwise->
<!-/siteedit:choose->
```

This is the rest of the case construct. Specifically, it treats ancestors (this page's parent, grandparent, and so on) a little differently, assigning a different class to those pages than to other pages. In either case, though, it creates a link to the page using the navigation label.

```
<!-/siteedit:forEach-->
```

This is the end of the forEach loop.

```
            </tbody>
          </table>
          </td>
        </tr>
      </tbody>
    </table>
    </body>
    </html>
```

And this is the rest of the code. Everything up to the </BODY> tag is output to the browser.

This code is used to generate HTML within your Web page. The actual HTML code generated will depend on the layout of your Web site. In our current example, from the index page, the generated code would look this:

Listing 4-8: The generated code for navigation widget on the Index page.

```
<table class="nav_side" cellspacing="0" cellpadding="0" border="0"
width="100%" height="100%">
    <tbody>
        <tr>
            <td valign="top">
            <table border="0" width="100%" cellspacing="0" cell-
padding="2">
                <tbody>
                    <tr>
                        <td class="nav-s-highlighted">Index</td>
                    </tr>
                    <tr>
                        <td class="nav-s-normal"><a
href="JSP1.jsp">Customers</a></td>
                    </tr>
                    <tr>
                        <td class="nav-s-normal"><a
href="About.html">About Us</a></td>
                    </tr>
                </tbody>
            </table>
            </td>
        </tr>
    </tbody>
</table>
```

InStep 4.5.a—The navigation site part language

> ## GOAL
>
> In this step, you'll learn more about the site part language used to create navigation widgets.

As I mentioned in the previous step, there is no formal documentation on the language used to create navigation widgets. I indicated that there were two parts to the definition: the site part and the tag that invokes the site part in a page. Each plays a different but important part in the process.

Invocation Tags

An invocation tag (siteedit:navbar, siteedit:navtab, siteedit:navtrail, or siteedit:sitemap) will appear in your HTML or JSP page to identify which of the pages in the Web site are to be processed, as well as the site part used to process them. While not completely intuitive, the various attributes for invocation tags can be deciphered by using the wizard to insert navigation site parts with various values and then looking at the resulting code. This is how I got most of my information on this particular feature, although I did have to do a little experimenting to see if certain combinations not normally provided by the wizard would work.

There are two sets of attributes for the invocation tags. One set is common to all the tags:

- *Spec:* Specification. This is the name of the file that contains the site part language that will actually create the widget. A set of pages will be created based on the other attributes in this group, and then that set of pages will be passed to the site part identified here.

- *Targetlevel:* A range of level numbers. Level 1 is the top of the site, and levels are numbered sequentially. Thus, a range of 1-3 would include the first three levels of the site. All pages within those levels will be included in the list. This is primarily used for site maps, although it can be used for navigation bars as well. Note: To use targetlevel in a navigation bar, you'll have to manually modify the invocation tag. The wizard only allows targetlevel on the sitemap part.

- *Target:* Mutually exclusive with targetlevel, target uses keywords to identify the pages to process. Values include home (top page of the Web site), topchildren (immediate children of the top page), parent (the current page's parent), ancestor (the current page's ancestors, all the way to the top), self (the current page), firstchild (the first child page of the current page), children (the current page's immediate children), siblings (all pages at the same level as the current page), previous (the previous page at this level), and next (the next page at this level).

- *Label:* Used only in conjunction with target when "prev" and/or "next" are defined. This value defines the text used on the previous and next labels.

The second set of attributes for the invocation tags is the special set:

- *Start, End, Separator:* Used only with navtrail parts. This defines the first character in the trail, the last character in the trail, and the character that separates the links.

- *navtabImg, navtabImgSel:* Used only with navtab parts. This attribute lists the GIF files used to build the tab portion of a screen. I don't use navtab parts, so I haven't done a lot of research on this particular attribute, but it looks pretty straightforward. Each attribute is a list of nine file names separated by a vertical bar, with each file name being the name of a GIF file. One set is used to draw the images for an unselected tab, the other for a selected tab.

Site Parts

Once the site part is invoked, then the site part language takes over. The site part language also consists of a number of siteedit tags. The tags inside a site part are even more vague than the invocation tags. As I noted earlier, some of the tags are based on the JSTL language, but many of them are more obscure.

They rely on an object structure that is simply not documented. I haven't been able to find anything on this anywhere, and I've tried. I've done file searches and scanned binary code, and still I've only come up with a few basic facts.

TAGS

A number of tags have been lifted almost directly from JSTL. These include forEach, choose, when, otherwise, and if. I haven't checked for others; if you feel ambitious, you might want to try an else tag, for example, but since else is not a part of the base JSTL, I would guess that it won't work here, either.

```
<!- siteedit:forEach var="varname" items="list" varStatus="statusvar" ->
```

The forEach tag is an iterator, and it will iterate over a list of objects. In each iteration, the variable varname will contain the next entry from list. The variable varStatus has two attributes-first and last-that can be checked to determine the position of the object in the list for pre- and post-processing.

```
<!- siteedit:if test"${ Boolean test }" ->
```

The code within this tag (that is, between this tag and the matching /siteedit:if tag) will be output if the Boolean test is true. Boolean tests include numeric comparisons such as node.childcount > 0, string comparisons such as item.label == 'Home', and even certain attributes, such as status.first and status.last.

```
<!- siteedit:choose ->
<!- siteedit:when test"${ Boolean test }" ->
<!- siteedit:otherwise ->
```

These tags define a classic case construct. The choose tag surrounds a number of when tags and an optional otherwise tag. Each when tag is tested, and if the Boolean test is true (see the if tag for more detail), the code in the tag is included. If no when test is matched and an otherwise tag is defined, the code in the otherwise tag is included.

OBJECTS

I have no idea how many objects are actually available to the site parts. In my research, I've turned up four so far. There could be others. So far, these are the objects I've been using:

- *sitenav:* This object contains the set of pages selected by the attributes of the invocation tag. The sitenav object has two sets of attributes. One set simply contains values as specified on the invocation tag. These match the special attributes I listed earlier: end, start, separator, navtabImg, navtabSelImg. The other set is actually a single attribute, either items or tops, depending on the attributes specified in the invocation tag. If you specify target, then the items attribute will contain a list of all pages selected. If you specify targetlevel, then the tops attribute will contain a list of nodes, each node being a page at the highest level you specified (this is primarily used for site maps).

- *node:* Used in sitemaps, a node represents a position in the Web site. It can have zero or more children. The number of children is located in childcount, while the children themselves are in the variable children, which is a list of nodes. A node also has an associated Web page, and the object that represents that page is located in the variable called item.

- *item:* An item represents a Web page. It has two fields and two Boolean attributes. The label field is the navigation label of the page, and the href field is the relative URL of the page. The two Booleans relate to the current page: The self Boolean means that this is the current page; the ancestor Boolean means this is a parent of the current page.

- *varStatus:* Used when processing a list, a varStatus object contains two flags-first and last-which indicate whether the item is the first or last entry in the list.

Step 4.6—Customizing your navigation widget

GOAL

In this step, you will customize one of the navigation bars in your Web site.

I've gone through quite a bit of explanation of the concept of site parts and how they are used to create navigation widgets. I've done this primarily so that you could customize the navigation widgets. The ones supplied by IBM are fine, but they really don't have a lot of Web appeal. They attempt a little eye candy with the graphical borders, but I'm not a big fan of gratuitous graphics—especially when you can get some really nice look-and-feel capabilities simply by using CSS.

So, in this last section of Step 4, I'm going to show you how to customize the navigation widget to generate code that is far more CSS-enabled and that delivers a far nicer look and feel. However, be warned that at the end of this step, the page won't look very nice. In fact, it will look *less* nice, because you haven't yet created the appropriate styles.

Typically, you would already have the style sheet in place. You would have created a throwaway Web page, just to get an idea of how you wanted your navigation to look. I'm going to assume we've already done that and know exactly what we want to generate. In fact, this is the code we want to generate:

Listing 4-9: This is the code you would like to see from the customized navigation widget.

```
<table class=ln>
<td>
  <span class=ln2>Index</span>
  <a href="Jsp1.jsp">Customers</a>
  <a href="About.html">About Us</a>
</td>
</table>
```

Note how brief the code is. Not only that, but there are additional benefits to this approach that you'll see in the next Step. By using a style sheet to format the links and by removing as much formatting as possible from the page itself, you will have a lot more flexibility in determining the final look and feel.

The downside is that, at least for a short time, the menu is going to look quite plain. But bear with me, because you're going to really appreciate the result.

There are several ways to customize the navigation. One way is simply to modify the IBM-supplied site part. However, that could have some unwanted side effects. Instead, I suggest copying the site part to a new file and modifying the new file. Then, you simply need to change the spec attribute on the invocation tag of your template, and the new navigation widget will be propagated throughout your site.

Copying a file is a fairly standard procedure. Select the file to be copied, use the main menu to copy it (Edit/Copy), select the target destination, and select Edit/Paste. Rename the file if necessary, and it will then be copied.

☐ **4.6(a) Select nav_side.html (in the theme folder).**

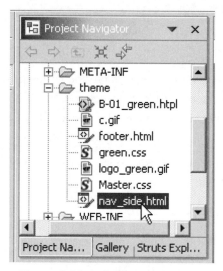

Figure 4-22: Left-click on the nav_side.html file to select it.

❏ **4.6(b) From the main menu, select Edit/Copy.**

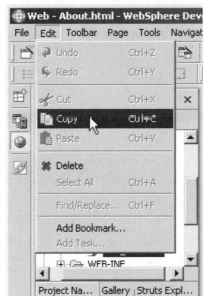

*Figure 4-23: Select Edit/Copy from
the main menu (Ctrl+C is a shortcut).*

The file is ready to be copied. In order to stay consistent, I'd like you to copy it into the theme folder, where all your other template information is located.

❏ **4.6(c) Select the theme folder.**

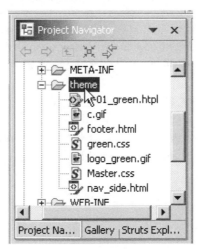

*Figure 4-24: Left-click on the
theme folder to select it.*

❑ **4.6(d) Select Edit/Paste from the main menu.**

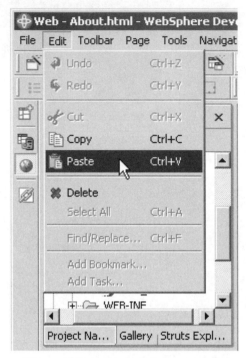

*Figure 4-25: Select Edit/Paste from the
main menu (Ctrl+V is a shortcut).*

Hint: Many of the normal Windows alternate methods for copying objects apply
here. For example, you can right-click on the nav_side.html and select Copy,
and then right-click on the theme folder and select Paste.

Since you will be attempting to copy in a file with the same name as an existing
file, you will see the Name Conflict dialog. At this point, you can rename the file.
Enter the name myns.html (short for My Navbar-Side). Press OK, and you'll see
the file appear in the folder, as shown in Figure 4-27.

❏ **4.6(e) Enter myns.html in the new name field and press OK.**

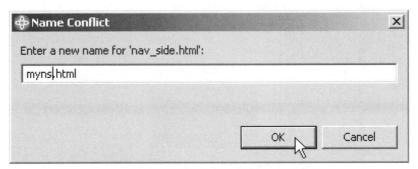

Figure 4-26: Enter the new name for the file, myns.html.

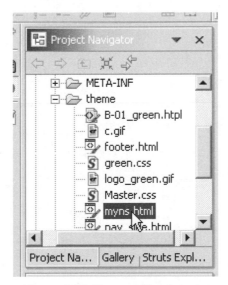

Figure 4-27: The new file appears
in the theme folder.

Now you can edit it. Double-click on the new file, and it will appear in the editor view as shown in Figure 4-28. The figure shows Preview mode, but you want to work in Source mode. Unless your editor comes up already in Source mode, press the Source mode tab to access the source, seen in Figure 4-29.

❑ **4.6(f) Double-click on myns.html to edit it.**

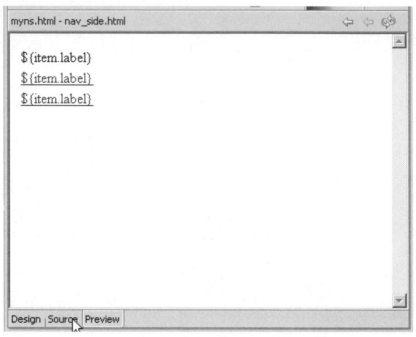

Figure 4-28: Here's the new navigation site part in Preview mode.

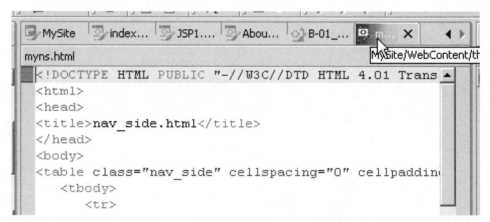

Figure 4-29: Here is the source, which is a bit cramped in the standard view.

Because of our 800×600 size, the code is somewhat difficult to see, so I want you to maximize the editor. Do this by double-clicking on the myns.html tab, which will be the rightmost tab above the editor view if you've been following along with the steps.

❑ **4.6(g) Double-click on the myns.html tab in the editor to maximize it.**

When the view maximizes, type in the code from Listing 4-9, as shown in Figure 4-30. There is also a text file on your CD-ROM, in the folder Imports, called Step4-6.txt. This file contains the code for the myns.html site part. You can open that file up in the text editor of your choice and just copy and paste it into the editor. Right-click in the editor and select Save to save the new code.

> **Note:** In this case, you completely replaced the existing code. You could have simply created a new file. But most often, you'll probably be working from a base and making minor edits, so I just wanted to show you how to do that.

Listing 4-10: This is the code for the myns.tml site part.

```
<!DOCTYPE HTML PUBLIC "-//W3C//DTD HTML 4.01 Transitional//EN">
<html>
<head>
<title>myns.html</title>
</head>
<body>
<table class=ln>
<td>
<!-siteedit:forEach var="item" items="${sitenav.items}"->
 <!-siteedit:choose >
  <!-siteedit:when test="${item.self}"->
  <br><span class=ln2>${item.label}</span>
  <!-/siteedit:when->
  <!-siteedit:otherwise->
  <br><a href="${item.href}">${item.label}</a>
  <!-/siteedit:otherwise->
 <!-/siteedit:choose->
<!-/siteedit:forEach->
</td>
</table>
</body>
</html>
```

❑ **4.6(h) Enter the code from Listing 4-9.**

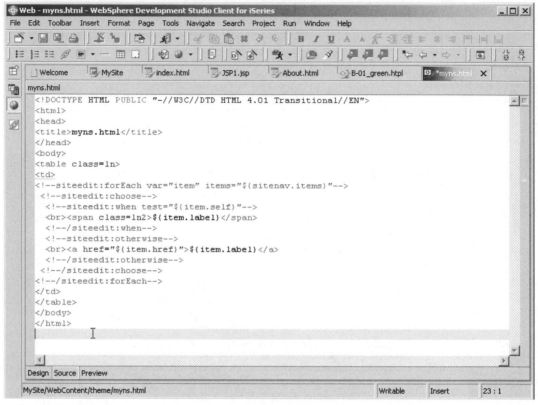

```
<!DOCTYPE HTML PUBLIC "-//W3C//DTD HTML 4.01 Transitional//EN">
<html>
<head>
<title>myns.html</title>
</head>
<body>
<table class=ln>
<td>
<!--siteedit:forEach var="item" items="${sitenav.items}"-->
 <!--siteedit:choose-->
  <!--siteedit:when test="${item.self}"-->
  <br><span class=ln2>${item.label}</span>
  <!--/siteedit:when-->
  <!--siteedit:otherwise-->
  <br><a href="${item.href}">${item.label}</a>
  <!--/siteedit:otherwise-->
 <!--/siteedit:choose-->
<!--/siteedit:forEach-->
</td>
</table>
</body>
</html>
```

Figure 4-30: Maximizing the view gives you enough room to comfortably type in the new code.

❑ **4.6(i) Right-click in the editor view and select Save.**

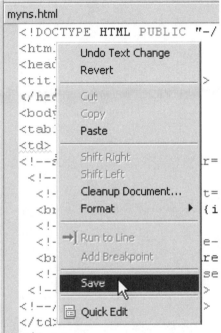

Figure 4-31: Right-click in the editor and select Save.

Now that you have a new site part, you need to include it in your Web pages. Since your Web pages are generated from a template, that means changing the template. This is good news, especially in larger Web sites, because it means you only have to change the code in one place.

❑ **4.6(j) Click on the B-01_green.html tab in the editor view.**

You'll see the source code shown in Figure 4-32. Since the code you need to change is at about line 30 and the screen shows only about 25 lines, you'll need to roll down a whole page.

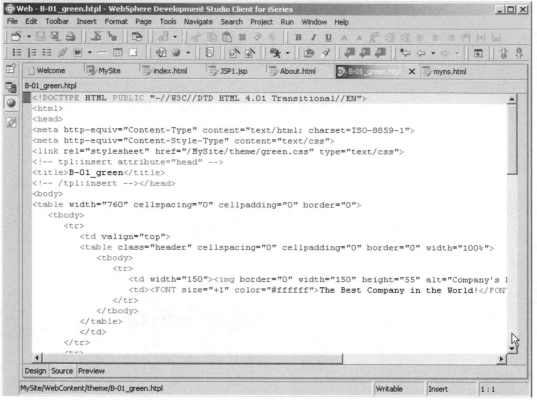

Figure 4-32: Roll down through the first page of the B-01_green.htpl template (shown in this figure).

❑ 4.6(k) Roll down a page.

This will bring up the second page of the template, as illustrated in Figure 4-33. About five lines down on that page, you'll see the siteedit invocation tag. You'll only see the left side of it. Scroll to the right a little bit to see where it references the nav_side.html site part, as shown in Figure 4-34. This is the only thing you need to change.

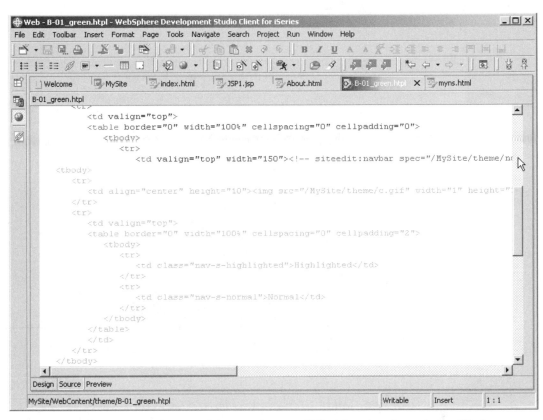

Figure 4-33: In the second page of the template, you'll find the siteedit tag in the fifth line.

```
"150"><!-- siteedit:navbar spec="/MySite/theme/nav_side.html" targetlevel="1-3"--><table
```

Figure 4-34: Currently, the invocation tag references nav_side.html.

Update the line to reference the new myns.html site part instead.

❑ 4.6(l) Update the invocation tag to reference myns.html.

```
"150"><!-- siteedit:navbar spec="/MySite/theme/myns.html" targetlevel="1-3"--><table clas
```

Figure 4-35: Change it to use myns.html instead.

That's the extent of what's required to change your entire Web site to use the new navigation site part. Save the new template code (right-click in the editor view and select Save).

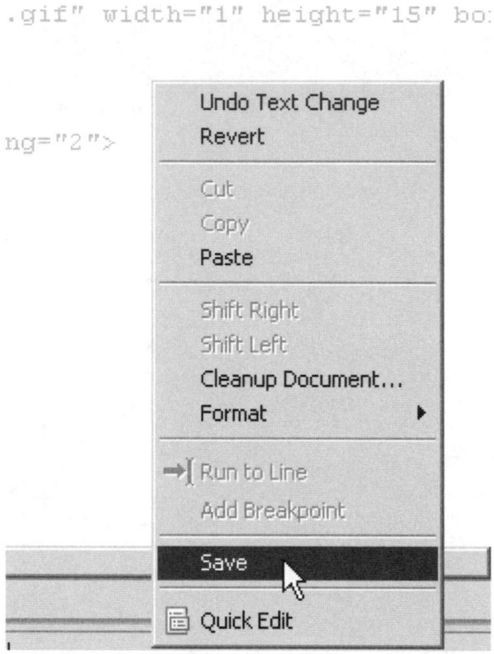

```
.gif" width="1" height="15" bo
```

```
ng="2">
```

Figure 4-36: Right-click and select Save.

❑ 4.6(m) Right-click in the editor view and select Save.

When you save the template, a status dialog will pop up, showing you all the work that is being done. Once that's finished, you can go back and see the effect on your Web site. Click on the About.html tab. Remember, template changes aren't immediately visible, so click on the Design mode tab and then back to the Preview mode. You'll see the new screen as shown in Figure 4-37.

❑ 4.6(n) Click on the About.html tab to see your results.

As I noted, the navigation widget isn't particularly pretty. But it's small, and it makes good use of styles, which will come in very handy in the next step.

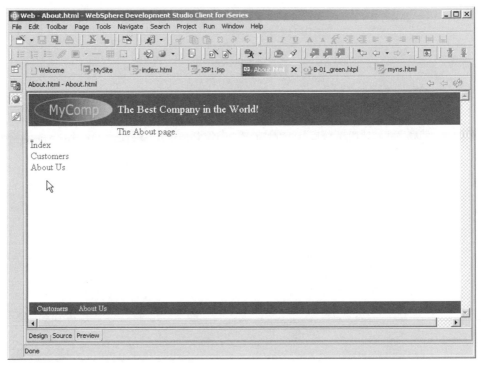

Figure 4-37: Here's the new About Us page with its new corporate logo and its navigation widget.

Caution: I'd like to caution you about some oddities with templates. First, the integration of custom site parts and templates via the wizards is not very good. In fact, I have so far been unable to successfully instruct the wizard to use a site part other than the IBM-supplied parts. Not only that, the templates themselves do not use the standard site parts used by the wizards. Because of this, I usually use the procedure outlined in this step: Start with the navigation site part included with the template, clone it, modify it, and then manually modify the invocation tag. Second, because of the way templates are created, they don't automatically show changes in your navigation site parts. As far as I can tell, the "example" code in the template is static code pulled in from somewhere else. Regardless of the changes you make to the navigation site part used in the template, you'll still see something like what is shown in Figure 4-38. The only way to really see the effect of your site part changes is to look at the generated pages in Preview mode. And remember to always "refresh" the Preview mode by switching to another mode and back again.

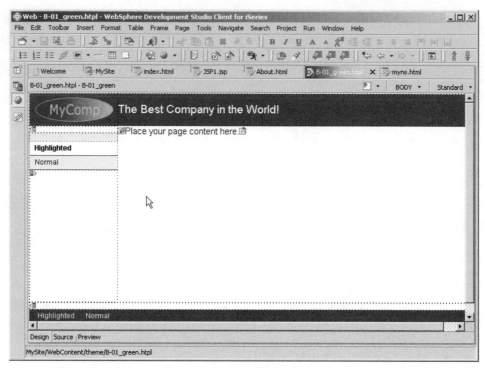

Figure 4-38: Templates do not reflect changes in their site parts; even after the changes, the template looks the same.

Step 5

CSS Designer

One of my favorite gems in the WDSC treasure chest is the CSS Designer. This often-overlooked feature is one of the best examples of interactive dialog design I've ever seen. The CSS Designer assists you in creating style sheets by using intuitive, context-sensitive dialogs. The Designer includes an excellent Preview mode that allows you to immediately see the effects of your changes either on a sample HTML page or even on your own HTML.

In this short step, you'll briefly use the CSS Designer to add some new styles to support the navigation site part you added in the previous step. The step itself won't show you much about the CSS Designer or styles in general, but even if you're not familiar with the language, just following along will get you acquainted with the basics.

Step 5.1—Adding new styles

GOAL

In this step, you will learn what a
template is composed of.

This step is not a primer on CSS; it assumes you already have some knowledge of
the underlying technology. In this step, you'll add a few new styles to an existing
style sheet. In the previous step, you created a navigation site part to generate the
following table:

**Listing 5-1: This is the code you would like to see from the customized navigation
widget.**

```
<table class=ln>
<td>
  <span class=ln2>Index</span>
  <a href="Jsp1.jsp">Customers</a>
  <a href="About.html">About Us</a>
</td>
</table>
```

If you review the generated code, you'll see two explicit classes, .ln and .ln2
("ln" stands for left navigation). You will need to add each of those styles. In
addition, you're going to be taking advantage of a feature of anchors (<A> tags)
that allows you to specify not only a "normal" style, but also a second style to use
when the user's cursor is on the link. This is the "hover" style, and careful style
design can yield some very useful effects. Because of the way CSS works, you can
modify the effect of all anchors by changing the style associated with the A style
selector, or you can change only the anchors in your table by specifying a nested
style. In this case, since the table has class ln, you can modify the anchors in that
table by creating style selector .ln A. In order to prevent the default behavior of
changing the font for visited links, you'll also add the selector .ln A:visited.
Finally, to take advantage of the special "hover" style, you need to specify the
style selector .ln A:hover.

But first, you need to decide whether to modify an existing style sheet or add a new one. There are currently two style sheets in the project: Master.css was added when you originally created the project, and green.css was added when you imported the template. Should you modify one of those or create a brand new one? Well, I think that the navigation widget is really part of the template, so it makes sense to me in this case to make changes associated with the navigation widget in the template's CSS file, green.css.

Therefore, you should start by editing the green.css style sheet. It is in the theme folder along with the rest of the template objects. Double-click on it to open it. The default editor for style sheets is the CSS Designer, so that should be the program that is loaded.

Note: If double-clicking does *not* bring up the CSS Designer, then you have somehow changed your default editor. To fix that, right-click on the style to bring up the pop-up menu and then select Open With/CSS Designer.

❑ **5.1(a) Double-click on green.css to bring it up in the CSS Designer.**

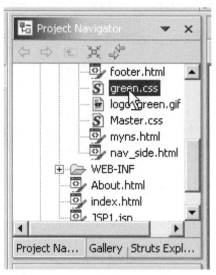

Figure 5-1: Double-click on green.css to bring it up in the CSS Designer.

When you do, you'll get a screen like the one in Figure 5-2. Given our limited real estate, it makes sense to maximize the CSS view. The CSS Designer is no different from any other editor; to maximize its view, just double-click on the associated tab in the editor view (in this case, the green.css tab).

❑ **5.1(b) Double-click on the green.css tab to maximize the CSS Designer.**

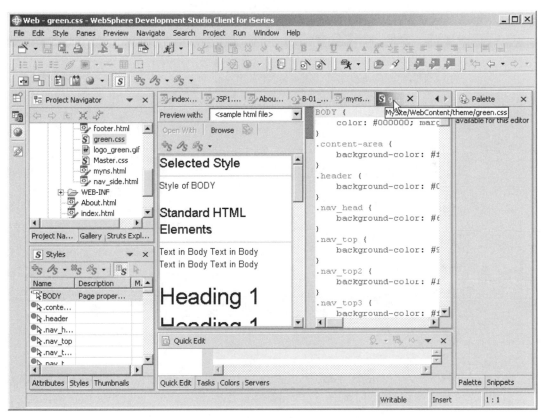

Figure 5-2: Double-click on the green.css tab to maximize the CSS Designer view.

Once you've done that, you'll see the screen in Figure 5-3. You'll note that there are two panes side by side. The right pane shows the actual source code of the style sheet, while the left pane shows the current effects of that style sheet on some sample HTML. Also, check out this very nice feature: You can click on a style in the right pane, and a visual representation of that style is displayed at the top of the left pane. In Figure 5-3, the style .nav_head was selected in the right pane, so the top of the left pane shows a paragraph using that style.

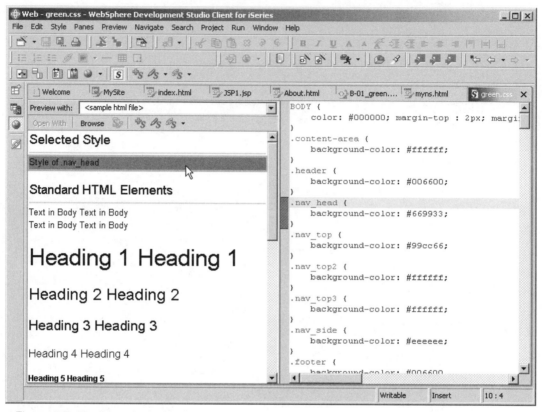

Figure 5-3: Having selected .nav_head in the right pane, the left pane shows an example of that style.

However, your current task is to add new styles, so the next step is to get those styles started. Listing 5-2 shows the five new style selectors you will be adding.

Listing 5-2: These are the five style selectors that need to be added.

```
ln {
    width: 100%;
    vertical-align: top;
    text-align: center;
}

.ln2 {
    width: 120px;
    color: #005000;
    font-size: 9pt;
```

```
        font-weight: bold;
        font-family: Verdana, sans-serif;
        text-decoration: none;
        background-color: #ffffff;
        border-style : solid;
        border-width : 2px;
        border-color : #005000 #ccffcc #ccffcc #005000;
        padding: 2px;
}

.ln A {
        width: 120px;
        color: #ffffff;
        font-size: 9pt;
        font-weight: bold;
        font-family: Verdana, sans-serif;
        text-decoration: none;
        background-color: #008800;
        border-style : solid;
        border-width : 2px;
        border-color : #ccffcc #005000 #005000 #ccffcc;
        padding: 2px;
}

.ln A:visited {
        color: #ffffff;
}

.ln A:hover{
        color: aqua;
        border-color : #005000 #ccffcc #ccffcc #005000;
        padding-left: 0px;
        padding-right: 4px;
          padding-top: 1px;
          padding-bottom: 3px;
          text-decoration: none;
          position: relative; top: 1px; left: 1px;
}
```

You can either type these in directly or use the wizard to add them. I'll walk you through the steps of using the wizard for one of them. From the main menu, select Style/Add. . . .

❑ **5.1(c) From the main menu, select Style/Add. . . .**

Figure 5-4: Select Style/Add . . . from
the main menu.

This will bring up the Set Selector dialog as shown in Figure 5-5. You're going to define the first style, so enter ".ln" as shown and press OK.

> **Note:** You'll notice that when you enter ".ln" in the name field, the radio button will automatically select Class, and the prompt for the field will change from "HTML tag name" to "Class name."

❑ **5.1(d) Enter ".ln" in the class name and press OK.**

Figure 5-5: Type in ".ln" and press OK.

This will bring up the Add Style wizard shown in Figure 5-6. While in this case you are adding a very simple style with only a couple of attributes, even the most complex style uses this same wizard. The menu on the left determines what is shown in the dialog on the right side of the wizard.

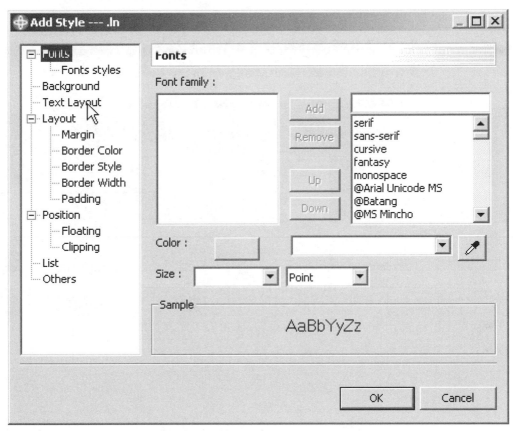

Figure 5-6: The Add Style wizard is showing the first page, Fonts.

In Figure 5-6, the first page of the wizard, Fonts, is displayed. When the wizard first comes up, the dialog usually displays the last selected menu option. Since this is the first time you've used the wizard, the Font page is shown.

The .ln style has only three attributes: vertical alignment, horizontal alignment, and width. The first two are in the Text Layout dialog, and the last one is in the Layout dialog. Start with the Text Layout page. To get to it, select Text Layout from the menu, and the dialog will change as shown in Figure 5-7.

❑ **5.1(e) Select Text Layout in the wizard's menu.**

Change the Vertical alignment value to Top by using the drop-down list, and then center your Horizontal alignment by clicking on the appropriate button as shown. Once that is done, you can switch to the Layout page by clicking on Layout in the menu as shown.

❑ **5.1(f) Change Vertical alignment to Top.**

❑ **5.1(g) Change Horizontal alignment to centered.**

❑ **5.1(h) Click on the Layout option in the menu.**

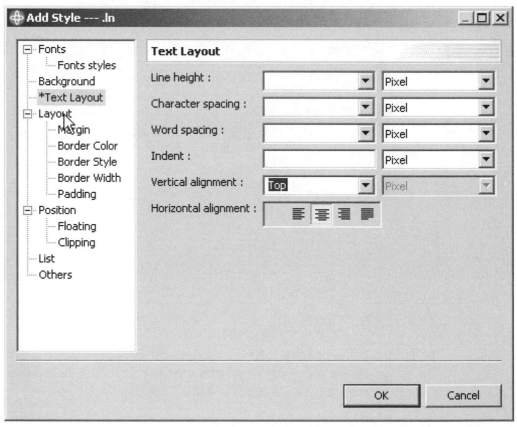

Figure 5-7: Set the values as shown and then click on Layout to move to the Layout page of the wizard.

As you can see in Figure 5-8, the Layout page is very simple. Note that it has a number of subpages (Margin, Border, and so on) that you are not interested in for this particular style. Instead, simply change the first value, Width, to 100% as shown. That's the last attribute for this style, so press OK to add the style to the style sheet.

❑ **5.1(i) Change width to 100% and press OK.**

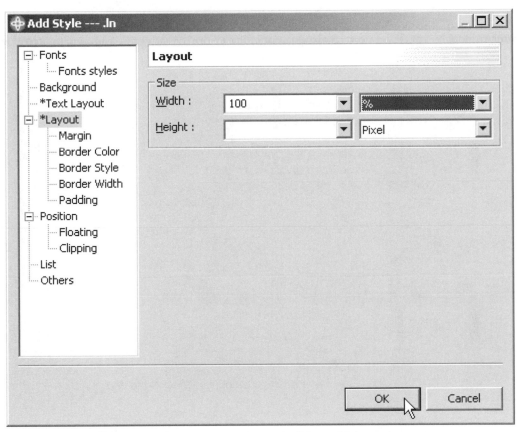

Figure 5-8: Change width to 100% and then press OK to add the style.

The style will automatically be added to the end of the style sheet, and the file will be positioned to the end, with your cursor on the new style, as shown in Figure 5-9.

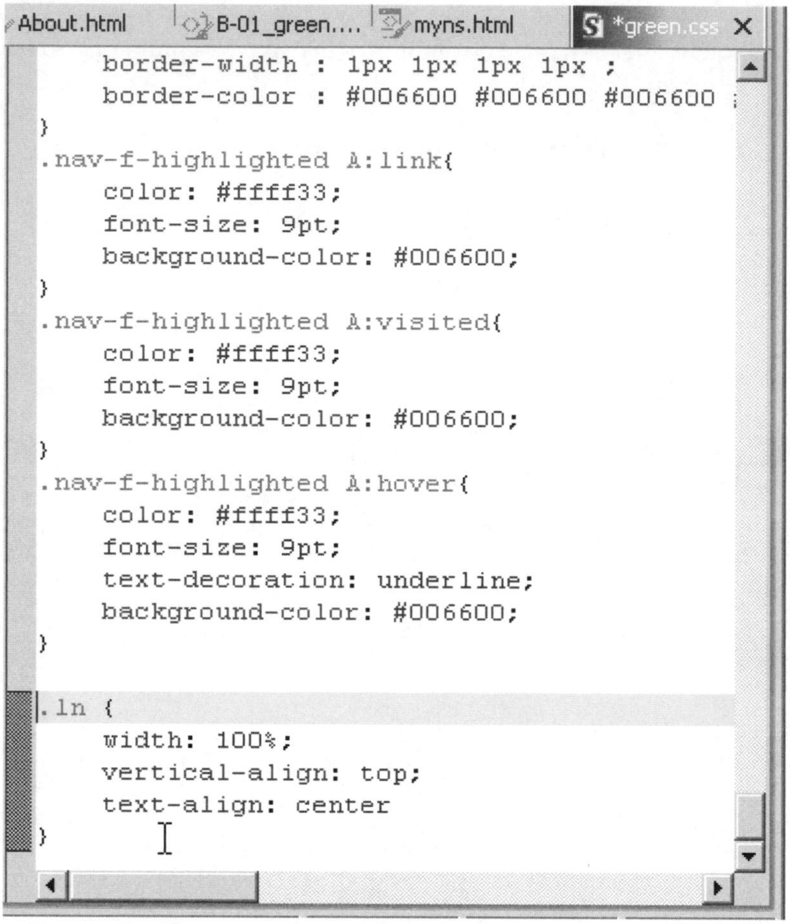

```
About.html        B-01_green....    myns.html          S  *green.css  X
      border-width : 1px 1px 1px 1px ;
      border-color : #006600 #006600 #006600 ;
 }
 .nav-f-highlighted A:link{
      color: #ffff33;
      font-size: 9pt;
      background-color: #006600;
 }
 .nav-f-highlighted A:visited{
      color: #ffff33;
      font-size: 9pt;
      background-color: #006600;
 }
 .nav-f-highlighted A:hover{
      color: #ffff33;
      font-size: 9pt;
      text-decoration: underline;
      background-color: #006600;
 }
 .ln {
      width: 100%;
      vertical-align: top;
      text-align: center
 }
```

Figure 5-9: The new style has been added at the end of the style sheet.

You now need to add the other four styles. You can either type them in or use the wizard to add them. There is also a text file on your CD-ROM, in the folder Imports, called Step5-1.txt. This file contains the new styles. You can open that file up in the text editor of your choice and just copy and paste it into the style sheet. Once you're finished, right-click in the editor and select Save to save the style sheet as illustrated in Figure 5-10.

❑ **5.1(j) Enter the rest of the new styles.**

❑ **5.1(k) Right-click in the editor and select Save.**

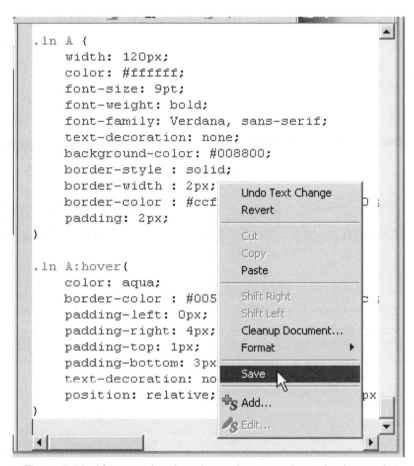

Figure 5-10: After entering the other styles, save the style sheet using the pop-up menu.

To see the finished product, switch back to the About Us page. Do that by clicking on the About.html tab as shown in Figure 5-11.

❑ **5.1(l) Click on the About.html tab.**

Figure 5-11: Click on the About.html tab to see the new styles in action.

You will get the screen shown in Figure 5-12. Remember that changes to the Preview mode are not automatic. You will probably have to refresh the display by clicking on a different mode, such as Design mode, and then back on Preview mode to get the display shown in Figure 5-13.

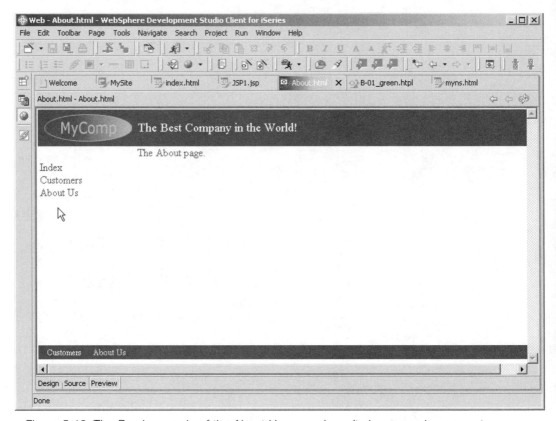

Figure 5-12: The Preview mode of the About Us page doesn't show any changes yet.

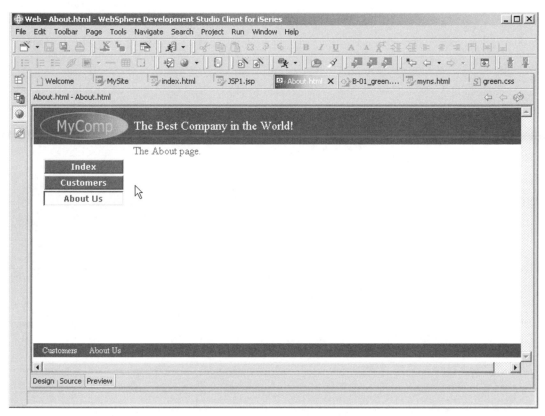

Figure 5-13: But after clicking to Design mode and back, the new navigation buttons appear.

The picture here doesn't really do the page justice. Because of the careful design of the .ln A and .ln A:HOVER style selectors, the buttons actually change as you roll over them. Figure 5-14 tries to give you a sense of how this looks and feels, but you really can't appreciate it until you see it live. And it's about time you did that, so on to Step 6 and the WebSphere Test Environment!

Figure 5-14: As you move your cursor over the links, they will change appearance with an almost 3-D quality.

Step 6

The WebSphere Test Environment

Unlike the CSS Designer, the WebSphere Test Environment (or WTE) is quite well-known in the IBM Java development community. Large, complex, and sophisticated, the WTE allows you to test your code on your workstation almost exactly as if you were running on a host machine such as the i5. And yet, using the WTE is almost completely transparent to the development process. Select an object, click on a menu option, and your application is running.

I'm amazed by how well IBM integrated this particular feature into the workbench. As I'll show you shortly, all of the setup tasks required to test your Web applications on a test server are handled completely automatically.

WTE's few idiosyncrasies are more an issue of J2EE deployment than anything, but they are usually one-time setup issues. For example, it's not particularly intuitive as to where log files might be located or where you would place an .ini file to configure an application. Once you get past these, however, the WTE is perhaps the best integrated Web application development environment you'll ever use. At the same time, this is *not* a task for an underpowered PC: To use this feature regularly, you will need at least 1GB of RAM and a 2GHz processor.

There are two separate and distinct modes of running the WTE: normal mode and debug mode. The two modes are completely different and serve different purposes. The normal mode's only use is for checking the look and feel of the Web site. Since you can't set breakpoints and can't really interrogate the state of the system, this mode is not much help in debugging.

Instead, you use the debug mode whenever you really need to query your code and find out what's going on. You can set breakpoints, inspect code, even change code on the fly when you are in debug mode. That being the case, you will probably find yourself spending most of your time in debug mode. In fact, nearly every time I've been running in normal mode, I've run across something and said to myself, "I wish I were in debug mode right now!"

✓ **Here is your step checklist:**

Step 6.1—Running the Web site in normal mode

GOAL

In this step, you will run your Web site using
the WebSphere Test Environment (WTE).

While the WTE has a great number of features, the WDSC developers have so
successfully encapsulated the complexity behind wizards that using the WTE
to run an application is almost trivial. This has positive and negative ramifica-
tions. On the positive side, it's easy to get going quickly, as we will do in this
step. Conversely, however, it is sometimes difficult to do things "outside of
the box" with the WTE. Simple tasks like locating log files can be difficult,
and sometimes integration with other Web products is not as easy as I'd like.
However, for most Web application development, the positives far outweigh
any negatives.

In this step, I will show you the fast-path way to get your Web site running on the
server in normal mode. This is primarily used to make sure the look and feel of
everything is correct; debugging will be addressed in the next step.

If you currently have the About Us page maximized as shown in Figure 6-1,
then double-click on the About.html tab to restore the workbench to its normal
state.

❑ **6.1(a) If About Us is maximized, double-click on the About.html tab.**

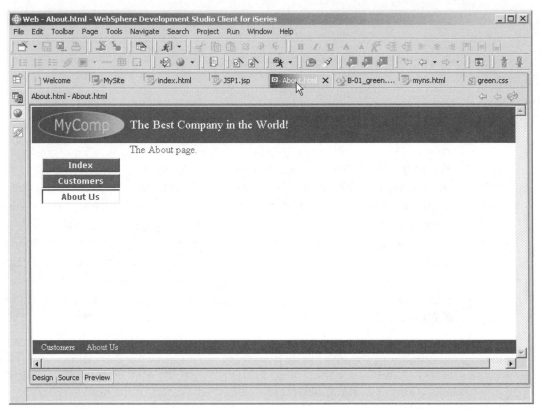

Figure 6-1: The About Us page may be maximized; if so, double-click on the About.html tab

At this point, you should see the standard workbench, and index.html should be in the Project Navigator in the upper left corner of the workbench. Right-click on it as shown in Figure 6-2 and select Run on Server . . .

❑ **6.1(b) Right-click on index.html and select Run on Server. . . .**

At this point, the only other thing you need to do is select a server on which to run. There are a number of options. You have a choice of both type and location of your runtime environment. For type, you can run on a WebSphere Version 5 or WebSphere Version 5 Express server. For location, you can do so either in the WTE or on an external server (either on your work-station or remote). If you choose an external server, it must be installed and configured correctly.

You can also run on WebSphere Version 4. However, when you created your project, you took the defaults, which means your project is J2EE 1.3, and WebSphere Version 4 only supports J2EE 1.2. Finally, a number of Tomcat options are available, all of which require Tomcat to be installed and running.

On subsequent launches, one of your options will be to use the server that you will be creating in this step, but since you haven't yet created a server configuration, your only option is to create a new server. The following pages will do that.

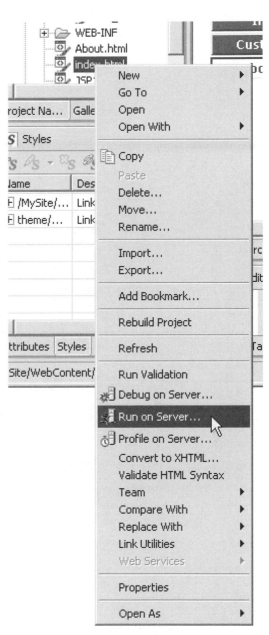

Figure 6-2: Right-click on index.html and choose Run on Server. . . .

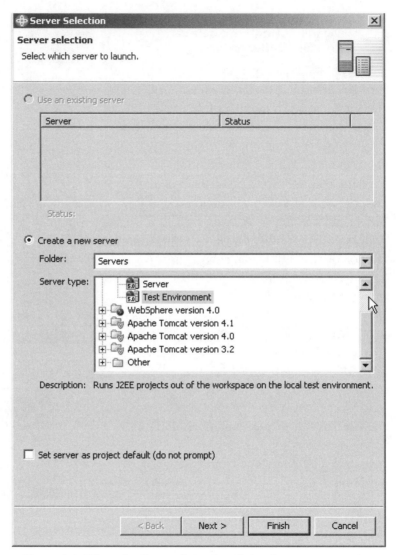

Figure 6-3: When the Server Selection dialog first comes up, there are no existing servers.

As you can see in Figure 6-3, there are no existing server configurations to choose from. Your only option is to create one. Which type you create is specified by selecting an option in the listbox marked Server type. The default is to create a configuration for a Version 5.0 Test Environment server (that is, a WebSphere Version 5 Base Edition server running inside the WTE).

Which server type to use is a matter of choice. Since WebSphere Express comes as a default product for most i5 users, I suggest using it as your standard test environment. Unless you have a specific need to use WebSphere Base Edition, stick with WebSphere Express.

> **Note:** The server type list that appears here will depend on the options taken at install time. I chose to install all the server environments; you may not have. If you don't have the WebSphere Express test environment installed, I suggest using the basic WebSphere test environment.

To do that, you'll need to select it. Roll the Server type listbox to the top, and you'll see an entry for Express Test Environment. Click on it, as shown in Figure 6-4, and the wizard will load the Express Test Environment, depicted in Figure 6-5. Once the hourglass disappears, the environment is loaded, and you can press the Finish button.

> **Release Note:** With V5.1.2, you also have the option to use a WebSphere Version 5.1 test environment. Because of difficulties I've had, especially with the JSP compiler, I still recommend using the V5.0 test environment.

❑ **6.1(c) Roll up the Server type listbox.**

❑ **6.1(d) Select Express Test Environment.**

❑ **6.1(e) Wait for the wizard to load the environment.**

❑ **6.1(f) Press Finish.**

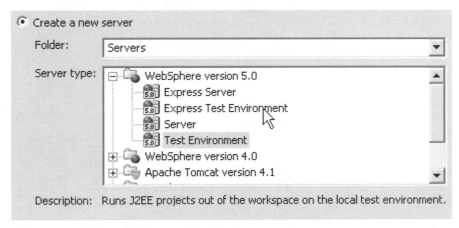

Figure 6-4: Select the Express Test Environment.

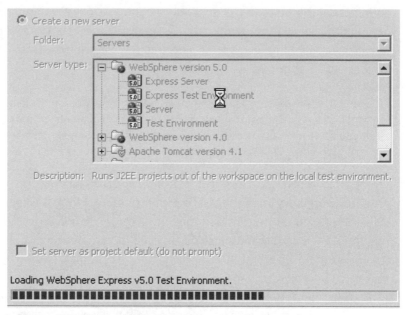

Figure 6-5: Wait until the Test Environment is loaded.

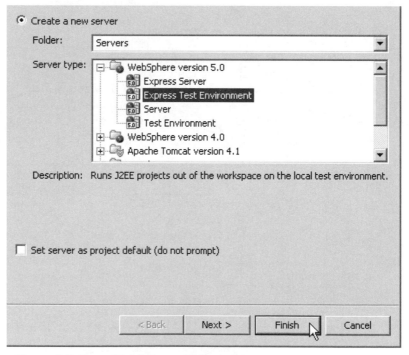

Figure 6-6: Press Finish to create the new server.

This creates a new server configuration for you to use. You could have created a server configuration manually by going through the Servers perspective (from the main menu, select Open Perspective/Servers). But the method we're using here not only creates the server, it also publishes your Web site (Figure 6-7) and launches the server (Figure 6-8). All you need to do is watch WDSC go through its paces.

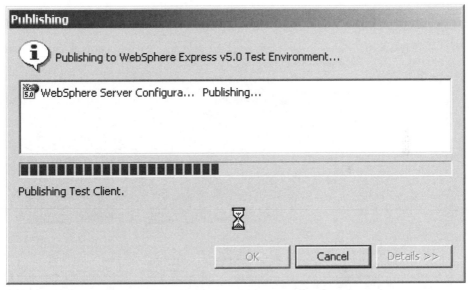

Figure 6-7: WDSC now publishes your Web site to the new server.

Figure 6-8: Next, the new server is launched (with the goal of running index.html).

Once this starts, your workbench will start to undergo some changes. First, the bottom center pane will switch to the console view. This is where all the output sent to stdout will appear. Unfortunately, if you're stuck with the 800×600 resolution we have been forced to work with, the view is so small that you can't actually see the information. One way around that is to resize the view, as shown in Figures 6-9 and 6-10.

Move your cursor onto the bar between the editor and console views; the cursor will become a vertical two-headed arrow.

❑ **6.1(g) Move your cursor onto the bar between the editor and console views.**

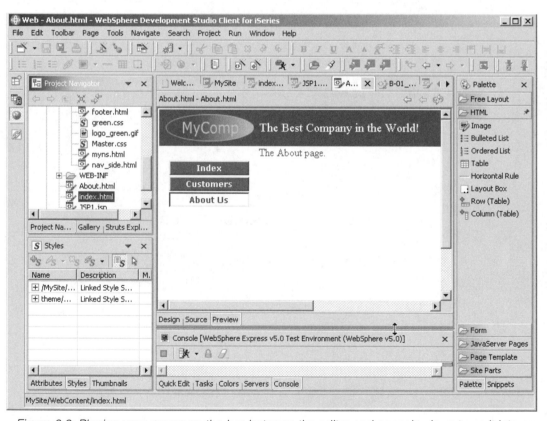

Figure 6-9: Placing your cursor on the bar between the editor and console views turns it into an arrow.

Now click and drag the bar upward a little bit and drop it. This will reduce the size of the editor view and increase the size of the console view.

❏ **6.1(h) Drag the bar upward and drop it to resize the views.**

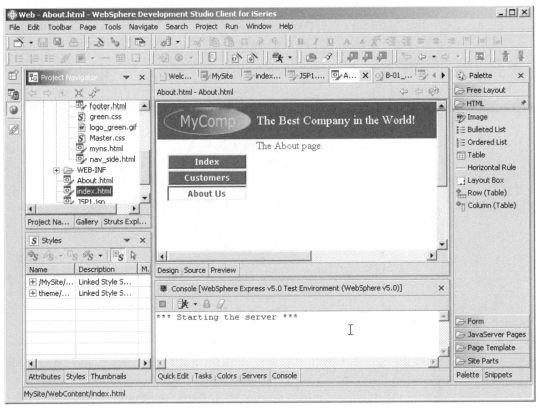

Figure 6-10: You can now see the output, such as the "Starting the server" informational message.

At this point, you'll start seeing a lot of messages, as shown in Figure 6-11.

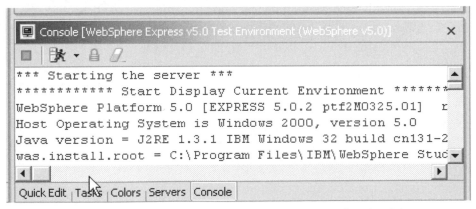

Figure 6-11: To see the messages, use the scroll bar to scroll to the right.

You now have to wait until all the messages are done before the server will start. You can tell when the server is started in one of two ways. First, you can look for the message "Server server1 open for e-business" as depicted in Figure 6-12. In the default resolution, you will have to scroll a little bit to the right to see the actual message text.

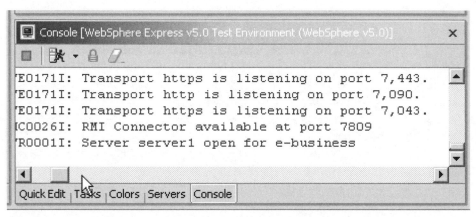

Figure 6-12: The message "open for e-business" indicates that the server has started.

The other sign that the server has started occurs when the Web Browser tab appears in the editor view. The Web Browser tab should appear on the far right (next to the green.css tab, if you've been following the script).

The Web Browser also contains a real image of the Web page, as shown in Figure 6-13. This is the fruit of all your labor to this point: a Web page with a reasonably nice-looking banner and navigation bar. And while there is currently little content, you can actually use the navigation widget to run through the pages of your site, as illustrated in Figures 6-14 and 6-15.

Figure 6-13: A new tab, the Web Browser tab, appears in the editor view.

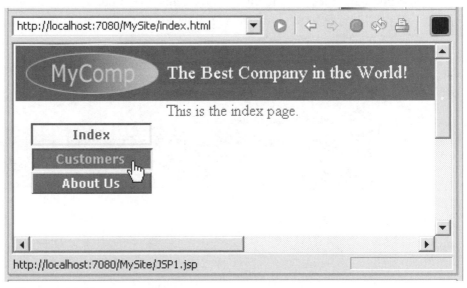

Figure 6-14: Here's your index page.

The index page allows you to go to the Customers or About Us pages. Click on Customers.

❑ **6.1(i) Click on Customers.**

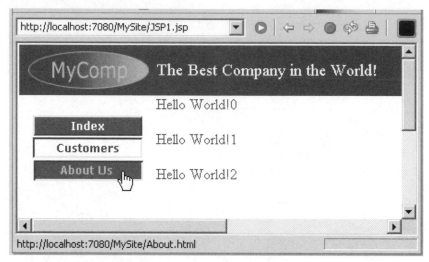

Figure 6-15: Clicking on the Customers link brings up the Customers page (JSP1.jsp).

Notice that the JSP actually runs the embedded code now, and you see "Hello World!" three times, with the iteration counter after each appearance. Next, click on About Us.

❑ **6.1(j) Click on About Us.**

Figure 6-16: Finally, you have your About Us page.

That's it. You've managed to run your three-page Web site (two static pages and one dynamic page) on a WebSphere Express server in the WebSphere Test Environment. Not bad so far!

This environment is very interactive, by the way. If you need to make a change to your JSP, all you need to do is save it to see the effects immediately in your server. If, for example, you accidentally typed "The Bust Company in the World," you can now go into the template, change the wording to "Best," and save it. Doing that will update all of the JSPs that use the template. The next time you load a page, the wording will be correct. It's phenomenally productive.

InStep 6.1.a—Normal vs. debug mode

GOAL

In this step, you will be introduced to debug mode.

You won't do anything in this step. I just want to make sure you're clear on the concept of debug mode. When you create a server configuration, it is neither a "normal" configuration nor a "debug" configuration. Any server configuration can be launched in either normal mode or debug mode.

But there is one crucial difference: Breakpoints are activated only in debug mode. The JVM is actually launched in a different way that enables it to communicate with the debugger, thereby allowing you to set breakpoints and then inspect the state of the JVM. In debug mode, you can also suspend threads and then inspect the state of the JVM that way (this comes in handy when an application hangs for no apparent reason).

Later, you'll be using debug mode to launch your server and test things. And in a normal development environment, that's where you will spend most of your time. But when you launch a server in debug mode, among the things that happens is that you are brought into the Debug perspective, and I wasn't prepared to do that just yet. You'll do it soon enough.

That completes the introduction. As I said, this was not a very ambitious step. But since I have been bitten more than once by being in normal mode when I really needed to be in debug mode, I figured it wasn't too early to at least present the terms. Now, let's move on and write some JSP code!

Step 7

Beans make
Web sites dynamic

There are many ways to create dynamic Web sites. Some require no Java at all; Common Gateway Interface (CGI) programs have been written in every language from Perl to RPG. With a CGI approach, you have programs that format and output all of the HTML tags in every Web page in your application.

Servlets are another approach. Servlets by themselves are little more than CGI programs written in Java. Sort of the worst of all worlds, servlets require lots of string manipulation as well the overhead of a Java Virtual Machine (JVM). Not exactly the best approach.

Next are the scripting languages. Scripting languages allow you to embed syntax into the HTML code of your Web pages. These scripts are interpreted by the Web application server. Various scripting languages exist, from PHP (based on a Perl-like syntax) to ColdFusion (a commercial, tag-based scripting language) to ASP/VB (Microsoft's scripting solution, using Visual Basic syntax in conjunction with the IIS server). Note: This is different from JavaScript, which is actually sent to the browser and interpreted on the client machine. Scripting languages are interpreted and processed on the host (the Web application server).

My favorite option and the one you'll be using here is JavaServer Pages (JSP). The JSP is an interesting and powerful hybrid. JSP scriptlets are embedded in standard HTML pages, which are then converted to executable Java servlets. Thanks to the coming of age of the JIT compilers for Java, what ends up happening is that the JSP pages eventually get converted to binary.

Now, the problem with *any* embedded language, from ASP to JSP, is that the programmer almost invariably puts too much code in the HTML page. The HMTL page should really be as simple as possible: It should simply retrieve data from what are essentially buffers and put that data out in the page. And in the proper JSP Model II design, that's exactly what happens, and that's what you'll be doing in this step. You will create buffers (called "Beans" in Java terminology) and send those to a JSP. Eventually, those Beans will be hooked up to back-end logic on the host. This staged, tiered design allows you to separate the workload. In a larger environment, the different tasks (UI design, Bean design, servlet design, back-end logic design) can be split among multiple people or multiple teams.

In this step, you'll create a couple of Beans to be attached to your JSP.

Step 7.1—Add Java to your application

GOAL

In this step, you will add a Java class
to your Web application.

In order to have proper JSP Model II architecture, you need Beans. To create your Beans, you'll use the Java editing capabilities of WDSC. The nice thing about WDSC is that it has a really great Java editor built in: the base Eclipse Java editor, which is very similar to VisualAge for Java (VAJ) because they were both essentially developed by the same folks[1]. So without further ado, I'm going to take you directly to adding Java classes to your application.

If you got here from the Checkpoint, you'll see the screen shown in Figure 7-1. The editor pane shows an error because the server isn't running. Don't worry; it won't affect your work.

---

[1] If you've never used Eclipse or VAJ or if you're just uncomfortable with PC-based tools in general, then you might want to find an introductory text. My own Eclipse: *Step by Step* book is actually a perfect companion piece to this book for people coming directly from the green-screen world.

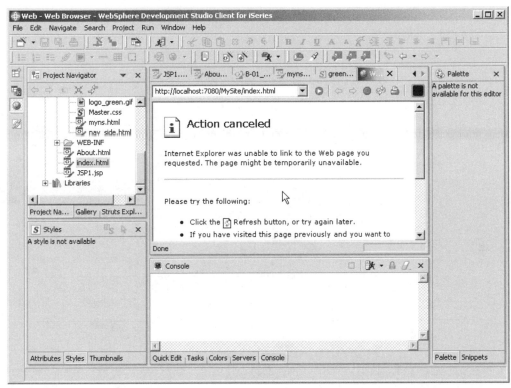

Figure 7-1: If you used the Chapter 7.1 Checkpoint restart, this is your first screen.

If you are simply moving ahead from Step 6, your editor view will resemble Figure 6-16, showing the About Us page. In either case, your Project Navigator will look like it does in Figure 7-2. (If either Gallery or Struts Explorer is visible instead of Project Navigator, just click on the Project Navigator tab at the bottom of the pane.)

The part of the project you want to concentrate on right now is not visible. It's the Java Source object, and it's currently near the top of the view. You'll need to use the scroll bar to roll the view up a page, as shown in Figure 7-2, or use another cursor movement technique to make the JavaSource folder visible, as it is in Figure 7-3.

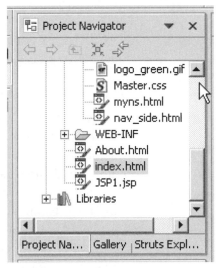

Figure 7-2: The Project Navigator should currently look like this.

Release Note: In V5.1.2, the name of this folder has been changed to Java Resources.

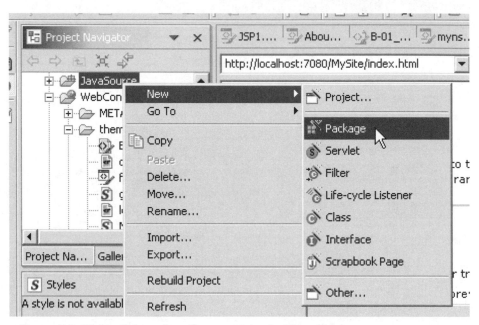

Figure 7-3: Right-click on Java Source and select New/Package.

Once you've made the Java Source visible, right-click on it and select New/Package from the pop-up menu to create a new package as shown in Figure 7-3.

❑ **7.1(a) Right-click on Java Source and select New/Package.**

You'll see the New Java Package wizard as shown in Figure 7-4. Package naming is an important topic, but in the interests of being concise, I'll leave it for another time. Remember that the standard naming convention for commercial packages is to use your domain name reversed. So, since the fictitious company in this firm is MyComp.com, I have used com.mycomp as the prefix for the package names. This prefix, common to all your packages, is sometimes called a "namespace." You should use whatever your own business uses. If you don't have a domain to use, feel free to use mycomp.com. If you do select a namespace other than com.mycomp for your packages, remember to take that into account when you follow the instructions on these pages.

❑ **7.1(b) Enter com.mycomp.beans and press Finish.**

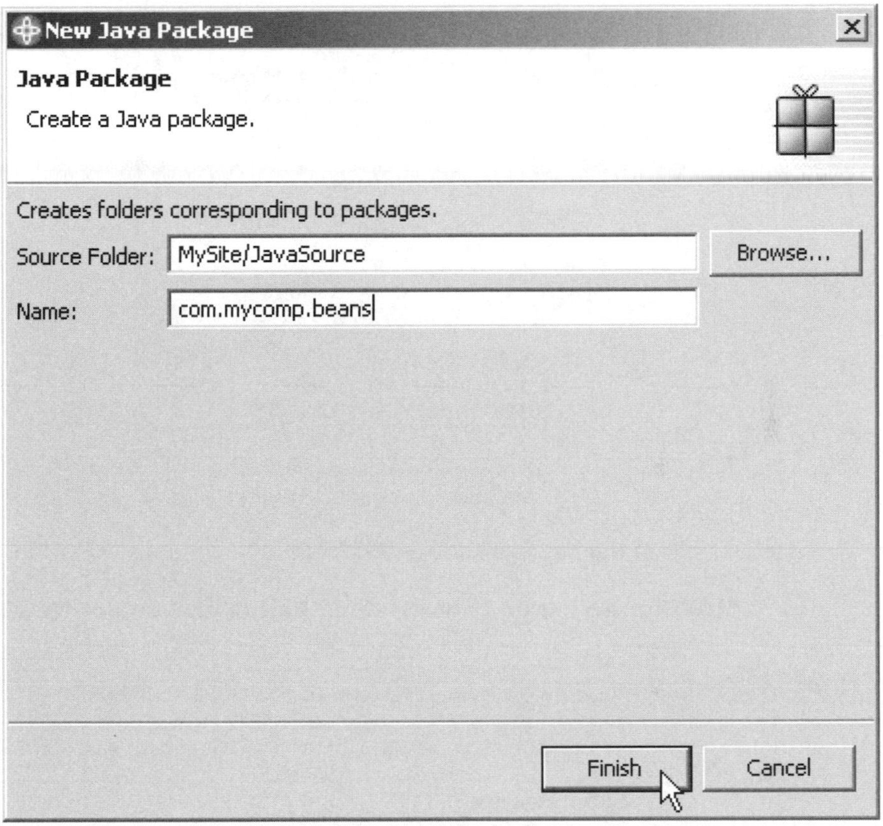

Figure 7-4: Enter a package name, such as com.mycomp.beans, and press Finish.

This will create a package named com.mycomp.beans, as shown in Figure 7-5.

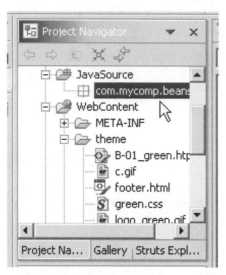

*Figure 7-5: The new package
appears under Java Source.*

Right-click on the new package and select New/Class, as shown in Figure 7-6.

❑ **7.1(c) Right-click on com.mycomp.beans and select New/Class.**

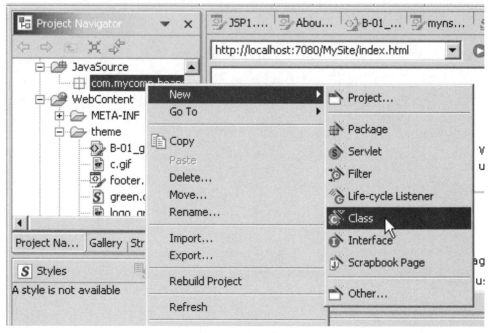

Figure 7-6: Create a new class within the new package.

At this point, you'll see the New Java Class wizard, shown in Figure 7-7. If you've followed the directions to this point, you can leave nearly everything at the defaults. The only thing you need to change is the Name field. Since the idea is that (eventually) you're going to create a small customer inquiry application, it makes sense to me that one of your first classes should be a Customer Bean. So enter the name Customer and press Finish.

❏ **7.1(d) Enter the name Customer.**

❏ **7.1(e) Make sure everything else matches Figure 7-7.**

❏ **7.1(f) Press Finish.**

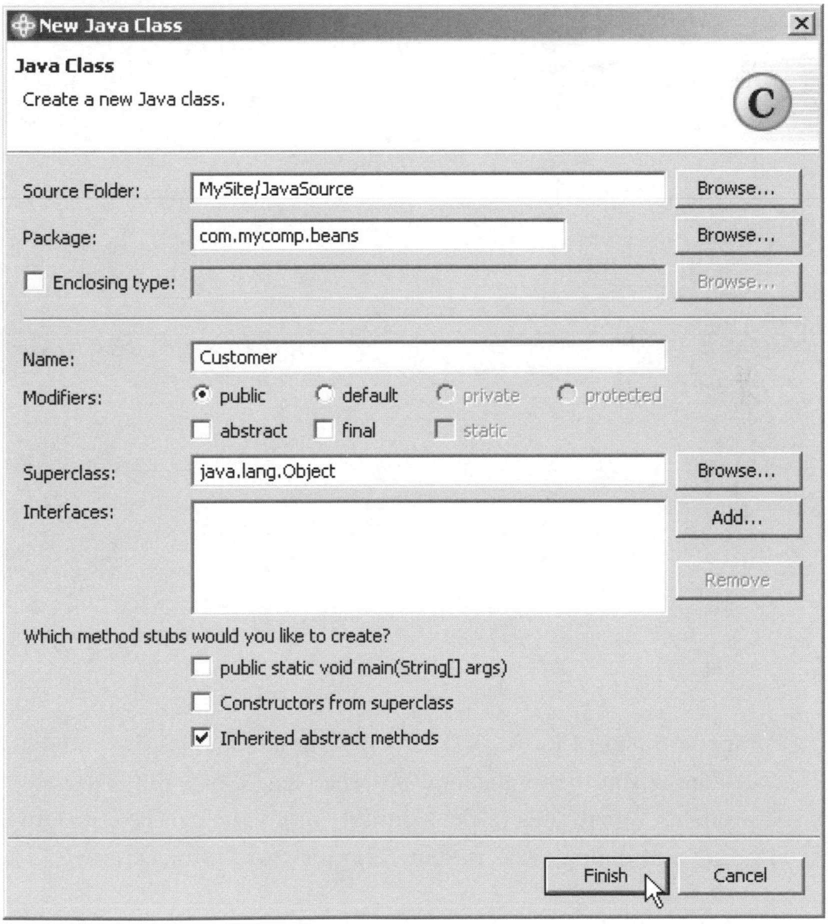

Figure 7-7: The New Java Class wizard has many settings, most of which you can leave at their defaults.

Note that this will create a class with many default characteristics. For example, the defaults should look as they do in Figure 7-7, with the class radio button set as public (don't set the abstract or final radio buttons). Remember, though, that the default settings really are whatever you set them to the last time you used the wizard. So always make sure to glance through the settings to be sure they're what you expect them to be.

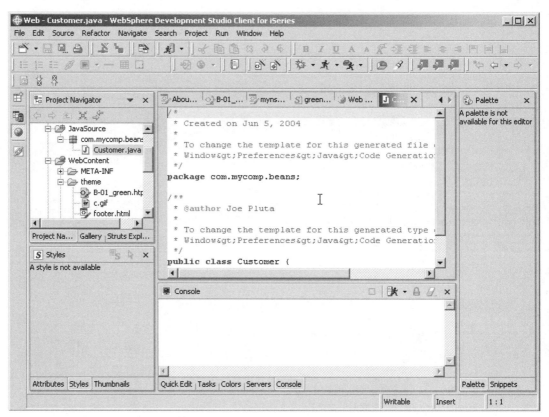

Figure 7-8: The Customer class has been added with the default settings of the New Java Class wizard.

When you press Finish, WDSC will generate a class for you, as shown in Figure 7-8. The wizard generates not only the basic class, but also some initial Javadoc comments. What goes in these initial comments can be configured using the Preferences dialog; read InStep 7.2.a for more information.

At this point, it's time to actually enter the class. You will entirely replace the existing code with the code I give you (that will be the norm throughout the book).

This is going to be a very simple Bean. The Customer Bean will have 10 fields that will be initialized by the constructor, and those fields will have accessors (getters). There are several ways to enter the code. If I were trying to teach you the Java editor, I would tell you to enter each of the fields and then use the Generate Getter and Setter wizard to create the getters. Since this is not a Java editor tutorial, I'll give you a couple of other choices. You can type in the code as shown in Listing 7-1, or you can import the code from the enclosed CD-ROM. There is a text file on the CD-ROM, in the folder Imports, called Step7-1-a.txt. This file contains the entire source code for the Customer class. You can open that file up in the text editor of your choice and just copy and paste it into the editor. Either way, once you're finished entering the code, right-click in the editor and select Save to save the code as illustrated in Figure 7-9.

❑ **7.1(g) Enter the code from Listing 7-1.**

❑ **7.1(h) Right-click in the editor and select Save.**

Listing 7-1: Key in this Customer class code or copy and paste it from the included CD-ROM.

```
package com.mycomp.beans;

public class Customer
{
        String number;
        String name;
        String address1;
        String address2;
        String city;
        String state;
        String zip;
        String phone;
        String fax;
        String email;

        public Customer(String number,
                                String name,
                                String address1,
                                String address2,
                                String city,
                                String state,
                                String zip,
                                String phone,
                                String fax,
                                String email)
        {
```

```
                    this.number = number;
                    this.name = name;
                    this.address1 = address1;
                    this.address2 = address2;
                    this.city = city;
                    this.state = state;
                    this.zip = zip;
                    this.phone = phone;
                    this.fax = fax;
                    this.email = email;
            }

        public String getAddress1() {
                    return address1;
            }

        public String getAddress2() {
                    return address2;
            }

        public String getCity() {
                    return city;
            }

        public String getEmail() {
                    return email;
            }

        public String getFax() {
                    return fax;
            }

        public String getName() {
                    return name;
            }

        public String getNumber() {
                    return number;
            }

        public String getPhone() {
                    return phone;
            }

        public String getState() {
                    return state;
            }

        public String getZip() {
                    return zip;
            }

    }
```

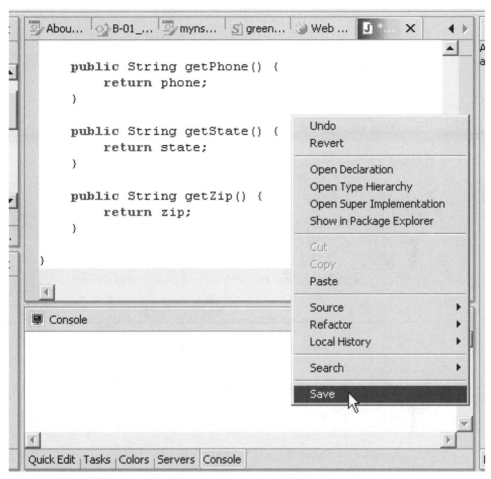

Figure 7-9: As usual, you can right-click and select Save to save the current file.

This application will need one other Bean, the CustomerList Bean. The CustomerList Bean allows you to build a list of customers and send just that Bean to a JSP. While you could do the work yourself using a TreeMap or ArrayList, the CustomerList Bean is a little cleaner, because it provides type safety: You can only add Customer objects, and when you retrieve an object, it is of type Customer. That avoids the messy casting required with the generic collection objects.

I'd like you to add a new class called CustomerList to the com.mycomp.beans package, and then enter the code from Listing 7-2. The code is also available on your CD-ROM in the folder Imports in a file named Step7-1-b.txt. Feel free to cut and paste that code into your class or even import it directly from CD. After entering the code, save it as usual (either through the pop-up menu or the main menu).

☐ **7.1(i) Add class CustomerList to your package.**

☐ **7.1(j) Enter the code from Listing 7-2.**

☐ **7.1(k) Right-click in the editor and select Save.**

Listing 7-2: Again, you can key in this CustomerList class code or download it from the CD-ROM.

```java
package com.mycomp.beans;

import java.util.*;

public class CustomerList {

        // The instance variables
        private Iterator i;
        private TreeMap customers;

        // The constructor simply creates an empty TreeMap
        public CustomerList()
        {
                customers = new TreeMap();
        }

        // Adding a customer puts it in the TreeMap keyed by customer number
        // It also clears the iterator and forces a reload
        public void addCustomer(Customer customer)
        {
                customers.put(customer.number, customer);
                i = null;
        }

        // getCustomer retrieve a single customer by key
        public Customer getCustomer(String number)
        {
                return (Customer) customers.get(number);
        }

        // rewind rebuilds the iterator over the current contents of the TreeMap
        public void rewind() {
                i = customers.keySet().iterator();
        }

        // hasNext checks for more data (it rewinds the iterator if needed)
```

```
public boolean hasNext() {
        // If an add has been performed
        if (i == null) rewind();
        return i.hasNext();
}

// This is a convenience method that does the class cast for you
public Customer nextCustomer() {
        return (Customer) i.next();
}

}
```

Once you've finished, your Project Navigator should display two Java classes, as shown in Figure 7-10.

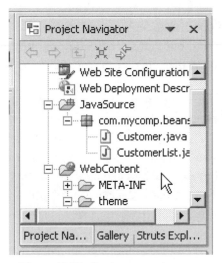

Figure 7-10: Customer and CustomerList have been added.

Step 7.2—Test the Beans

GOAL

In this step, you will test your Beans.

There are many schools of thought on testing. In this case, I find the easiest way to test a Bean is to use a small test class. Some people like to include a main() method in every Bean that can be run to test the Bean. Others are enthusiastic in their praise of JUnit, and as it turns out, WDSC has some JUnit integration built in. For more on that, see InStep 7.2.a.

Personally, I don't like either of those approaches. The main() method technique means a lot of baggage dragged along with every class, which is packaged, shipped, and deployed even though it may never be used. JUnit is a better approach, but that's really all about unit testing, whereas I like to create test classes that I can use throughout the life of my development.

In this particular case, I am going to build a test class that does two things: create a CustomerList object preloaded with some dummy data, and format the contents of a CustomerList. The ability to create a dummy CustomerList will come in handy not only in this phase, but later as you add the CustomerList to the JSP and as you add the servlet into the JSP Model II architecture. The formatting piece, on the other hand, may come in handy as you start building your JSPs.

In order to separate the testing from the Beans, I usually create a simple package called test. Since this package is not designed to be deployed, I don't worry about giving it a "standard" name, such as com.mycomp.test. I just call it test. In this case, I would then add a class called TestCustomerList (Listing 7-3), with methods like make() and format(). As usual, the code is on the CD-ROM in case you aren't interested in using this book as a typing lesson. This class is located in file Step 7-2.txt in the Imports folder.

❑ **7.2(a) Right-click on Java Source and select New/Package.**

❑ **7.2(b) Enter "test" and press Finish.**

□ **7.2(c) Right-click on test and select New/Class.**

□ **7.2(d) Enter the name TestCustomerList.**

□ **7.2(e) Make sure everything else matches Figure 7-11.**

□ **7.2(f) Press Finish.**

Figure 7-11: Add the TestCustomerList class to package test.

❑ **7.2(g) Enter the code from Listing 7-3.**

❑ **7.2(h) Right-click in the editor and select Save.**

Listing 7-3: Here's the code for the TestCustomerList class.

```
package test;

import com.mycomp.Beans.*;

public class TestCustomerList {

        private static final String[][] cdata =
        {
                {       "123456", "Manx Catering", "1234 Main St.",
                        "",       "Fairfield",      "VA", "24435", "540-555-6634",
                        "540-555-9919", "bob@manx.com"      },
                {       "777777", "Lucky Gambling Supply", "554 Federal St.",
                        "", "Washington", "DC", "20515", "202-224-3121",
                        "202-225-6827", "cincinnati@thekid.com" },
                {       "001987", "The Lefthand Store", "7332 Prairie",
                        "", "Springfield", "XX", "99999", "877-555-5432",
                        "800-555-2121", "ned@flanders.com" },
        };

        public static CustomerList make()
        {
                CustomerList cl = new CustomerList();
                for (int i = 0; i < cdata.length; i++)
                {
                        cl.addCustomer(new Customer(
                          cdata[i][0], cdata[i][1], cdata[i][2], cdata[i][3],
                          cdata[i][4], cdata[i][5], cdata[i][6], cdata[i][7],
                          cdata[i][8], cdata[i][9]));
                }
                return cl;
        }

        public static String format(Customer c)
        {
                return "Customer: " + c.getNumber() +
                        "\nName: " + c.getName() +
                        "\nAddress1: " + c.getAddress1() +
                        "\nAddress2: " + c.getAddress2() +
                        "\nCity: " + c.getCity() +
                        "\nState: " + c.getState() +
                        "\nZip: " + c.getZip() +
                        "\nPhone: " + c.getPhone() +
                        "\nFax: " + c.getFax() +
                        "\nEmail: " + c.getEmail();
        }

        public static void main(String[] args)
        {
```

```
        CustomerList cl = make();
        while (cl.hasNext())
        {
                System.out.println(format(cl.nextCustomer()));
                System.out.println();
        }
        System.exit(0);
    }
}
```

Now that the class is entered, you can run it. There are a number of ways to do this. The first time, I find it easiest to simply use the main menu. From the main menu, select Run/Run As/Java Application (as shown in Figure 7-12), and the workbench will run your program. Under the covers, the workbench creates an object called a "Launch Configuration," which you can use later or even modify and use for other things. This is one of the very nice ease-of-use features that WDSC uses to make your job that much simpler.

> **Note:** I have intentionally placed a mistake in this class in order to show you how to handle errors. You can see the expected error in Figure 7-13. If you see any other error, carefully check and make sure your code exactly matches (including case!) the code shown in Listing 7-3.

> **Release Note:** n V5.1.2, the Java Application option is much farther down the list than in earlier releases.

❑ **7.2(i) From the main menu, select Run/Run As/Java Application.**

Figure 7-12: You want to run this class as a Java application.

Since you've entered the code exactly as I told you to, you shouldn't be surprised that it doesn't quite work correctly. In fact, you'll get an error message in your console view (in the bottom center pane) that looks like the one in Figure 7-13.

Figure 7-13: The error occurred in nextCustomer, and clicking will take you there.

What this tells you is that you are getting a ClassCastException. Somewhere in your code, you are attempting an explicit downcast, and the object being cast is of an incorrect type. Where is the error occurring? Well, the stack trace indicates that it's in the method nextCustomer in the class com.mycomp.beans.CustomerList. But here's a really user-friendly feature of the console: The stack trace contains hyperlinks. Click on the offending method as shown (or any other method in the stack), and the editor pane will open the associated source member and position you on the line in error, as illustrated in Figure 7-14.

❑ **7.2(j) Click on com.mycomp.beans.CustomerList.nextCustomer.**

Figure 7-14: Clicking on a method in the console opens the source member and positions you to the method.

Based on the error and the code in question, it's clear that i.next() is not returning an object that can be cast to Customer. Why is this? Well, I used a TreeMap to hold the Customer objects. Before you read the entries in the CustomerList, you are supposed to call the method rewind() to create an iterator over the TreeMap.

Unfortunately, the current code gets the iterator over the keys, not the objects, and because of that, the iterator does not return Customer objects; it returns the keys to those objects. To fix this code, I need to use the iterator over the objects. This is a simple change to the rewind() method.

Change the following line in rewind()

```
i = customers.keySet().iterator();
```

to

```
i = customers.values().iterator();
```

That does the trick. So, change the code and then save the member as shown in Figure 7-15.

❑ **7.2(k) Modify the rewind() method and save the source.**

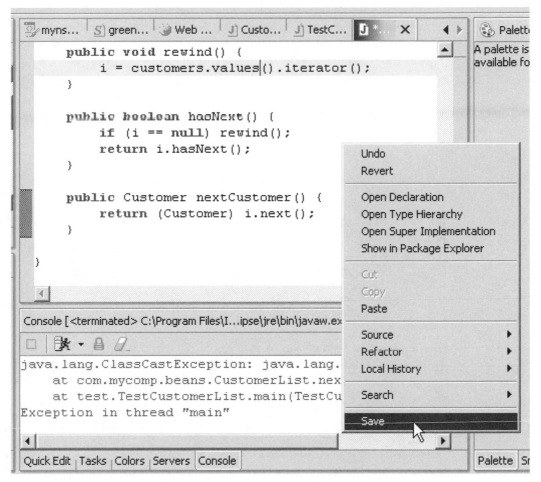

Figure 7-15: Save the code after changing the rewind() method.

Now you can re-run the application. Earlier, I mentioned that WDSC had, unbeknownst to you, created and saved a Launch Configuration, which you would be able to use later. Well, later is now. WDSC tries very hard to anticipate what you will do next, usually by assuming that you're going to do the same thing you did last time or something very similar. Because of this, repeating a previous action is often as easy as the click of a button. In this case in particular, re-running the same application as last time is simply a matter of clicking on the Run tool in the main toolbar, as shown in Figure 7-16. Now, in case you've forgotten what the default action is, holding your cursor over the tool will bring up a tool tip telling you what the workbench intends to do should you press the tool button. If for whatever reason you don't like the default action for the Run tool, use the small down arrow to the right of the tool to pop up a menu with your options. Many of the tool buttons work that same way.

In this case, the default behavior is exactly what you want, so just click on the little running man, and the TestCustomerList application will be launched.

❑ **7.2(l) Click on the Run tool.**

Figure 7-16: The default for the launch tool is to run the TestCustomerList application.

This will run the application. If everything has gone smoothly, you will get no errors. Instead, you will see the customer list printed in the console, as shown in Figure 7-17.

Figure 7-17: This time, it works—no red messages! Blue is standard console output.

As always, if there isn't enough room to really review the console output, you can double-click on the title bar for that view and maximize it, as shown in Figure 7-18.

So now you have a Customer class and a CustomerList class, as well as a test class with one method that creates a dummy CustomerList and another that dumps a CustomerList. Now it's time to start creating the JSPs that will use these classes.

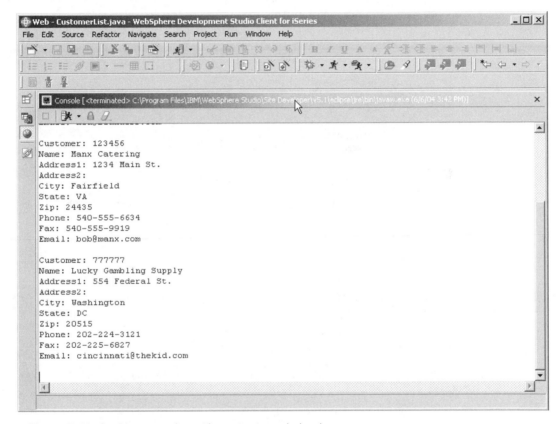

Figure 7-18: And here you have the output maximized.

InStep 7.2.a—Code review

You can feel free to skip this step. If you would like to see the code in detail and get an idea of why I did things the way I did, then by all means take the time to peruse this InStep. But if you want to keep going with the exercises, please go ahead. You can come back to this InStep at any time.

Listing 7-4: This is a very abbreviated version of the Customer class.

```
package com.mycomp.beans;

public class Customer
{
        // Instance variables
        String number;
(...)
        String email;

        // The constructor simply sets all the instance variables
        public Customer(String number,
(...)
                                            String email)
        {
                this.number = number;
(...)
                this.email = email;
        }

        // And the rest of the Bean is getters
        public String getAddress1() {
                return address1;
        }

(...)

        public String getZip() {
                return zip;
        }

}
```

This is the Customer class. There's not a lot to it. There are probably four or five architectures for Beans, including ones with setters and getters, ones that do or do not accept parms on the constructor, and so on. Personally, I'm currently a little on the fence as to when you should have getters and when you shouldn't. I'm starting to lean toward package-level (default) access for Beans; classes in the package can have knowledge of their internals, but those outside cannot. That way, Beans that are only used inside a single package can be created without accessors of any kind.

In this case, though, the Bean definitely goes outside of package scope (it's pretty much an entity Bean), so it will need getters. But I like the idea of no setters and only a single constructor that sets all the instance variables, and since that's practical in this instance, that's the design I'll use.

Listing 7-5: Here's the CustomerList class.

```
package com.mycomp.beans;

import java.util.*;

public class CustomerList {

        // The instance variables
        private Iterator i;
        private TreeMap customers;

        // The constructor simply creates an empty TreeMap
        public CustomerList()
        {
                customers = new TreeMap();
        }

        // Adding a customer puts it in the TreeMap keyed by customer number
        // It also clears the iterator and forces a reload
        public void addCustomer(Customer customer)
        {
                customers.put(customer.number, customer);
                i = null;
        }

        // getCustomer retrieve a single customer by key
        public Customer getCustomer(String number)
        {
                return (Customer) customers.get(number);
        }

        // rewind rebuilds the iterator over the current contents of the TreeMap
        public void rewind() {
                i = customers.keySet().iterator();
        }

        // hasNext checks for more data (it rewinds the iterator if needed)
        public boolean hasNext() {
                // If an add has been performed
```

```
            if (i == null) rewind();
            return i.hasNext();
    }

    // This is a convenience method that does the class cast for you
    public Customer nextCustomer() {
            return (Customer) i.next();
    }

}
```

This class is pretty straightforward. It's a classic pattern—basically, a List object with a built-in iterator. The problem I have with most of the Java collection classes is the fact that they tend to require and return objects of class Object. That's great for flexibility, but a pain in the butt for programming, since you always have to cast things, and of course, you can accidentally put the wrong object type in the wrong container, and then bad things happen. It would be nice to have type-specific collections.

The good news is that Java 1.5 does just that with the introduction of Generics, and if it's good enough for Java, it's good enough for me. And while I don't have the ability to use the new syntax, I can at least write my classes with the concept of type-specific collections. So, my CustomerList has addCustomer, which adds a Customer object, and getCustomer and nextCustomer, which return Customer objects.

OK, so on to the fun. I decided to use a TreeMap for my internal structure. That's for two reasons. First, I know I'll get the objects in key order. The nice thing is that if I decide to change the order for some reason, it will be relatively easy to do so: I'll simply use a different field for the key. Second, I wanted to be able to get at a Customer by key. Although I don't use it in this simple example, if I wanted to add a detail page, it would be nice to be able to use the customer number to get the Customer object the user clicked on.

The only other piece of logic was one that I needed to add to get around a problem with synchronization. If you create an iterator over a collection and then change the collection (add or delete something, for example) and access the iterator again, an exception is thrown. This is a relatively inexpensive way to handle the situation, but it means you have to be careful about synchronizing puts and gets. To do that, my put routine (addCustomer) sets the iterator to null whenever a new Customer is added. This then forces a rebuild of the iterator the next time someone calls hasNext.

It's not a perfect solution by any means; it could conceivably cause some strange results. But at least it won't throw an exception.

Listing 7-C: Here's the TestCustomerList class.

```
package test;

import com.mycomp.beans.*;

public class TestCustomerList {

        private static final String[][] cdata =
        {
                {       "123456", "Manx Catering", "1234 Main St.",
                        "",      "Fairfield",      "VA", "24435", "540-555-6634",
                        "540-555-9919", "bob@manx.com"     },
                {       "777777", "Lucky Gambling Supply", "554 Federal St.",
                        "", "Washington", "DC", "20515", "202-224-3121",
                        "202-225-6827", "cincinnati@thekid.com" },
                {       "001987", "The Lefthand Store", "7332 Prairie",
                        "", "Springfield", "XX", "99999", "877-555-5432",
                        "800-555-2121", "ned@flanders.com" },
        };

        public static CustomerList make()
        {
                CustomerList cl = new CustomerList();
                for (int i = 0; i < cdata.length; i++)
                {
                        cl.addCustomer(new Customer(
                                cdata[i][0], cdata[i][1], cdata[i][2], cdata[i][3],
                                cdata[i][4], cdata[i][5], cdata[i][6], cdata[i][7],
                                cdata[i][8], cdata[i][9]));
                }
                return cl;
        }

        public static String format(Customer c)
        {
                return "Customer: " + c.getNumber() +
                        "\nName: " + c.getName() +
                        "\nAddress1: " + c.getAddress1() +
                        "\nAddress2: " + c.getAddress2() +
                        "\nCity: " + c.getCity() +
                        "\nState: " + c.getState() +
                        "\nZip: " + c.getZip() +
                        "\nPhone: " + c.getPhone() +
```

```
                                "\nFax:  " + c.getFax() +
                                "\nEmail: " + c.getEmail();
        }

        public static void main(String[] args)
        {
                CustomerList cl = make();
                while (cl.hasNext())
                {
                        System.out.println(format(cl.nextCustomer()));
                        System.out.println();
                }
                System.exit(0);
        }
}
```

This class isn't too sophisticated. Basically, it has an array with three elements, each element of which is an array of 10 strings representing a customer. There is a static method "make" that creates a new CustomerList object. It then generates a new Customer object for each entry in the array and adds that Customer to the CustomerList.

The program has a main method, which calls "make" to get the dummy CustomerList and then runs through the list using the hasNext method. Each Customer is formatted (using the "format" method) and then printed to the standard output stream.

I could have embedded some or all of this testing code in the classes Customer and CustomerList, but I chose not to; I don't like having all that extra baggage. At the same time, the make method will definitely come in handy for testing, as you'll see in subsequent steps.

Step 8

Adding Beans to your JSPs

Now that you've created a JavaServer Page (JSP), the next item on the agenda is to make it display data. First-generation JSPs did all the work themselves. You would see tons of embedded Java code in scriptlets that did everything from database access to formatting to display. These pages were big, ugly, and difficult to debug. And interestingly enough, at the end of the day, they often called servlets to actually perform updates.

Step 8.1—Rename the JSP

When you originally added this JSP, you named it JSP1.jsp. That was fine for that time, but at this point, it makes sense to rename it. Is renaming this particular file required? No, but there will come a time when you want to rename a file, so this is a good exercise.

First, close all your open files to remove some of the clutter. Use File/Close All from the main menu as shown in Figure 8-1.

❏ **8.1(a) Select File/Close All from the main menu.**

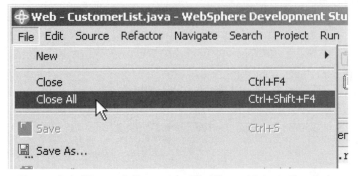

Figure 8-1: Close all files using File/Close All from the main menu.

Now that all your files are closed, you need to re-open the Web Site Designer. You accomplish that by double-clicking on the Web Site Configuration object. It's the first thing in your folder, as shown in Figure 8-2.

Release Note: In V5.1.2, the name Web Site Configuration has been changed to Web Site Navigation.

□ **8.1(b) Double-click on the Web Site Configuration object.**

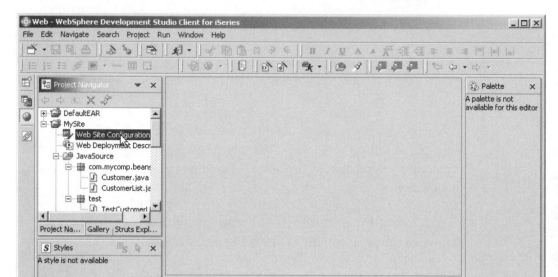

Figure 8-2: Double-click on the Web Site Configuration object to bring up the Web Site Designer.

Once the Web Site Designer is started, you'll see the layout of your Web site. There are three pages: Index, Customers, and About Us. Roll your cursor over the Customers page and an information pop-up will appear identifying the name of the JSP as JSP1.jsp, as you can see in Figure 8-3. The pop-up also shows the navigation label (which is also shown in the graphical depiction of the page) and any template that is associated with the page.

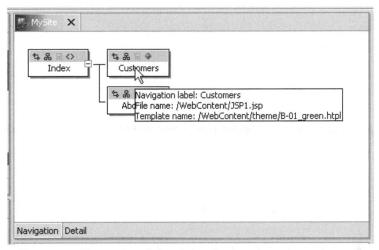

Figure 8-3: The pop-up information for the page shows the name JSP1.jsp.

To rename the file, right-click on it and select Rename, as shown in Figure 8-4.

❑ **8.1(c) Right-click on the Customers page and select Rename. . . .**

Release Note: In V5.1.2, the order of the menu options has been changed. Rename is way near the bottom of the list.

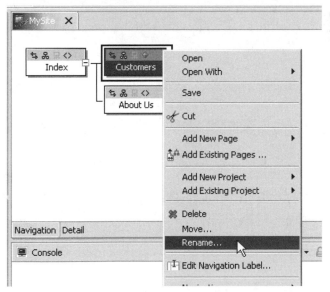

Figure 8-4: Right-click on the Customers page and select Rename. . .

This will cause a small text box to appear, "floating" above the Customers page as shown in Figure 8-5. Type in the new name for the file, "CustList.jsp" and press the Enter key.

Release Note: In V5.1.2, an actual Rename dialog appears.

❑ **8.1(d) Type CustList.jsp in the text box.**

❑ **8.1(e) Press the Enter key.**

At this point, many things will happen as the workbench makes all the necessary adjustments to your Web site. If you think about it, there are a number of changes, including changing any pages that point to this page. Wherever the link used to read JSP1.jsp, it must now change to CustList.jsp. However, those links were created by the navigation site part, so what really has to happen is that the workbench has to go through each page with a navigation site part that points to this page and regenerate the navigation site part.

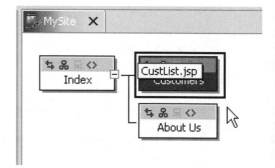

Figure 8-5: In the text box that appears above the page, type in CustList.jsp and then press the Enter key.

The first dialog that will pop up is the one shown in Figure 8-6.

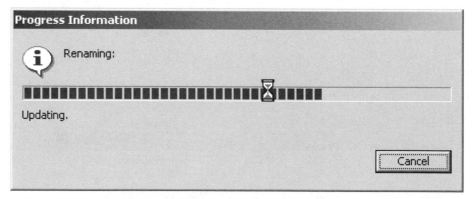

Figure 8-6: This is the primary dialog, which indicates that a page is being renamed.

Next, a pop-up like the one in Figure 8-7 appears, confirming that you actually want to change the Web site. Since there are some outstanding changes, WDSC wants to either commit to them or discard them prior to beginning the mass move operation.

You'll see this whenever you rename or move a file in your Web site. If there are outstanding changes, you will be asked to either commit to or discard them. In this case, the only resource in the list is the Web site configuration object itself (this makes sense; by changing the name of the JSP file, you changed the Web site). By default, it is already selected. Leave the dialog the way it is and press OK.

❑ **8.1(f) Leave the dialog as it appears in Figure 8-7 and press OK.**

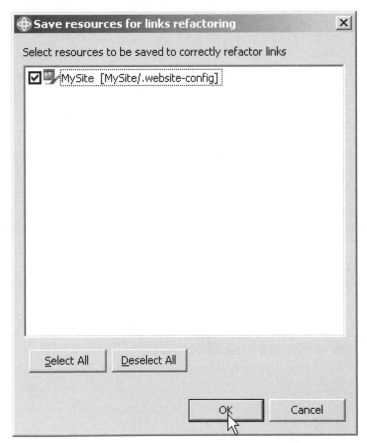

Figure 8-7: This box confirms that you want to change your Web site. You do, so press OK.

The next box appears after any outstanding changes have been saved. This box asks if you want to change the links of any pages that point to this page. Typically, you will always do this, so the workbench gives you a time-saving option. If you uncheck the "Show this message…" box, this prompt will not appear again. However, I kind of like having the workbench ask me before it does things, so I leave this box checked.

❑ **8.1(g) Press the Yes button.**

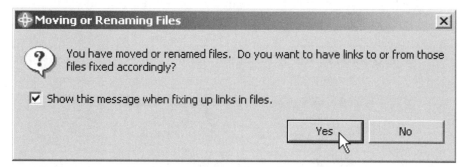

Figure 8-8: This prompt asks whether you want pages that point to this link to be updated to the new page name.

Once you've pressed Yes, the rest of the work occurs. Links are processed, tables are updated, site parts are generated, and so on. Depending on the size of your Web site, this could take a while. On our example site, it will take a few seconds. During that time, the dialog in Figure 8-9 (the same one from Figure 8-6) will indicate the current status of the operation.

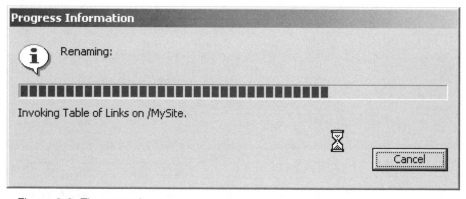

Figure 8-9: The renaming process continues.

Once done, the workbench will return. You may not see a lot of visible changes, but you will be able to roll your cursor over the Customers page and see in the pop-up information box that the page name has changed to CustList.jsp. And that's exactly what you were trying to accomplish.

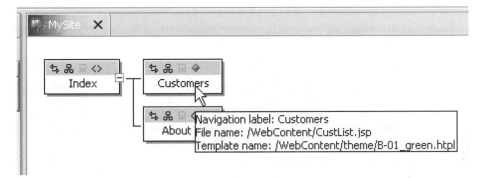

Figure 8-10: The page has been renamed to CustList.jsp, as you can see from the pop-up.

Step 8.2—Add a Bean to your JSP

GOAL

In this step, you will add a CustomerList bean to your JSP.

In the true JSP Model II architecture, the application would build a CustomerList and pass it to the JSP as a Bean. The JSP would then display the contents of that Bean and eventually use it to perform other tasks. Later in the book, I'll present the JSP Model II architecture in detail. But for now, picture it this way:

1. A servlet is invoked.

2. That servlet gathers data from the host and places it into Beans.

3. It invokes the appropriate JSP page.

As you might guess, this is the simplified version. It leaves out a number of details, including security and even passing data back to the host. But for many inquiry applications, this is really all that is needed. For this design, the JSP uses the useBean tag to identify a Bean that it expects to get from the servlet. You haven't yet created a servlet, but eventually you will have to create one because in the JSP Model II architecture, it's up to the servlet to decide what data will be shown on the JSP. The JSP simply shows whatever was passed to it.

At this moment, however, you're at a bit of a design impasse. You don't have a working JSP to test the servlet, and you don't have a servlet to pass data to the JSP. You have Beans, and you know they work, but you don't have a servlet to populate those Beans. How do you get around this bottleneck?

First, you can simply run the JSP with an empty Bean. One of the nice features of the useBean tag is that it will instruct the server to automatically create a Bean if one does not exist, and that's what will be passed to the JSP. It is crucial with this technique that you make sure your Bean will function even when empty. Later, you'll load the Bean with some dummy data for testing purposes, but for now, I just want you to add the Bean to the page.

To do that, first bring up the page in Page Designer. The easiest way to get there from your current position is to double-click on the Customers page in the Web Site Designer view, as seen in Figure 8-11.

❑ **8.2(a) Double-click on the Customers page.**

The last time you were looking at this page, you were in Preview mode, so that's the view that will be brought up, as illustrated in Figure 8-12. Click on the Design tab to get into WYSIWYG design mode. While I do much of my work in Source mode, Design mode is sometimes a little easier when you want to add a specific widget in a specific spot on the page. In this case, I want you to add the Bean in the very first available spot on the

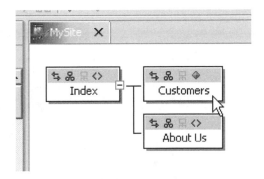

Figure 8-11: Double-click on the Customers page to bring it up in Page Designer.

page. Since this page was generated from a template, there are only certain places where widgets can be added, and I find it a little easier to identify the editable location in the Design mode. Don't worry; we'll be in Source mode soon enough.

❑ **8.2(b) Click on Design mode.**

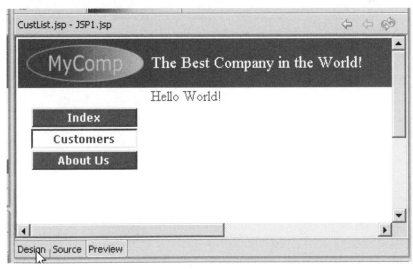

Figure 8-12: Click on Design mode to get to the WYSIWYG editor.

Your workbench should now look like the one in Figure 8-13. I purposely expanded the scope of this figure a little bit to show you the Project Navigator view immediately to the left of the Page Designer view. I'm glad the views are positioned this way; the positioning makes it easy to drag a class from the Project Navigator into the Page Designer, where it will be turned into a Bean.

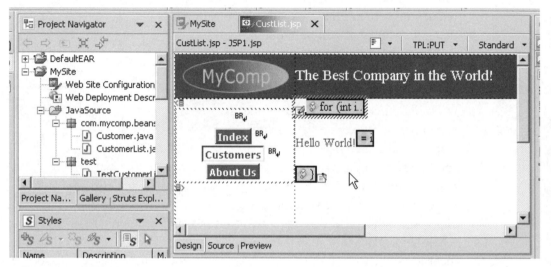

Figure 8-13: The Project Navigator and the Page Designer are side by side, making it easy to drag classes into the JSP.

This is one of the reasons I like to create my own class for every Bean I send to a JSP. The class CustomerList is right there in my project now, and I can click on it as shown in Figure 8-14 and then drag it over to the JSP as shown in Figure 8-15 and drop it.

❑ **8.2(c) Click on the CustomerList class and start dragging it to the left.**

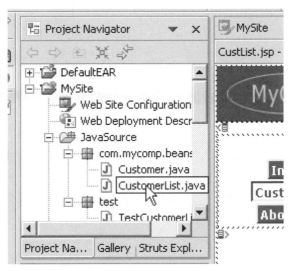

*Figure 8-14: Click on CustomerList to drag it
over to the JSP.*

Note that in Figure 8-15 I am dropping the class right after the little icon that represents the start of the editable area (the icon is a pencil on a scrap of paper, denoting an editable fragment). By dropping it right there, I am guaranteeing that the Bean is executed before any other of my code. Note that the drag-and-drop cursor will be a "no drop" (the international circle with a slash through it) until it enters the editable area; thus, I can find the beginning easily by simply moving the cursor slowly over the editable area icon until it changes to a droppable cursor (the box with the plus sign).

❑ **8.2(d) Drop the CustomerList class into the editable area of the JSP.**

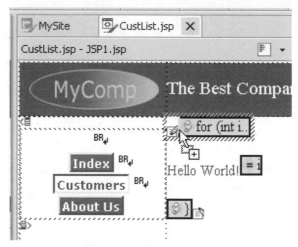

Figure 8-15: The cursor changes to the "drop" cursor once it enters the editable area.

After you drop the class, you'll see it added as a Bean icon, as shown in Figure 8-16.

Figure 8-16: The newly added Bean has its own icon. The icon is, not surprisingly, a small coffee bean.

This adds the Bean with default values, which are pretty useless, actually. There is no ID specified and no scope defined. My company standard is to use session scope, but the ID of the Bean requires a little more care. Remember that the ID of the Bean is really the name of the variable that will be created. So you want to be sure to specify a meaningful name. At the same time, you want to avoid collisions with other Beans, since this value is the "key" by which the application server accesses the Bean. If you were to place two different Beans in the session with the same name but different types, chances are you'd get some subtle (or not so subtle!) errors. Also, you have to be careful not to conflict with any "special" names that are part of the JSP, such as "session" or "request."

In this case, I want you to add the Bean with the ID of "customers," which for now is safe within our application. Also remember that I usually use session scope, so I want you to set that as well. All of these values can be set using the Attributes view, available in the lower left pane of the workbench. Click on the Attributes tab as shown in Figure 8-17.

❑ **8.2(e) Click on the Attributes tab.**

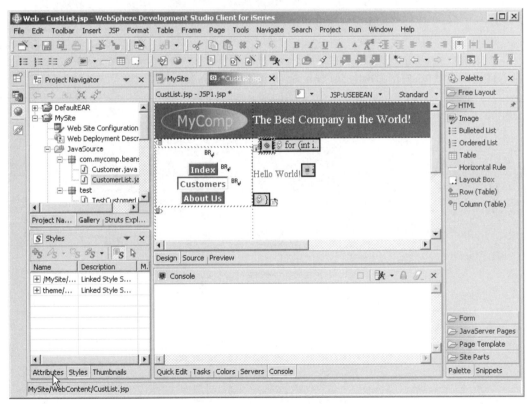

Figure 8-17: Click on the Attributes tab to access the attributes of the newly added Bean.

This will bring up the Attributes view. Due to the space constraints, the pane is too small for the entire Attributes view. You can maximize the pane as always by double-clicking on the title bar, or you can just enter the fields as I have shown in Figure 8-18.

❏ **8.2(f) Type "customers" into the ID field.**

❏ **8.2(g) Set the scope value to Session.**

Once you've done this, the Bean properties will change on the Design mode, which is currently displayed in the editor. However, the work you now have to do will be a lot easier using the Source mode, so you should now click on the Source tab as shown in Figure 8-19.

Figure 8-18: Enter "customers" as the ID and select Session for scope.

❏ **8.2(h) Click on the Source tab.**

Figure 8-19: Click on the Source tab.

You'll need all the room you can get, especially at this resolution, so maximize the view by double-clicking on the CustList.jsp tab as shown in Figure 8-20.

❏ 8.2(i) Double-click on the CustList.jsp tab.

Figure 8-20: Double-click on the CustList.jsp tab to maximize the source view.

At this point, you'll see the useBean tag you just added. You will also see the old code you entered back in Step 2.5. You will replace this code with new code that will create a table of customers. First, you'll create a table and a couple of heading rows. Then, you'll create a loop while there are more customers in the CustomerList Bean. For each customer, you'll output a row with a few of the fields. Finally, you'll close the loop and output the end of table tag. The final code looks like the code in Listing 8-1.

Listing 8-1: This is the JSP code that will generate a table of customers.

```
<jsp:useBean class="com.mycomp.beans.CustomerList"
id="customers" scope="session"></jsp:useBean>
<table>
<tr><th colspan=3>Customer List</th></tr>
<tr><th>Number</th><th>Name</th><th>Email</th></tr>
<%while (customers.hasNext()) {
   com.mycomp.beans.Customer c = customers.nextCustomer(); %>
<tr><td><%=c.getNumber()%></td><td><%=c.getName()%></td><td>
   <%=c.getEmail()%></td></tr>
<%}%>
</table>
```

Enter this code as shown between the <tpl:put> and the </tpl:put> tags in the JSP, as shown in Figure 8-21.

Tip: Sometimes it gets difficult to enter code into a page that was generated from a template. The editor occasionally gets confused marking the "non-editable" area, and you can't get your code in. If that ever happens, you can always modify the source code using a text editor; in fact, that's one of the options if you right-click a JSP or HTML page in the Project Navigator. Just be very careful to leave all of the <tpl:> tags in place, or else your results are unpredictable.

❏ **8.2(j) Enter the code from Listing 8-1.**

```
CustList.jsp
    <br><a href="/MySite/About.html">About Us</a>
</td>
</table>
<!-- /siteedit:navbar --></td>
                <td valign="top" class="content-area" height="300"><%-- tpl:put name="b
<jsp:useBean class="com.mycomp.beans.CustomerList"
id="customers" scope="session"></jsp:useBean>
<table>
<tr><th colspan=3>Customer List</th></tr>
<tr><th>Number</th><th>Name</th><th>Email</th></tr>
<%while (customers.hasNext()) {
  com.mycomp.beans.Customer c = customers.nextCustomer(); %>
<tr><td><%=c.getNumber()%></td><td><%=c.getName()%></td><td><%=c.getEmail()%></td></tr>
<%}%>
</table>
<%-- /tpl:put --%></td>
            </tr>
        </tbody>
    </table>
    </td>
    </tr>
    <tr>
        <td valign="top"><!-- siteedit:navbar spec="/MySite/theme/footer.html" target="s
<table class="footer" cellspacing="0" cellpadding="0" width="100%" border="0">

Design  Source  Preview

MySite/WebContent/CustList.jsp                                    Writable   Insert   54 : 9
```

Figure 8-21: This is the JSP with the code for processing the CustomerList Bean.

Once you've entered the code, you can go back to the Preview mode to take a look at your handiwork. Just click on the Preview mode tab at the bottom of the editor pane as illustrated in Figure 8-21.

❑ **8.2(k) Click on the Preview mode tab.**

Figure 8-22: The Preview mode shows your table headings, but no data.

When you see the Preview mode, you'll see the headings but no data. That's because Preview mode doesn't try to show you the scriptlets or anything; it only shows you the actual HTML code from the JSP. To get a little better idea of what the page might look like with data, you can use the Design mode. Click on the Design mode tab at the bottom of the editor, as shown in Figure 8-22.

❑ **8.2(l) Click on the Design mode tab.**

If you take a look at the Design mode (Figure 8-23), you'll see the outlines of the table. You'll see not only the heading rows, but also the detail row with scriptlets in each cell. This gives you a little better idea of what your page will ultimately look like. But there's no easy way to see the final product except by running it, so that's the next step.

First, save the current changes by right-clicking in the editor view and selecting Save, as shown in Figure 8-23. Note that you can only save changes when you're in the Design or Source modes; the Preview mode has no Save option in the pop-up menu.

❑ **8.2(m) Right-click in the editor view and select Save.**

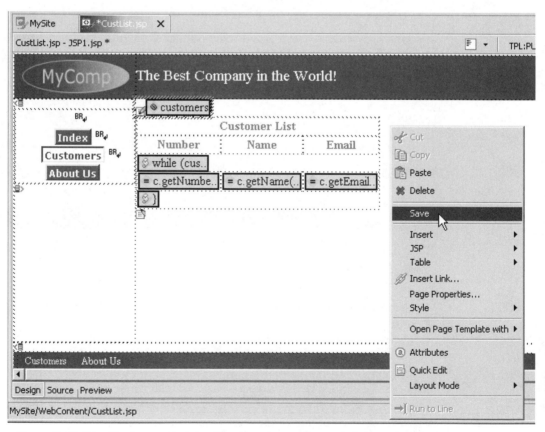

Figure 8-23: The Design mode tab allows you to see the scriptlets—as well as to save your changes.

Once you've saved, the next thing to do is to run the application on the server. You'll have to return to a non-maximized view, so double-click on the CustList.jsp tab, as shown in Figure 8-24.

❑ **8.2(n) Double-click on the CustList.jsp tab.**

Now you can run the application. As you did last time, locate index.html in the Project Navigator. Then, right-click on it and select Run on Server... from the pop-up menu.

Figure 8-24: Double-click on the CustList.jsp tab to restore it to normal size.

❑ **8.2(o) Find index.html, right-click on it, and select Run on Server....**

The primary difference between this time and the first time you ran on the server back in Step 6-1 is that this time you already have a server configuration available. Because of this, the radio button "Use an existing server" should be selected and, in the corresponding list box, a launch configuration titled WebSphere Express V5.0 Test Environment should be available with a status of Configured. That's exactly what you want, so press the Finish button to start up the server.

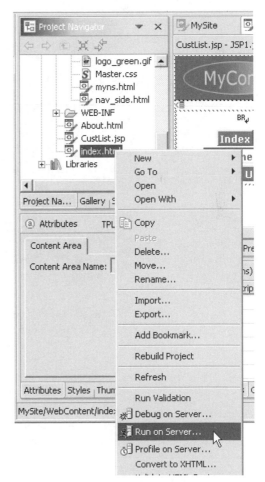

Figure 8-25: Run index.html on the server.

❑ **8.2(p) Leave the Server selection parameters as shown in Figure 8-26.**

❑ **8.2(q) Press Finish and wait for index page to appear.**

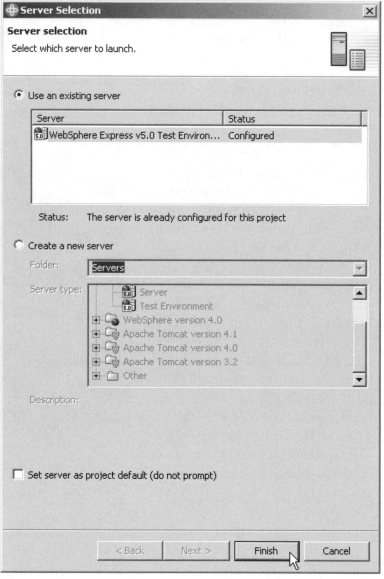

Figure 8-26: The only difference between now and Step 6-1 is that a server is already configured.

The server will start, and you'll go through the same startup procedure you did in Step 6-1. Eventually, the index page will come up as shown in Figure 8-27.

Figure 8-27: The index page comes up.

You can click on the Customers button to run the new JSP.

❑ **8.2(r) Click on Customers to see your results.**

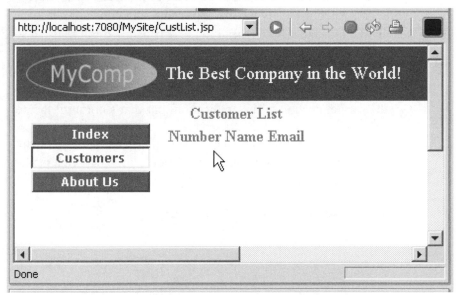

Figure 8-28: And here is the revamped CustList.jsp, but without data.

It seems to come up just fine. Now it's time to see some data!

Step 8.3—Default the data

GOAL

In this step, you will add a small amount of code to see what the JSP actually looks like with data.

There are a number of ways to get around this particular problem. One way is to have the Bean fill itself with data if it is created with the default constructor. That's because the useBean tag will automatically create the Bean that way if needed. Another way is to pass parameters on the useBean tag; these tags set values if the tag creates the Bean. This typically is the case when the JSP is invoked stand-alone—that is, if the JSP is not invoked from a servlet that creates the Bean prior to invoking the JSP. Invoking a JSP standalone is primarily something you would do in a test step like this one.

Either case above involves special coding in the Bean to support the test case. And while you could probably have a helper class that doesn't get loaded, it simply seems like unnecessary overhead to me. Instead, I'd rather use a separate test class that would create some dummy data. Something like the TestCustomerList class from Step 7.2! And in fact, that's what you'll do: You'll insert a call to the "make" method of TestCustomerList. Of course, this call will have to come out before you test the servlet portion of the application, but that's not until the next step.

For this step, I want you to update CustList.jsp by adding a line that will initialize the customers Bean with dummy data. Click on the CustList.jsp tab to make it active, as in Figure 8-30.

❑ **8.3(a) Click on the CustList.jsp tab.**

Figure 8-29: Click on the CustList.jsp tab to activate it.

The last time you were in this particular member, you were in Design mode, so that should be the mode you return to, as shown in Figure 8-30. That's not where you need to be, however. You need to be in Source mode, so click on the Source tab as illustrated.

❑ **8.3(b) Click on the Source tab.**

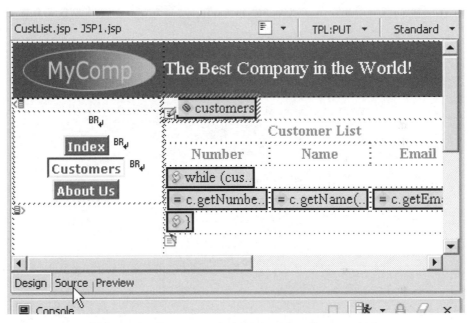

Figure 8-30: Click on the Source mode tab to get into Source mode.

Now that you're in Source mode, it's easy to make the change. Right after you initialize the Bean (that is, right after the useBean tag), enter the following scriptlet:

```
<%customers=test.TestCustomerList.make();%>
```

This will load the customers Bean with the results of the make method, which as you might recall from Step 7-2 is simply a CustomerList object with a few lines of dummy data. Of course, you can feel free to add your own data to this class, but this is just a temporary class for testing only. Eventually, you're going to get this data from a database file, so you don't need to spend a lot of time getting realistic data at this point.

Once you've added the line of code as shown in Figure 8-31, save the member. You can use the right-click method as also shown in Figure 8-31.

❑ **8.3(c) Enter the code as shown.**

❑ **8.3(d) Right-click and select Save.**

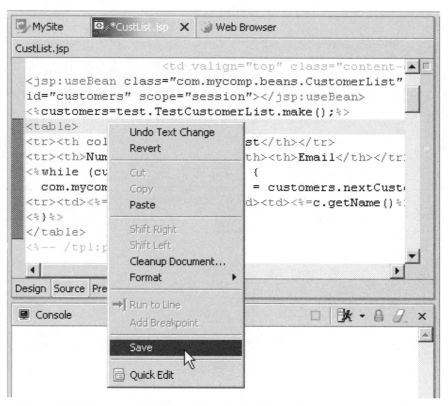

Figure 8-31: After entering the scriptlet, right-click in the editor and select Save.

This will save the code. You can now test it.

Run the index page on the server, using the same technique that was outlined in steps 8.2(o) through 8.2(q). This will bring up the index page, from which you can select the Customers link and see the results as shown in Figure 8-32.

Note: If you started from Checkpoint 8-3, the server will not be running, so you'll have to wait a moment as it comes up and initializes. If not, the index page should come up immediately.

Whether you had to restart the server or you had one already started from a previous step, the JSP will come up with dummy data in it. Maximize the page to get the view shown in Figure 8-32.

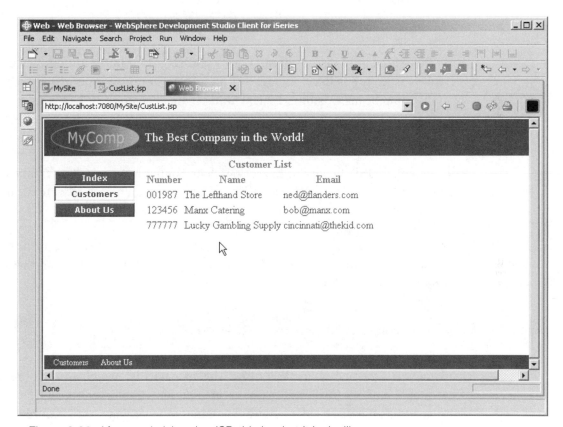

Figure 8-32: After maximizing the JSP, this is what it looks like.

And you're done with this step. You've successfully created a JSP that works within your Web site framework and puts out formatted data. The data is still dummy data from a test class, but don't worry about that for a little while yet.

InStep 8.3.a—Code review

I'll go through the JSP code line by line in this InStep. If you want to understand the reasoning behind the code, this is the place. But don't feel you have to read it; if you want to continue with the primary steps, you can come back to this chapter later.

```
<jsp:useBean class="com.mycomp.beans.CustomerList"
id="customers" scope="session"></jsp:useBean>
```

First, let's look at the jsp:useBean tag. If you're unfamiliar with the concept, what this is saying is that I expect to find a Bean in my session of the type com.mycomp.beans.CustomerList, with the name "customers." This information becomes very important later, when writing the servlet. That's because the servlet must put this Bean in the session using that same name (customers).

If I invoke this JSP directly or the servlet does not put a Bean in the session with the correct name, then the Web application server will automatically create an instance of the Bean for me. The result is what you see back in Figure 8-28: headings with no rows.

For testing purposes, I decided to load the Bean in the JSP myself. I did that by adding the following line:

```
<%customers=test.TestCustomerList.make();%>
```

This line calls the make() method from TestCustomerList, which you may recall from Step 7 builds a CustomerList with three dummy Customer objects. Because of this, adding the make call changes the output to what you see in Figure 8-32, which is headings followed by three lines of customer data.

```
<table>
<tr><th colspan=3>Customer List</th></tr>
<tr><th>Number</th><th>Name</th><th>Email</th></tr>
```

Next are the headings. This is standard HTML. I have the <table> tag, which begins the table, followed by two heading rows. The first heading line has a heading cell with colspan=3 specified, which causes it to span three columns. The next line has three individual heading cells: Number, Name, and Email. By using heading cells (<TH>) rather than data cells (<TD>), I can easily specify different formatting for the headings than for the detail. You'll see this in more detail in Step 16.

```
<%while (customers.hasNext()) {
    com.mycomp.beans.Customer c = customers.nextCustomer(); %>
```

This is the primary business logic of the JSP. What it does is loop through the customers in the list. As long as there is more data (hasNext returns true), it will grab the next Customer object from the CustomerList object, using the nextCustomer method.

```
<tr><td><%=c.getNumber()%></td><td><%=c.getName()%></td><td><%=c.getE
mail()%></td></tr>
```

This line outputs the detail rows. It is executed for every Customer object. What it does is call the appropriate getter for each of the three fields I want to show (number, name, and email) and output them to the browser inside of a data cell.

```
<%}%>
```

This simply closes the while loop.

```
</table>
```

And this ends the table.

Note that there's really very little Java code in the JSP. Some people insist on using certain structured tags to iterate through Beans, but frankly, I think the standard tag libraries are anything but standard. And while you have to know basic

Java syntax to understand the loop, that's all you have to know. You don't have to look up the syntax of yet another tag language.

Am I any more correct than someone who swears by the JSP Standard Tag Library (JSTL)? No, it's really more a matter of programming style. It's just that I don't really want to add another syntax to my poor aching brain. And it's not that the syntax is difficult, it's just one more piece that I don't want to have to remember.

Step 9

JSP Model II

It is time to rest your weary fingers for just a few moments while I go into some detail on the JSP Model II architecture. Never fear, this step is still hands-on. Later in the step, you will create a servlet and a servlet proxy and use them to invoke the JSP you so lovingly modified in the previous step.

Up until this point, I've given you instructions on using WDSC to create an application that is essentially non-interactive. Even the JSP you created doesn't really do anything. And while you've seen a lot of features of WDSC, nothing until this point has been really focused on business application design. From this point forward, that will change. The rest of this book is dedicated to creating a real business application.

And while we were able to generate a lot of pretty pages using the wizards, before we can go any further on this project, we need to start making some design decisions. This is where the work gets more difficult, as a bad decision now can affect the success of the entire endeavor. That being the case, it's time to address the first of the big issues in any Web application: the application architecture.

Specifically, I'd like to talk about what the JSP Model II is and why you are going to use it in this book and also about the concept of a "servlet proxy," which helps you avoid many of the pitfalls inherent in programming with servlets. By the end of this step, you'll have a client/server architecture in place that will allow you to create robust business applications.

Step 9.1—Why JSP Model II?

> ## GOAL
>
> In this step, I will introduce you to JSP Model II and explain why I chose it as the underlying architecture for the examples in this book.

There is no single correct architecture. What might be right for one application may not be right for another. At the same time, there are ways to identify which architecture is right for you. The reasons usually come in two varieties: strategic and tactical.

Strategic reasons involve identifying the best architecture for your business in the long term. These reasons include things like flexibility and maintainability, features that generally tend to add a little design time to the application but make it easier to later expand the application in response to changing business needs. I try to incorporate as many of these features in my designs as possible—or at least not design them out.

Tactical reasons, on the other hand, tend to be based on such short-term issues as initial cost and available talent. For example, you may not have any Java talent on your staff. That might cause you to decide to go with an RPG-CGI approach or a screen scraper, simply so you don't have to add Java expertise. Whether or not I not agree with such decisions, you have to ultimately decide what makes sense in your environment.

Since I don't have a crystal ball that shows me your particular business environment, I am going to err on the side of strategic planning and show you what I consider to be the best-of-breed design. To me, that's the JSP Model II architecture.

In the JSP Model II architecture, everything centers on the servlet. The servlet is actually the controller for the entire system. The sequence works like this:

1. The servlet is invoked.

2. The servlet builds Beans and places them in the session.

3. The servlet invokes a JSP.

4. The JSP renders the contents of the Beans (including input capabilities).

5. The user enters data into the JSP's form and presses a submit button.

6. The contents of the form are sent back to the servlet for processing.

RPG programmers should find this extremely familiar. It's a pretty faithful imitation of the 5250 I/O cycle: call program, move data into screen variables, EXFMT, wait for user input, retrieve data from screen.

How does this compare with other architectures? A pure servlet architecture (like any CGI approach) generally involves a lot of formatting within the application program itself. With servlets, that means outputting all the HTML tags yourself, which is more work than you really want to do.

CGI of any type means that you cannot separate the tasks of servlet programming and UI design. Any change to the UI means a change to the application. Having separation here is crucial to good project management. It means you don't have to have one person who knows both application and GUI design, which is a good thing: It's amazing how rarely those two abilities reside in the same individual. It also means that theoretically you could bring in a consultant or a mentor to help you with one area where you are currently lacking in specific expertise.

The thing I like best about the JSP Model II architecture is my ability to control the application flow like I would with any other business application architecture: based on business logic. In the older JSP-only architecture, which didn't include controlling servlets, it was up to each JSP to identify the next JSP in the line. In most cases, the best you could do was go to one JSP or another based on which button the user pressed. That means you already had decided what the next page was before you had even been able to validate the user's data.

And while this worked to some degree in simple applications, complex applications required either layers of indirection or lots of preprocessing in each JSP. And since JSPs are not that easy to debug (that was especially true in the early days of the architecture), this meant a lot of debugging work for the developers.

Instead, with the JSP Model II design, the servlet decides which JSP is next. How this is done depends on the specific design. For example, Struts uses a combination of an XML definition file and code within the servlet to determine what the next page is. I usually have one of two designs: one in which there is a servlet for each application and one in which there is a single controller servlet for the entire user session. Which design to use depends on where in the architecture the application panel designs are made. When completely controlled by the RPG programs on the host, users tend to be locked into a specific sequence of screens until they log out. In that case, I tend to use a single controller. When users have more ability to jump between running applications, I tend to use one servlet per application.

And while this book looks to be using the latter approach, the design issues are still valid, regardless of the architecture. In this case, I have created a proxy for the servlet, and that's a crucial design decision. I'll review the reasons for that particular decision in the next step.

Step 9.2—Why use a servlet proxy?

> ## GOAL
> In this step, I discuss the architectural decisions behind the servlet proxy.

What is a servlet proxy? Well, what is a proxy? A proxy is something that acts on something else's behalf. Not to be confused with a proxy server, a proxy is an object that essentially processes a request for another object. The term is most often used in multi-tiered architectures, where an object on one machine is really a sort of surrogate for an object on another machine. Remote Method Invocation (RMI) is an example of just that sort of design: When you call a method on the proxy object on the local machine, the proxy actually forwards the request to another object on the remote machine.

In this case, though, the proxy is going to serve as a go-between from the multi-threaded servlet object to a single-threaded session object. The most important benefit of this architecture is the ability to use instance variables, which allow you to develop stateful applications.

A quick glimpse into servlets: No matter how many users are invoking a servlet, only one instance of the object is in memory. The initial design decision was made to enhance performance. By creating only one servlet object and having many sessions use it simultaneously, there is no need to synchronize the usage of the servlet. This means that one user session won't hold up another one, even if it needs to do something that takes time. And while this is a good concept in theory, it has certain drawbacks. The biggest drawback is that servlets cannot use instance variables, because those variables are shared among all sessions executing the servlet. A side effect of this design is that you can't store state information in a servlet.

This is fine for stateless connections, which were pretty much the norm in the early days of Web application design. However, as the browser becomes the de facto replacement for the green-screen, the concept of a pure stateless session is less prevalent. Instead, the concept of the session has received more attention.

When a user invokes a servlet, the servlet can create an HTTP session object, which is then alive for the duration of the browser session. How the Web application server maintains that HTTP session is implementation-specific, but generally it involves a cookie on your workstation. This cookie tells the Web application server which session object to activate for this request.

The traditional way to provide state is to store all your variables in this session object. The getAttribute and setAttribute methods allow you to store variables in the HTTP session. However, you must pass the HTTP session object to all of the methods in your servlet, and you must get these values from the session. That's a lot of hash table look-ups and, because the methods work only with objects of type Object, a lot of class casting as well.

To get around this problem, I have designed something called a "servlet proxy." The servlet proxy is an object that performs all the processing of the requests that a servlet would normally perform. The servlet does almost nothing except use the request to get the HTTP session, get the servlet proxy from the HTTP session, and then pass the request to that servlet proxy. Note that my terminology is somewhat backward: It might be more accurate to call the servlet proxy an "application" and the servlet an "application proxy," but I like the fact that the term "servlet proxy" indicates that the object is intimately associated with a servlet.

The beauty of this design is that the servlet itself is very simple. All it does is go to the HTTP session object, get a servlet proxy or create one if none exists, and then pass the HTTP request to the servlet proxy. From that point on, the servlet proxy handles everything. And since there is exactly one servlet proxy per user session, the programmer can use instance variables just like in any other application. This can greatly minimize the extraneous code required to constantly get and set attributes in the HTTP session.

I know it sounds like it might be unnecessary overhead, but once you take a look at the actual code, you'll see just how simple it is. And now that I've given you the overview, it's time to get back to the hands-on work.

Step 9.3—Remove the test data from the JSP

GOAL

Since the data will be coming from the servlet now, you should first remove the line of code in the JSP that creates dummy data.

Remember that back in Step 8-3 you added a scriptlet to your JSP to create dummy data. Since from now on all data will come from your servlet, you need to remove that line. So edit that JSP (click on the CustList.jsp tab in the editor). You'll see the source code in Figure 9-2. Scroll through the source until you're down around line 45; that should be just above the scriptlet you added in Step 8-3. You're looking for the following line:

```
<%customers=test.TestCustomerList.make();%>
```

Hint: When you are in a source editor, your current position in the source (line number and column) is displayed in the very bottom right corner of the workbench.

❑ **9.3(a) Click on the CustList.jsp tab.**

❑ **9.3(b) Scroll until line 47 is displayed.**

Figure 9-1: Click on the CustList.jsp tab.

Figure 9-2: This is the beginning of the source. Scroll until you get to line 47.

Now that you've located the scriptlet, I'll show you a little trick for quickly commenting out a scriptlet without actually removing it from the source.

Just go into the line right after the begin scriptlet tag (<%) and enter in two forward slashes (//). This should change the color of the code within the scriptlet, indicating that the code is now a comment. These slashes will also be generated when the JSP is converted into Java, so doing this will effectively comment out the line. Typically, you would do this if you intended to go back and re-insert the line later, so it really isn't appropriate here, but I wanted to show you the technique.

You can also use a scriptlet comment by adding two dashes (—) after the begin scriptlet tag, but you have to be careful to also add two dashes *before* the end scriptlet tag (%>); otherwise, the compiler will consider the rest of your JSP a comment.

❑ **9.3(c) Comment out the scriptlet.**

❑ **9.3(d) Right-click and select Save.**

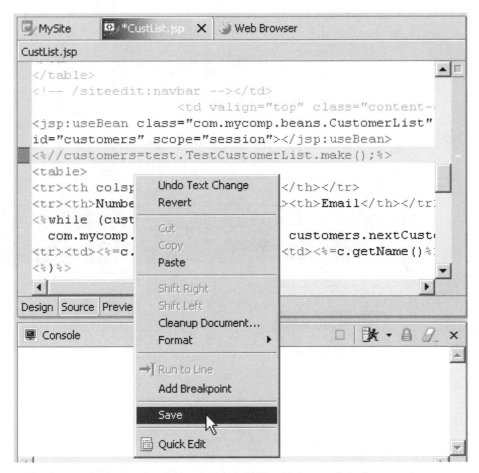

Figure 9-3: After commenting out the scriptlet with forward slashes as shown, save the member.

The modified JSP is ready for testing.

Run the index page on the server, using the same technique you performed in steps 8.2(o) through 8.2(q). This will bring up the index page as shown in Figure 9-4. From that point, select the Customers link and see the results as shown in Figure 9-5.

Note: If you started from Checkpoint 9-3, the server will not be running, so you'll have to wait a moment as it comes up and initializes. If not, the index page should come up immediately.

☐ **9.3(e) Launch the index page.**

☐ **9.3(f) Click on Customers to run the modified JSP.**

Figure 9-4: On the index page, click on Customers to bring up the JSP.

The dummy data will be gone.

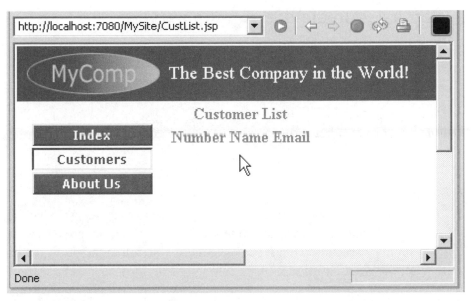

Figure 9-5: The customer list is empty because you removed the scriptlet that created dummy data.

Step 9.4—Create and run the servlet

> ### GOAL
>
> In this step, you will create the two classes required for the servlet (the servlet and the servlet proxy) and run them.

I told you that you would be using my servlet proxy design. That means that you will need to add two classes: the servlet and the servlet proxy. The servlet is very simple; essentially, it just passes requests through to the proxy, which actually does all the work.

It should be noted that, even though the servlet proxy is designed to handle some pretty complex code, it's going to be quite simple for now. This is especially true in this step, because you still won't be accessing data on the host. Instead, you will take advantage of the same test class that you have throughout the development of this application (this is one of the reasons I really prefer the technique of a class specifically for generating dummy data). As the application gets more complex, you'll see that only the proxy will require substantially more code; the servlet will stay nearly unchanged.

To start this step, I want to create a second package that is dedicated to applications. All of the servlet and servlet proxy code will live in this package. Why do I have it separate from the Beans? Because the Beans are all that the JSPs know about; they're really the model portion of the Model-View-Controller (MVC) interface. The JSPs are the view, and the servlet proxies are the controllers.

So create the new package by right-clicking on the JavaSource folder in your project and selecting New/Package, as shown in Figure 9-6.

> **Release Note:** If you're using V5.1.2, remember that the JavaSource folder was renamed Java Resources.

❑ **9.4(a) Right-click on JavaSource and select New/Package.**

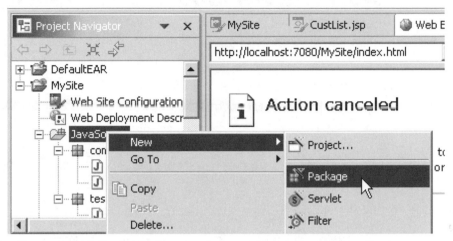

Figure 9-6: Right-click on the JavaSource folder and select New/Package.

> **Note:** You'll only see "Action canceled" in the browser if you started this step from Checkpoint 9-4. Otherwise, you should see the customer list JSP shown in Figure 9-5.

Now you can add the new package. Type com.mycomp.app in the Name field and press the Finish button as shown in Figure 9-7.

> **Note:** Even if you are using your own package names, I still suggest you select a name ending in .app for this package to identify it as the application package and to clearly differentiate it from the Beans packages.

❑ **9.4(b) Type com.mycomp.app into the Name field.**

❑ **9.4(c) Press Finish.**

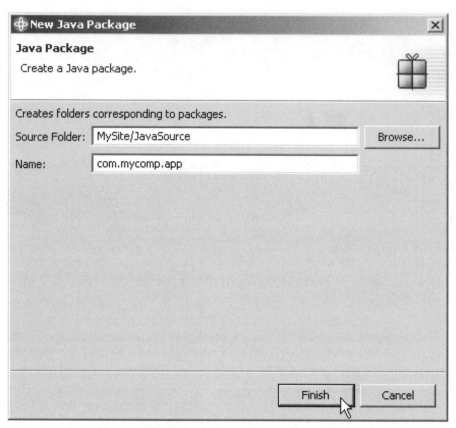

Figure 9-7: Type com.mycomp.app into the Name field and press Finish.

You've added the package, so now you need to add the classes. I'll walk you through the first one; it's the same thing you've been doing. Right-click on the package to bring up the pop-up menu, and from that menu, select option New and then Class, as shown in Figure 9-8.

❑ **9.4(d) Right-click on the package you just added and select New/Class.**

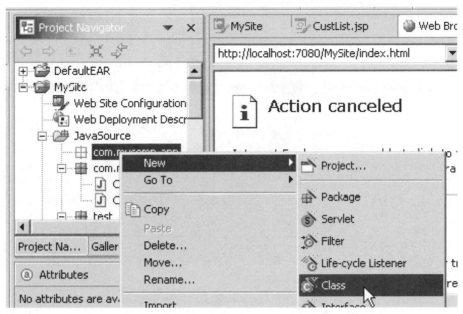

Figure 9-8: Right click on com.mycomp.app and select New/Class.

This brings up the New Java Class wizard shown in Figure 9-9. Since you have all the code already, you don't need to use any of the fancy features of the wizard; simply type in the name of the class (CustListProxy) and press the Finish button.

❑ **9.4(e) Type CustListProxy into the Name field.**

❑ **9.4(f) Press Finish.**

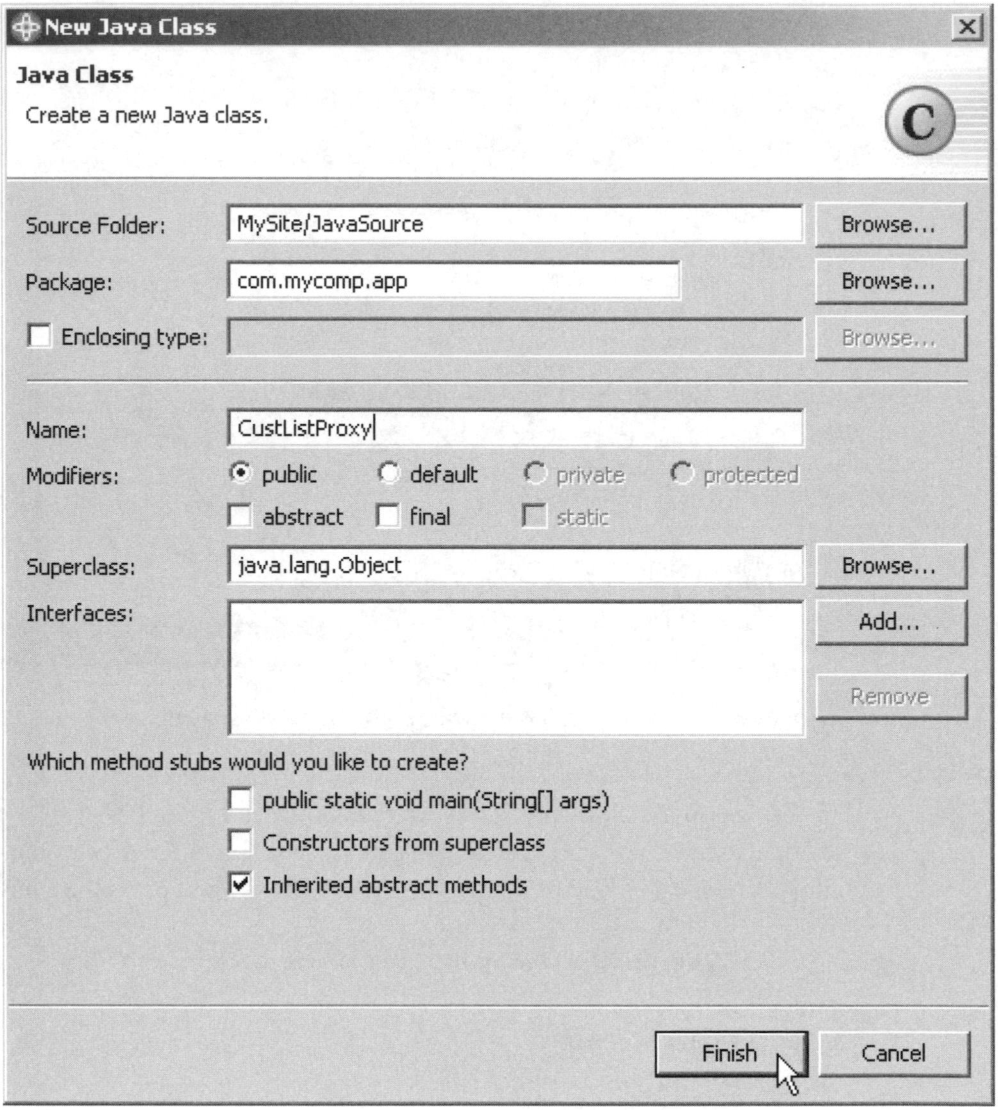

Figure 9-9: Type CustListProxy into the Name field and press Finish.

This creates the class for you. Now I want you to overlay the source with the contents of Listing 9-1.

Listing 9-1: This is the CustListProxy, which will actually process the requests.

```java
package com.mycomp.app;

import com.mycomp.beans.*;

import java.io.*;
import javax.servlet.*;
import javax.servlet.http.*;

public class CustListProxy {

    private HttpServlet servlet;
    private HttpSession session;
    private HttpServletRequest req;
    private HttpServletResponse res;

    public CustListProxy(HttpServlet servlet, HttpSession session) {
        this.servlet = servlet;
        this.session = session;
    }

    protected void doGet(HttpServletRequest req,
        HttpServletResponse res)
    throws ServletException, IOException {
        this.req = req;
        this.res = res;
        doRequest();
    }

    protected void doPost(HttpServletRequest req,
        HttpServletResponse res)
    throws ServletException, IOException {
        this.req = req;
        this.res = res;
        doRequest();
    }

    private void doRequest() throws ServletException, IOException {
        CustomerList cl = test.TestCustomerList.make();
        session.setAttribute("customers", cl);
        servlet.getServletContext().
            getRequestDispatcher("CustList.jsp").
                forward(req, res);
    }
}
```

You may enter the code from above, or you can copy it in from the CD-ROM (as always). In the Imports folder is a file named Step9-4-a.txt, which contains the code displayed in Listing 9-1. You can open it with a text editor and cut and paste it into the editor view. After entering the code, right-click in the editor and select Save to save the member as shown in Figure 9-10.

❑ **9.4(g) Enter the code from Listing 9-1 into the editor view.**

❑ **9.4(h) Right-click in the editor view and select Save.**

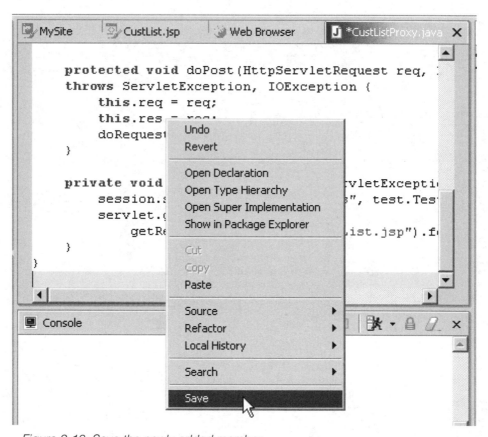

Figure 9-10: Save the newly added member.

Now do the same thing for CustList. Repeat steps 9.4(d) through 9.4(h), except change the class name to CustList and use the source from Listing 9-2 (which is also available on the CD-ROM in the Imports folder as Step9-4-b.txt).

Listing 9-2: This is the CustList class—the actual servlet, which passes the request to CustListProxy.

```
package com.mycomp.app;

import java.io.*;
import javax.servlet.*;
import javax.servlet.http.*;

public class CustList extends HttpServlet {

    private static final String PROXY = "CustListSession";

    protected void doGet(HttpServletRequest req,
        HttpServletResponse res)
    throws ServletException, IOException {
        CustListProxy proxy = getProxy(req);
        proxy.doGet(req, res);
    }

    protected void doPost(HttpServletRequest req,
        HttpServletResponse res)
    throws ServletException, IOException {
        CustListProxy proxy = getProxy(req);
        proxy.doPost(req, res);
    }

    private CustListProxy getProxy(HttpServletRequest req)
    {
        HttpSession session = req.getSession(true);
        CustListProxy proxy = (CustListProxy)
            session.getAttribute(PROXY);
        if (proxy == null)
        {
            proxy = new CustListProxy(this, session);
            session.setAttribute(PROXY, proxy);
        }
        return proxy;
    }
}
```

The only thing left is to run the code. Figure 9-11 shows how to run the servlet itself (be sure to run CustList, which is the servlet, not CustListProxy). Running the servlet is just like running the index page. And if the server is still running (that is, you haven't started from a Checkpoint), then you'll almost immediately be brought to the Web browser, as shown in Figure 9-12. If you did start from the Checkpoint, wait a few moments while the server starts up; *then* you'll be presented with Figure 9-12.

□ **9.4(i) Run the servlet CustList on the server.**

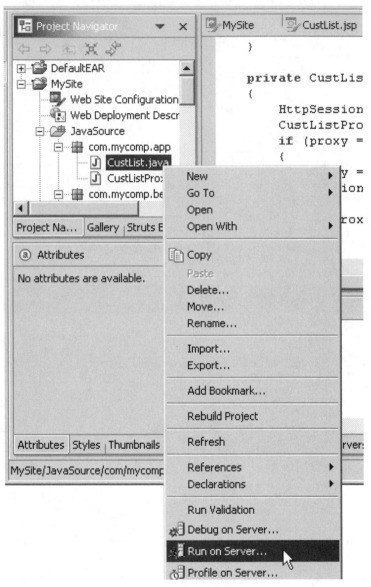

Figure 9-11: Start up the server by using Run on Server, but this time, use it on the CustList servlet.

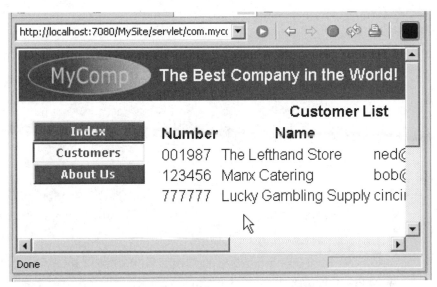

Figure 9-12: The JSP looks like this after being launched by the servlet.

The JSP comes up fine, and the dummy data is there. However, you may notice some differences in the fonts and colors between this screen and earlier screens. Why is that? Well, one clue can be found in the console output shown in Figure 9-13. There is a line that says "java.lang.ClassNotFoundException: theme." That indicates that somehow the JSP thinks it needs a class called theme. This is really a misleading error; the truth is a little more complex, and it involves relative paths versus absolute paths.

I'll explain it in more detail in Step 9.5.

```
Console [WebSphere Express v5.0 Test Environment (WebSphere v5.0)]
: [MySite] [/MySite] [Servlet.LOG]: InvokerServlet: init
: Application started: DefaultEAR
: Transport http is listening on port 7,080.
: Transport https is listening on port 7,443.
: Transport http is listening on port 7,090.
: Transport https is listening on port 7,043.
: RMI Connector available at port 7809
: Server server1 open for e-business
: [MySite] [/MySite] [Servlet.LOG]: com.mycomp.app.CustList: init
: [MySite] [/MySite] [Servlet.LOG]: /CustList.jsp: init
: [Servlet Error]-[theme]: Failed to load servlet: java.lang.ClassNotFoundException: theme
CompoundClassLoader.java:351)
CompoundClassLoader.java:261)
iled Code))
```

Figure 9-13: The console output of the project shows something named "theme" is missing.

InStep 9.4.a—Code review

> **GOAL**
>
> In this InStep, you will review the code for the servlet and servlet proxy and learn how they interact.

This is another code review InStep. As always, you can skip this and come back later if you want to keep moving ahead with the examples. If you aren't worried about the little details of the code, just go on ahead with Step 9.5. Come back and review this later.

But if you want to know why I did what I did, please follow along! In this case, since the code is a bit long, I'll simply embed my narrative comments into the listing. Let's do this backward and start with the servlet.

```java
package com.mycomp.app;

import java.io.*;
import javax.servlet.*;
import javax.servlet.http.*;
```

Standard stuff: the package declaration and the imported definitions.

```java
public class CustList extends HttpServlet {
```

And this is your standard servlet definition. A servlet must extend the HttpServlet class.

```java
    // Unique ID for the CustListProxy object
    private static final String PROXY = "CustListProxy";
```

This is the first bit of custom code. It identifies the name of the attribute that we will use to identify the proxy object. This value must be unique, but nobody needs to know what it is.

```
// The doGet and doPost methods simply get the current proxy and
// forward the request to it.
protected void doGet(HttpServletRequest req,
    HttpServletResponse res)
throws ServletException, IOException {
    CustListProxy proxy = getProxy(req);
    proxy.doGet(req, res);
}

protected void doPost(HttpServletRequest req,
    HttpServletResponse res)
throws ServletException, IOException {
    CustListProxy proxy = getProxy(req);
    proxy.doPost(req, res);
}
```

These are the standard methods called by the Web application server on a request. All they do in this servlet is get the servlet proxy object from the session and then pass the request on to it.

```
// This is the only real code. We get the HttpSession (creating one
// if none exists), then look and see if a CustListProxy exists.
// If not, we create a new one and store it in the session.
// Return the proxy to the caller.
private CustListProxy getProxy(HttpServletRequest req)
{
    HttpSession session = req.getSession(true);
    CustListProxy proxy = (CustListProxy)
        session.getAttribute(PROXY);
    if (proxy == null)
    {
        proxy = new CustListProxy(this, session);
        session.setAttribute(PROXY, proxy);
    }
    return proxy;
}
```

And this is the actual logic. First, get the HTTP session. The getSession method will automatically create a new one if one does not exist. Next, we use getAttribute to see if a proxy has already been established for this session. If one exists, the proxy will be non-null and we simply return it to the user. If, however, the getAttribute returns null, that means there is no proxy yet and we need to create one. We do that and then store it in the session using setAttribute. The return statement will return the newly created proxy.

```
}
```

And finally, we have the curly brace that ends the source for this class. The CustList servlet, then, is pretty straightforward. And indeed, this code is the model that I use for all my non-trivial servlets now. Basically, this is just an adapter class, which allows me to take a multi-threaded request and delegate it to an instantiated object, thereby allowing me to save state and so on using standard OO techniques.

On now to the class that does the work, the proxy.

> **Note:** Even though the proxy does the work, the work that it does is still quite trivial at this point in the process. When you actually attach the business logic in Step 15, this logic required for class will become more substantial.

```
package com.mycomp.app;

import com.mycomp.beans.*;

import java.io.*;
import javax.servlet.*;
import javax.servlet.http.*;
```

Once again, the standard beginning: the package declaration and imported definitions. Note that we need to include the Beans package as well, since this class is all about creating Beans.

```
public class CustListProxy {
```

The CustListProxy is just an object; it has no superclass. As you create more proxy classes, though, you may want to encapsulate the constructor and the doGet/doPost methods in a single abstract superclass, with an abstract doRequest method. There are pros and cons to that technique, primarily having to do with the common instance variables, but that's another topic for another day.

```
// Instance variables
private HttpServlet servlet;
private HttpSession session;
private HttpServletRequest req;
private HttpServletResponse res;
```

Speaking of instance variables, here they are. Pretty much every servlet proxy will need these variables. The first two are assigned at creation time and allow you to access the servlet and session, both of which are required when forwarding the request. The other two variables are set with each request. They are also required when you forward to the JSP, but you may also need them to retrieve user data entered on forms, as well as possibly using them for error reporting (note that for brevity's sake I've done almost zero error-handling in this application).

```
// Constructor: Save initial parameters
    public CustListProxy(HttpServlet servlet, HttpSession session) {
       this.servlet = servlet;
       this.session = session;
    }
```

The constructor is very simple, especially in this trivial case. It simply stores the initialization parameters. In more complex applications, this would be where you do session initialization, such as creating connections or performing authentication tasks.

```
// doGet and doPost both do the same thing:
    //    Save request information
    //    Invoke doRequest
    protected void doGet(HttpServletRequest req,
       HttpServletResponse res)
    throws ServletException, IOException {
       this.req = req;
       this.res = res;
       doRequest();    protected void doPost(HttpServletRequest req,
                      HttpServletResponse res)
    throws ServletException, IOException {
       this.req = req;
       this.res = res;
       doRequest();
    }
    }
```

In this particular case, I've decided to funnel both GET and POST requests through the same handler. There might be situations where you don't do this, which is another reason I didn't bother creating the abstract superclass. That's more of an application design issue.

```
// In this initial version, use the make() method from the test
   package
// to create a dummy CustomerList. Put that into the session and
   then
// forward the request to the appropriate JSP.
private void doRequest() throws ServletException, IOException {
   CustomerList cl = test.TestCustomerList.make();
   session.setAttribute("customers", cl);
   servlet.getServletContext().
      getRequestDispatcher("CustList.jsp").
         forward(req, res);
}
```

And finally, the actual work is done. As I said earlier, this is a pretty trivial application at this point. All it does is invoke the make method from the test package and pass that to the JSP. However, it does illustrate a couple of key points:

1. Note the name "customers". This must directly match the name specified in the useBean tag in the JSP. Refer back to InStep 8.3.a for another look at the useBean tag, looking specifically at the ID attribute.

2. The name of the JSP is specified relative to the application root. The application root is what is returned from the call to getServletContext.

This may seem like a lot of work just to display what we already displayed in the JSP *without* using a servlet. But that's the point of the exercise: By building the application infrastructure gradually, you can check your progress at each point.

First, you created the Beans and tested them. You also wrote a class that created a dummy Bean that you could test.

Next, you inserted that dummy Bean into your JSP. This allows you to completely design and test the JSP without worrying about the servlet interface.

Now, in this step, you create a scaled-down servlet that invokes the test method to create the same dummy data that you used in the initial JSP test. You have a ready-made unit test case now, because the output of the JSP launched from the servlet should be identical to what the JSP looked like without the servlet.

Personally, I prefer this sort of gradual build-and-test philosophy. I was able to do all of this without ever hitting the host. Now I know my infrastructure works, and if I have any other errors, it will be because of the host side of things.

Step 9.5—Absolute style

> ### GOAL
> In this step, you will learn the safest way to specify links to style sheets and fix your pages accordingly.

In the course of events so far, you've done several different things. One was to create a simple Web site with three pages: index.html, about.html, and JSP1.jsp (now renamed to CustList.jsp). In so doing, you let WDSC pretty much have its way in creating the pages, and it defaulted a number of things, including the reference to a style sheet called Master.css. A little later, you started using some advanced capabilities of WDSC and added a template to your pages along with a customized navigation widget. This brought in a second style sheet, green.css. Finally, you built a servlet and some Beans in your initial steps toward writing real Web applications, and now your JSP is launched through a servlet instead of from a hyperlink.

The problem is that the various stages aren't entirely consistent in how they handle certain things; in particular, the style sheet references are not consistent, and that's leading to the problem we are seeing. Let's recap that issue. Run the index on the server and then click on the Customers link to bring up the JSP. You'll get the screen shown in Figure 9-14. This is the result of running the JSP directly from a hyperlink. Next, run your servlet (CustList.java) on the server. You'll get the page shown in Figure 9-15. This is what you get when you forward your request from a servlet to the JSP.

❏ **9.5(a) Run index.html on the server and click on Customers.**

❏ **9.5(b) Run CustList.java on the server.**

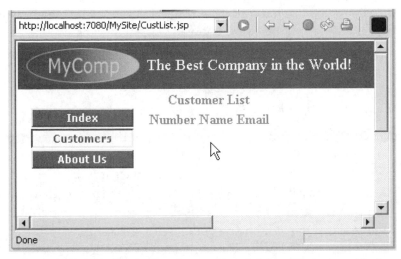

Figure 9-14: *CustList.jsp run from a hyperlink has this look and feel (and no data).*

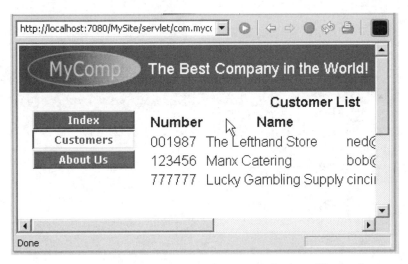

Figure 9-15: *CustList.jsp launched from a servlet has different fonts and contains data.*

There are two things to note when you compare these two images:

The first thing you'll notice is that the first image has no data because you removed the code that would pre-initialize the JSP. Now, the only way the JSP can show any data is if it is already loaded into the session. The servlet does this, so that's why the second page has data.

The second thing you'll see is that the title and the customer list table are in completely different fonts in the two versions. In most cases, this would be because of a style sheet issue. So what is the issue? Well, the clue is in the error you saw at the end of the last step, in Figure 9-13.

```
Failed to load servlet: java.lang.ClassNotFoundException: theme
```

This error says the application server tried to load a servlet but encountered an error when looking for the theme class. That's interesting; a closer look at the source of the JSP may shed further light on the topic. Normally, to go to the source of the JSP, you would just click on the CustList.jsp tab to bring it up into the editor. However, it will be easier to see what you're doing if you have the whole view in front of you, so double-click on it instead. This will not only switch to the source, but maximize the view as well. So double-click at the place shown in Figure 9-16.

❑ **9.5(c) Double-click on the CustList.jsp tab.**

Figure 9-16: Double click on CustList.jsp to bring the source up in a maximized view.

You should be in Source mode for this particular member, as shown in Figure 9-17, because that's where you last left it. If for some reason you're not in Source mode, simply click on the Source mode tab at the bottom of the editor window.

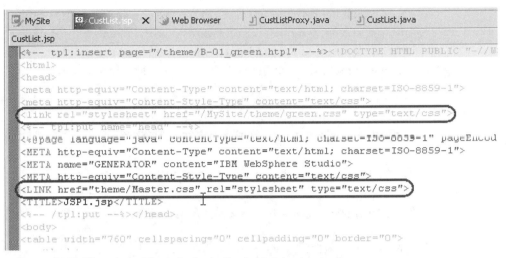

Figure 9-17: The circled lines indicate the two style sheet references.

In Figure 9-17, you'll see two lines circled. One is the reference for the template's style sheet, green.css. This line is grayed out because it came from the template and you cannot edit it. Remember, template lines are non-editable. The second line is the reference to the page's style sheet, Master.css. This was generated when you created the page way back in Step 2.5. If you compare the two, you'll notice the only difference between these two lines of code (other than the order of the tags, which doesn't matter) is the formatting of the href tag. The href tag tells the application server where to find the style sheet. In this case, we have two slightly different syntaxes:

A. /MySite/theme/green.css

B. theme/Master.css

The only difference between these syntaxes (other than the actual name of the style sheet) is that the first reference starts with /MySite/ and the other one does not. The first one is for the template style sheet, and it's clear that worked, because if it hadn't, you wouldn't see the nice formatting of the link buttons. Since the buttons appear properly, you can assume this reference works. Links in which the first character is a forward slash are called "absolute links," and they always work.

The second reference uses a relative link—one that does *not* start with a slash—and for some very convoluted reasons, relative links don't work when JSPs are served by servlets. The underlying issue is that the "base" page, which is the page from which the browser attempts to request the style sheet, is different when talking to a servlet, which in turn forwards a JSP. For more information on that phenomenon, feel free to read InStep 9.5.a, but to fix the problem, I want you to change the relative link in the JSP to an absolute link.

As it turns out, it's easier to fix than it is to explain. Simply look for the link for Master.css and change it from what's shown in Figure 9-18 to /MySite/theme/Master.css. Then save the source.

❑ **9.5(d) Change reference to /MySite/theme/Master.css.**

❑ **9.5(e) Right-click in the editor and select Save.**

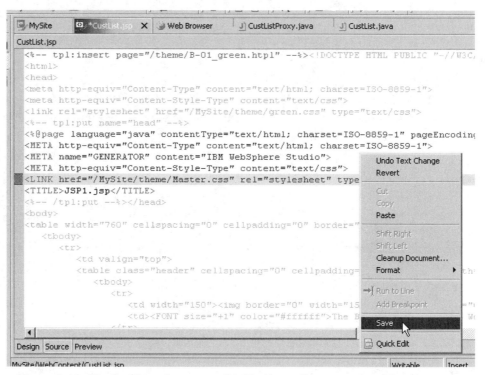

Figure 9-18: Change the reference to /MySite/theme/Master.css and Save.

Click on the Web Browser tab to get back to the Web browser. Click on the Refresh tool as shown Figure 9-19, and you will see the updated JSP in Figure 9-20. Note that the fonts and colors change back to the style you saw when you launched the JSP directly from the menu.

❑ **9.5(f) Click on the Web Browser tab.**

❑ **9.5(g) Click on the Refresh tool.**

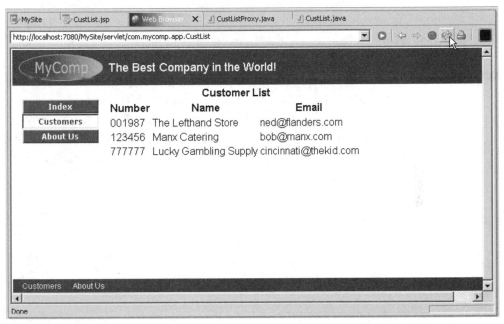

Figure 9-19: The JSP still has the wrong fonts, but click on the Refresh tool...

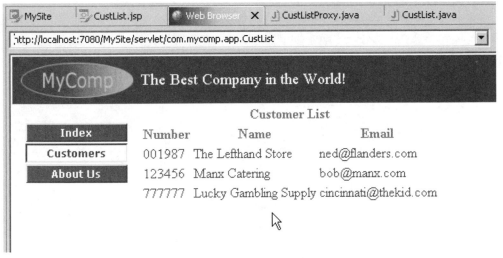

Figure 9-20: ...and voila! The fonts and colors change!

And now you've fixed the style sheet problem! My only problem at this point is that I actually think these are pretty ugly fonts. But we'll leave that particular problem alone for now.

I think it's important to point out that I have changed the style reference only in the JSP. The style references in the two static HTML pages remain as originally generated, with relative links. That should not matter because those pages should always be served via hyperlink rather than forwarded through a servlet, so the issue of the base page should not come into play. If at some later date you change your application so that you are using the servlet to forward to static HTML pages as well, you'll likely see the same strange behavior with your style sheets. If that begins to happen, you'll need to go in and make the same changes to your static HTML pages as you just did to this JSP.

InStep 9.5.a—Absolute and relative links and servlets

GOAL

This InStep discusses the differences between relative and absolute paths and how Web application servers interpret them.

In Step 9-5, you had two different link syntaxes for style sheets:

A. /MySite/theme/green.css

B. theme/Master.css

Since the first reference starts with a forward slash, it is an "absolute link." That means the application server will look for the style sheet in a specific place, no matter where the page is served from. The value "MySite" tells it to look in this application, and the value "theme" tells it to look in a folder theme located in the Web Content folder for this application.

The second reference does not start with a forward slash, so it's a "relative link," which means the application server starts its search from where the current page was served. Up until this point, that worked fine because the CustList.jsp page was served from the root of the Web Content folder. However, things get a little messy when you use servlets, and application servers behave a little differently when it comes to relative links for servlets.

Look carefully at Figure 9-15. In the address bar, you'll see that the URL for the CustList JSP is as follows:

```
http://localhost:7080/MySite/CustList.jsp
```

That indicates that the page is served from the root of the MySite application. However, if you look at the URL for Figure 9-16, it's different. In the figure, the URL is cut off, but if you were to maximize the screen, you would see that the full URL is this:

```
http://localhost:7080/MySite/servlet/com.mycomp.app.CustList
```

Note that according to the URL, the servlet (com.mycomp.app.CustList) is served from a folder called servlet. And this is where things get a little confusing. There is no folder called servlet. Instead, this was a convention adopted years ago to tell the application server that you weren't trying to load a page; you were trying to load a servlet. All Web application servers honor this convention; it's a sort of shorthand to tell the server that you're specifying a servlet class name. The server then will go and search in the application in a special location ("/Web Content/WEB-INF/classes") for the class. It can also locate the class in any of the JAR files specified in the classpath at startup time (which includes all JAR files located in "/Web Content/WEB-INF/lib"). Confused yet?

OK, so now let's say the servlet outputs HTML. Before JSPs, this was the way servlets used to work: They output HTML. If your HTML includes a *relative* link to a style sheet, then you must take into account that your URL includes that "/servlet" pseudo-folder in the path. If you want to access a style sheet in a folder called "theme" (for example), then you can't use href="theme/mystyles.css". The Web application server thinks the servlet was loaded from the servlet pseudo-folder, so you would instead have to use href="../theme/mystyles.css".

Well, here's where it gets ugly. Let's say that you request a servlet and the servlet then forwards your request to a JSP. This is the standard procedure for JSP Model II architecture: request to servlet, servlet formats Beans, servlet forwards to JSP. However, the Web application server gets confused at this point. It will load the JSP from the correct spot, but it still *thinks* it's working in the servlet context, so now all the links that used to work just fine fail because the Web application server thinks it's working from the servlet folder.

Not only that, each Web application server handles things a little differently. Some take this pseudo-folder into account, some don't, and some get really confused. The WTE is so confused that it doesn't even look for a style sheet in a folder named "theme." Instead, it attempts to load another servlet, and it thinks the name of the servlet class is "theme." That's where the ClassNotFound exception comes from.

So the moral of the story is that relative links tend to be a bad idea when you're mixing servlets and JSPs. This is a particularly sneaky little problem, and I discovered it the hard way a few years ago when it suddenly started occurring in a working product.

But a number of workarounds exist. The easiest by far is to always use absolute links. There are obvious issues with that approach, of course. The most egregious problem is that you must include the application context with every link. For example, in this application, every link will have to begin with "/MySite", which is the application's context. This can make for some real pain and suffering should you ever need to rename your application (though I'm pretty confident that WDSC, at least, would be smart enough to fix all of the links).

Another approach is to make sure all your JSPs are at the same level as your servlets and then always use "../" as the beginning of your relative links. This is a particularly sneaky approach, and it actually adds more mystery to the mystery, if you will. What you've done is counteract a strange behavior caused by a non-intuitive convention (the magic "servlet" pseudo-folder) by introducing your own non-intuitive convention. While it might have a certain appeal as a sort of "fight fire with fire" approach, it really causes more problems.

A third possibility is to map your servlets. Servlet mapping is well outside the scope of this book, but it's something you should probably start to think about anyway. Briefly, in servlet mapping, you specify a URL pattern, and if the URL matches the pattern, the request is routed to the corresponding servlet. At that point, you're in that context. With a little foresight, you can map your servlets in such a way that the servlet and the JSP are at the same level so that you can test the JSP in a standalone environment, and any relative links will still work when the JSP is launched from the servlet. In a way, it's sort of a more-involved version of the second option, but since all the names are now under your control (no more magical "servlet" pseudo-folder), I find it appeals to my sense of order.

In order to keep things simple, the application in this book does not map servlets. Instead, it takes advantage of an application server feature that allows any servlet to be served by its class name alone. This removes the need for mapping. While fine for development environments, this is actually a slightly sloppy way to program, not to mention a moderately severe security risk. Simply by knowing the name of the class, users could access servlets that you didn't intend for them to access.

There's one even more obscure method, the <BASE> meta tag. You can use this tag in your HEAD section to tell the JSP where to resolve all pointers from. However, the same issues occur if you rename your application.

Anyway, as I said, this book is hardly a tome on Web application design. But I thought you might want to understand why you had to do what you did in Step 9-5.

Step 9.6—Change the index

> ## GOAL
>
> You've been running the servlet using the pop-up menu; in this Step, you'll change your Web application to invoke the servlet rather than the JSP.

You would think this would be easy, right? Just change the URL on the index page to point to the servlet rather than the JSP, and you're done! But wait, it's not quite that easy because the navigation buttons on the index page—and indeed on the entire Web site—are generated via a navigation site part.

Uh oh.

Some intense research proves that there is no easy way around this problem. It would be nice if the Web Site Designer provided the capability to override the URL, but there's no way. I even went so far as to scour the little text files that WDSC likes to use to store information, and I got nowhere. As it turns out, the information is stored in a file called .website-config that is stored at the project level, and the only thing that can be changed in that file is the title—what we've been calling the navigation label.

So, it would seem that, for now, there is a fatal design problem with WDSC that will not allow us to properly include servlets as part of a Web application. You can get around this problem, but most of the ways are kludgy at best. For example, you could create a dummy page that forwards to the servlet and use that in the Web Site Designer. Or you could leave the Web site layout the way it is and try to redirect the URL using a mapping in the Web Deployment Descriptor. This option has a certain appeal because it seems at first glance to be moving away from the concept of serving servlets by class name, which, if you read the InStep in the previous chapter, you've been advised is something of a security risk. However, the more I think about it, the more I wonder whether that will cause problems. The JSP will be mapped to call my servlet, but what will happen when my servlet attempts to forward the request to the JSP? It seems like the water is getting murkier here.

No, I'd rather not cheat that way. I want to keep CustList.jsp in place so that I can use the Web Site Designer to manage my navigation. That means CustList.jsp has to stay part of the Web site; otherwise, the links on the JSP won't get updated when a new page is added. At the same time, I want all references that used to point to CustList.jsp to now point to the servlet, com.mycomp.app.CustList. How can I do that?

Well, where is that navigation widget generated? In the navigation site part, the one I designed. So why not go right to the source and fix the site part? This is where really knowing the product comes in handy. Because, knowing the syntax of the site part, it is feasible to fix the navigation site part to put in the right link. It will, at least for now, involve a little hard-coding, but it can be done.

To do so, simply open the site part for editing. The site part is myns.html, located in the theme folder. Double-click to open it, as shown in Figure 9-21.

❑ **9.6(a) Double-click on myns.html to open it.**

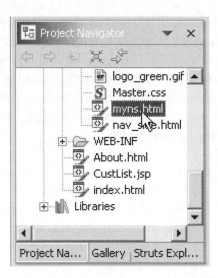

Figure 9-21: Double-click on the site part to open it.

The site part should be in Source mode, as depicted in Figure 9-22. If not, simply click on the Source mode button at the bottom of the editor view. Now you can enter in the new source for the site part. The code for the enhanced site part is in Listing 9-3.

Listing 9-3: This is the enhanced navigation site part, with the modified code in gray.

```
<!DOCTYPE HTML PUBLIC "-//W3C//DTD HTML 4.01 Transitional//EN">
<html>
<head>
<title>myns.html</title>
</head>
<body>
<table class=ln>
<td>
<!--siteedit:forEach var="item" items="${sitenav.items}"-->
 <!--siteedit:choose-->
  <!--siteedit:when test="${item.self}"-->
  <br><span class=ln2>${item.label}</span>
  <!--/siteedit:when-->
  <!--siteedit:otherwise-->
   <!--siteedit:choose-->
    <!--siteedit:when test="${item.href == '/MySite/CustList.jsp'}"-->
   <br><a href="/MySite/servlet/com.mycomp.app.CustList">${item.label}</a>
    <!--/siteedit:when-->
 <!--siteedit:otherwise-->
  <br><a href="${item.href}">${item.label}</a>
    <!--/siteedit:otherwise-->
   <!--/siteedit:choose-->
  <!--/siteedit:otherwise-->
 <!--/siteedit:choose-->
<!--/siteedit:forEach-->
</td>
</table>
</body>
</html>
```

If you analyze the code, you'll see that I replaced the original code for a link with a choose block that looks specifically for the value '/MySite/CustList.jsp' and replaces it with a link to "/MySite/servlet/com.mycomp.app.CustList". This will cause the correct link to be generated. If there were more JSPs that needed this sort of fix, you could write more when statements. I realize that this is a somewhat hard-coded approach, but it's the best I can do at this time. What really needs to happen is IBM needs to enhance WDSC to allow you to define your own URLs for the linkages. But for now, this is a reasonable compromise.

As always, I've included a shortcut around the typing portion of the exercise. In the Imports folder on your CD-ROM is a file called Step9-6.txt; it contains the complete source code for the enhanced site part, and you can simply cut and paste it into the editor.

❏ **9.6(b) Enter the code from Listing 9-3.**

❏ **9.6(c) Right-click in the editor and select Save.**

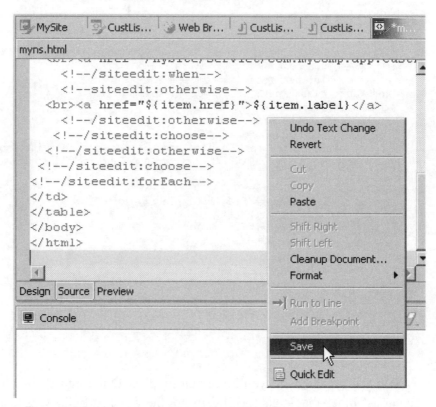

Figure 9-22: After entering the code, right-click in the editor and select Save.

When you do this, you may see a little bit of activity, since the tool has to go through and modify all pages that contain that site part. Since there are only three such pages, it won't take that long.

Once the conversion is done, start up the index as normal. If you'd like to review this process, the steps are 8.2(o) through 8.2(q). You should get the screen shown in Figure 9-23.

❑ 9.6(d) Run Index.html on the server.

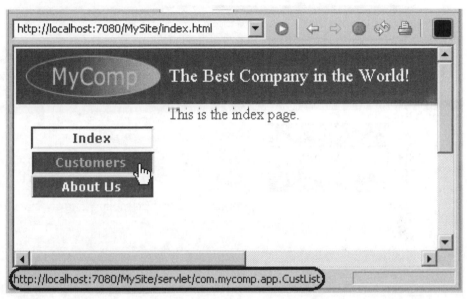

Figure 9-23: This is the index page. Note the circled value.

In Figure 9-23, you'll see that the cursor is hovering over the Customers link. This causes the target of that link to be shown at the bottom of the window. Notice that it is no longer /MySite/CustList.jsp, but instead is /MySite/servlet/com.mycomp.app.CustList. This shows that the site part worked correctly and that the surrogate link to the servlet was properly introduced. Feel free to click on the Customers link, which should bring you to the panel shown in Figure 9-24. Once again, note the link in the address bar; it should match what you saw in Figure 9-23.

❏ **9.6(e) Click the Customers link.**

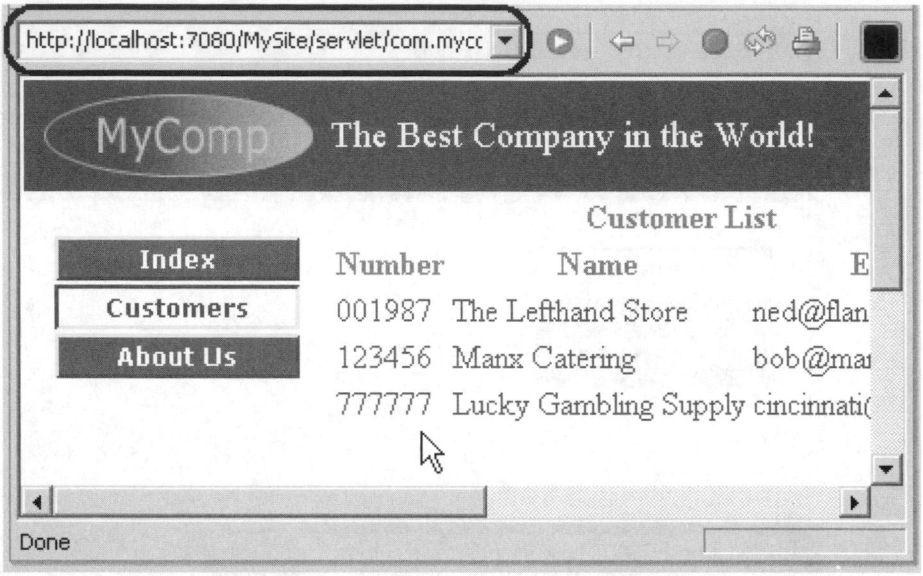

Figure 9-24: The new index indeed launches the servlet correctly.

Is this the best way to get around the problem? I don't think so. I'd rather be able to customize the link, the same way I am able to customize the navigation label. It might even be nice to be able to associate a JSP with a servlet that is its controller. That association could be an object, and the object would even allow parameters to be passed to the servlet.

Multi-page applications also present issues. For example, let's say each line was clickable and would bring up the detail for that customer. If that were the case, then what would you like to see in the navigation bar? My compromise is to enable *all* of the buttons in the navigation widget; clicking on the Customers button will return you to the first page of the Customers application (the initial customer list).

That's it for attaching a servlet to the application. You've done everything you can on the Web portion of the program. Now you need a short course in debugging, and then you can move on to the host side of things.

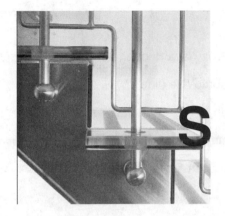

Step 10

Debugging

The primary reason to go through all the work of getting your application up and running inside of an IDE such as WDSC is to take advantage of the debugger. And while many IDEs have debugging capabilities, in my opinion the integration of the debugger in WDSC is phenomenal. The ability to set not only breakpoints, but conditional breakpoints and watchpoints, is a powerful feature, as is the ability to set breakpoints on specific exceptions.

I also particularly like to take advantage of the ability to set breakpoints in JSPs. That single feature can make the difference between an easy job and a tedious one. I'm disappointed that JavaScript debugging seems to be available only in the advanced edition of the product; the lack of JavaScript debugging is one of the last great obstacles preventing the development of a true killer app for the browser.

But even with its limitations, WDSC is still the best-of-breed IDE when it comes to being able to debug servlet-based applications, and in this step I'll introduce you to the basic capabilities of the debugger.

There are no Checkpoints in this chapter; just run right through. You're not doing anything drastic, just setting a breakpoint and modifying a variable, so it really shouldn't take long at all.

Step 10.1—Set a breakpoint

GOAL
In this step, you will set a breakpoint.

Setting (or "adding") a breakpoint means to identify a line of code where execution will be halted. Most debugging tools have the ability to set simple breakpoints: "Stop at line such-and-such." There are more sophisticated ways to halt the machine as well. Breakpoints can be conditional, meaning that they only stop when a certain condition is met. More powerful debuggers have watchpoints, which will stop execution whenever the contents of a variable change. Professional-quality Java debuggers usually have exception breakpoints as well: the ability to halt execution whenever a certain exception occurs.

WDSC has all of these capabilities. I typically only use simple breakpoints and on occasion the exception breakpoint. I'll show you the simple breakpoint in this step and then an exception breakpoint a little later.

Setting a breakpoint in WDSC is really easy. When you bring up a member in the source editor, there is a gray border on the left of the view that is roughly the same width as a scroll bar. It's easy to overlook. However, this column is where all of your debugging action takes place. Start by opening up CustListProxy.java. Double-click on the source member as shown in Figure 10-1.

❑ **10.1(a) Double-click on CustListProxy.java to open it in the editor.**

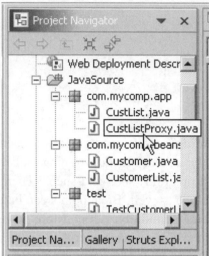

Figure 10-1: Double-click on CustListProxy.java. This will open it in the editor.

You can see the gray border on the left of the source code. The hard part is telling exactly where in the source code my cursor is when I'm way over on the left. This is especially true when the code gets indented a bit. To get around that, the Java editor has a nice feature: Click anywhere on a line and the line is highlighted across the editor view, as shown in Figure 10-2.

The line on which you are setting the breakpoint is near the end of the source member, so you'll have to scroll down into the source to find the correct line.

❑ **10.1(b) Scroll down to the setAttribute line (line 45).**

❑ **10.1(c) Click on the line to highlight it.**

Figure 10-2: After scrolling down, click on the setAttribute line to select it.

Note that the line is now highlighted, and you can tell where in the left column to click to work with the highlighted line.

There are many ways to set a breakpoint. The easiest is simply to double-click in the gray area; this will set an unconditional breakpoint. I'll use the pop-up menu in this case, because you can then see some other options. To get the pop-up menu to pop up, you simply right-click in the gray area to get the menu shown in Figure 10-3 and then select the Add/Remove Breakpoint option.

❑ **10.1(d) Right-click in the gray column to bring up the breakpoint menu.**

❑ **10.1(e) Select Add/Remove Breakpoint.**

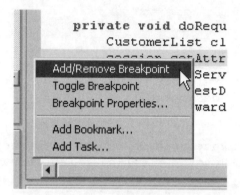

Figure 10-3: This menu allows you to
add or remove breakpoints, as well
as toggle them on and off.

You'll see the screen return with a small blue ball icon that indicates a breakpoint
is set.

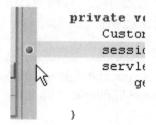

Figure 10-4: A break-
point is set at this line.

You have successfully set a breakpoint in your servlet proxy object. Now it's time
to use it.

Step 10.2—Running in debug mode

> ### GOAL
> Start the server in debug mode and get your
> first look at the debug perspective.

Up until now, you've been running the server in normal mode, with "normal mode" basically meaning "not debug mode." The two modes are mutually exclusive; if you try to start a server in debug mode and it is already started in normal mode, you will get an error message (I'll show you the error a little later).

Starting a server in debug mode is almost exactly the same as starting it in normal mode. You select a file to run and then use the pop-up menu to select Debug on Server. . . , rather than the Run on Server . . . option you've been using up until this point. To get started, launch the index page in debug mode by right-clicking on it and selecting Debug on Server. . . , as shown in Figure 10-5.

❑ **10.2(a) Right-click on Index.html and select Debug on Server. . . .**

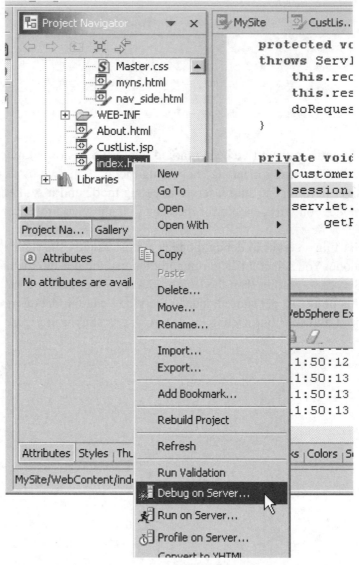

Figure 10-5: Starting the server in debug mode is nearly identical to starting it in normal mode.

The server selection prompt will appear just as it always does. You're using the same server (you're simply in debug mode now), so just press Finish.

❑ **10.2(b) On the Server Selection dialog, just press Finish.**

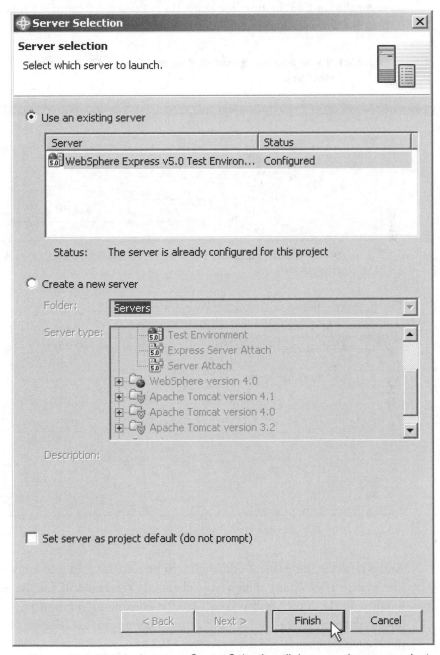

Figure 10-6: This is the same Server Selection dialog you always see. Just press Finish.

At this point, if the server is already running in normal mode, you will get an error dialog like the one in Figure 10-7. Pressing Restart on this dialog will stop the server and then restart it in debug mode.

❑ **10.2(c) If the Server Error dialog of Figure 10-7 appears, press Restart.**

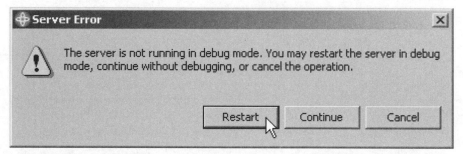

Figure 10-7: This dialog appears if the server is already running in normal mode; press Restart.

The progress dialog will appear. Wait for it to finish.

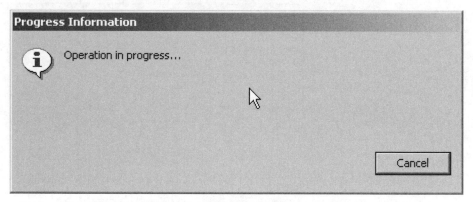

Figure 10-8: The standard progress dialog appears.

And when it is done, the workbench will be transformed into something that looks like Figure 10-9. Many things have changed. You can still see the source in a short window in the center, and you can see the console on the bottom. Other views have appeared, though, which are entirely debug-related. For more information on the Debug perspective, refer to InStep 10.2.a.

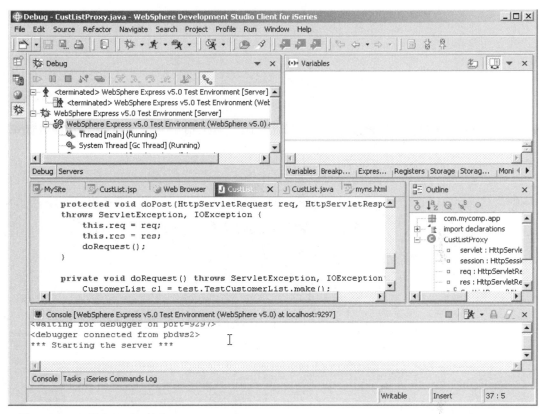

Figure 10-9: This is the debug perspective.

The server is not loaded yet; the console at the bottom shows that it is in fact just starting. Notice that the lines before the "*** Starting the server ***" message refer to debuggers and ports; these indicate that the JVM is actually starting up in debug mode. This is really the only outward difference when you start a server in debug mode, at least until you start running servlets and JSPs.

The server will continue to send messages to the console, similar to the way it works in normal mode, until the server is actually "open for e-business," as the message says. At that point, the middle pane (which is where the editor view is now located) will change from source code to the Web Browser view, and you will see the screen shown in Figure 10-10.

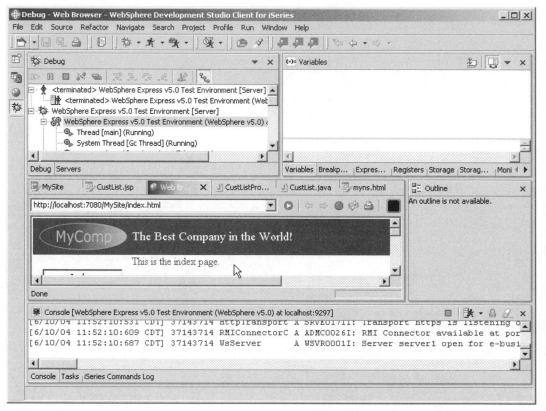

Figure 10-10: The server is now in debug mode, and your index page has been displayed.

This is not a particularly easy-to-use screen. It's too bad that publishing constraints force us to use 800×600, but of course you have no such limitations. But if you do happen to be stuck with 800×600 as we are in the book, then I'll show you a way to get a little extra room.

Remember that WDSC is built on top of Eclipse, and Eclipse allows you to resize all of the panels. In this case, the Debug perspective has what amounts to three rows, one on top of the other. I'll show you how to shrink the upper and lower rows, thereby giving the middle row more room.

Phase one: Grab the bar between the console and the Web browser and drag it down about halfway. You'll know your cursor is in the right place to grab the bar when it turns into a two-headed vertical arrow like the one in Figure 10-11. Dragging the bar is like any other click-and-drag maneuver.

❑ **10.2(d) Click the bar between the console and browser and drag it down.**

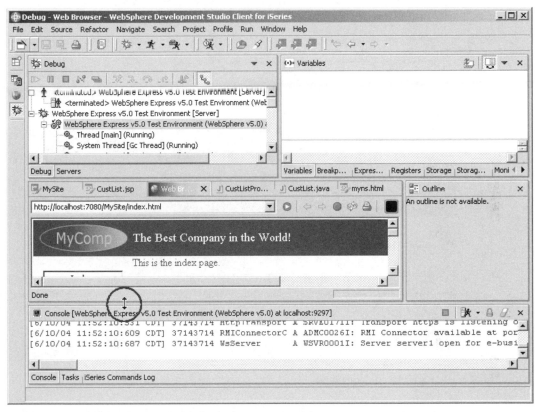

Figure 10-11: Click the bar, hold down the mouse, and. . .

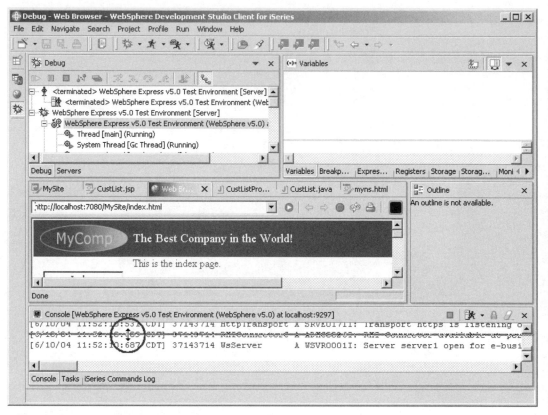

Figure 10-12: . . .drag it down.

Do the same thing with the bar above the browser, but drag it up instead and not quite as far.

❑ **10.2(e) Click the bar above the browser and drag it up.**

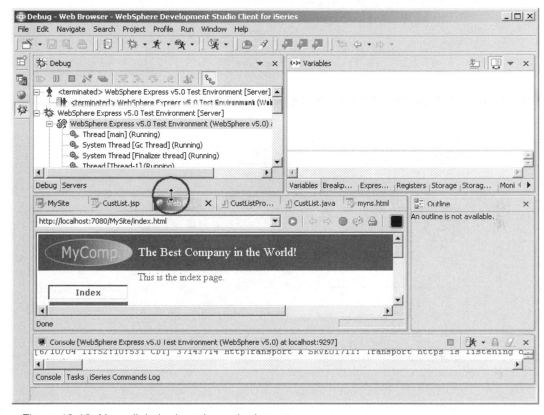

Figure 10-13: Now click the bar above the browser . . .

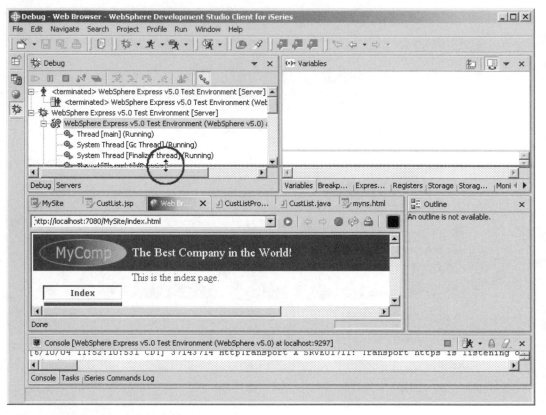

Figure 10-14: . . .and drag it up.

Very good. You have increased the room for your browser dramatically, and it's much easier to see what you're trying to accomplish. Next, I would like you to click on the Customers link to launch your CustList servlet, as shown in Figure 10-15.

□ **10.2(f) Click on the Customers link.**

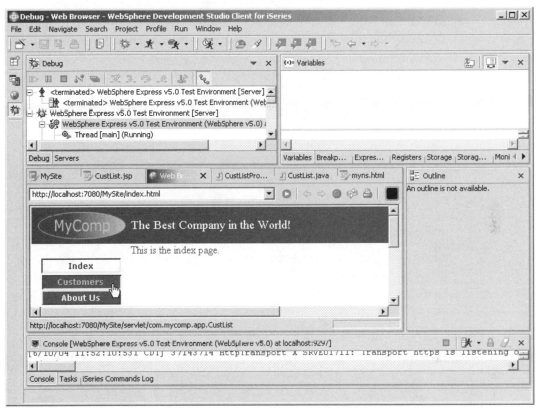

Figure 10-15: Launch the CustList servlet by clicking on the Customers link.

At this point, you might expect to hit your breakpoint, but you won't. Instead, there's a special built-in feature of the WebSphere Test Environment (WTE) that will suspend execution whenever you start a servlet. You'll get a dialog like the one in Figure 10-16.

By default, the "Step into" radio button is set, which will allow you to enter the servlet at the first executable step and debug it. This is a nice convenience feature that makes it unnecessary to have to set breakpoints. However, I typically have breakpoints set as in this example, so I set the radio button to "Skip" and press OK as shown in the figure.

Notice also that there is a "Disable step-by-step mode" checkbox. Checking this box will prevent this dialog from coming up on every servlet and JSP. This can be helpful when you have a long conversation to get through before debugging. If you do check this box, the only way to force the WTE to start prompting you again is to click on the Enable Step-by-Step Debug tool on the Debug View toolbar.

❑ **10.2(g) Select the Skip radio button and press OK.**

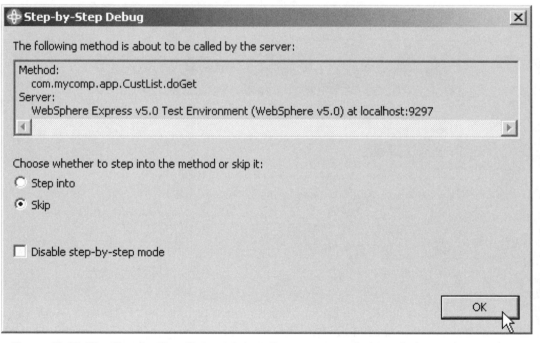

Figure 10-16: The Step-by-Step Debug dialog allows you to walk through the servlet step by step.

At this point, your CustList servlet will finally be launched, and the next thing you'll see is the breakpoint display in Figure 10-17.

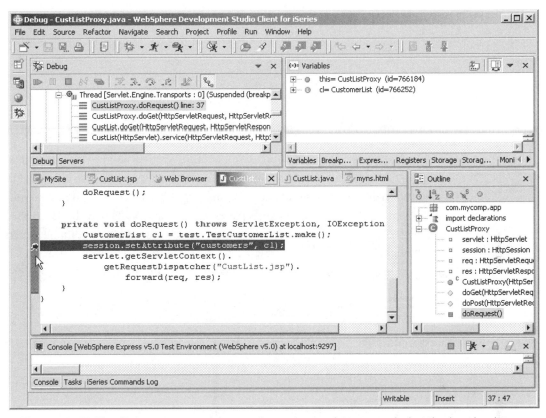

Figure 10-17: The Debug perspective now shows the servlet suspended at the breakpoint.

The servlet is suspended. If you look in the upper left pane, you'll see a suspended Thread and the entire stack of that thread, with the method where the thread is suspended at the top. In the left center pane is the source, and the dark blue arrow superimposed on the blue dot indicates that this is where the code is suspended. The line itself is also highlighted.

You're now in complete control of the application. The browser page is waiting for you to come back, and the JVM is simply holding. You can do whatever you want—review code, inspect and even to a limited degree change the contents of variables, set and remove breakpoints, whatever you think is necessary. I'll walk you through a couple possible activities in the next steps. First, though, the next InStep goes into more detail on the Debug perspective.

InStep 10.2.a—The Debug perspective

GOAL

Review the contents of the Debug perspective.

The Debug perspective is an impressive panel. It has everything you could need when debugging an application, including views to start and stop servers. That's actually pretty important when you manage to completely hose a server while debugging it. In any event, there is so much in this panel that it required its own InStep. Like any InStep, you can just skip this section if your primary focus is to get things up and working. The next "hands-on" step is Step 10.3, so flip ahead to there if you're in a hurry. But if you stick around, I'll walk you through the high points of the Debug perspective.

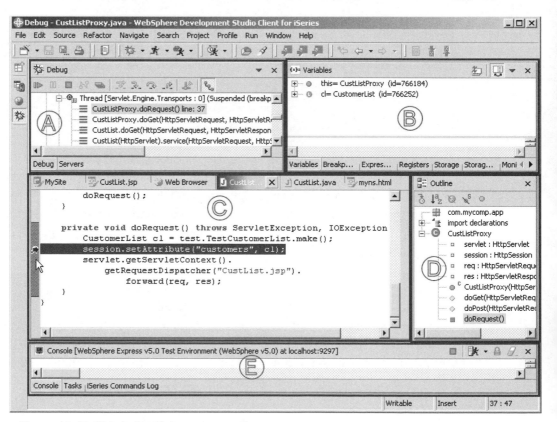

Figure 10-18: This is the Debug perspective.

We'll ignore the areas that most perspectives share: the main menu bar, the main tool bar, and the perspective bar. If you want to know more about them, please refer back to InStep 2.1.a, where I describe them related to the Web perspective.

Next, though, are the other areas.

A: This pane by default contains the Debug view. The Debug view indicates which servers are currently running or terminated and shows the threads of the ones that are active. This view can be used to suspend a thread of a server in a loop, and it's the primary view for performing operations like step into, step over, and resume. The other view in the pane is the Servers view, which allows the user to start and stop application servers.

B: This is the inspection pane. Typically, it shows the Variables view, which allows the user to inspect the instance and automatic variables of the current class and method. Other views include the Breakpoints view and a number of storage inspection views. There are also views designed to allow you to see the results of an expression.

C: This is the primary editor pane. All editors show up in this pane. You can further subdivide this pane, stacking editors side by side or top to bottom. This allows you to edit multiple members simultaneously or easily cut and paste between them.

D: This is the outline pane. This pane usually shows the outline (as appropriate) of whatever panel is active in the Editor view.

E: Console output shows up here. This is the place where you can output data for the user to see. Typically, this pane shows the output from the stdout stream, but it can also be used to show current tasks outstanding as well as the iSeries command log.

Step 10.3—Inspecting and changing variables

> ### GOAL
> **Review a complex variable and update one of its members before resuming the application.**

Probably the most important thing to be able to do when you're debugging a program is to view the contents of variables. In rare cases, you may even need to modify them in order to see how a certain bit of code works. WDSC allows a very powerful inspection capability as well as a serviceable update feature. This step will walk you through the process of inspecting variables and then changing one so that the output of the JSP changes.

First, though, you're going to need some room to work, so I want you to maximize the Variables view, in the upper right pane, by double-clicking on its title bar as shown in Figure 10-19. For more information on the Variables view and other views in the Debug perspective, refer back to InStep 10.2.a.

❑ **10.3(a) Double-click on the Variables view title bar to maximize it.**

Figure 10-19: Double-click on the title bar to maximize this view.

Now that the view is maximized, you can start inspecting the variables. Typically, you will see a variable named "this" (which represents the class instance you are currently debugging) as well as any local automatic variables for the method you are debugging. In Figure 10-20, you can see that the current method has only one automatic variable, cl. This makes sense, because back in Step 10.1 you set your breakpoint on the line after this variable was defined.

Where are the instance variables? If you were to expand the variable this, you would see the instance variables. But right now, you're more interested in the CustomerList object stored in variable cl. Expand that variable by clicking on the plus sign, as shown in Figure 10-20.

❑ **10.3(b) Expand the variable cl.**

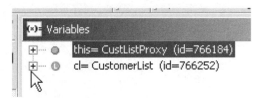

Figure 10-20: Click on the plus sign to expand the CustomerList object stored in variable cl.

After expansion, you'll see that the CustomerList object has two instance variables, a variable named customers that contains a TreeMap and a variable named i that has a null in it. This matches the way CustomerList is defined. Right now, there are Customer objects in the CustomerList object, so let's take a look at them. Expand the customers variable (Figure 10-21).

❑ **10.3(c) Expand the customers variable.**

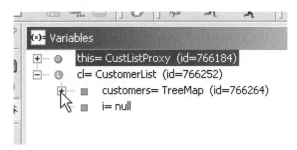

Figure 10-21: Expand the customers variable, which currently contains a TreeMap.

Now things get a little trickier. You knew how CustomerList was supposed to be defined, because you wrote the class. But right now, you're trying to decipher a TreeMap, and you may or may not have a lot of experience with it.

From experience, I know that a TreeMap has a variable root, which is the base of the TreeMap. From there, you can find all of the nodes. But to see how this works, you only need to change one, so this should be pretty easy. Expand the root variable as shown in Figure 10-22.

❑ **10.3(d) Expand the variable root.**

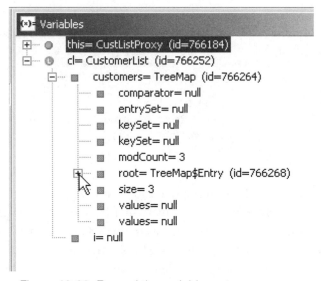

Figure 10-22: Expand the variable root.

You may notice that root is a variable of type TreeMap$Entry. From my experience, that means that when you expand it, you will see a variable called value that actually contains one of the entries in the TreeMap. There will also be a variable named key that contains, not surprisingly, the key of the object. And our specific example does not disappoint. The variable key contains a String, "123456", and the variable value contains an object of type Customer. That's exactly what was expected.

Expand the variable value as shown in Figure 10-23.

❑ **10.3(e) Expand the variable value.**

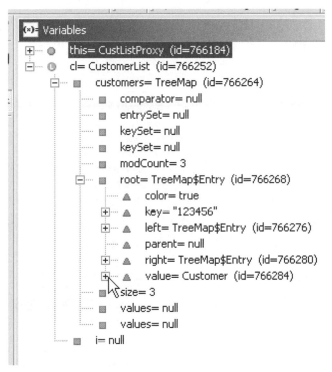

Figure 10-23: Expand the variable value, which contains the Customer object for this entry.

After expanding the Customer, you'll see all of its instance variables, from city to ZIP. At this point, you can change one or more of the values by double-clicking on it.

> **Note:** You can change only primitive variables, such as integers. The only exception to that rule is the ever-unique String object. You can always change the contents of a variable of type String—which is good, because that's what you're going to do.

Double-click on the name field to edit it, as shown in Figure 10-24.

❑ **10.3(f) Double-click on the name field.**

Figure 10-24: Double-click on the name to edit it.

Thatwill bring up the Set Variable Value dialog, shown in Figure 10-25. Just type in the new value and press OK.

❑ **10.3(g) Type "Joe's Pizza Emporium" and press OK.**

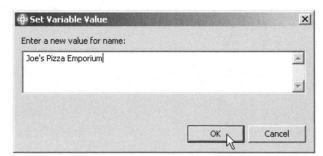

Figure 10-25: The Set Variable Value dialog allows you to change values on the fly.

After you hit OK, you'll be returned to the workbench, where you'll see that the name has changed, at least in the Variables view. However, there's only one way to make sure that the change actually took effect: Resume the application. And to get to the other Debug views, you'll need to restore the current view to normal size. To do so, just double-click the title bar again as shown in Figure 10-26.

❑ **10.3(h) Double-click the title bar to restore the view to normal size.**

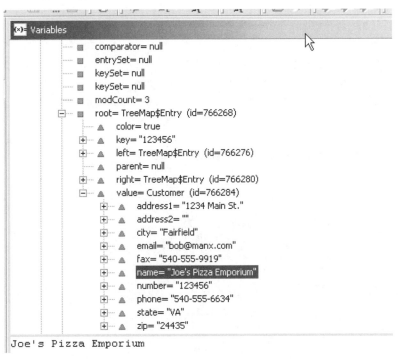

Figure 10-26: Double-click on the title bar of the Variables view to restore it to normal size.

The editor view should still be showing the source for the CustListProxy class. Since you want to see the browser results, you need to make the browser visible by clicking on the Web Browser tab, as shown in Figure 10-27.

❑ **10.3(i) Click on the Web Browser tab to make the browser visible.**

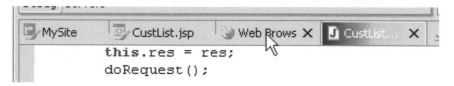

Figure 10-27: Click on the Web Browser tab to show the browser.

This will change the editor view to display the browser. Now you need to resume the application. Figure 10-28 shows the top of the Debug perspective, with the Debug view on the left and the Variables view on the right. The Variables view shows the change you just made, while the Debug view has a small tool called "Resume" that will allow the servlet to continue. Click on this tool.

❑ **10.3(j) Click on the Resume tool.**

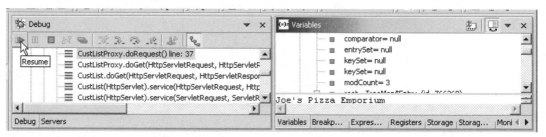

Figure 10-28: Click on the Resume tool (upper left of the Debug view) to resume the application.

Once the resume button is pressed, the system will churn along. But before it displays the results of the JSP, you will once again see the Step-by-Step Debug dialog as shown in Figure 10-29. The difference is that this time the method that is going to be called is org.apache.jsp._CustList._jspService.

> **Note:** This is just another reminder that JSPs are compiled down to and run as servlets. They may look more like HTML than anything else, but JSPs are actually run just like servlets. Unless you have disabled step-by-step mode, when a JSP is about to be run, you will get the Step-by-Step Debug dialog for that JSP's service method, _jspService.

❑ **10.3(k) Select Skip and press OK.**

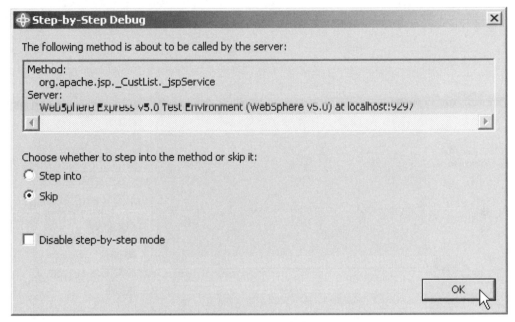

Figure 10-29: This dialog comes up for JSPs as well as servlets.

Finally, the page will come up! But this time, rather than Manx Catering in the second line, you'll see Joe's Pizza Emporium, as displayed in Figure 10-30. Note the circled value. That's the value you entered when the servlet was suspended at the breakpoint. That's what debugging is supposed to be able to do.

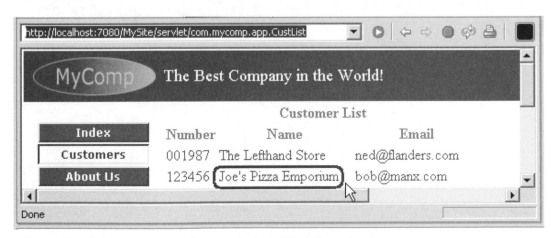

Figure 10-30: And now, Manx Catering is Joe's Pizza Emporium!

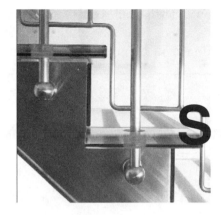

Step 11

Setting Up the iSeries

It's hard to believe, but you've gone about two thirds of the way through this book, and we're only just now beginning to deal with the iSeries. That's been by design; the idea is that you should be able to create and test most of the components of your Web application without having to worry about the iSeries side of things. A few classes to create dummy data should be sufficient for you to do most of the look-and-feel design work.

But now it's time to start putting the back-end onto your wonderful UI. What you're going to do over the next several chapters is learn about all the iSeries-specific extensions to the WDSC workbench. You're going to learn how to edit, compile, and debug programs on the host, and then through the magic of JTOpen, you will be able to access those programs from your Web application.

> **Note:** JTOpen is the open-source version of IBM's Java Toolkit, a powerful and extensive set of APIs that allow Java programs to access just about any feature of the iSeries. You can find out more about JTOpen at a very nice Web page with a somewhat ungainly Web address: http://www-124.ibm.com/developerworks/oss/jt400/.

And the beauty of it all is that almost nothing will change on the Web side of things! This separation of layers is the way that we can take advantage of all the strengths of the various languages we have available, yet not hold up one part of the design worrying about the other parts.

This step will specifically introduce all the setup tasks required (setting up connections, creating libraries, and so on) for host programming. Subsequent steps will introduce editing and compiling. Finally, you'll design and write the back-end business logic to support your JSP. Once that's done, you'll tie all the pieces together, and at the end, you'll have a working application. So let's move on!

Step 11.1—iSeries extensions

This is more of an introductory step than anything else. In it, I will explain the relationships between Eclipse, the various non-iSeries WebSphere Studio products, and WDSC.

WDSC is huge. It's far more comprehensive than any other IDE out there. This is a *Step by Step* book, so we don't have time to go into every facet of the tool. This is not a reference manual; it's a targeted how-to book focused on a specific, albeit major, task: to create a Web-based application with an RPG back-end. But there is so much more to the package.

For example, the non-iSeries things we haven't spent a lot of time on include the Java visual editor, Struts and JSF support, Web Services tools, XML and SQL support, and profiling and testing tools. The advanced edition even has EJB support. All of these are powerful tools in their own right, and I encourage you investigate them when you find the time. They're all there, and they're all free (well, except for the EJB stuff).

And then there are all the enhancements specific to the iSeries. Collectively known as "the iSeries extensions," these include a number of features:

Remote System Explore (RSE): This is the meat of the iSeries extensions. It contains all the tooling for connecting to the iSeries (as well as other machines in your network) and for editing, compiling, and debugging host programs. This feature is central to everything you do with your iSeries, and it will be our primary focus for the rest of the book.

iSeries Debugger: This feature is quite nice. It's sort of a bridge between the WDSC workbench and the standard debuggers on the host. In fact, in order to use the debugger, you'll need to have authority to things like STRDBG and STRSRVJOB.

iSeries Projects: This unique WDSC feature allows you to essentially identify a library that you want to work on offline, which is a great feature for people who work on laptops. By caching information from the host, you can actually disconnect your laptop from the network and work on your projects at home or even while traveling. We won't need this feature for this project, but we may cover it in more detail in another book.

WebFacing: This superb tool quickly puts a JSP front-end on an existing green-screen program. However, WebFacing is focused on making existing monolithic green-screen applications Web-ready, while this book is focused on creating multi-tiered Web applications from the ground up.

Web Tooling: iSeries-specific features continue to be built in to the standard Web tooling features of WSSD/WSAD. So when you're performing one of the base functions, such as editing a JSP, you'll automatically have access to iSeries enhancements, such as the iSeries components. While these are pretty powerful, they require special iwcl tags that are used to embed the iSeries components in the JSP source. My concern is that these tags will not work with either Struts or the new JSF support.

CODE and VisualAge for RPG (VARPG): These standalone tools are leftovers from the earlier WebSphere Development Tools. And just as VisualAge for Java was phased out in favor of Eclipse's JDT, so too shall these venerable tools get phased out. CODE is still the GUI design tool of choice for display files; WDSC has a long way to go to catch up there. And VARPG has a unique thick-client, event-driven architecture that may prevent it from being supplanted in the immediate future.

Note: CODE is a generic term for two distinct tools: CODE Editor and CODE Designer. The editor is being superseded by WDSC, but it probably won't be removed from the tool suite immediately. It may continue as a separate installed item for some time, primarily for those people who want a GUI editor but cannot afford the hardware requirements of WDSC. The designer is the primary tool used to customize WebFacing applications, but it's also the only way to edit display files, so I suspect it will hang around as long as the editor, and for the same target audience.

Each of these is a powerful and important tool in its own right. Some of them, though, like WebFacing and iSeries Projects, simply don't help us in our task, while the Web Tools enhancements are a little too non-standard for use today. So the following steps will concentrate on those areas that do help in the development of a Web application, namely the RSE and the iSeries Debugger.

Step 11.2—Remote System Explorer

The RSE is the primary perspective for iSeries developers. I'll explain it in more detail in a moment, but it essentially combines the Remote System Navigator and the editor views so that you can find objects on your host machine and then edit them.

Be sure you have all of the appropriate host servers running. Some people just run the command STRHOSTSVR *ALL and STCPSVR *ALL on their iSeries, but if you're a little more security conscious than that, you can enable only the required servers: DDM, File, and Remote Command (although to be honest, these three open up some pretty big holes in your security if you're not careful).

Once you've done that, you're ready to get RSE up and running. This actually was the perspective you saw when you first started WDSC way back in Step 2, but since then, you've spent most of your time in the Web perspective and recently in the Debug perspective. But it's time to get iSeries-specific. First, I'd like you to close everything down by selecting File/Close All from the main menu as shown in Figure 11-1. This will close all your open files—including your Java files, JSPs, and even the Web Site Designer—so that you'll have a clear plate to work from.

❏ **11.2(a) Select File/Close All from the main menu.**

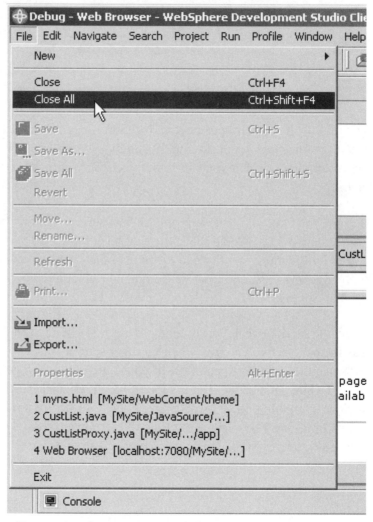

Figure 11-1: Close all your open files.

After that, switch to the RSE perspective. The easiest way to do that is to click on the Remote System Explorer Perspective icon in the perspective bar, as shown in Figure 11-2.

❑ 11.2(b) Click on the Remote System Explorer Perspective icon.

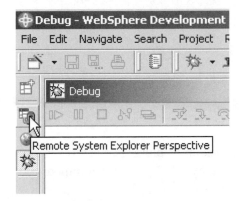

Figure 11-2: Click on the Remote System Explorer Perspective icon in the perspective bar.

That will bring you to a lovely, empty workbench like the one in Figure 11-3.

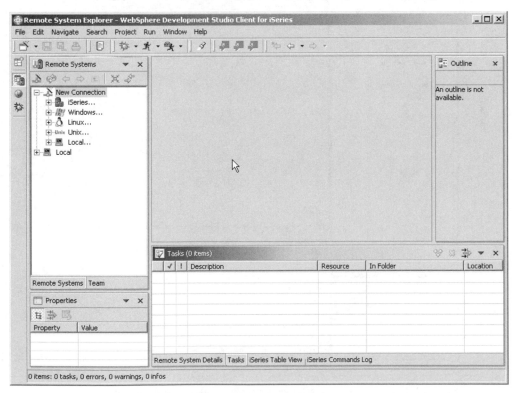

Figure 11-3: The Remote System Explorer perspective is empty and ready to go.

InStep 11.2.a—The Remote System Explorer perspective

GOAL

Review the contents of the Remote System Explorer perspective.

The Remote System Explorer perspective is similar to the other two perspectives you've used. Many of its parts are common to the other perspectives, such as the main menu, main tool bar, and perspective bar. As I've noted already, those rarely change from one perspective to another. There are also five primary panes, labeled A through E in Figure 11-4 below.

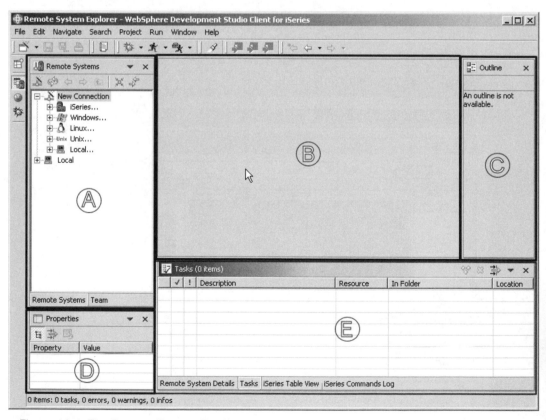

Figure 11-4: The Remote System Explorer perspective has five primary panes.

A: This pane by default contains the Remote Systems view. This is where you will spend most of your time when you're working with the iSeries (other than the time you actually spend editing code). This view allows you to find, create, delete, move, and edit just about any object on the host system. You'll notice that there are icons not only for iSeries, but also for Windows, Linux, Unix, and Local; that's because you can use WDSC to communicate with any one of these system types. So, in a heterogeneous environment, you can use WDSC to move objects from one system to another.

B: This is the primary editor pane. All editors show up in this pane. You can further subdivide this pane, stacking editors side by side or top to bottom. This allows you to edit multiple members simultaneously or easily cut and paste between them.

C: This is the outline pane. It usually shows the outline (as appropriate) of whatever panel is active in the Editor view.

D: This is the properties pane. It shows the Properties view, which provides information about the selected object.

E: This is the log pane. Unlike other perspectives, quite a bit actually ends up here. Everything from compile error listings to source code prompting can be found here at one point or another.

Step 11.3—Create your own perspective

> ## GOAL
> Create the iEdit perspective, giving yourself
> more real estate.

More than once I've lamented that the 800×600 resolution we're stuck with in order to fit in a book is a little too small to do serious work. In fact, I highly recommend 1280×1024, more than twice the real estate, as the minimum size to use WDSC on a daily basis. However, up until now, I've managed to creatively shoehorn things into the available space, occasionally maximizing a view to get things done, but in general working within the bounds I've been given.

No more. It's just not feasible to do serious iSeries work—both navigating through the iSeries libraries and at the same time editing code—within the strictures of 800 pixels. It's just not wide enough. Truth be told, even 1280×1024 can be a little constricting when dealing with two source members side by side, and in order to get around that restriction, I've taken advantage of the flexibility of Eclipse, the underlying foundation of all the WebSphere Studio products.

You see, while Eclipse allows the tool designers to create perspectives, it allows you, the tool *user*, to modify those perspectives and even create new ones of your own. And that's exactly what this step is all about: creating your own perspective. Technically, I'm really just modifying an existing perspective, but it's the same idea.

The primary goal in this step is to get as much room for the editor pane as possible. We're going to do this in three ways: We're going to shrink one view, close another view that we really don't use, and then modify some others to be something called "fast views," a really cool concept. Interestingly enough, I'll be showing you how to do each of these things in reverse order. First, a fast view.

Every view has the capability of becoming a fast view. You do this by right-clicking on the view's title bar and then selecting Fast View from the pop-up menu, as shown in Figure 11-5.

❑ **11.3(a) Right-click on the title bar of the Remote Systems view.**

❑ **11.3(b) Select Fast View.**

Figure 11-5: Right-click on the title bar and select Fast View.

What happens is that the view is removed from the workbench, and an icon representing that view shows up in the perspective bar on the left of the workbench, as shown in Figure 11-6. Click on the icon, and the view appears in a sort of "slide-out" view on the left, as shown in Figure 11-7.

❑ **11.3(c) Click on the Remote Systems fast view icon.**

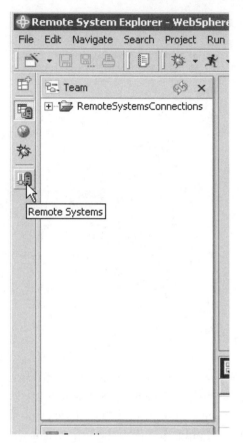

Figure 11-6: The view appears in the perspective bar; click the icon to make the view appear.

This slide-out view tends to appear only temporarily. For example, the Remote Systems view you see is usually used to locate and open a source member. Typically, if you select a member to edit, the Remote Systems fast view disappears again. Or, if you want to hide the view manually, simply click on the icon in the perspective bar again, as shown in Figure 11-7.

❑ **11.3(d) Click on the Remote Systems fast view icon again.**

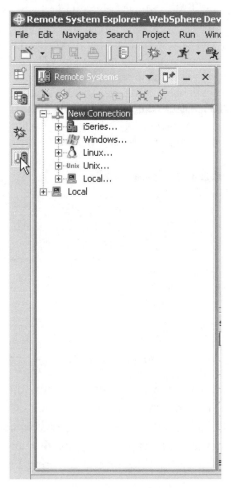

Figure 11-7: The fast view opens;
close it by clicking the icon again.

You will return to the workbench (which will once again look like it did in Figure
11-6). Note that the Team view now appears in the upper left pane. The upper left
pane used to be shared by two views: the Remote Systems view and the Team view.
The Team view, whose primary purpose is integration with CVS or some other
source management system, has been hidden until this point. Now that you've turned
the Remote Systems into a fast view, the only thing left in that pane is the Team
view, so you can see it. You could turn the Team view into a fast view as well, but

since I don't use this view, I've decided to just remove it from my perspective. Just close it using the little standard close widget (the X in the upper right corner).

Warning: If you close a view in this manner, the only way to make it appear again is through the main menu. The main menu Window has a submenu called Show View… that will allow you to re-display a view. But it's not quite that simple; you need to know the name of the view you are looking for, and the nature of the view isn't always entirely obvious from the name. Another option (provided you haven't actually saved the perspective) is to reset it; use the option Window/Reset Perspective to reset all views in the perspective to their last saved position.

❑ 11.3(e) Close the Team view.

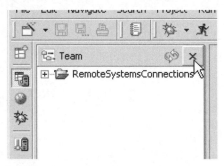

Figure 11-8: Close the Team view.

This closes the last view in that pane, so now the bottom left pane expands to fill the vacancy. Thus the Properties view, which originally was only in the bottom left pane, now fills the whole left side of the workbench. Since my primary goal is to make the editor as wide as possible, this view too must go. Turn it into a fast view by right-clicking on the title bar and selecting Fast View (Figure 11-9).

❑ 11.3(f) Right-click on the title bar of Properties and select Fast View.

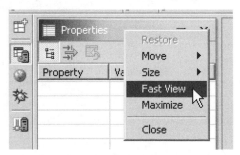

Figure 11-9: Right-click on the title bar of the Properties view and select Fast View.

The right side of the editor is the Outline view. I use it occasionally, so rather than close it, I turned it into a fast view. As you did with the others, right-click title bar and select Fast View (Figure 11-10).

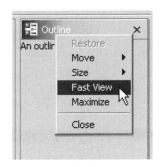

At this point, I now have a very clean-looking workbench, as shown in Figure 11-11. There are only two panes, one over the other. All other views have been turned into fast views. The only issue is that I'd like a little bit more of the workbench dedicated to the editor. So now I can resize the panes, shrinking the lower panes a little bit.

Figure 11-10: Turn the Outline view into a fast view.

Click on the bar between the two views as shown, and start dragging it down.

❑ **11.3(g) Click on the bar between the editor and log panes.**

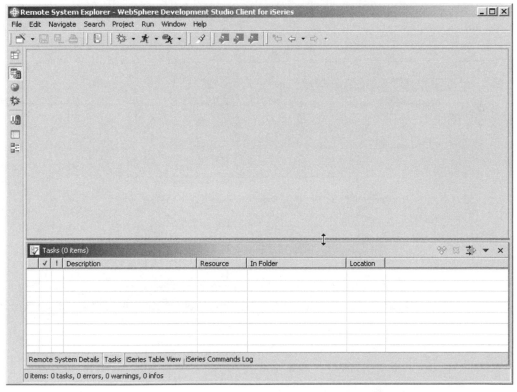

Figure 11-11: Click on the bar between the two panes and start dragging it down.

Drag down a little way and then let go at the position shown in Figure 11-12. This will expand the top pane (the editor pane) at the expense of a couple of lines in the log pane. (To see the result of the drag, look at how the log pane is smaller in Figure 11-13).

❑ **11.3(h) Drag the bar down a bit and drop it.**

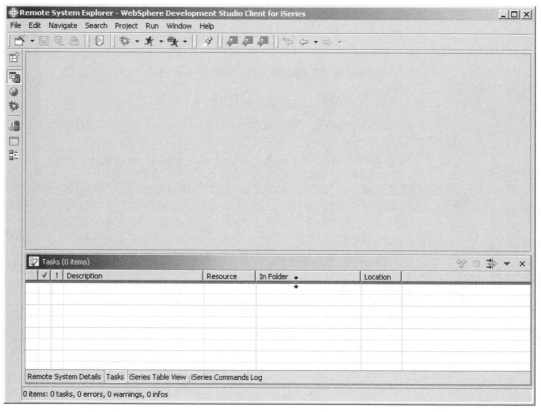

Figure 11-12: Drag the bar down a little bit and release it to resize the panes.

Now that you're done creating your custom perspective, you can save it. Figure 11-13 shows how: Select Window/Save Perspective As... from the main menu.

❑ **11.3(i) Select Window/Save Perspective As... from the main menu.**

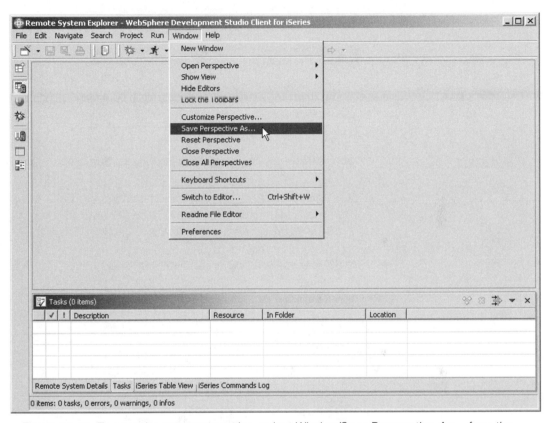

Figure 11-13: To save the new perspective, select Window/Save Perspective As... from the main menu.

I call this particular perspective iEdit, because I like to use it whenever I'm editing iSeries source code.

☐ **11.3(j) Type "iEdit" into the name field.**

☐ **11.3(k) Press OK.**

Figure 11-14: Key "iEdit" into the Name field and press OK.

The biggest annoyance is that it will keep the same icon as the original perspective, the Remote Systems perspective. If you have the iEdit perspective and the Remote Systems perspective both open at the same time, you will see two of the same icon in the perspective bar. But you can cursor over them to display a "tool tip" with the perspective name.

OK, now you've got your custom perspective in place. Things will start to move along quickly now.

Step 11.4—Connect to the host

> **GOAL**
>
> Create a connection to the host.

Prerequisites: Unlike most of the steps in this book, this step requires a couple of prerequisites that are outside the scope of the book itself. First, you'll need to make sure you have either the IP address or a resolvable name for your iSeries host. The book uses a host named WDSCHOST. Second, you'll need a valid user profile on the iSeries, with authority to the STRDBG, STRSRVJOB, and ENDSRVJOB commands. In the book, I use a user profile called WDSCUSER. These prerequisites were spelled out in Step 1, but I wanted to make sure they were reiterated here.

The first thing to do is to make the Remote Systems view visible. Because I wanted the extra real estate for the editor (you'll see why as we start editing), I traded off that extra room for the minor inconvenience of having to click the fast view icon on the left whenever I need this view.

> **Note:** The initial screen for each step may be different depending on whether you use Checkpoints or not. If you use Checkpoints, you'll sometimes find that you need to make the Remote Systems view visible, as you will in this step.

> **Note:** This step will create a connection to your host called WDSCHOST. As indicated in the prerequisites section of Step 1, you must have made an appropriate entry in your HOSTS file. If you already have a connection that you would like to use instead, you can skip to Step 11.5. Just remember to use your connection name rather than WDSCHOST throughout the rest of the book.

❑ **11.4(a) Click on the Remote Systems fast view icon.**

Figure 11-15: Click on the Remote Systems fast view icon to make the view visible.

The Remote Systems view contains two entries, Local on the bottom and New Connection on the top. The New Connection entry is expanded with sub-entries for iSeries, Windows, Linux, Unix, and Local. You want to create an iSeries connection, so "expand" the iSeries entry (click on its plus sign).

> **Release Note:** I find it sort of amusing that in V5.1.2 they moved iSeries from the top to the bottom of the list. I can't see any reason for doing it; I'd love to know the rationale behind the decision.

❑ **11.4(b) Click on the plus sign (+) to the left of iSeries.**

*Figure 11-16: Click on the plus
sign to the left of the iSeries entry
to create a new iSeries connection.*

This will bring up the personal profile wizard. Since you haven't yet created a
profile, you will need to create one. I created one called WDSC User, although I
could have used my name or some other uniquely identifying value.

❑ **11.4(c) Type "WDSC User" into the Profile field and press Next.**

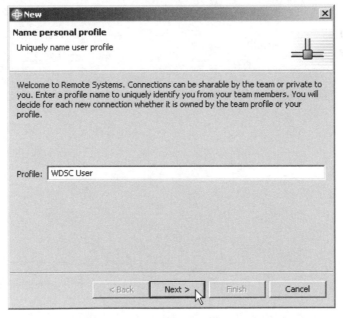

*Figure 11-17: Type in a unique profile name and press
Next.*

The next dialog you see will be the Remote iSeries System Connection wizard. In this page, the only important information is the name of the host. The Parent profile is also important if you're in a team environment, but right now we're not considering team development issues. The connection name and description are pretty much just free-form entry fields. Enter as shown and hit Finish.

❑ **11.4(d) Leave the Parent profile as WDSC User.**

❑ **11.4(e) Type "WDSCHOST" into the Connection name field.**

❑ **11.4(f) Type "WDSCHOST" into the Host name field.**

❑ **11.4(g) Type "WDSC Host" into the Description field.**

❑ **11.4(h) Press Finish.**

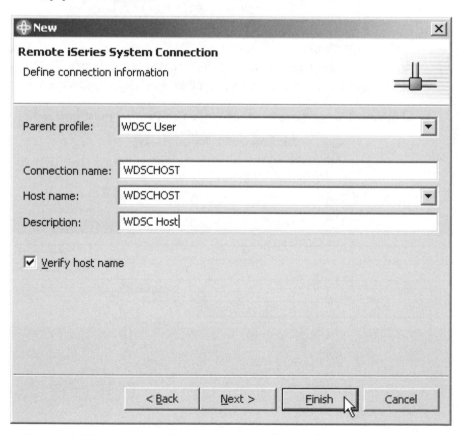

Figure 11-18: Update the dialog as shown and press Finish.

This will create the connection. When it's completed, your Remote Systems view will look like the one shown in Figure 11-19.

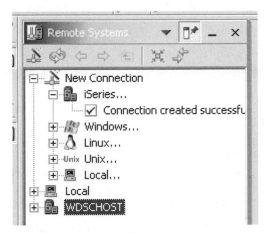

Figure 11-19: WDSCHOST has been created (as the little status message tells you).

Step 11.5—Create a library

We're starting to pick up the pace here. The next task is to create a library, and it's very simple.

If necessary, click on the Remote Systems fast view to open the view and then expand the WDSCHOST connection as shown in Figure 11-21.

❏ **11.5(a) Click on the Remote Systems fast view.**

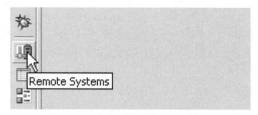

*Figure 11-20: Click on the Remote
Systems fast view to open it.*

❏ **11.5(b) Expand the WDSCHOST connection.**

*Figure 11-21: Expand the
WDSCHOST connection.*

You should now see the Remote Systems view depicted in Figure 11-22. Right-click on the iSeries Objects entry as shown and select New/Library....

❑ **11.5(c) Right-click on iSeries Objects and select New/Library....**

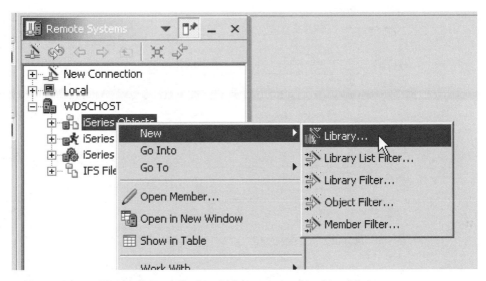

Figure 11-22: Right-click on iSeries Objects and select New/Library....

This will bring up the Create Library (CRLIB) wizard. As shown, enter WDSCLIB into the Library field, select the Test radio button, and type in "WDSC Test Library" for the text. Press Finish to create the library.

❑ **11.5(d) Type "WDSCLIB" into the Library field.**

❑ **11.5(e) Select the Test radio button.**

❑ **11.5(f) Type "WDSC Test Library" into the Text field.**

❑ **11.5(g) Press Finish.**

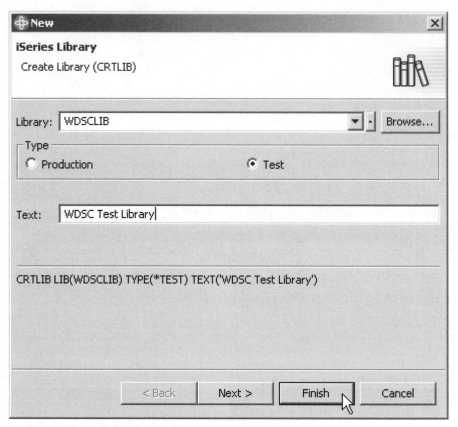

Figure 11-23: Fill in the dialog as shown and press Finish to create the WDSCLIB library.

At this point, you will be asked to log into the system. Enter your user ID and password as shown in Figure 11-24.

❑ **11.5(h) Enter your user ID and password and press OK.**

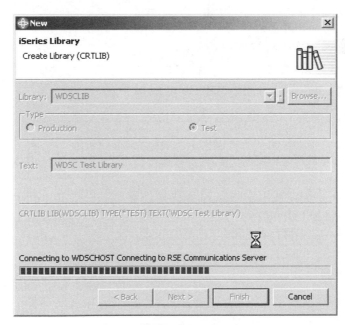

*Figure 11-24: Enter your user ID and password
and press OK.*

The Create Library dialog will display the status of the operation as it continues along, as shown in Figure 11-25.

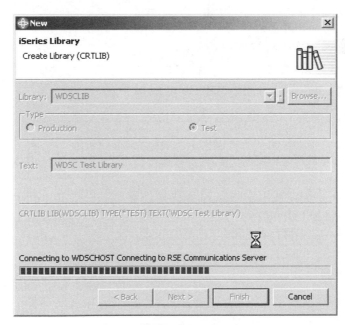

*Figure 11-25: The CRTLIB dialog will show the status
of the operation.*

When the operation is complete, the dialog will disappear (and so will the Remote Systems fast view), and you should see some text in the iSeries Commands Log view at the bottom of the workbench as shown in Figure 11-26.

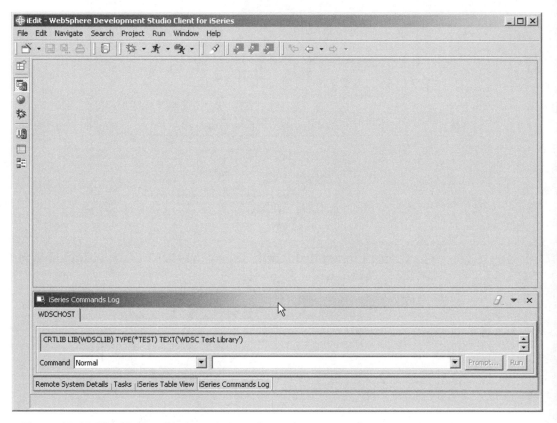

Figure 11-26: The iSeries Commands Log shows the results of commands, but it's too small to see much.

The iSeries Commands Log view is too small to really see the results, so you may want to maximize it by double-clicking on the title bar. You'll get the screen shown in Figure 11-27.

❑ **11.5(i) Double-click the title bar of the iSeries Commands Log.**

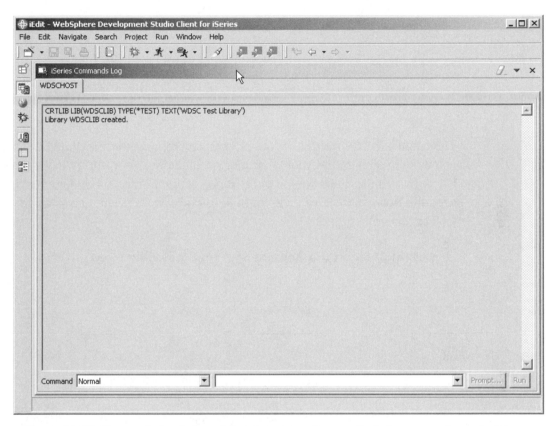

Figure 11-27: The maximized view of the view shows the result of all commands run to this point.

You can see the result of the CRTLIB command. If, for example, you didn't have authority to the CRTLIB command, you would see the corresponding error message in this view. Double-click on the title bar again to restore the workbench.

❑ **11.5(j) Double-click it again.**

Step 11.6—Modify the connection's library list

GOAL

Add the newly created WDSCLIB to the
WDSCHOST connection.

The connection controls how your programs compile and run. One of the things you need to do is set up your environment, including your library list. In this step, I'll show you the quick way to put a library in the library list of a connection. You need the Remote Systems view for this, so click on the Remote Systems fast view icon as shown in Figure 11-28.

❑ **11.6(a) Click on the Remote Systems fast view icon.**

Figure 11-28: Open the Remote Systems view by clicking on the fast view icon.

This will open the Remote Systems view.

Note: If you run this step from its Checkpoint, you will see the Enter Password prompt shown in Figure 11-29. That's because no connection to the host has been made. Throughout the steps, if you start from a Checkpoint, you will get this prompt when you log on. This behavior can be changed in the Preferences, but since I always need to have access to the host, I don't bother.

❑ **11.6(b) If prompted, enter your user ID and password.**

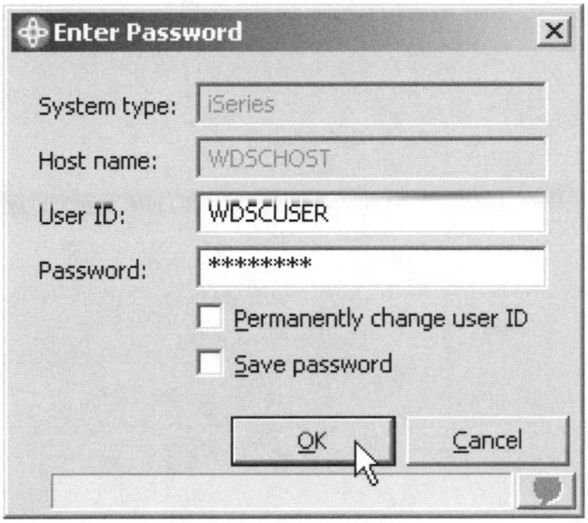

Figure 11-29: If prompted, enter your user ID and password.

Now, you will see the WDSCHOST connection you created in Step 11.4. To change the library list, you need to edit the connection's properties. Do this by right-clicking on the WDSCHOST connection and selecting Properties, as shown in Figure 11-30.

❏ **11.6(c) Right-click on the WDSCHOST connection and select Properties.**

Figure 11-30: Right-click on the connection and select Properties to edit the properties.

This will bring up the Properties dialog. The default is to show the Connection page of the dialog (illustrated in Figure 11-31), which essentially contains the information you entered when you originally created the connection. But you want the information in the Subsystems page, so click on the Subsystems option as shown.

❑ **11.6(d) Click on the Subsystems option.**

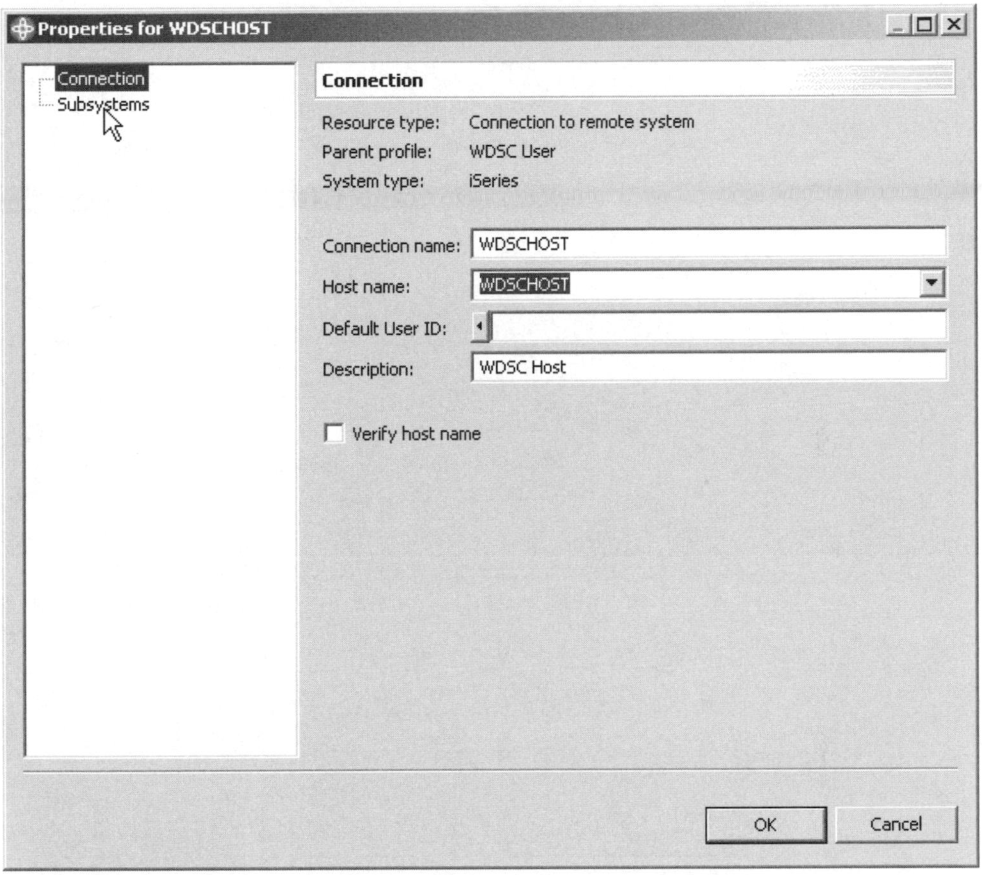

Figure 11-31: This is the Connection page; click on the Subsystems option to bring up the Subsystems page.

The Subsystems page has two panes, one for iSeries objects and one for iSeries commands, as shown in Figure 11-32. The pane you want is iSeries Commands, so click on the iSeries Commands tab to bring up the right pane.

❑ **11.6(e) Click on the iSeries Commands tab.**

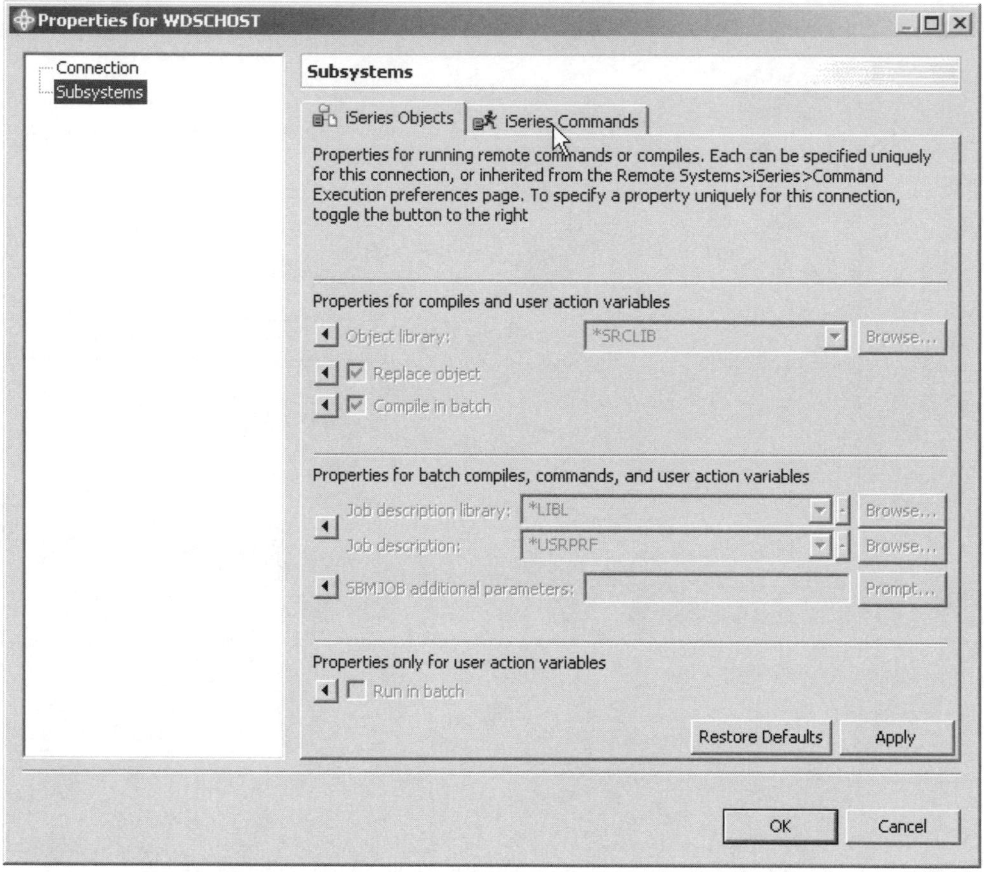

Figure 11-32: Click on the iSeries Commands tab.

This will bring up the iSeries Commands pane. As you can see in Figure 11-33, the pane has a library list you can modify, a place to enter the current library, and a spot for an initial command. I highly recommend the initial command option; in my environment, I have a command that allows me to set the initial library list quite easily. However, that would involve actually writing and installing the command, so instead you're just going to add the new WDSCLIB to your library list.

To do this, type "WDSCLIB" into the Library field and press the Add(B) button.

❑ **11.6(f) Type "WDSCLIB" into the Library field and press Add(B).**

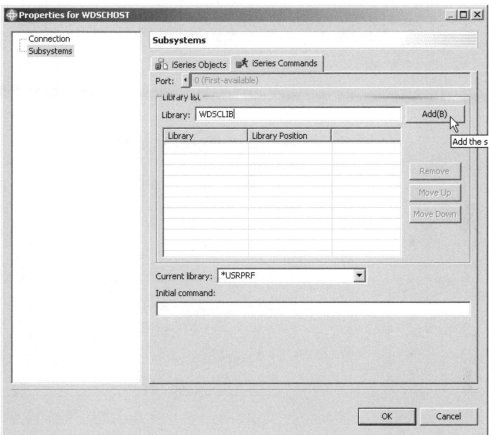

Figure 11-33: Type the library name and press Add(B) to add it to the connection's initial library list.

This will update the panel as shown in Figure 11-34. Press OK.

❑ **11.6(g) Press OK.**

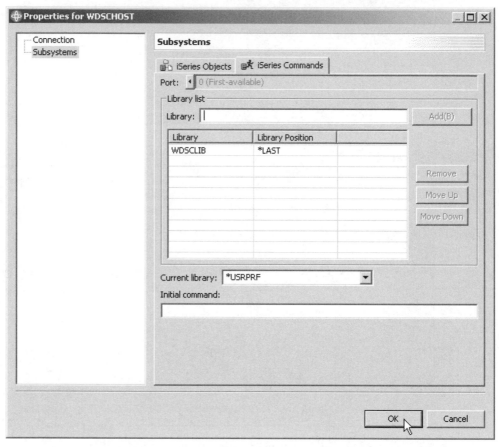

Figure 11-34: WDSCLIB is now part of the connection's library list. Press OK.

From this point on, whenever you connect to the host using this connection, the connection job will have WDSCLIB in its library list.

Warning: This does not take effect immediately. In fact, the only way to make it take effect is to disconnect and reconnect. If you're coming in from Checkpoint 11-6, you don't have a connection, so there's no problem. But from any other point, you should disconnect. Do this by right-clicking on the WDSCHOST connection and selecting Disconnect All.

Step 11.7—Create a source file and member

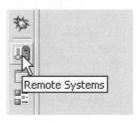

GOAL

Create a source physical file in the new library and add a source member to it.

This is the last environment step for a little while. You need to add a source file and then add a member to that source file. That done, you can start editing and compiling. To create the file, though, you need the Remote Systems view, so click on the Remote Systems fast view icon as shown in Figure 11-35.

❑ **11.7(a) Click on the Remote Systems fast view icon.**

Figure 11-35: Open the Remote Systems fast view.

The WDSCHOST connection should be expanded (if not, expand it using the plus sign to the left). Expand the iSeries Objects entry to access the host as shown in Figure 11-36. In some circumstances, the entire tree may already be open. If you can see the entry labeled WDSCLIB.*lib.test, skip to Step 11.7(e).

❑ **11.7(b) Expand the iSeries Objects entry.**

Figure 11-36: Expand the iSeries Objects entry to access the host for this connection.

One of the entries under iSeries Objects will be the library you just added, WDSCLIB. You can now access the objects in that library by expanding the entry as shown in Figure 11-37.

❑ **11.7(c) Expand the WDSCLIB library entry.**

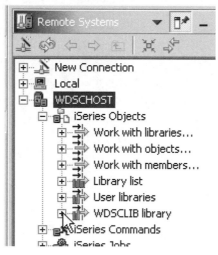

Figure 11-37: Expand the WDSCLIB library entry to get at the objects within.

Note: If you run this step from its Checkpoint, you will see the Enter Password prompt shown in Figure 11-38.

Release Note: In V5.1.2, you will not get the Enter Password prompt until you try to create the source member in Step 11.7(i).

❑ **11.7(d) If prompted, enter your user ID and password.**

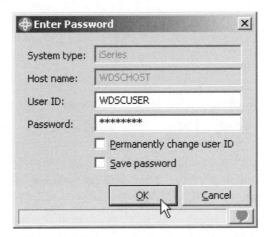

Figure 11-38: Enter your user ID and password.

When the WDSCLIB entry opens, you will see an entry inside it called WDSCLIB.*lib.test. This represents the library up on the host. Now you can add the source file. To do that, right-click on WDSCLIB.*lib.test entry and select New/Source Physical File... as shown in Figure 11-39.

❑ **11.7(e) Right-click on WDSCLIB.*lib.test and select New/Source Physical File....**

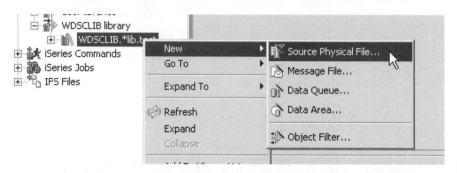

Figure 11-39: Right-click on WDSCLIB.*lib.test and select New/Source Physical File....

This brings up the Create Source Physical File (CRTSRCPF) wizard. Enter the values as shown in Figure 11-40 and press Finish to create the file. I don't intend this to be a philosophical discussion about naming conventions, but lately I've found myself more and more often trying to use a single source file (QSOURCE) for just about everything. This is by no means a hard-and-fast rule, though, so if you're mortally offended, feel free to name the file whatever you'd like to name it. However, I'm going to continue on under the assumption that you're OK with QSOURCE.

❑ **11.7(f) Type "QSOURCE" into the File field.**

❑ **11.7(g) Leave the record length at 112.**

❑ **11.7(h) Type "WDSC Test Source" into the Text field.**

❑ **11.7(i) Press Finish.**

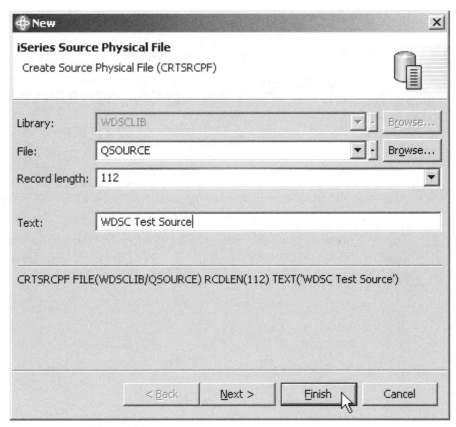

Figure 11-40: When you press Finish, these values will create a source file named QSOURCE.

Now that you've added a source file, you need a source member. This member is going to be a very simple one called CONCAT, which will be a program that will concatenate two strings together. This is our only throw-away program actually, but it will serve as a guide to editing, compiling, and debugging.

To add the new member, right-click on the newly added source file and select New/Member… as shown in Figure 11-41.

❑ **11.7(j) Right-click on QSOURCE and select New/Member….**

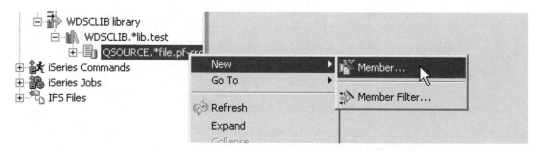

Figure 11-41: Right-click on the file you just added, QSOURCE, and select New/Member….

This will bring up the Add Physical File Member (ADDPFM) wizard. Enter a member name of CONCAT, leave the member type at its default of RPGLE, put in a description, and press Finish.

❏ **11.7(k) Type "CONCAT" into the Member field.**

❏ **11.7(l) Leave the Member type as RPGLE.**

❏ **11.7(m) Type "Concatenate Two Strings" into the Text field.**

❏ **11.7(n) Press Finish.**

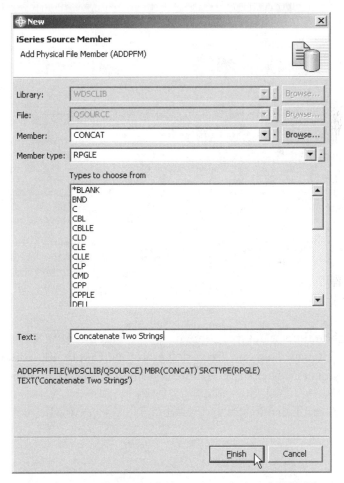

Figure 11-42: This will add the new member CONCAT with a type of RPGLE.

The next thing you will see will be the LPEX editor for the RPGLE source member CONCAT, as shown in Figure 11-43.

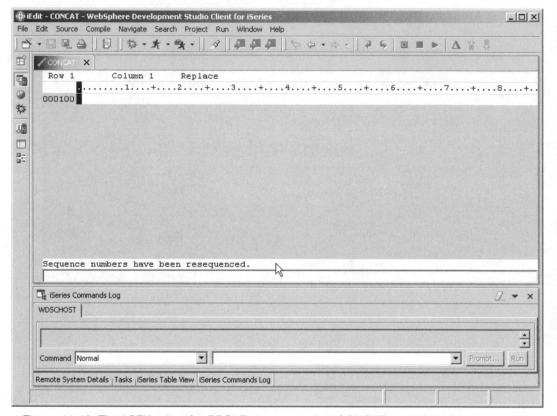

Figure 11-43: The LPEX editor for RPGLE shows member CONCAT open for editing.

I should point out that some people refer to the LPEX editors as jLpex, because LPEX was the name given to the original CODE/400 editor (though not the designer). The code in WDSC is written in Java, hence the "j" in jLpex.

You're finally done with the setup. Now you can edit, compile, and test a program!

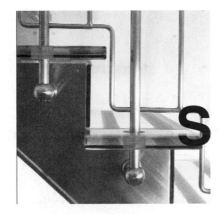

Step 12

Editing, compiling, and debugging

The pace is going to accelerate from here on in. I'm going to assume you know RPG and are at least familiar with RPG IV syntax. I'm going to assume you know what a physical file is, what the *ENTRY PLIST does, and what a program status data structure is.

To those of you who would complain because I use a prototype for the program rather than a PLIST, I apologize. However, not everybody out there uses prototypes, and this book isn't about RPG, it's about WDSC. In fact, I'm using fixed-format RPG IV rather than free-form. And while some RPG wunderkind may consider this form of the language obsolete, I'm confident that they will still remember the syntax.

Given the scope of this book, not only do I not have time to teach advanced RPG, I'm barely going to touch the surface of some of the more powerful tools of WDSC, the jLpex editors. That's because this is a *Step by Step* book, not a reference manual, and by design it has to move fast.

I'll show you how to enter some code and how to use the two built-in verification processes to speed the development cycle. I'll show you how to compile a program on the host and even how to run your own PDM-like commands. Then, I'll walk you through a quick debugging session so you can see how the debugger works.

As I said, it's fast-paced, and it covers a lot of ground in a very short time. Necessarily, I'm going to have to skip a few things that you might want to know more about. Things like CODE/400 and the Data perspective are great tools, but not specifically relevant to the task at hand, which is creating a client/server application.

In Step 13, I'll give you a list of the areas we won't be covering, so that you can do a little more research on your own.

Step 12.1—Editing and verifying

The pace continues to accelerate. This is a relatively long step, but even so, you'll just be skimming the surface of the subject, which happens to be the jLpex RPG editor. This remarkable piece of software manages to keep most of the features of the old SEU yet provide a wealth of new functionality of the type you would expect in a GUI editor. In this regard, I'm told it compares favorably with CODE/400, although the jLpex editor is still a little slower and a little quirkier.

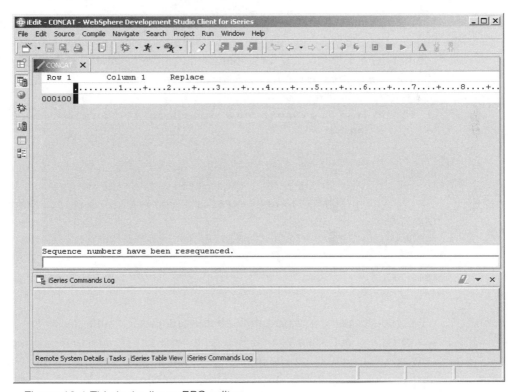

Figure 12-1:This is the jLpex RPG editor.

Figure 12-1 shows the editor. You'll note that the editor is column-oriented, as many text editors are. The heading across the top of the editor gives the column numbers. But watch how quickly that changes. Cursor over to column 6 and type a "d" for a Definition specification.

❏ **12.1(a) In column 6, type "d."**

The heading will immediately become context-sensitive, as shown in Figure 12-2.

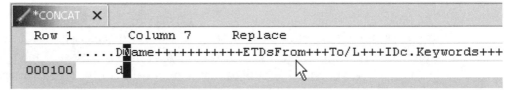

Figure 12-2: The heading is context-sensitive, based on the specification type of the current line.

This is very nice. It makes it quite easy to type in source, especially since a cursor moves along the heading in sync with your cursor on the actual source line. I want you to type in a Definition for a standalone variable named Input1 with a length of 10. You can check out Figure 12-3 for an example.

❏ **12.1(b) Type in a D-spec for a standalone, 10-character variable named Input1.**

```
*CONCAT  X
  Row 2          Column 7       Replace   2 changes.
           .....DName+++++++++++ETDsFrom+++To/L+++IDc.Keywords++
  000100      d Input1             s            10
  000101      d
```

Figure 12-3: Even though you can't see it very well in grayscale, the line is color coded when it is parsed.

What you can't see very well in the book's grayscale is that the code is in black as you're typing, but when you hit Return and the line is parsed, the editor automatically color codes the line. Note that the editor also creates a new line with the specification type already filled in. This is sometimes a help and sometimes an annoyance, but I live with it.

Hint: You can change this behavior (along with a multitude of other options) in the WDSC preferences. Use menu option Window/Preferences, and then use the left-side navigation tree to drill to Remote Systems/iSeries/LPEX Editor Parsers/ILE RPG. The option you need to turn off is Repeat previous specification type.

Next, I want you to try a line command. These are just like you remember them from SEU. Type a "c" on the line number of the line you entered for Input1 and a "b" on the line number of the empty D-spec the editor generated, as shown in Figure 12-4.

Note: You must type the line command directly on top of the line number. The line number will then disappear, showing only the line command.

Warning: Line commands will work only if your cursor is currently located in the line number column when you press Enter. Also, while the jLpex editors do indeed handle a large number of SEU line commands, I encourage you to use the more "notepad-like" techniques, such as cut and paste, to change your text. This will allow you to use the same basic coding keystrokes whether you're working on RPG, Java, or HTML.

❑ **12.1(c) Type "c" on line 100 and "b" on line 101. Press Enter.**

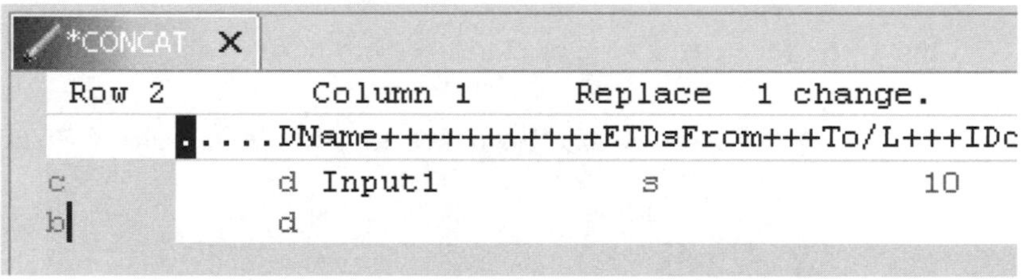

Figure 12-4: Type standard SEU line commands over the line numbers.

So the old SEU commands work just fine. And now I'll show you what I really find amazing about the jLpex editor—the melding of the old and the new. Besides the SEU line commands, you can also use standard GUI IDE commands. For example, you can mark a line using the mouse, as in Figure 12-5, and then right-click on the marked selection and select Copy from the pop-up menu.

There are other techniques as well. For instance, you can use Alt+L to mark a line, Ctrl+C to copy the line, and Ctrl+V to paste it. Just remember that Ctrl+V posts exactly where your cursor is, so if you aren't at the first position of a line, the paste will occur right in the middle of that line, splitting it in two.

❑ **12.1(d) Mark the line of code you just generated (line 101).**

❑ **12.1(e) Right-click on the marked code and select Copy.**

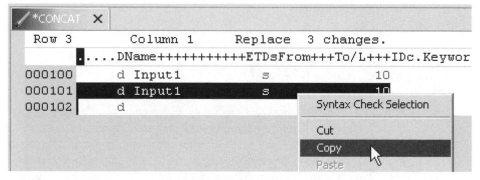

Figure 12-5: Mark the newly copied line, right-click on the selection, and select Copy.

Now you can paste the line. To paste over the empty D-spec, simply mark that line, right-click, and select Paste, as shown in Figure 12-6.

❑ **12.1(f) Mark the empty D-spec (line 102).**

❑ **12.1(g) Right-click on the marked code and select Paste.**

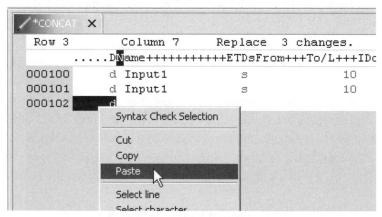

Figure 12-6: Mark the empty D-spec, right-click on it, and select Paste.

OK, edit those lines: Rename one variable Input2 and one Output and resize the Output variable to be 20 long (so it can hold the concatenation of the two input variables, of course!).

Now I'd like to show you a slightly cumbersome but still effective feature of the editor. Enter an empty line (you'll have to delete the "d" that the editor insists on putting in), and then enter a "c" for a Calculation specification. Make sure your cursor is on the empty C-spec and press F4.

❏ **12.1(h) Enter a blank line.**

❏ **12.1(i) Enter an empty C-spec.**

❏ **12.1(j) Press F4.**

The bottom pane of the editor will become a prompt—sort of a cross between a wizard and the green-screen prompting you're used to in SEU—as seen in Figure 12-8. Once again, real estate is our enemy, and the bottom pane is too small to be usable. Double-click on the title bar of the prompt to maximize it as shown in Figure 12-9.

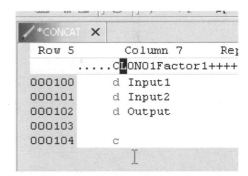

Figure 12-7: Enter a blank line, enter an empty C-spec, and press F4.

❏ **12.1(k) Double-click on the title bar to maximize the iSeries Source Prompter.**

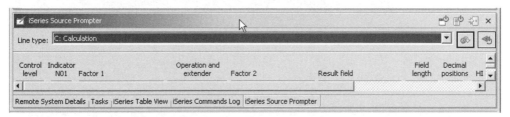

Figure 12-8: The small prompt for a Calculation specification is unusable.

You can see the entries for Factor 1, Factor 2, and so on. A nice feature is the operation code drop-down list; all valid opcodes are available. Key "*entry" in Factor 1, select PLIST from the opcode drop-down, and then press Enter.

☐ **12.1(l) Type "*entry" into Factor 1.**

☐ **12.1(m) Select PLIST from the opcode drop-down.**

☐ **12.1(n) Press Enter.**

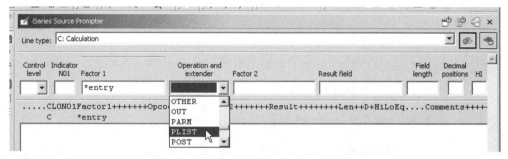

*Figure 12-9: Type "*entry" in Factor 1, select the opcode PLIST, and then press Enter.*

This will add the line. Of course, you can't see it because the Source Prompter is maximized. Real estate gets us again. Double-click on the title bar again to restore the workbench.

I should point out that although the prompter is functional, you probably won't use it often. The main editor window shows a format line at the top of the screen that depends on the line your cursor is on. You can also specify your own tab stops, so you may never need the F4 Prompt capability.

☐ **12.1(o) Double-click the Prompter's title bar again.**

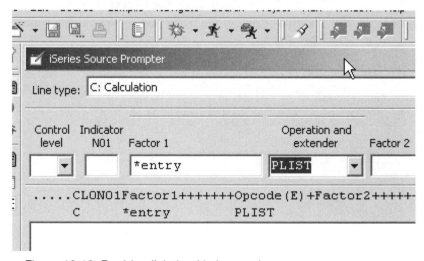

Figure 12-10: Double-click the title bar again.

Enter in a line defining Input1 as a parm, and then copy it twice after the PLIST line as shown in Figure 12-11.

❑ **12.1(p) Enter a C-spec defining Input1 as a parm.**

❑ **12.1(q) Copy it twice after the PLIST, using line commands.**

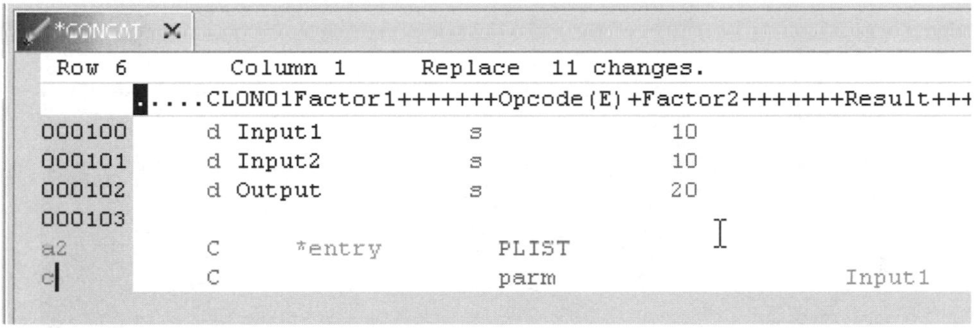

```
*CONCAT  ✕
  Row 6          Column 1        Replace   11 changes.
        .....CLON01Factor1+++++++Opcode(E)+Factor2++++++Result+++
000100      d Input1          s            10
000101      d Input2          s            10
000102      d Output          s            20
000103
a2          C      *entry         PLIST              I
c|          C                     parm                    Input1
```

Figure 12-11: Enter Input1 as a parm and then use line commands to make two copies.

Now I want to show you how the editor works to help you enter your source code correctly. There are two levels of verification. One is purely syntactical and happens as the editor parses each line. Enter the line as shown in Figure 12-12. Note that I've used a minus sign (-) instead of an equals sign (=) in the expression. This is an error, and the editor tells us so in no uncertain terms.

❑ **12.1(r) Type "eval Output - Input + Input2" and press Enter.**

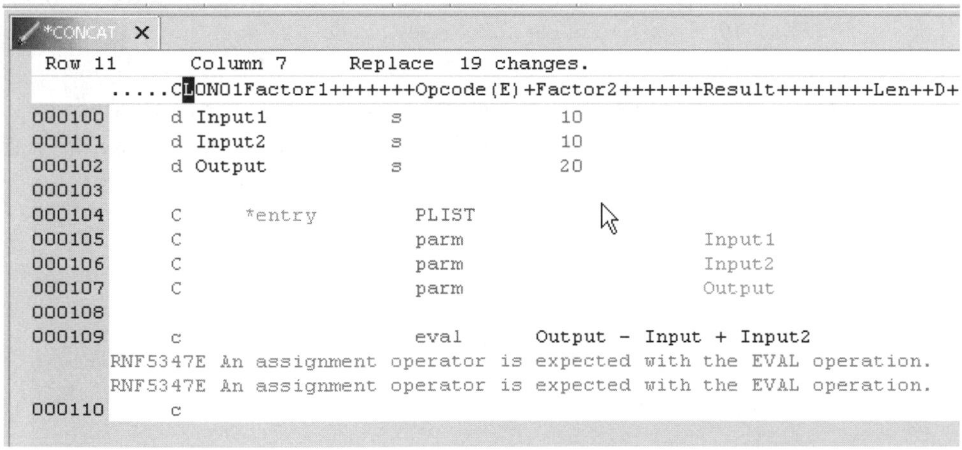

```
*CONCAT  ✕
  Row 11         Column 7        Replace   19 changes.
        .....CLON01Factor1+++++++Opcode(E)+Factor2++++++Result++++++++Len++D+
000100      d Input1          s            10
000101      d Input2          s            10
000102      d Output          s            20
000103
000104      C      *entry         PLIST          ⌐
000105      C                     parm                    Input1
000106      C                     parm                    Input2
000107      C                     parm                    Output
000108
000109      c                     eval       Output - Input + Input2
       RNF5347E An assignment operator is expected with the EVAL operation.
       RNF5347E An assignment operator is expected with the EVAL operation.
000110      c
```

Figure 12-12: Type the expression as shown, using a minus sign (-) instead of an equals sign (=), and press Enter.

The syntax checker will tell you there is an error. Fix the error, add the "return" opcode on the next line, and then save the source using the same technique we've used throughout the book: right-click in the editor and select Save.

❑ **12.1(s) Right-click in the editor view and select Save.**

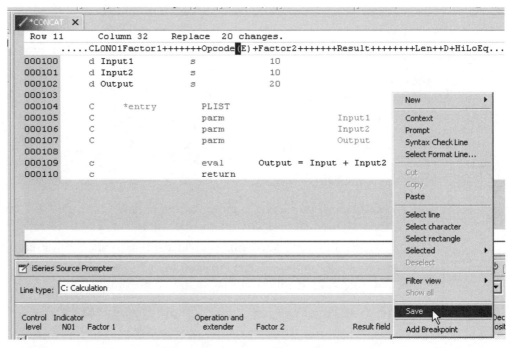

Figure 12-13: Right-click in the editor view and select Save.

This will save the source in the source member on the host, so if you are getting here from a Checkpoint, you will see the infamous Enter Password dialog, as shown in Figure 12-14. By now, you know what to do.

❑ **12.1(t) If prompted, enter user ID and password.**

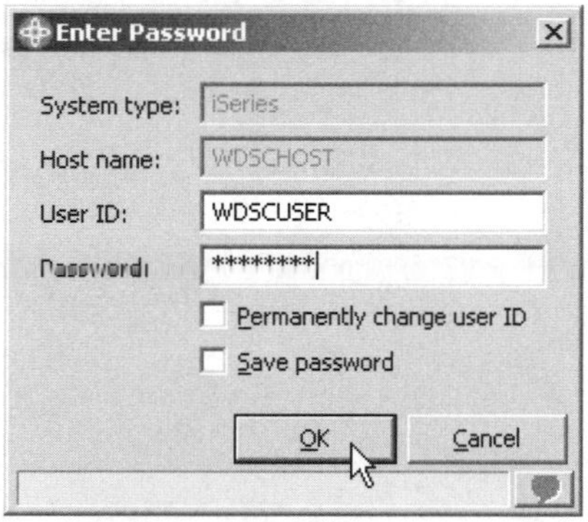

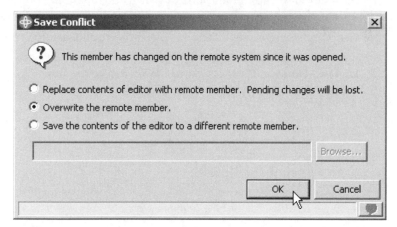

Figure 12-14: Enter your user ID and password.

You may see the Save Conflict dialog shown in Figure 12-15. This is one of the very annoying quirks of WDSC and one of the things that makes all of us who use it shake our heads. There really is no conflict, but WDSC insists there is, so we have to work around it. Select the radio button for "Overwrite the remote member" and press OK.

❑ **12.1(u) Select Overwrite the remote member and press OK.**

Figure 12-15: To circumvent the phantom Save Conflict, select Overwrite and press OK.

Finally, you can invoke the *other* verification process. This one is a bit more stringent. From the main menu, select Source/Verify as shown in Figure 12-16.

❑ **12.1(v) From the main menu, select Source/Verify.**

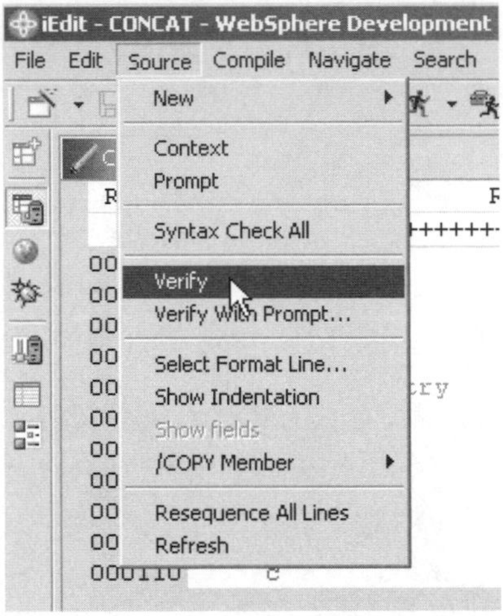

Figure 12-16: From the main menu, select Source/Verify.

This will perform what is in essence a complete compile, only without creating any object. All errors will be checked just as if you did a compile; for nearly any situation, if the code passes the verification, it should compile. But what if there are errors? They show up in the iSeries Error List view in the bottom pane, as shown in Figure 12-17. However, there's an even slicker trick: Double-click on any one of the errors in the error view, and you'll see the results as pictured in Figure 12-18.

❑ **12.1(w) Double-click on an error in the error list.**

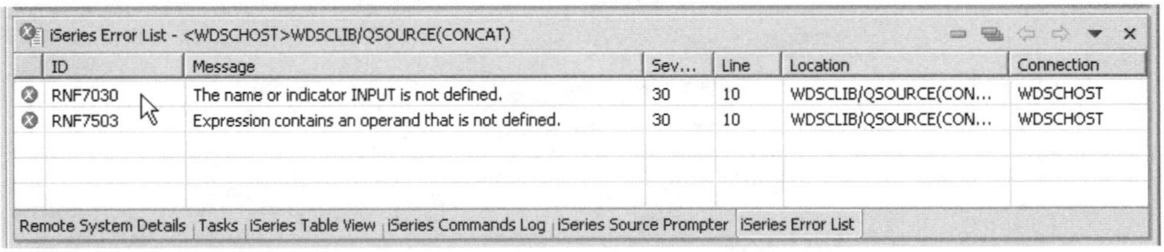

Figure 12-17: Double-click on one of these errors to copy them all into the source member.

You'll see that the errors are now copied into the source member, located after the line that caused the error. In your case, you only have two errors, and they're both because of the same problem: You typed Input rather than Input1. But that's OK; just fix the error and resave the source.

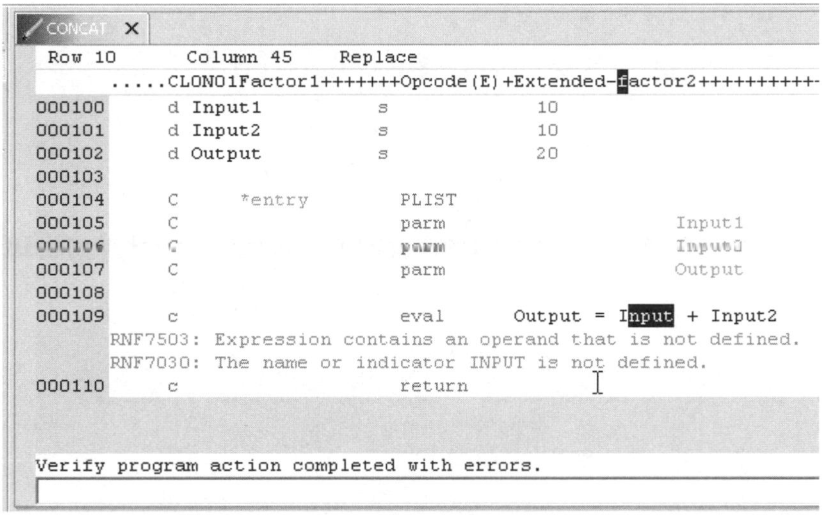

Figure 12-18: Here are the errors, embedded in the source for easy reference.

❑ 12.1(x) Fix the error and re-save the source.

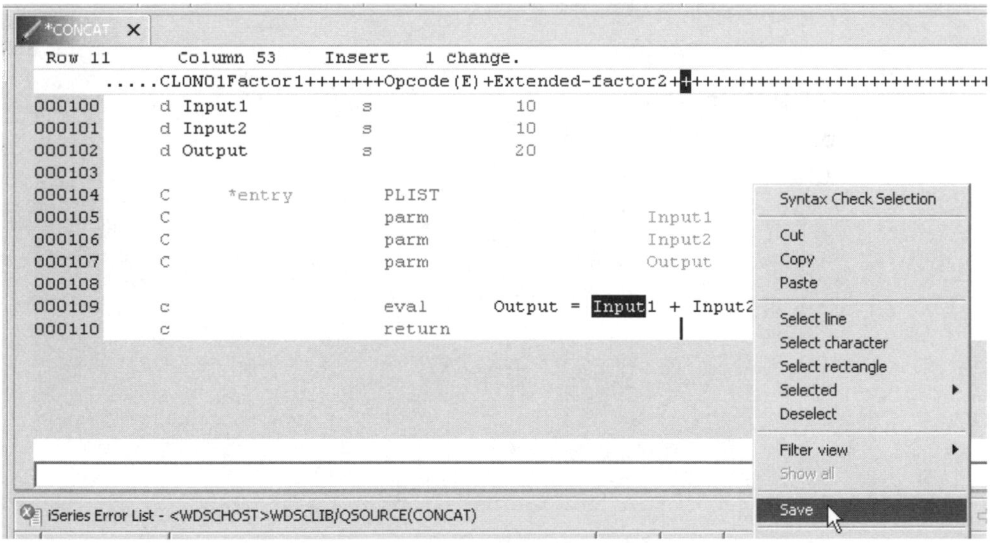

Figure 12-19: Fix the error and re-save the source.

With the error fixed, you can run the verification again as shown in Figure 12-20, and you should see the results depicted in Figure 12-21, with no errors found.

❏ **12.1(y) Re-verify the source.**

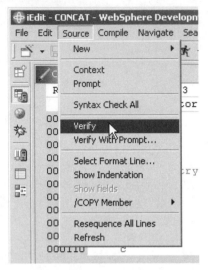

Figure 12-20: Select Source/Verify again to re-verify the source.

```
CONCAT  X
  Row 11        Column 44      Replace
      .....CLONO1Factor1+++++++Opcode(E)+Extended-factor2++++++++++++++++
 000100     d Input1        s           10
 000101     d Input2        s           10
 000102     d Output        s           20
 000103
 000104     C    *entry        PLIST
 000105     C                  parm                    Input1
 000106     C                  parm                    Input2
 000107     C                  parm                    Output
 000108
 000109     c                  eval        Output = Input1 + Input2
 000110     c                  return



 Verify program action completed with no errors.

```

Figure 12-21: This is the completed program with no errors.

You should have no errors. If you do, continue the process until all the errors are corrected. Once they are all fixed, you can move on to the compilation process in the next step.

Step 12.2—Compiling on the host

OK, your source verifies, but now how do you compile it on the host? Pretty much the same way. You can use a main menu option; in fact, there is a main menu option called Compile that's dedicated to compiling on the host. However, in one of the more subtly annoying design decisions, the Compile menu isn't always available.

> **Note:** If you are *not* restarting this chapter from a Checkpoint, then you probably won't have any of these issues. However, you may still want to read through this next section, just so you get an idea of how the workbench behaves when it is not connected to the host.

This next section applies only if you're not connected to the host. You're probably not connected to the host if you haven't seen the ubiquitous Enter Password dialog since you started WDSC; that just means you haven't done anything that requires host access. Editing, for example, doesn't require host access.

There's another way to see if you're connected to the host. First, make sure the CONCAT member is selected by clicking on its tab (Figure 12-22).

❑ **12.2(a) Click on CONCAT in the editor.**

Figure 12-22: Click on CONCAT to select it.

Now, if you go to the main menu bar and click on Source, a whole drop-down list of options will appear, as shown in Figure 12-23.

❑ **12.2(b) Click on the Source menu.**

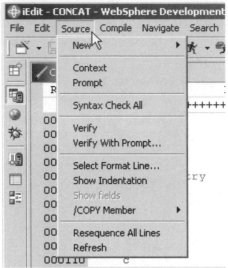

Figure 12-23: These options are available from the Source menu.

Now, though, click on the Compile menu.

Release Note: In V5.1.2, the Compile menu does not even appear. This behavior, which I call "jittery menus," is something I'd like to see removed in later releases. I don't mind disabling options, but removing options (and menus!) completely is a trend I'd like to see stopped.

❑ **12.2(c) Click on the Compile menu.**

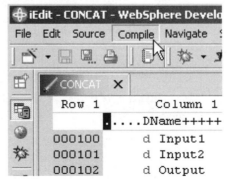

Figure 12-24: There are no options available in the compile menu.

No options whatsoever appear in the Compile menu—no errors, no attempt to log on, not even grayed-out options. That's due partially to the way Eclipse works and partially to the way the WDSC designers deployed it: The options aren't added unless you're currently on an object that can be compiled. However, the reason CONCAT can't be compiled is not because it's the wrong type of object but because you aren't currently connected. This isn't particularly intuitive, and new users may have difficulty determining why they suddenly can't compile.

This strange circumstance would occur if you had to end WDSC (for whatever reason) and then restart it. You go home at the end of the day, come back, restart the program, and then try unsuccessfully to do a compile. It would happen to you specifically if you started this step from its Checkpoint, since the first thing you're supposed to do in this step is compile the program. However, I'll show you two easy workarounds.

One is to re-save the source. Type a space somewhere safe and then right-click in the editor and Save (or press Ctrl+S). The first thing you'll see is the Enter Password dialog. After the save is complete, the Compile menu will be populated again. Or you can use the technique I'll show you now: Just open the Remote Systems view.

❑ **12.2(d) Click on the Remote Systems fast view icon.**

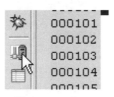

Figure 12-25:
Click on the
Remote Systems
fast view icon.

That will force a connection to the host. Enter your user ID and password (Figure 12-26), and you'll be connected.

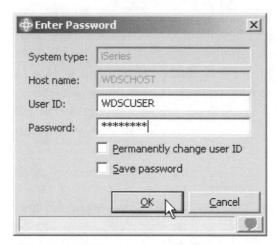

Figure 12-26: Enter your user ID and password.

Now that you're connected, click on the Compile menu again and you'll see that options have appeared.

❑ **12.2(e) Click on the Compile menu again.**

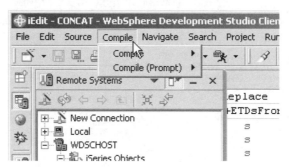

Figure 12-27: Options now appear in the Compile menu!

At this point, you can use the Compile option from the main menu to compile your program. I'd like to present another option, however. If you look at Figure 12-28, you'll see how you can right-click on the source member in the Remote Systems view and get a nice pop-up menu that has, among its options, Compile. (It also has User Actions, which I'll discuss a little later.)

You can, therefore, right-click on the source member and select the Compile/ CRTBNDRPG option to compile the program (Figure 12-28).

❑ **12.2(f) Right-click on the CONCAT source and select Compile/CRTBNDRPG.**

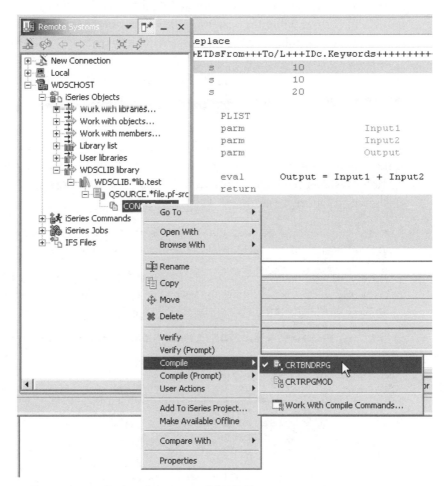

Figure 12-28: Right-click on the CONCAT source member and select Compile/CRTBNDRPG.

This will submit the compile to batch on the host. During the compile, you may see some progress reports, and finally you will see the display shown in Figure 12-29, indicating that WDSC is retrieving the events file.

Figure 12-29: WDSC indicates that it is retrieving the events file.

The reason this happens is because there is an option now on most compile commands to output a small status file. Actually, it's more like a member in a file named EVFEVENT. And while the design is a little bizarre, the effect is that WDSC can retrieve a log of errors from the compile. You must specify OPTION(*EVENTF) on your compile command; and while this is done automatically for you on standard compile commands, you must address the EVENTF option if you create your own user actions for compiling.

After the file has been retrieved, one way to tell the compile was successful is to look at the iSeries Error List. If you have no errors, the compile was successful. A more active approach is to refresh the library view, which you can do from the Remote Systems view by simply right-clicking on the library and selecting Refresh as shown in Figure 12-30.

Note: You may need to make the Remote Systems view visible again by clicking on the appropriate Fast View icon in the left navigation bar.

Note: Under some circumstances, the object WDSCLIB.*lib.test may be shown as WDSCLIB.*lib.dsclib. I don't know why this occurs, but the Refresh method in 12.2(g) will correct the problem.

❏ **12.2(g) Right-click on WDSCLIB.*lib.test and select Refresh.**

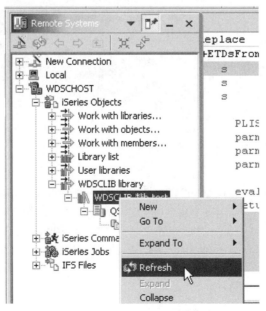

Figure 12-30: Right-click on WDSCLIB.*lib.test and select Refresh.

You'll get a listing such as the one shown in Figure 12-31. Note not only the presence of the brand new CONCAT program object (CONCAT.*pgm.rpgle), but also the appearance of the EVFEVENT file. This came about magically as a result of the compile command, which unbeknownst to you, was submitted with OPTION(*EVENTF).

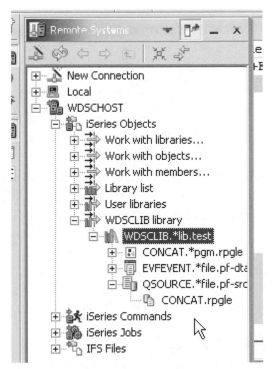

Figure 12-31: The new CONCAT program shows up, along with the EVFEVENT file.

There is one other way to see what has happened on the host. First, let's get some real estate by closing the Remote Systems view. Click on the Remote System fast view icon as shown in Figure 12-32. Because of another quirk in the GUI , you may have to hit it twice. I'm not sure why.

❏ **12.2(h) Click the Remote Systems fast view icon.**

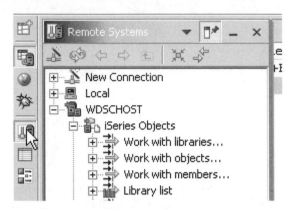

Figure 12-32: Click the Remote Systems fast view icon (twice if necessary).

At the bottom of the workbench is the iSeries Error List. The title bar even shows which error list is showing—in this case, WDSCLIB/EVFEVENT(CONCAT), which is the error listing from the last compile of CONCAT in WDSCLIB. Since you've only compiled CONCAT once and there are no errors, it's a reasonably safe bet that the compile went fine. But for proof positive, take a look at the iSeries Commands Log. Click on it as shown in Figure 12-33.

❏ **12.2(i) Click on the iSeries Commands Log tab.**

iSeries Error List - WDSCLIB/EVFEVENT(CONCAT)				
ID	Message	Sev...	Line	Location

Remote System Details | Tasks | iSeries Table View | iSeries Commands Log | iSeries Source Prompter | iSeries Error List

Figure 12-33: Click on the iSeries Commands Log tab to review host activity.

As always, we're short on screen space, and in this case it's really a problem, so just double-click on the title bar to maximize the window.

❑ **12.2(j) Double-click the title bar to maximize the iSeries Commands Log.**

Figure 12-34: Double-click the title bar to maximize the iSeries Commands Log view.

You'll see a screen as shown in Figure 12-35. This is a log of all the activity that has occurred on the host in reaction to this session of WDSC; essentially, it's a dump of the joblog for the host server job.

If you started this step from its Checkpoint, the list will be very short, like the one in Figure 12-35. The first entry should interest you: It's an ADDLIBLE WDSCLIB command. I'll leave it as an exercise to the reader to determine why that happened.

If you've been on WDSC for a while, just plowing through Step after Step without stopping, then your log will be quite extensive. Regardless, the last entry in the log should be something like this, indicating that the compile was successful: "CRTBNDRPG PGM(WDSCLIB/CONCAT)... Program CONCAT was successfully created in library WDSCLIB...."

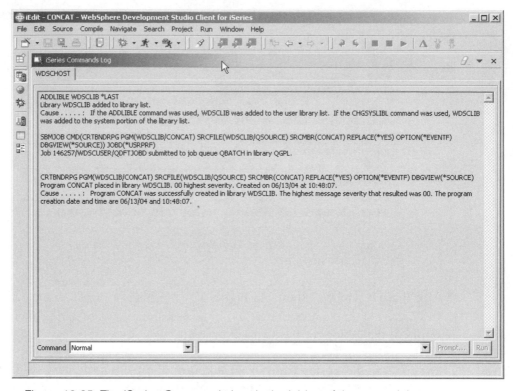

Figure 12-35: The iSeries Commands Log is the joblog of the server job.

After you're done looking, double-click the title bar to restore the workbench view and then proceed to the next Step, debugging a host job.

Note: This view can get unwieldy, since it reports everything you do. The small "eraser" icon near the upper right of the view will clear the screen if you ever want to get rid of the messages.

❑ **12.2(k) Double-click the title bar again to restore the workbench.**

InStep 12.2.a—User actions

> ## GOAL
> This is a quick introduction to user actions.

Given our primary goal of getting through this project as quickly as possible, I try not to veer off too often into subjects that really don't have any bearing on the tasks at hand. However, I believe this particular feature is one that you should know about. This InStep simply introduces the feature rather than actually create one, but if you've ever created a user option with PDM, you'll be able to master this quickly.

Hint: User actions work only on source members, not programs! One way to avoid this problem is to create source-only object filters.

If you've worked with PDM on the iSeries, you may know that you can add your own user-defined options. If you're not familiar with this ability, bring up a PDM display (WRKLIBPDM, WRKOBJPDM, or WRKMBRPDM) and hit F16. That will take you to a page that will allow you to define your own PDM options. You can then use those options on any PDM display.

WDSC has a similar, even more powerful capability called "user actions." If you right-click on a member or an object in the Remote Systems view, the pop-up menu has a submenu called User Actions. That submenu contains all currently defined user actions as well as an option to maintain those actions.

If you were to select that option on your current workspace, you'd see that the submenu contains only the Work with User Actions option, as shown in Figure 12-36. That's because you haven't defined any options yet. However, if you select the Work with User Actions option, you'll get a screen like the one in Figure 12-37.

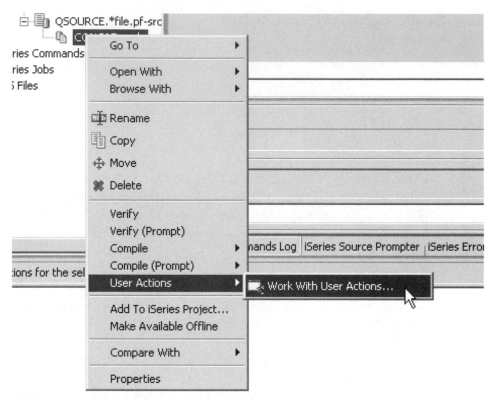

Figure 12-36: The pop-up menu for objects in the Remote System view shows all available user actions.

This wizard allows you to create your own user actions. You can select from a wide variety of substitution variables, as well as make certain options available only for certain source or object types. A number of checkboxes relate to option processing, including forcing a prompt or refreshing the list after an option has been executed.

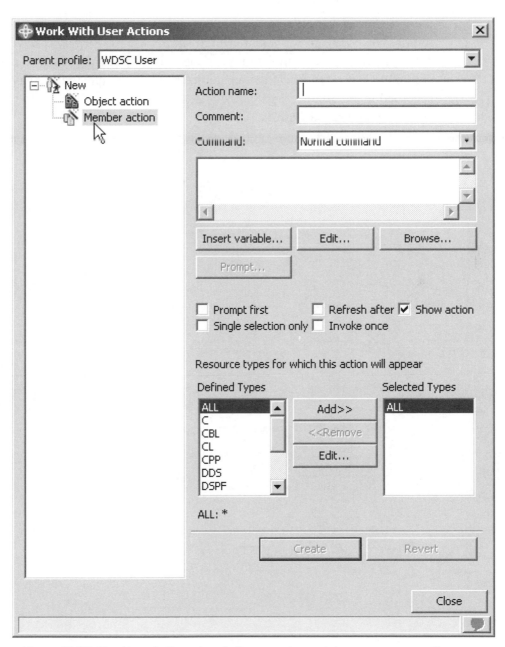

Figure 12-37: The User Action wizard allows you to create your own user actions.

In one of my workspaces, I have multiple user options, including one that invokes my own CRTOBJ command, which is tailored for my environment. The important thing to note is that if you are compiling objects and you want to see the errors returned to WDSC, it is not sufficient to simply use the OPTION(*EVENTF) when you invoke the compiler in your custom compile program. You must also accept OPTION(*EVENTF) as a parameter on your command and have that specified in the user action. If you do not, WDSC will not look for the results and you won't see any errors.

Step 12.3—Debugging on the host

> ## GOAL
> ### Debug a program on the iSeries.

The last task in this Step is to debug the small program you wrote. This is a very simple program, designed to take three parameters. The first two are 10-character input parameters, which the program concatenates and then stores in the third 20-character output parameter.

In order to debug a program, you need to set up a debug configuration for it, which specifies how the program will be submitted to batch: command to execute, parameters, job description, and so on. Once the configuration is created, you can use it to launch your program.

Note: Sometimes, developers use wrapper programs that call the program they want to test—for example, to pass parameters to the program or to perform special overrides or other pre-testing behaviors. In order to do this, you simply need to launch the wrapper program rather than the test program.

Debug configurations are great time-savers, especially in a real development environment. The first time you test a program, you'll follow the scenario in this step: Get your program ready to test, and once it compiles cleanly, go into debug mode, creating the debug configuration as you go. It may seem like a lot of work just to call a program. After that, however, you will have a debug configuration ready and you won't have to go through these additional beginning procedures; instead, you can just select the debug configuration from the debug drop-down.

Hint: You can reuse an outdated configuration for a different program by editing the configuration. Use the Debug... option from the debug drop-down to open the Create, Manage and Run Configurations wizard. Just remember, it will no longer call the original program.

In fact, as an additional time-saver, the debug icon will default to the last debug configuration you used, so simply clicking on it will launch the previous program again. However, since this is the first time you will be debugging this particular program, you will need to create a debug configuration for it. You start that process by clicking on the drop-down arrow to the right of the Debug tool on the main toolbar, as shown in Figure 12-38.

❑ **12.3(a) Click on the Debug drop-down.**

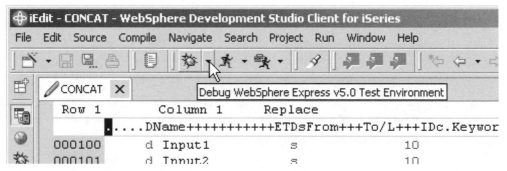

Figure 12-38: Since this is the first time debugging this application, use the Debug dropdown.

Now you have a submenu, Debug As, with a number of options. You will be debugging this as an iSeries Batch Application, so select that option as shown in Figure 12-39.

Release Note: Remember that the options change in V5.1.2; iSeries Batch Application is the second option.

❏ **12.3(b) Select Debug As/iSeries Batch Application.**

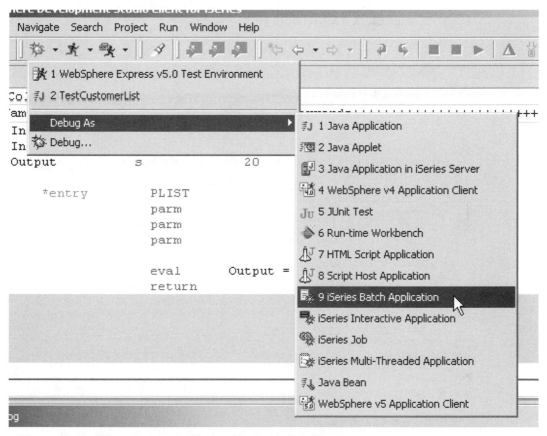

Figure 12-39: Select Debug As/iSeries Batch Application.

This will begin the process of creating a new debug configuration. The configuration wizard is shown in Figure 12-40. While you have a wide variety of options to choose from, the only options you really need to worry about are the name of the configuration (so you can use it again) and what that configuration launches.

The name is simple: Type "CONCAT" into the Name field. What the configuration launches is a little more complex: You need to click on the How to Start tab, as shown in the figure.

❑ **12.3(c) Type "CONCAT" into the Name field.**

❑ **12.3(d) Click on the How to Start tab.**

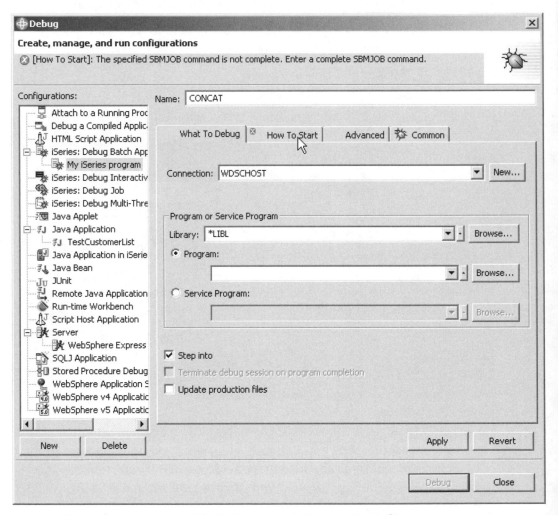

Figure 12-40: Enter the name (CONCAT) and then click on How to Start.

Not surprisingly, this will switch to the How to Start pane. What you'll see (as depicted in Figure 12-41) is the command the configuration currently intends to run and a big button marked Prompt…, which will run the iSeries command prompter to allow you to build your command.

> **Hint:** If you fill in the program name on the previous pane (What To Debug), that program name will be pre-filled here. This can be a big time-saver, especially if you don't need any parameters: You won't even need to prompt the SBMJOB command. Another point on that first screen is the Update production files checkbox, which corresponds to UPDPROD on the OS/400 STRDBG command.

Click on the Prompt… button as shown in the figure.

☐ **12.3(e) Click on the Prompt... button.**

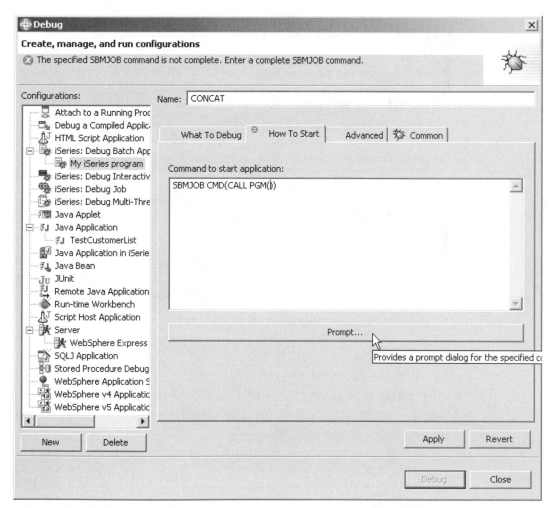

Figure 12-41: Click on the Prompt... button

Interestingly enough, if you've started this step from the Checkpoint, you'll get the Enter Password dialog at this time as shown in Figure 12-42. Up until now, WDSC hasn't needed the iSeries, but when it comes to prompting CL, WDSC knows it ought to make use of the host. As always, if the dialog appears, enter your user ID and password and hit OK.

Note: If you are prompted for user ID and password, you may need to hit the Prompt… button again. And it can take a little while for the SBMJOB dialog to appear. During that time, there isn't any good indication that the workbench is still active. Be patient.

❑ **12.3(f) If necessary, enter your user ID and password.**

Figure 12-42: The ever-popular Enter Password dialog; if you see it, enter your user ID and password.

This will cause the Submit Job (SBMJOB) wizard to pop up. This wizard will prompt you for all the appropriate parameters for a SBMJOB command. In this case, you're going to take nearly all the defaults. But the first thing you have to do is enter the command you want to run in this job.

The command prompter supports nested prompting. If you have a command that takes another command as its parameter, like SBMJOB does, then you can prompt for the command parameter. It's a little convoluted, but it works. You've probably done it before when prompting the SBMJOB command in the green-screen. The same concept applies here. You position your cursor somewhere in the command parameter, which at this point simply reads CALL PGM(), and then hit F4.

❑ **12.3(g) Put your cursor in the Command to run parameter and press F4.**

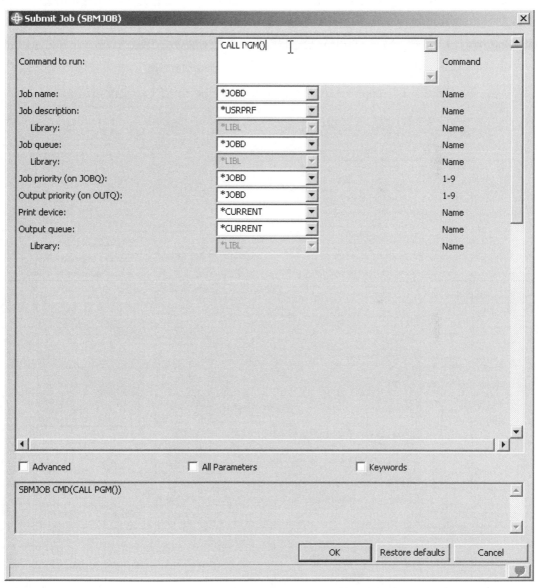

Figure 12-43: Pressing F4 inside the Command to run parameter brings up another prompt.

This will bring up a new prompt window—in this case, the Call Program (CALL) wizard, as shown in Figure 12-44. This is a far simpler command, with only the program and library to call and the parameters to pass. As I noted at the beginning of this step, there are two input parameters and one output parameter. To simulate that in this very bare test scenario, I want you to add three constants. It's quite simple. First, enter the program name CONCAT in the Program field. Then type "ABC" in the Parameters field and press the Add button.

❑ **12.3(h) Enter CONCAT in the Program field.**

❑ **12.3(i) Type "ABC" in the Parameter field and press Add.**

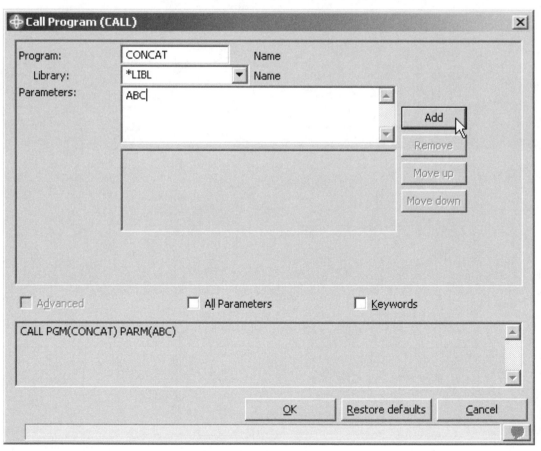

Figure 12-44: Set the program name to CONCAT and then add the first parameter, ABC.

Add the second parameter, DEF, as in Figure 12-45 and the third parameter, three dots, as in Figure 12-46.

❑ **12.3(j) Add the second parameter, DEF.**

❑ **12.3(k) Add the third parameter, three dots (…).**

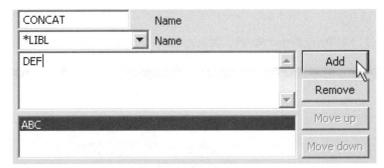

Figure 12-45: Add the second parameter, DEF.

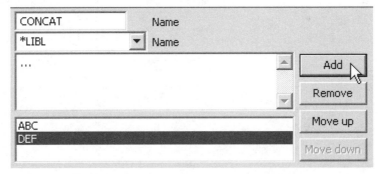

Figure 12-46: Add the third parameter, three dots.

The CALL command is now set up. The two input parameters are ABC and DEF, and the output parameter, which we don't care so much about, is initialized to three dots. Click OK as shown in Figure 12-47.

❑ **12.3(l) Press OK.**

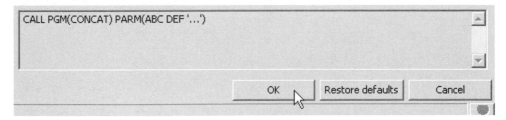

Figure 12-47: Now that the CALL command is complete, press OK.

The completed command will be returned to the Command to run field in the SBMJOB wizard as shown in Figure 12-48. At this point, you could just press OK, or you could set as many of the other parameters as you deem necessary. I usually set the Job name parameter, so I can easily find my job in a heavily loaded host.

❑ **12.3(m) Enter CONCAT into the Job name parameter and press OK.**

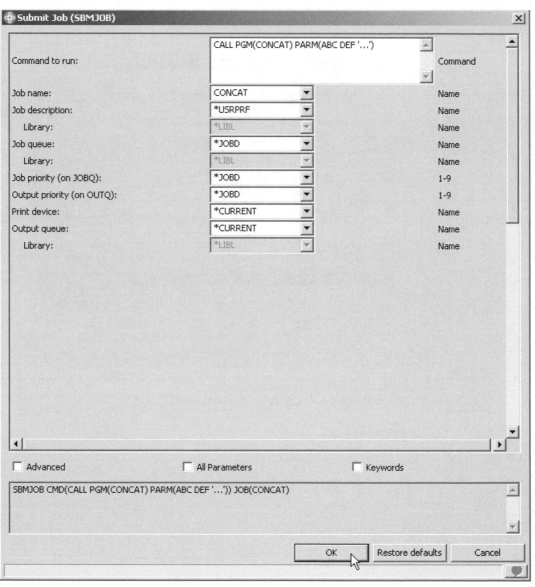

Figure 12-48: I usually set the Job name parameter so I can find the job easily if I need to.

Pressing OK will return the entire SBMJOB command back to the How to Start pane, as shown in Figure 12-49. While there are a lot of other settings that you can change, the parameters you just changed in this walkthrough are typically enough for most situations.

If you were just editing the debug configuration (you might do this if you wanted to change some parameters, for instance), then you would hit the Apply button. This would change the configuration without launching it, and you could then press Close to get out of the dialog (if you make a mistake, press Revert to undo any changes). In this case, though, you *want* to launch the program, so hit the Debug button. This will both save your configuration and launch the program.

❑ **12.3(n) Press Debug to launch the program.**

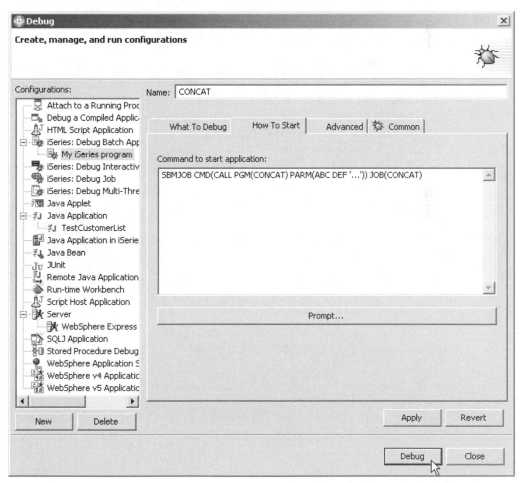

Figure 12-49: Pressing Debug will save the configuration and launch the program.

That's all you need to do. WDSC will take care of the rest. You'll see a status bar briefly on the bottom of the Debug launch dialog, but not for long.

Launching CONCAT...

Figure 12-50: The program is being launched on the host!

Very quickly, you should see the Debug perspective as shown in Figure 12-51. Notice that this is the same perspective that you used back in Step 10. The only major difference is that the Debug view shows an iSeries program stack rather than a JVM stack. The program is loaded and stopped at the first statement, and you can now do whatever you need to do to debug the program.

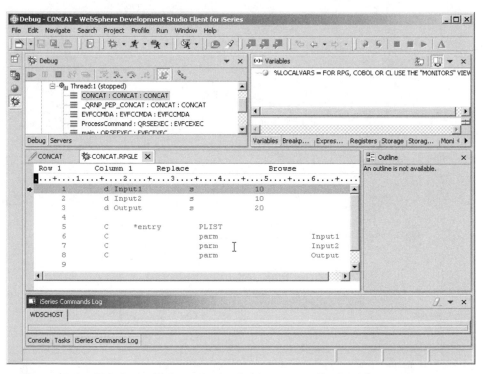

Figure 12-51: This is the Debug display for the remote iSeries job.

One difference in actual operation is in the variables display. In the olden days of RPG, all variables were global, so the Variables view would be all but useless.

There is a nice message in the box that reminds you of that fact. Instead, you'll use the Monitors view, which will allow you to monitor the contents of a variable.

Note: I'm not sure why the Variables view does not work for procedures. The whole RPG procedure concept still has a few hitches, so for now you have to use the Monitor view to look at anything. Unfortunately, the Monitor view does not differentiate between a local variable and a global variable of the same name. You can monitor both, but it's impossible to tell in the Monitor view which is which.

☐ **12.3(o) Press the Monitor tab on the inspection view.**

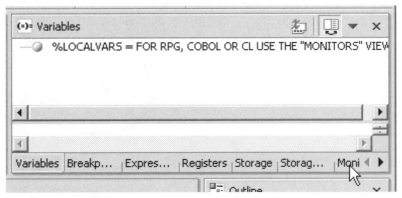

Figure 12-52: The Variables view is useless in RPG, so use the Monitors view.

Now you select what you want to monitor. One very nice thing is that as you move your cursor through the program, if you let it rest on a variable, WDSC will pop up the current value of the variable, as shown in Figure 12-53.

```
  CONCAT        CONCAT.RPGLE   X

  Row 1          Column 2        Replace
..ᐧ..+....1....+....2....+....3....+....4...
➤        1         d Input1           s
         2         d Input2           s
         3         d Output           s
         4               ┌ OUTPUT = ...        ┐
         5         C       *entry          PLIST
         6         C                       parm
         7         C                       parm
         o         c                       norm
```

Figure 12-53: Rest your cursor on a variable and WDSC will pop up its value.

To monitor a variable, first double-click on it to select it (or use your mouse to click and drag over the variable name). Once the name is highlighted, right-click and select Monitor Expression from the pop-up menu.

❑ **12.3(p) Double-click the variable name Output to highlight it.**

❑ **12.3(q) Right-click and select Monitor Expression.**

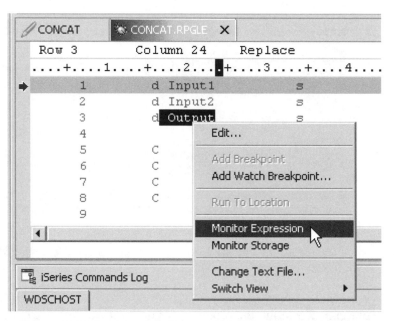

Figure 12-54: Double-click Output to highlight it, and then right-click and select Monitor Expression.

The variable will appear in the Monitors view as shown in Figure 12-55. Note that the variable name is all uppercase, since RPG is case-insensitive. The current value of three dots is shown as well.

Figure 12-55: The variable Output is being monitored; its current value is three dots (…).

You can set breakpoints and watch breakpoints just like in any other language. Given the global nature of RPG variables, watch breakpoints are often lifesavers during the debugging process. You set a watch breakpoint on a variable much the same way you monitor the variable: highlight it, and then right-click and select Add Watch Breakpoint….

❑ **12.3(r) Right-click and select Add Watch Breakpoint….**

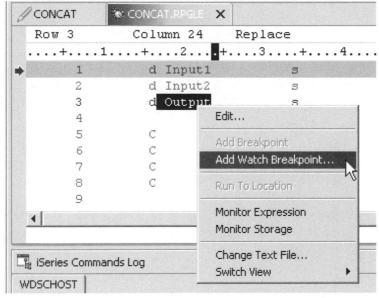

Figure 12-56: Right-click and select Add Watch Breakpoint….

The Add a Watch Breakpoint dialog will appear. As long as I've used WDSC, I've never changed anything in this particular dialog. I simply leave the defaults and press Finish.

❑ **12.3(s) Leave the defaults and press Finish to set the watch break-point.**

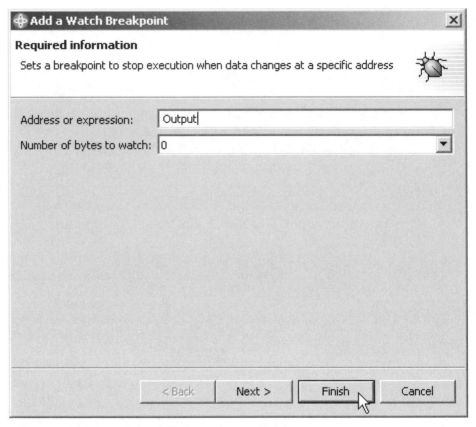

Figure 12-57: Leave the defaults and press Finish.

Now that your watch breakpoint is set, you can run your program. As with a Java program or a servlet, click on the Resume button as shown in Figure 12-58 to resume the RPG program.

❑ **12.3(t) Press Resume.**

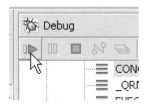

Figure 12-58: Click Resume to run the program.

Almost immediately, you should see the watch breakpoint Debugger Message shown in Figure 12-59. Press OK to continue.

❑ **12.3(u) Press OK.**

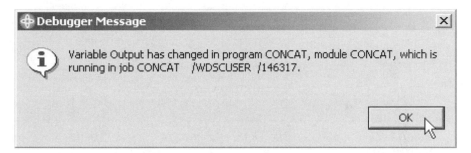

Figure 12-59: This is your watch breakpoint. Press OK.

At this point, your workbench will look like the one in Figure 12-60. In the Monitors view, you'll see that Output has changed to ABC DEF, as you would expect. Also, the program is currently suspended at the "return" opcode, which is the line *after* the line that changed Output.

This is all perfect. In a live environment, you'd be checking variables and testing conditions to see what your program was doing, but this quick demonstration should show you the very basics of how debugging works. It's really not that different from STRISDB, just a little more colorful.

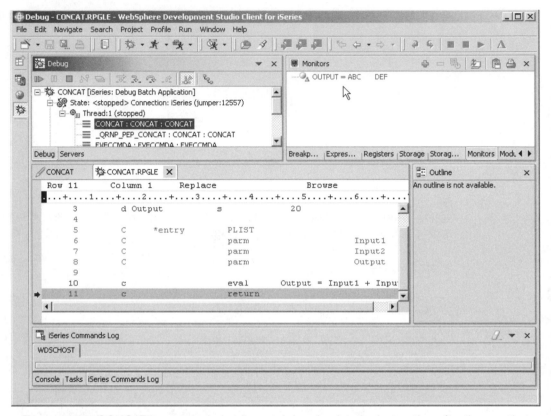

Figure 12-60: CONCAT is suspended at its watch breakpoint, the instruction after the one that changed Output.

You can end this program by pressing the Resume tool again, as shown in Figure 12-61.

❑ **12.3(v) Press Resume again.**

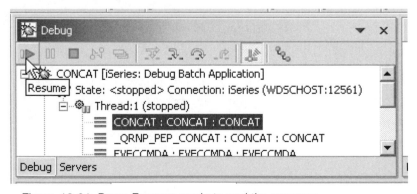

Figure 12-61: Press Resume again to end the program.

That doesn't stop the server job, though. The only way to do that is to shut down the connection or manually cancel the job. To manually terminate the job, right-click on it in the Debug view and select Terminate and Remove.

❑ **12.3(w) Right-click on the server job and select Terminate and Remove.**

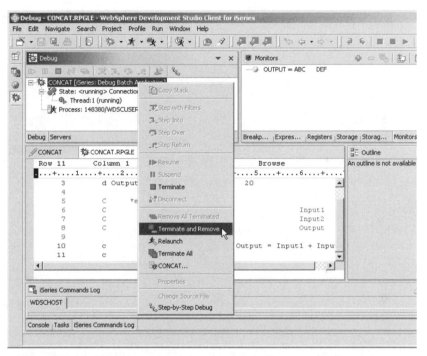

Figure 12-62: This shuts down the server job that was used to debug CONCAT.

That will clean up the server job. This little clean-up tip will make life a bit easier when you have lots of people debugging lots of programs.

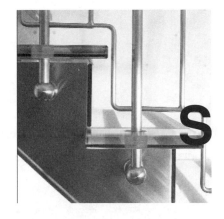

Step 13

Things we won't get to see

This is a somewhat different step than the others you've read up to this point. You've been going at a great pace, using many different features of WDSC. And in the next several steps, you'll take all that knowledge and turn it into a real application.

But because of the great breadth of the WDSC product, there's no way one single example like the one we've been building could take advantage of all of its great features. But I want you to know that these things exist, so this step contains a list of some of the features that just didn't make the cut.

And, no matter how wonderful WDSC is, there are also some things it *doesn't* do, and we'll address some of those as well. If you want to skip this step completely and go straight to Step 14, you won't lose anything; you can come back to this step whenever you'd like.

If you do plan to read this step—and especially if you plan to do some poking around—you might want to use a test workspace. Close your current WDSC session and then copy ch1301 from the Checkpoints folder on your CD-ROM. Use this as your workspace for this chapter and start there. When you're done playing around, just end the session and go back to your original workspace. Otherwise, you may end up with a bunch of junk in your workspace that you didn't really want.

Just a thought.

Step 13.1—Preferences

GOAL

This chapter will introduce the
Preferences panel.

A whole world of features and functionality is buried beneath the unassuming menu option of Window/Preferences.

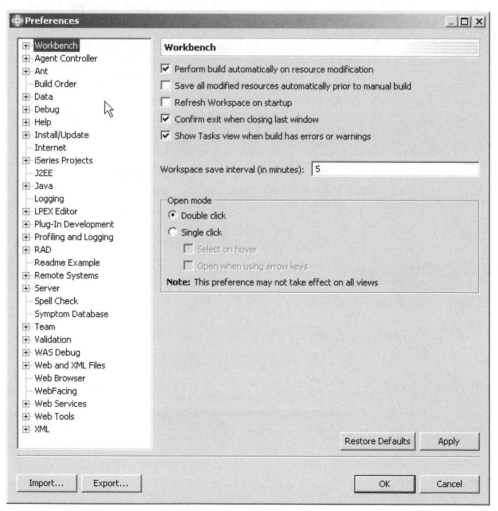

Figure 13-1: WDSC's main preferences panel offers plenty of functionality.

As you can see, there are pages and pages of preferences setting. Everything from font and color settings to keyboard shortcuts to code templates can be set here. Need to set up an Internet proxy? This is the place to do it. Want to customize the step filters for WebSphere debugging? Look no further.

And while Eclipse provides a bunch of these preferences (to the point that it was sometimes called the Black Hole of Preferences), WebSphere Studio and specifically WDSC added whole new categories of preferences, such as ILE RPG.

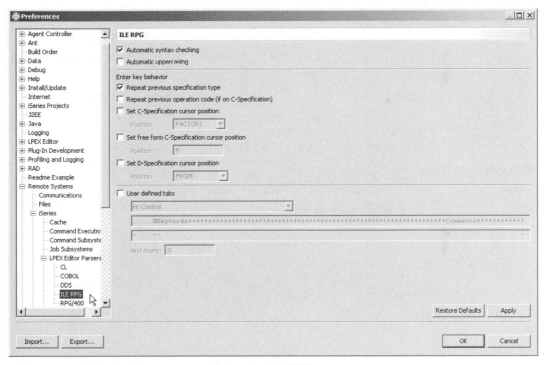

Figure 13-2: This preferences page is just for ILE RPG.

When you have time, I suggest you go in and get familiar with these settings. Since each programmer is different, you may find uses for options that I will never use. At the same time, I'd like to point out a couple of specific options:

1. To change the font for the Java editor, use Workbench/Fonts.

2. To change the font for the jLpex editors, use LPEX Editor/Appearance.

3. To make the editors re-sequence source members on save, go to Remote Systems/iSeries/LPEX Editor Parsers.

4. Add user-defined tabs to various RPG specifications.

As you can see, the various settings are fairly widespread and not that easy to find. The Preferences dialog is sort of like the junk drawer of WDSC; every miscellaneous thing goes here, and it's gotten somewhat out of control. For example, there is a preferences category called LPEX Editor, which you might expect to contain these options. For whatever reason, it does not, and you have to find them under the Remote Systems category. This alone took me a couple of hours to find.

One other hint: If you have Client Access on your machine and you have loaded at least one session, several excellent monospaced fonts appear, including IBM3270, which can be shown reasonably well in sizes as low as 6 point.

Warning: Some of these settings can have drastic affects on your workbench. I highly recommend that you have a "sandbox" workspace for this sort of research. I in fact have a workspace called "sandbox" just for that purpose.

Step 13.2—The Data perspective

> ## GOAL
> The goal of this chapter is to give you a quick glimpse of the Data perspective, WDSC's SQL tool.

If you're into SQL, this is your perspective. Through this perspective, you can create data definitions for any files on your system and then generate statements and execute them.

The perspective is very flexible, with the ability to use just about any JDBC driver, which in turn allows you to access just about any database. Once you've mastered the mechanics of the perspective, you can generate statements of all kinds, which you can then use to generate stored procedures or embedded SQL. However, the more advanced features require additional components such as the DB2 Application Development Client.

Also, this perspective is not exactly for the casual user. You'll need to be pretty comfortable with some of the more arcane SQL terms, such as Data Definition Language (DDL). Before you can execute a simple query, you need to create a connection, import a table into a project, and generate the DDL for the table. And even then, the viewing capabilities are pretty limited.

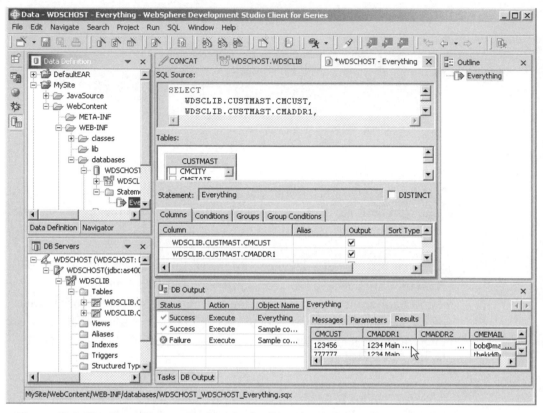

Figure 13-3: The Data perspective is quite flexible, but you'll need to really know your SQL to take advantage of it.

The Data perspective seems to me to be directed toward people who do all their database access via SQL or JDBC. That's not my ideal environment; I prefer to use SQL for ad hoc access and traditional RPG I/O for transactional access. Thus, any perspective based on SQL that I'd want to see would have some great capabilities of easy, fast access to the database.

Right now, I'd say Operations Navigator does a better job of ad hoc database access, and it offers a number of database viewing plug-ins. For now, the Data perspective is still a work in progress for me.

Step 13.3—Advanced editing features

GOAL

This step lists some of the other features in RSE's LPEX editors.

The RPG editor is a lot more advanced than I've been able to show you. It offers some great capabilities, such as prompting for BIFs, that I just don't have the space to go over in detail. For example, you can use certain templates to generate code (they can be found in the Preferences sections). Although the supplied templates are for free-form RPG, you can also add them for ILE COBOL or C++.

If you're familiar with the Java editor, you're probably aware of the code completion capabilities, something every good Java editor must have; hit Ctrl+space just about any time during entering Java source and you will get context-sensitive selections of what you can and cannot do at that point. The RPG editor has a similar capability.

Used in conjunction with the Outline view (another thing I've neglected), the code completion feature will even list the available fields, very similar to its Java cousin.

And since the RPG editor is just another LPEX editor, it gains all of the features of LPEX.

I should mention that the term LPEX is used throughout WDSC to refer to the editors. I, on the other hand, like to use the term jLpex because it more clearly identifies the fact that these editors are written in Java and are part of the Eclipse (and thus WDSC) environment. The *original* LPEX (or Live Parsing Editor) was found in CODE/400 and was written in C. It is faster and more stable than the jLpex editors, but jLpex is catching up. So, when you see jLpex in this book, I am referring to the Java version of the LPEX editors, which WDSC always refers to as LPEX.

In any case, with the LPEX editors, color coding is available for dozens of syntaxes, including assembly language and JCL. Each syntax has dozens of styles that you can color code, ranging from literals to opcodes to errors. Given enough time, you can make some mighty ugly screens!

Not only that, but you can add user actions. These are pieces of code that you write that will be invoked by the editors in response to various conditions. In these actions, you can actually interact with the user through prompts and then modify the source currently being edited. It's sort of like a super-macro language that allows you to greatly extend the editors.

The more you learn about the editing capabilities of WDSC, the more you realize how truly powerful the platform is.

Step 13.4—iSeries projects

GOAL

This step introduces iSeries projects.

One of the favorite features of the WDSC developers themselves, an iSeries project is an interesting way to do offline development. Many people love the ability to cache a bunch of file definitions onto their laptop and then go off and do development without being connected to an iSeries.

iSeries projects allow you to do just that sort of disconnected development. You identify a library you are working with and then download all the definitions to your local copy of WDSC. From that point on, you can work with the source as you would if you were connected. You can make changes, verify source, and so on. Of course, you can't really compile anything or run it locally; you have to "push" it back to the host to do that. But you can at least write the code.

The WDSC team is continuing to listen to input from the field as to how best to implement this feature. The fact that changes are pushed to a single host library makes the concept less useful in a production environment, but the team continues to enhance the capabilities of the tool, and I hope to see some improvements in this area. Until then, however, the projects are more of a luxury item for me than one I would use in a day-to-day environment.

Step 13.5—CODE and VisualAge for RPG

> ## GOAL
> This step offers a look at CODE and VisualAge for RPG, two legacy tools still shipped with WDSC.

These tools are very powerful development systems in their own right. However, they were written in the days before WDSC, before Eclipse was the framework. They are standalone tools and as such will never be really integrated into the WDSC workbench. Even a slight amount of non-integration can be a problem (for example, the Image Designer is still somewhat clumsy). These two products are so standalone that they are difficult to even think of as part of the package.

CODE Editor and Designer

CODE in particular has capabilities that just aren't available in WDSC yet. For example, the CODE Editor has a tool that converts fixed-format RPG IV to /free syntax. I don't know why this logic has not been ported into WDSC, but at this writing, it still has not, so CODE is the only way to automatically convert to /free syntax.

> **Release Note:** V5.1.2 of WDSC has finally incorporated this feature.

Similarly, the CODE Designer provides GUI development capabilities that WDSC does not match. Expect to see CODE in each release of WDSC until they finally manage to port those features into the Eclipse framework. However, CODE isn't necessary for new browser-based development, so it didn't get coverage in this book.

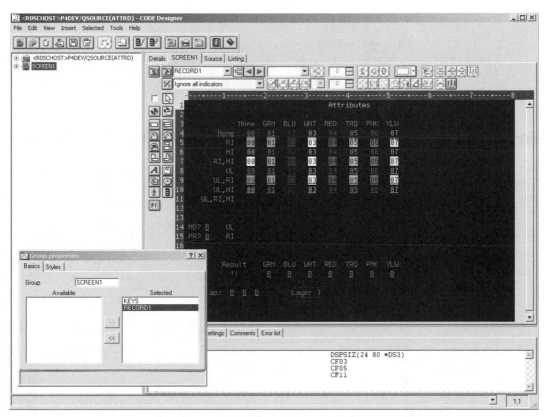

Figure 13-4: You can do a lot with CODE. This is the CODE Designer screen.

VisualAge for RPG

VisualAge for RPG (VARPG) is a completely different animal. It extends the RPG language to the PC along with event-driven code capabilities and a sophisticated thick-client GUI designer. These features allow an RPG programmer to start developing real thick-client applications—and with a reasonably short learning curve! Once again, that particular feature set wasn't what was needed for this project, so the product really didn't get any particular attention in the mainstream of this book, but feel free to fire it up and play with it; it will be a great learning experience.

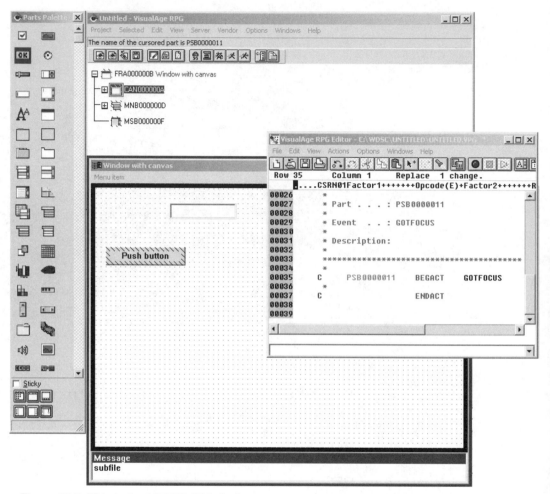

Figure 13-5: This is the VARPG GUI designer.

Step 13.6—WebFacing

GOAL

This last step gives a quick introduction to WebFacing.

WebFacing is one of the major features of WDSC, at least from an iSeries perspective, and I don't even have a screen shot for it. That's because WebFacing addresses a completely different business issue than this book does. I wrote a book, *e-Deployment: The Fastest Path to the Web*, that addresses this other issue, that of putting existing legacy applications on the Web.

WebFacing is IBM's transition path for moving existing legacy applications to the Web. You download the definitions from the host into WDSC and then WebFacing will generate JSPs and an XML file that controls them. This information gets sent back up to the host in the form of a J2EE project, which you can then install into a Web application server such as WebSphere. Your applications will then appear in the browser.

It's sophisticated, but as I indicated, it's really not the focus of this book. This book focuses on new development in a true client/server environment as opposed to graphically enabling existing monolithic applications. If, in addition to writing new applications, you also have existing legacy applications that you would like to quickly Web enable, you should take a look at what WebFacing has to offer.

If you find WeFacing intriguing, you might also want to take a look at my version of this technique. You can see demonstrations at my Web site, www. plutabrothers.com/PBDWeb/p1e.html.

Step 14

Importing a JAR file

Time for the home stretch. The next three steps will finish up the application. You're going to import a JAR file, build your business logic, attach it to your application, and then pretty things up.

This step shows you how to incorporate an external JAR file into your application. The beauty of Java is that you can take advantage of the entire spectrum of open-source code available out there. If so inclined, you can also purchase commercial JAR files to make your job easier. For example, some commercial vendors provide incredible graphics packages that allow you to generate a graphical image on the fly as a GIF or JPEG image and present it to your user.

Frankly, I'm overwhelmed by the amount of free software out there, much of which is written by computer enthusiasts who just want to make great code available to everyone. Some of this stuff is nothing short of amazing, but there's always the tradeoff that, if the stuff breaks, you have to either rely on the good graces of the developer to get things fixed or go in and fix it yourself.

And then there is perhaps one of the most powerful open-source packages ever written: the JTOpen toolbox from IBM. Originally called JT400 because of its AS/400 heritage, JTOpen still retains many naming conventions that recall that history. But even so, the JTOpen package is one of the great pieces of free software available. And not only that, it's supported by IBM!

The JTOpen package is crucial to the design of this application because, among its many capabilities, JTOpen allows you to quickly and easily call an RPG program on the host. So let's get the JAR file in your project and get moving!

Step 14.1—Importing a JAR file

> **GOAL**
>
> Import the Java Toolbox JAR file into your project.

You can import a file into your project in a variety of ways. One is to simply drag and drop the file from Windows Explorer into your /WEB-INF/lib folder under Web Content. We're going to do it a little more carefully, but the result is the same.

You may note that I said the /WEB-INF/lib folder. Why do you put things there? Well, that's one of the "magic" folders in the J2EE architecture. Any JAR file placed in that folder will be available to the application's class loader. That means all the classes in the JAR file can be used by your application.

One nice thing about WDSC is that it recognizes this folder naming convention, and if you copy a JAR file into the folder, it is used for compiling, testing, and deployment. So this is by far the easiest way to use an external JAR file. There are other methods, including setting up the project build path, and each technique has its positive and negative points. But this technique is straightforward and easy to use, so it's my method of choice for the task at hand.

You need only two things to import a JAR file: the name of the JAR file and the fully qualified name of the folder the JAR file resides in. I have included the appropriate JAR file on the CD that comes with this book. On the CD, look for a folder called jtopen_4_3_1. This folder contains the entire downloadable code for JTOpen version 4.3.1, including a folder called lib. In that folder will be a JAR file called jt400.jar. That's the JAR file I'd like you to use.

The procedure is quite simple. First, though, you need to be in the Web perspective. Click on the Web Perspective icon in the perspective bar (Figure 14-1).

❑ **14.1(a) Click on the Web perspective icon.**

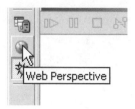

Figure 14-1: Switch to the Web perspective by clicking on the Web Perspective icon.

Next, locate and expand the WEB-INF folder under Web Content.

❑ **14.1(b) Expand the WEB-INF folder.**

Figure 14-2: Expand WEB-INF by clicking on the plus sign (+).

You'll see two folders, classes and lib; lib is where you want the new JAR file. Right-click on the lib folder and select Import . . . as shown in Figure 14-3.

❑ **14.1(c) Right-click on lib and select Import. . . .**

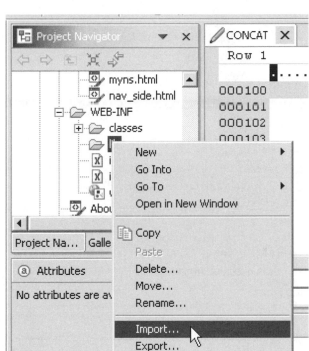

Figure 14-3: Right-click on the lib folder and select Import . . .

The Import wizard will appear. The first thing the wizard wants to know is where your file is coming from. In this case, it's on disk, so select File System and then press Next.

❑ **14.1(d) Click on the File System option and press Next.**

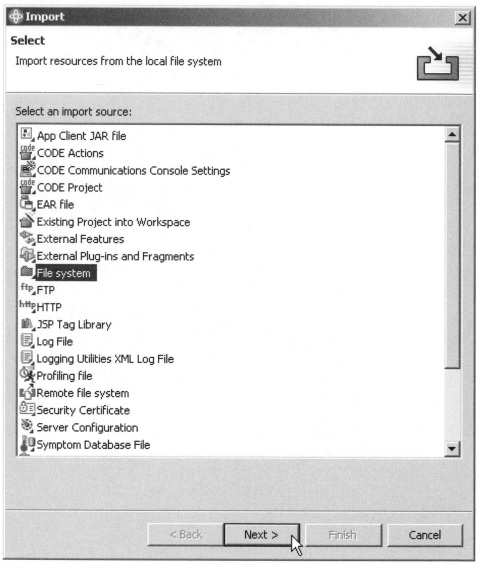

Figure 14-4: Click on File System and press Next.

Now you'll see the File System Import wizard. This is where you need to know the folder and file name. Remember, I said the JAR file was on the accompanying CD, so make sure the CD is in the drive. Also, be sure you know which drive your

CD-ROM is in. I'll assume your CD is in drive D, so enter D:\jtopen_4_3_1\lib into the From directory field as shown in Figure 14-5. Then press the Tab key.

❑ **14.1(e) Enter D:\jtopen_4_3_1\lib into the From directory field and press the Tab key on your keyboard.**

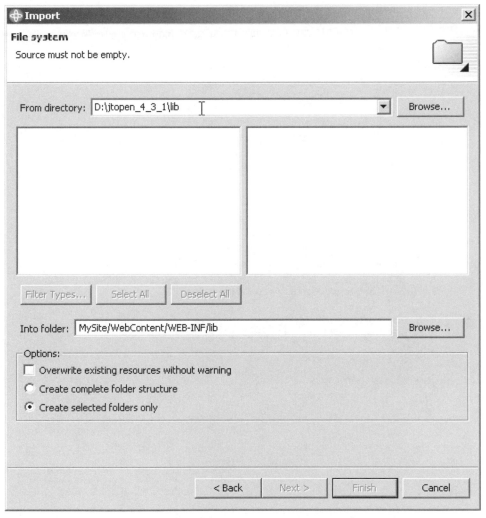

Figure 14-5: Enter D:\jtopen_4_3_1\lib into the From directory field and press the Tab key on your keyboard.

This will cause the lib folder to appear in the left list box. Click on the lib folder (do not check the box next to it).

❑ **14.1(f) Click on the lib folder without checking the box.**

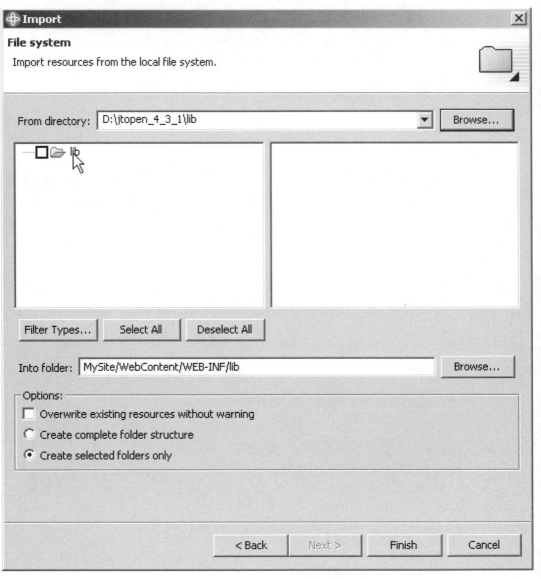

Figure 14-6: Click on the lib folder to show its contents in the right pane.

A list of the eligible files in that folder will then appear in the right list box, as shown in Figure 14-7. Click on the checkbox to the left of jt400.jar and press Finish. Leave the Overwrite existing resources without warning checkbox unchecked, and be sure the Create selected folders only checkbox is selected. A progress bar like the one in Figure 14-8 will appear at the bottom of the wizard, and when the import is done, the dialog will disappear.

❑ **14.1(g) Check the box next to jt400.jar and press Finish.**

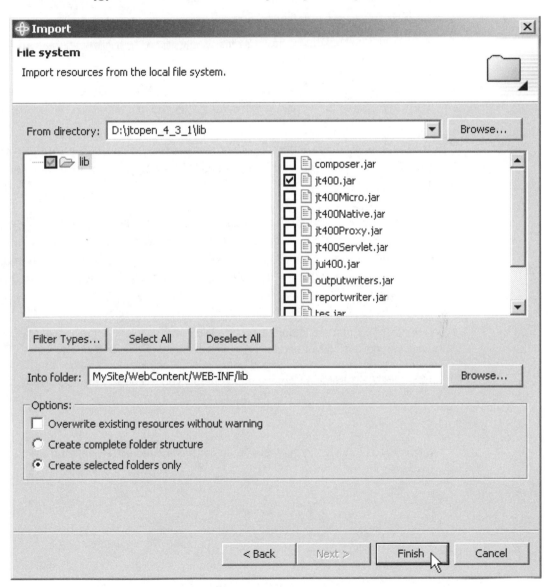

Figure 14-7: Check the box next to jt400.jar and press Finish.

> **Note:** Figure 14-8 is really just the bottom of Figure 14-7; WDSC adds the progress bar when you click Finish.

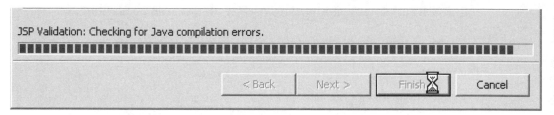

JSP Validation: Checking for Java compilation errors.

| < Back | Next > | Finish | Cancel |

Figure 14-8: The progress bar indicates the status of the import.

The JAR file is now available to your project. Also, because you imported it into the lib folder, the JAR file will be included whenever you export the project as a WAR or EAR file.

Just to double-check, expand the /WEB-INF/lib folder as well as the Libraries folder at the bottom of the project. Both should now contain jt400.jar. The Libraries folder contains all JAR files used by this project, both internal and external, while the /WEB-INF/lib folder contains only those JAR files imported into the project itself.

> **Note:** JAR files that are imported into the WEB-INF/lib folder actually take up space on your disk drive, and they are also included in any EAR or WAR file you may generate when you export your project. The decision whether to import into WEB-INF/lib or not depends on how you will deploy the application.

> **Release Note:** In V5.1.2, the Libraries folder has moved underneath the Java Resources folder.

❑ **14.1(h) Expand /WEB-INF/lib.**

❑ **14.1(i) Expand Libraries.**

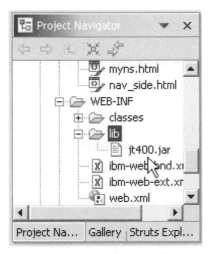

Figure 14-9: The jt400.jar file appears not only in the /WEB-INF/lib folder. . .

Figure 14-10: . . .but in the Libraries folder as well.

Step 14.2—Test the Toolbox

Now you can test the toolbox by using this simple program. TestCONCAT is neither robust nor sophisticated; it sets up a program call, converts two Java strings to EBCDIC, calls the program, converts the EBCDIC results to a Java string, and displays the results. The classes used in this program (and a couple of other closely related classes) are all that are used to write the actual client/server application.

This procedure should be very familiar by now. First, add a new class called TestCONCAT to the test package.

❑ **14.2(a) Right-click on the test package and select New/Class.**

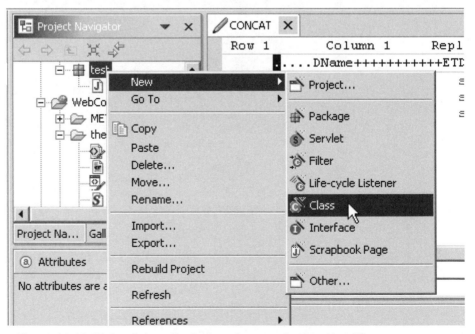

Figure 14-11: Right-click on the test package and select New/Class.

❑ **14.2(b) Enter TestCONCAT into the Name field and press Finish.**

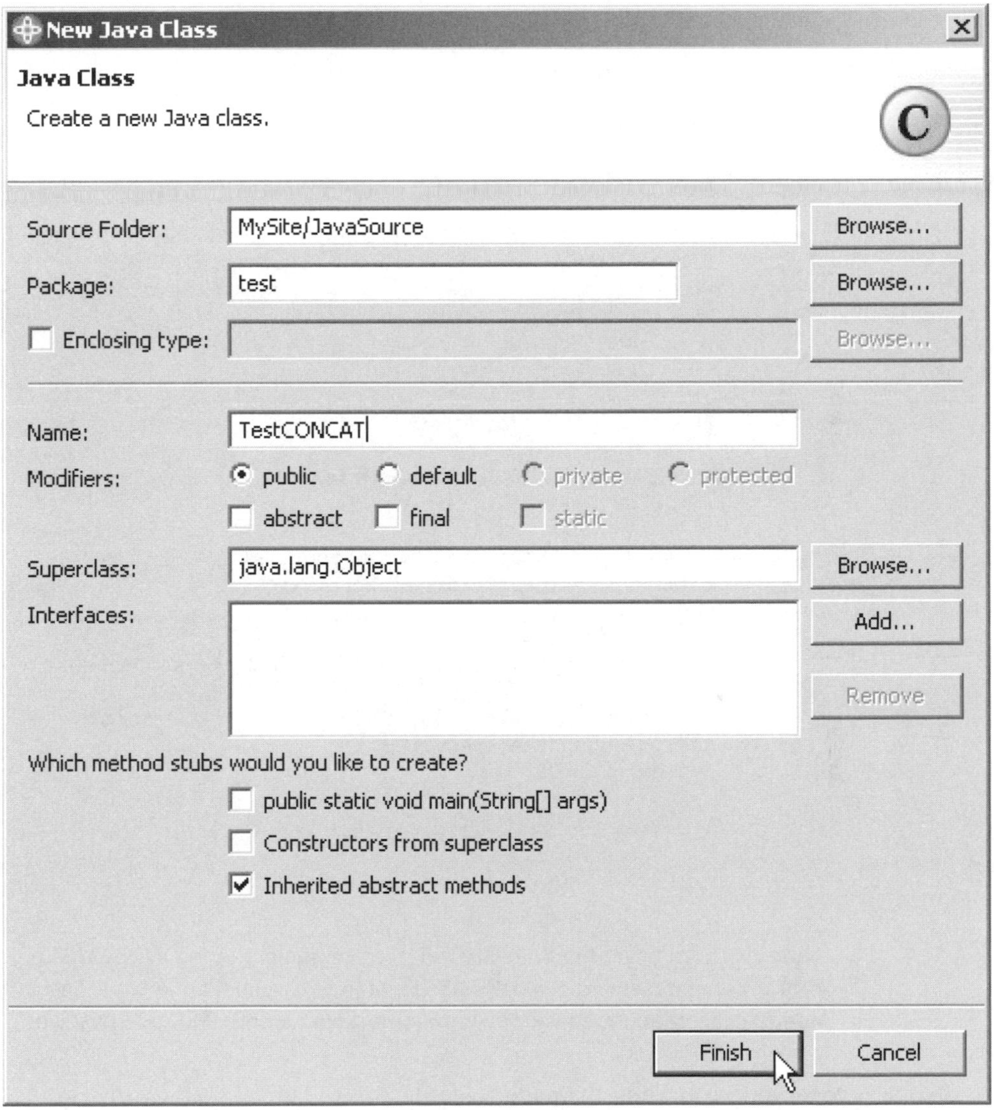

Figure 14-12: Name the class TestCONCAT, leave the other fields at their defaults, and press Finish.

At this point, enter the code from Listing 14-1 or copy it in from the CD-ROM. The code for this class is located in file Step14-2.txt, in the folder Imports.

Listing 14-1: This is the code for the TestCONCAT class.

```
package test;

import com.ibm.as400.access.*;

public class TestCONCAT {

    public static void main(String[] args) throws Exception {

        AS400 host = new AS400("WDSCHOST", "WDSCUSER", "WDSCUSER");
        String path = "/QSYS.LIB/WDSCLIB.LIB/CONCAT.PGM";
        ProgramParameter[] parms = new ProgramParameter[] {
            new ProgramParameter(10),
            new ProgramParameter(10),
            new ProgramParameter(20)
        };
        ProgramCall concat = new ProgramCall(host, path, parms);

        AS400Text text10 = new AS400Text(10);
        AS400Text text20 = new AS400Text(20);

        parms[0].setInputData(text10.toBytes("ABC"));
        parms[1].setInputData(text10.toBytes("123"));
        concat.run();
        String result =
            (String) text20.toObject(parms[2].getOutputData());

        System.out.println("ABC CONCAT 123 = " + result);
        host.disconnectAllServices();
        System.exit(0);
    }
}
```

Note: If you're using the WDSCHOST system name and the WDSCUSER profile with a password of WDSCUSER, then you're fine. Otherwise, line 9 needs to be changed to your own system name, user profile, and password.

Once you've entered the code, save it.

❑ **14.2(c) Enter the code from Listing 14-1; then right-click and select Save.**

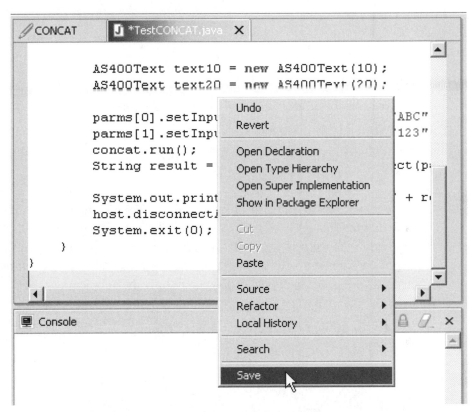

Figure 14-13: After entering the code, right-click and Save.

The last task is to test the program by running it. You can run the program by using the "running man" icon on the main tool bar. Since this is the first time you've run the program, you'll need to set up a launch configuration. This is easily done by using the drop-down arrow just to the right of the running man. Click on that drop-down arrow as shown in Figure 14-14.

❑ **14.2(d) Click on the drop-down arrow to the right of the running man.**

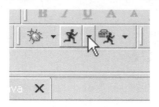

*Figure 14-14: Click on
the drop-down arrow to
the right of the running
man.*

In the menu that appears, select Run As/Java Application, as shown in Figure 14-15. Note that in Figure 14-15, the submenu appears to the *left* of the primary menu, as opposed to the right as is usually the case. This is purely a matter of screen real estate; the submenu wouldn't fit to the right, so it's placed to the left of the main menu. There is no functional difference in how the submenu works.

❑ **14.2(e) Select Run As/Java Application.**

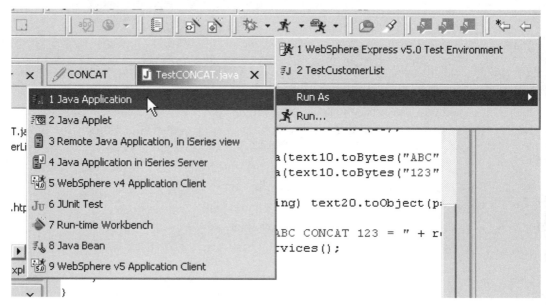

Figure 14-15: Select Run As/Java Application.

Under the covers, this will actually create a new launch configuration for the TestCONCAT program. But you're not worried about that; all you want to see is the results, which should appear in the console window at the bottom of the screen as they do in Figure 14-16.

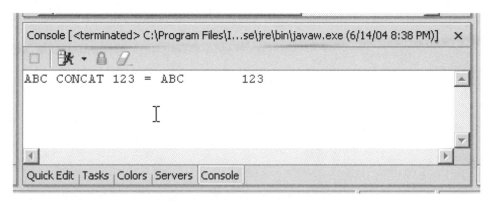

Figure 14-16: ABC concatenated with 123 . . . brilliant!

And that's all there is to it! You've managed to call an RPG program on the host and pass it two variables, receiving one in return—all in about 30 lines of code, and all without using any wizard-generated code.

Sure, you could probably have done it faster using the Web Interaction Wizard, but you own all of this code, and you should understand each line and be able to tweak it as necessary in your application. I can't always say that for code that comes from a code generator.

In any case, you're ready for the big time. Step 15 actually creates live business logic that you can use to fill your Beans. Time to move on!

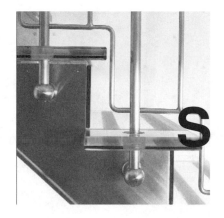

Step 15

Attaching to business logic on the host

I told you we would be moving quickly. Step 14 didn't take long at all, and now you're here on Step 15, ready to finish the bulk of the heavy lifting. It is this step that actually cements the two worlds, GUI and green, together.

In this step, you'll create a database on the iSeries, and then you'll create a program that accesses the database and is designed for client/server processing. Finally, you'll modify your servlet to invoke this program to load the Beans for your JSP. Once done, you will have a true multi-tiered, multi-language, client/server application.

It would actually be easier to create the database using the green-screen, because the GUI tools just haven't caught up yet. In fact, there's no way to easily verify that the database got built correctly (you could use the Data perspective, but that would add another 20 steps to the procedure).

Even though creating the database has a lot more steps than are strictly necessary, you'll be done quickly, and once that's done, the rest of the code is not much more complex than the sample program you wrote in Step 14. On the host side, you're going to read records and return them one at a time in a data structure. If you hit end of file, you'll return an EOF code. The servlet side has a little more additional work: You'll need to initialize the connection and then call the host program until you get an EOF code. On each successful call, you'll use an AS400Structure object to parse the data structure into individual fields and then use those fields to create a Customer.

That's about it. The application is really basic.

Step 15.1—Create the database

> **GOAL**
>
> **Create and populate a simple Customer Master file.**

Using the tools you have learned to date, you'll quickly create a physical file and a program that writes a few records to that file. First, you'll need to get back into the iEdit perspective. Do that by clicking on the iEdit icon in the perspective bar.

❑ **15.1(a) Click on the iEdit icon in the perspective bar.**

Figure 15-1: Switch to the iEdit perspective by clicking on its icon.

Next, you'll need to bring up the Remote Systems view, so click on its fast view icon.

❑ **15.1(b) Click on the Remote Systems fast view icon.**

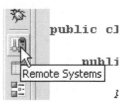

Figure 15-2: Make the Remote Systems view visible by clicking on its fast view icon.

As you've encountered before, if you're starting from a checkpoint, you'll have to log in.

> **Release Note:** In V5.1.2, you won't be prompted until after Step 15.1(g).

❑ **15.1(c) If prompted, enter your user ID and password and press OK.**

Enter Password		✕
System type:	iSeries	
Host name:	WDSCHOST	
User ID:	WDSCUSER	
Password:	********	

☐ Permanently change user ID

☐ Save password

[OK]   [Cancel]

Figure 15-3: Log in if necessary.

Now you're going to have to add a couple of members and compile them. This is a straightforward process: Add the member, enter the code, compile the object. As with all other source code in the book, you can import the code from the accompanying CD-ROM.

❑ **15.1(d) Right-click on QSOURCE and select New/Member....**

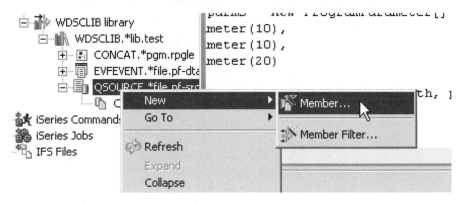

Figure 15-4: Create a new member using the pop-up menu.

❑ **15.1(e) Enter CUSTMAST into the Member field.**

❑ **15.1(f) Enter PF into the Member type field.**

❑ **15.1(g) Type "Customer Master" into the Text field and press Finish.**

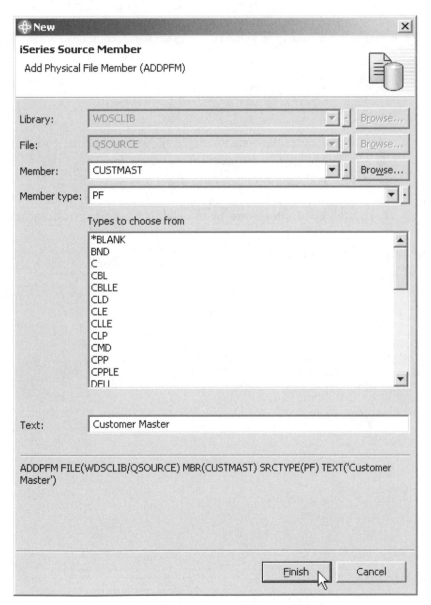

Figure 15-5: Enter the fields as shown and press Finish.

Listing 15-1: Here's the DDS for the Customer Master file.

```
A            R CUSTMASTR
A              CMCUST        6S 0
A              CMNAME        30
A              CMADDR1       30
A              CMADDR2       30
A              CMCITY        25
A              CMSTATE        3
A              CMZIP          9
A              CMPHONE       15
A              CMFAX         15
A              CMEMAIL       64
A            K CMCUST
```

You can now enter the code as shown in Listing 15-1 or copy the code in from the CD. The file to copy is named Step15-1-a.txt in folder Imports. After you've entered the code, right-click in the editor and select Save.

❑ **15.1(h) Enter the code from Listing 15-1, right-click, and select Save.**

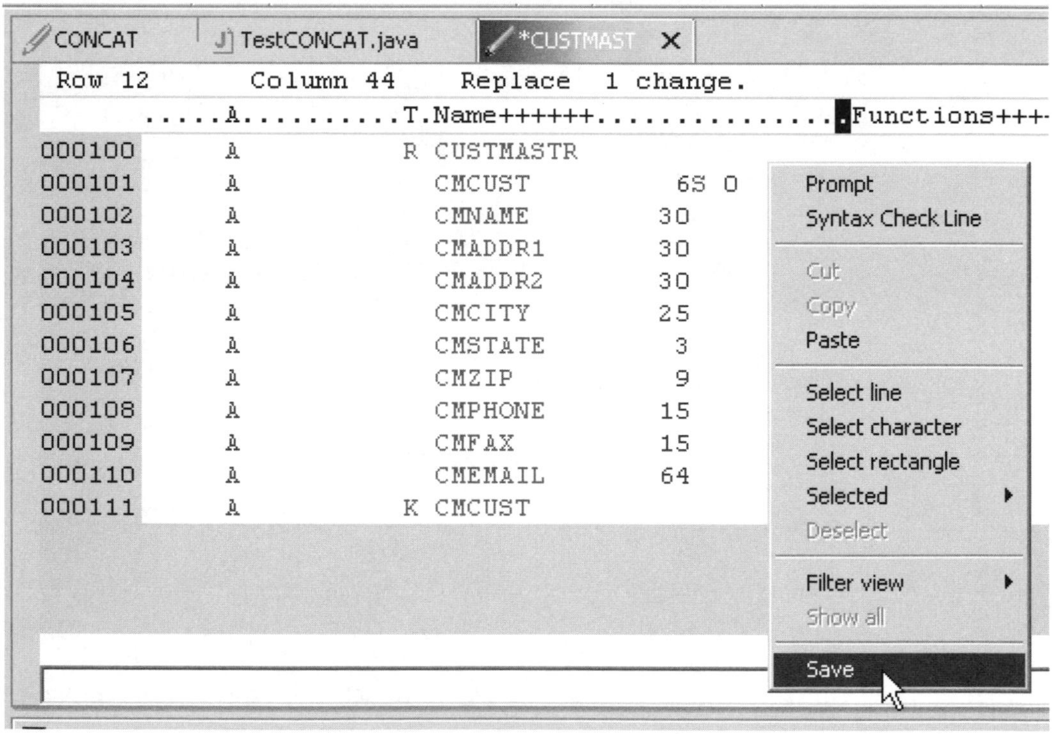

Figure 15-6: After entering the code, right-click and select Save.

Now you can create the physical file. Using the main menu, select Compile/Compile/CRTPF.

❑ **15.1(i) From the main menu, select Compile/Compile/CRTPF.**

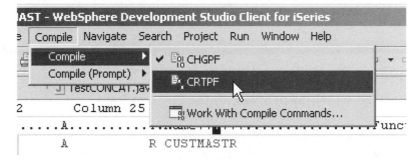

Figure 15-7: From the main menu, select Compile/Compile/CRTPF.

You should see no errors in your iSeries Error List, as shown in Figure 15-8.

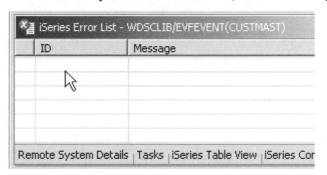

Figure 15-8: An empty error list indicates the compile was successful.

It's time to do the same steps for the RPG program that populates the file.

❑ **15.1(j) Click on the Remote Systems fast view icon.**

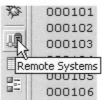

Figure 15-9: Bring up the Remote Systems view.

❑ **15.1(k) Right-click on QSOURCE and select New/Member....**

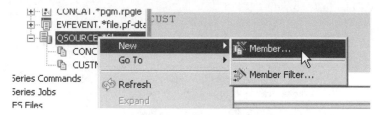

Figure 15-10: Create another new member.

❑ **15.1(l) Enter INZCM into the Member field.**

❑ **15.1(m) Enter RPGLE into the Member type field.**

❑ **15.1(n) Type "Initialize Customer Master" into the Text field.**

❑ **15.1(o) Press Finish.**

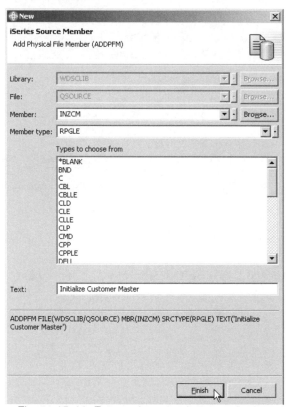

*Figure 15-11: Enter values as shown and press
Finish to create the RPGLE member INZCM.*

Listing 15-2: Program INZCM writes some records to CUSTMAST.

```
    fcustmast  o   e           disk

    c                    eval      CMCUST  = 123456
    c                    eval      CMNAME  = 'Manx Catering'
    c                    eval      CMADDR1 = '1234 Main St.'
    c                    eval      CMADDR2 = ' '
    c                    eval      CMCTTY  - 'Fairfield'
    c                    eval      CMSTATE = 'VA'
    c                    eval      CMZIP   = '24435'
    c                    eval      CMPHONE = '540-555-6634'
    c                    eval      CMFAX   = '540-555-9919'
    c                    eval      CMEMAIL = 'bob@manx.com'
    c                    write     CUSTMASTR

    c                    eval      CMCUST  = 777777
    c                    eval      CMNAME  = 'Lucky Gambling Supply'
    c                    eval      CMADDR2 = ' '
    c                    eval      CMCITY  = 'Washington'
    c                    eval      CMSTATE = 'DC'
    c                    eval      CMZIP   = '20515'
    c                    eval      CMPHONE = '202-224-3121'
    c                    eval      CMFAX   = '202-225-6827'
    c                    eval      CMEMAIL = 'thekid@cincinnati.com'
    c                    write     CUSTMASTR

    c                    eval      CMCUST  = 001987
    c                    eval      CMNAME  = 'THe Lefthand Store'
    c                    eval      CMADDR1 = '7332 Prairie'
    c                    eval      CMADDR2 = ' '
    c                    eval      CMCITY  = 'Springfield'
    c                    eval      CMSTATE = '-'
    c                    eval      CMZIP   = '99999'
    c                    eval      CMPHONE = '877-555-5432'
    c                    eval      CMEMAIL = 'ned@flanders.com'
    c                    write     CUSTMASTR

    c                    eval      *inlr = *on
```

Enter the code as shown in Listing 15-2 or copy the code in from the CD. The file to copy is named Step15-1-b.txt in folder Imports. After you've entered the code, right-click in the editor and select Save.

❏ **15.1(p) Enter the code from Listing 15-2, right-click, and select Save.**

```
CONCAT    TestCONCAT.java    CUSTMAST    *INZCM ×
Row 37        Column 66      Replace   1 change.
      .....CLON01Factor1+++++++Opcode(E)+Extended-factor2+++++++++++++++++++++++++++++Comme:
000122    c                    eval      CMEMAIL = 'thekid@cincinnati.com'
000123    c                    write     CUSTMASTR
000124
000125    c                    eval      CMCUST  = 001987
000126    c                    eval      CMNAME  = 'THe Lefthand Store'
000127    c                    eval      CMADDR1 = '7332 Prairie'
000128    c                    eval      CMADDR2 = ''
000129    c                    eval      CMCITY  = 'Springfield'
000130    c                    eval      CMSTATE = '--'
000131    c                    eval      CMZIP   = '99999'
000132    c                    eval      CMPHONE = '877-555-5432'
000133    c                    eval      CMEMAIL = 'ned@flanders.com'
000134    c                    write     CUSTMASTR
000135
000136    c                    eval      *inlr = *on
```

Context menu items:
New ▶
Context
Prompt
Syntax Check Line
Select Format Line...
Cut
Copy
Paste
Select line
Select character
Select rectangle
Selected ▶
Deselect
Filter view ▶
Show all
Save
Add Breakpoint

```
iSeries Error List - WDSCLIB/EVFEVENT(CUSTMAST)
ID        Message                              Sev...  Line   Location
```

Figure 15-12: Enter the source from Listing 15-2, right-click, and press Save.

Finally, create the RPG program. Using the main menu, select Compile/Compile/CRTBNDRPG. Note that the menu changes to include compile commands appropriate for the source member type.

❏ **15.1(q) From the main menu, select Compile/Compile/CRTBNDRPG.**

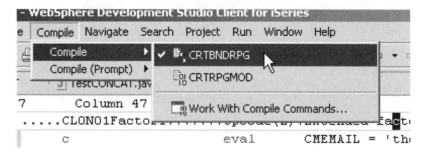

Figure 15-13: Compile the RPGLE program using the CRTBNDRPG command.

This compile command, though, returns an error in the iSeries Error List, as shown in Figure 15-14. However, that is just an informational error message and does not affect the program; you can ignore it.

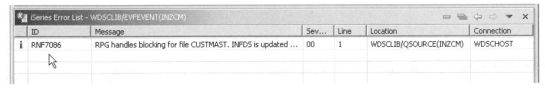

Figure 15-14: Ignore this informational message.

Running the program will require one last trip to the Remote Systems view.

❑ **15.1(r) Click on the Remote Systems fast view icon.**

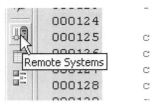

Figure 15-15: Click on the Remote Systems icon.

Your new program and file will not appear until you refresh the library's contents. Do this by right-clicking on the library and selecting Refresh, as shown in Figure 15-16.

❑ **15.1(s) Right-click on the entry WDSCLIB.*lib.test and select Refresh.**

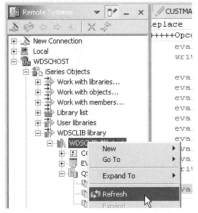

Figure 15-16: The Refresh option will show any new objects in the library.

The new objects appear. The new members also appear in QSOURCE. At this point, you can now run your new program. Do that by right-clicking on the program and selecting Run/Normal as shown in Figure 15-17.

> **Release Note:** In V5.1.2, Run/Normal no longer exists as an option; as far as I can tell, it has been replaced by Run As/iSeries application in RSE Job.

❑ **15.1(t) Right-click on the program INZCM and select Run/Normal.**

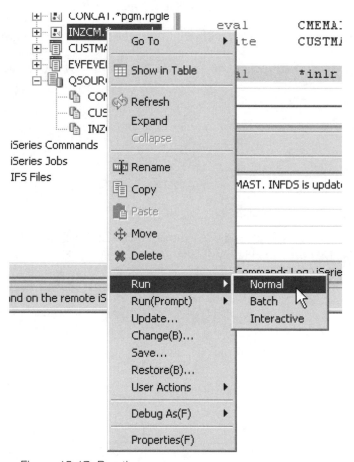

Figure 15-17: Run the new program.

As I said earlier, there's no easy way right now to see that the database has been properly populated. You can indirectly check what has happened by looking at the log. Click on the log, expand it, and then roll down to see the last thing that happened.

❏ **15.1(u) Click on the iSeries Commands Log tab.**

❏

Figure 15-18: Open the log view by clicking on the iSeries Commands Log tab.

15.1(v) Double-click the title bar to maximize the view.

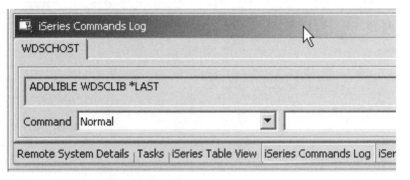

Figure 15-19: Maximize the view.

❏ **15.1(w) Scroll down to the bottom.**

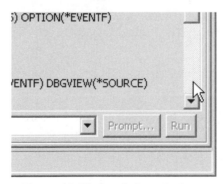

Figure 15-20: Scroll down to the bottom.

You'll see a view like the one in Figure 15-21. The important line is the bottom line: Command has completed. This indicates that the call to INZCM completed successfully. Remember to restore the view after you've seen it.

❏ **15.1(x) Double-click the title bar again to restore the workbench.**

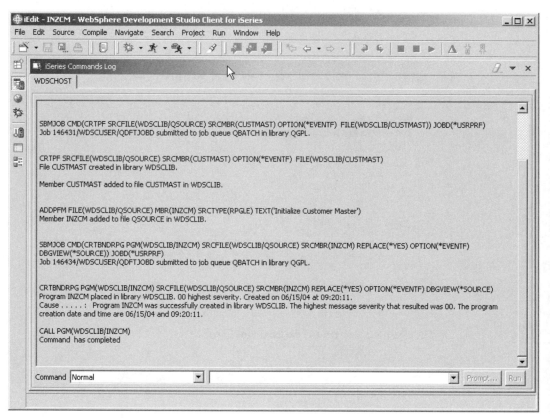

Figure 15-21: The log file shows a successful completion message.

Now, you can assume that the command worked or you can double-check using a green-screen, as shown in the following figures. Execute the command DSPPFM WDSCLIB/CUSTMAST to see these pictures.

```
                    Display Physical File Member
File . . . . . . :   CUSTMAST           Library  . . . . :   WDSCLIB
Member . . . . . :   CUSTMAST           Record . . . . . :   1
Control  . . . .    _____          Column . . . . . :   1
Find . . . . . .    _____
*...+....1....+....2....+....3....+....4....+....5....+....6....+....7....+...
123456Manx Catering                 1234 Main St.
777777Lucky Gambling Supply         1234 Main St.
001987THe Lefthand Store            7332 Prairie
                    ****** END OF DATA ******
```

Figure 15-22: These are the leftmost 80 characters of the CUSTMAST file.

```
                    Display Physical File Member
File . . . . . . :   CUSTMAST           Library  . . . . :   WDSCLIB
Member . . . . . :   CUSTMAST           Record . . . . . :   1
Control  . . . .    _____          Column . . . . . :   79
Find . . . . . .    _____
.8....+....9....+....0....+....1....+....2....+....3....+....4....+....5....+.
            Fairfield          VA 24435    540-555-6634    540-555-
            Washington         DC 20515    202-224-3121    202-225-
            Springfield        -- 99999    877-555-5432    202-225-
                    ****** END OF DATA ******
```

Figure 15-23: And these are the next 80 characters.

```
                    Display Physical File Member
File . . . . . . :   CUSTMAST           Library  . . . . :   WDSCLIB
Member . . . . . :   CUSTMAST           Record . . . . . :   1
Control  . . . .    _____          Column . . . . . :   157
Find . . . . . .    _____
...6....+....7....+....8....+....9....+....0....+....1....+....2....+..
9919    bob@manx.com
6827    thekid@cincinnati.com
6827    ned@flanders.com
                    ****** END OF DATA ******
```

Figure 15-24: And finally, here's the tail end of the file.

Step 15.2—Writing the business logic

> **GOAL**
>
> Write the business logic program that will return the customer data.

You're almost done! This is the last piece of RPG code to write. This program is designed to return the records in the customer file. How you choose to write this program is going to depend entirely on your style. If you ask three programmers the proper way to do this, you will get three different answers. It's really a matter of personal style.

I'm going to make this particular example as simple as possible. This program has two parameters: a data structure for the customer record and a return code that indicates whether the read was successful or not. The program will be very simple: It will read records and, while not at the end of file, will return a value of '0' in the return code. When the program hits end of file, it will return a value of '1' in the return code and will reset the file to the beginning for the next read.

The beginning of this step should be very familiar by now.

❑ **15.2(a) Click on the Remote Systems fast view icon.**

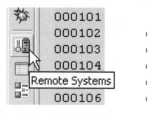

Figure 15-25: Bring up the Remote Systems view.

If you're starting from a Checkpoint, you'll have to log in.

Note: As in the previous step, in V5.1.2 you won't be prompted until after Step 15.2(g).

❑ **15.2(b) If prompted, enter your user ID and password and press OK.**

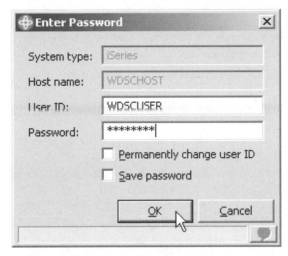

Figure 15-26: Log in if necessary.

❑ **15.2(c) Right-click on QSOURCE and select New/Member... .**

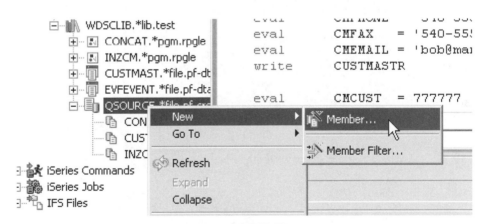

Figure 15-27: Add a new member to QSOURCE.

❑ **15.2(d) Enter SVRCM into the Member field.**

❑ **15.2(e) Enter RPGLE into the Member type field.**

❑ **15.2(f) Type "Customer Master Server" into the Text field.**

❑ **15.2(g) Press Finish.**

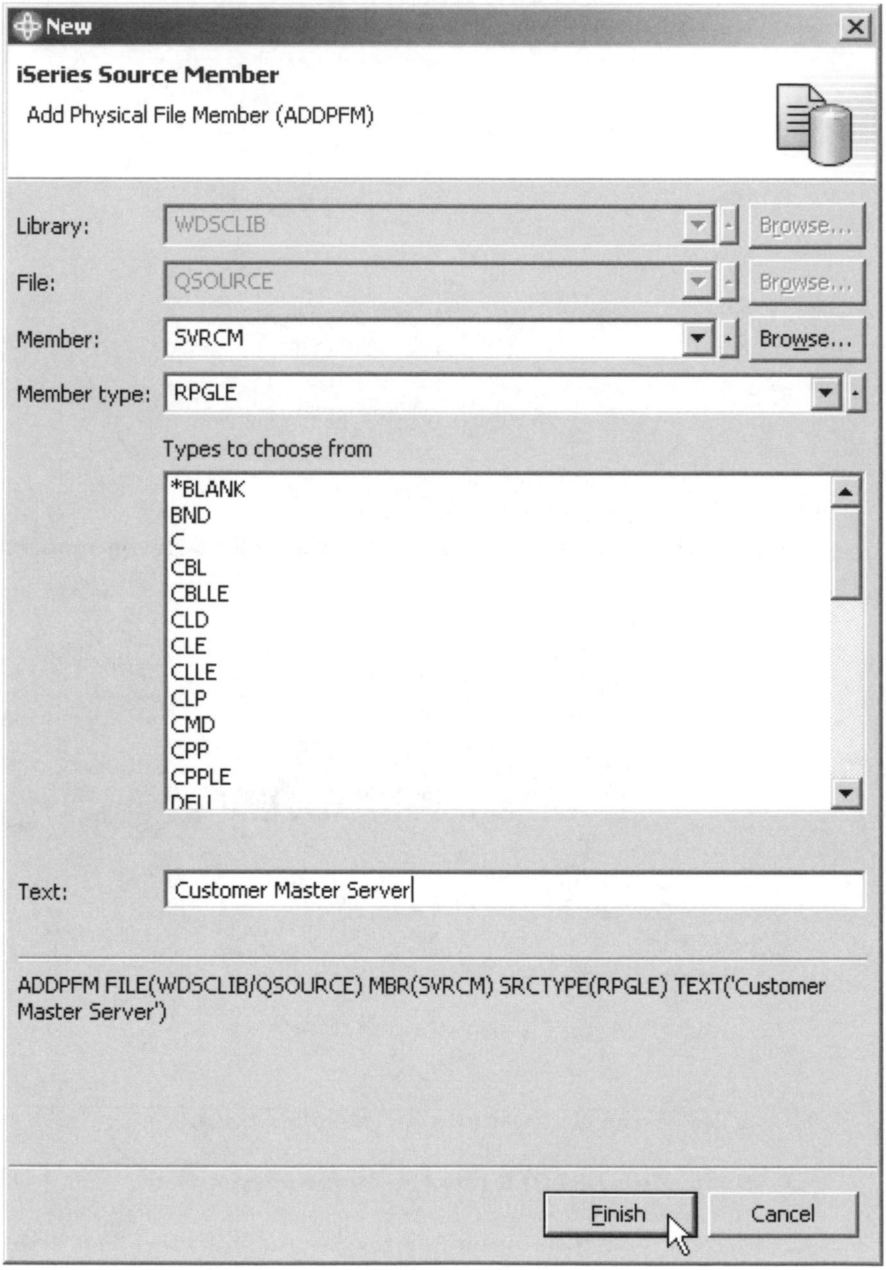

Figure 15-28: Enter the fields as shown and press Finish.

Listing 15-3: This is the Customer Master server program.

```
fcustmast   if    e           k disk
d dscust          e ds                     extname(custmast)
d eof             s             1

c       *entry         plist
c                      parm                      dscust
c                      parm                      eof

c                      read      custmast
c                      eval      eof = %eof(custmast)
c                      if        eof = '1'
c       *start         setll     custmast
c                      endif

c                      return
```

Enter the code as shown in Listing 15-3 or copy the code in from the CD. The file to copy is named Step15-2.txt in folder Imports. After you've entered the code, right-click in the editor and select Save.

❑ **15.2(h) Enter the code from Listing 15-3, right-click, and select Save.**

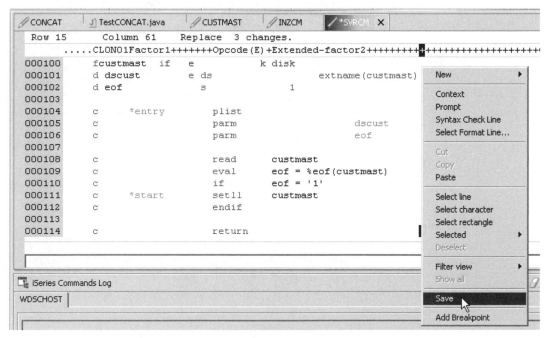

Figure 15-29: Enter the code from Listing 15-3, right-click, and Save.

❑ **15.2(i) From the main menu, select Compile/Compile/CRTBNDRPG.**

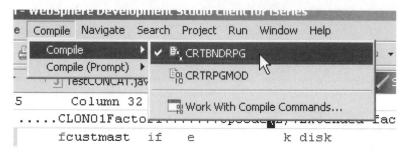

Figure 15-30: Compile the program using the main menu option.

And that's it! You'll notice in Figure 15-31 that there are a lot of errors. However, these are all informational errors. To be sure, double-click on the title bar to maximize the view.

❑ **15.2(j) Double-click on the title bar to maximize the iSeries Error List.**

	ID	Message
i	RNF7066	Record-Format CUSTMASTR not used for input or output.
i	RNF7031	The name or indicator CMEMAIL is not referenced.
i	RNF7031	The name or indicator CMFAX is not referenced.
i	RNF7031	The name or indicator CMPHONE is not referenced.

iSeries Error List - WDSCLIB/EVFEVENT(SVRCM)

Figure 15-31: Maximize the view.

When you're satisfied that the list is all warning errors (as shown in Figure 15-32), double-click the title bar again to restore the workbench and continue to the next step.

> **Hint:** Another option is to filter the messages. The downward-pointing arrow icon in the upper right corner of the error list (next to the "X") allows you to filter errors by severity. Uncheck the information errors option to hide information errors.

❑ 15.2(k) Double-click on the title bar to restore the workbench.

iSeries Error List - WDSCLIB/EVFEVENT(SVRCM)

	ID	Message	Sev...	Line	Location	Connection
i	RNF7066	Record-Format CUSTMASTR not used for input or output.	00	1	WDSCLIB/QSOURCE(SVRCM)	WDSCHOST
i	RNF7031	The name or indicator CMEMAIL is not referenced.	00	10	WDSCLIB/QSOURCE(SVRCM)	WDSCHOST
i	RNF7031	The name or indicator CMFAX is not referenced.	00	9	WDSCLIB/QSOURCE(SVRCM)	WDSCHOST
i	RNF7031	The name or indicator CMPHONE is not referenced.	00	8	WDSCLIB/QSOURCE(SVRCM)	WDSCHOST
i	RNF7031	The name or indicator CMZIP is not referenced.	00	7	WDSCLIB/QSOURCE(SVRCM)	WDSCHOST
i	RNF7031	The name or indicator CMSTATE is not referenced.	00	6	WDSCLIB/QSOURCE(SVRCM)	WDSCHOST
i	RNF7031	The name or indicator CMCITY is not referenced.	00	5	WDSCLIB/QSOURCE(SVRCM)	WDSCHOST
i	RNF7031	The name or indicator CMADDR2 is not referenced.	00	4	WDSCLIB/QSOURCE(SVRCM)	WDSCHOST
i	RNF7031	The name or indicator CMADDR1 is not referenced.	00	3	WDSCLIB/QSOURCE(SVRCM)	WDSCHOST
i	RNF7031	The name or indicator CMNAME is not referenced.	00	2	WDSCLIB/QSOURCE(SVRCM)	WDSCHOST
i	RNF7031	The name or indicator CMCUST is not referenced.	00	1	WDSCLIB/QSOURCE(SVRCM)	WDSCHOST

Figure 15-32: After checking to make sure these are all warnings, double-click to restore the view.

Step 15.3—Modify the servlet

> ### GOAL
> Modify your servlet to call the SVRCM program.

This is the last piece of the puzzle. In this step, you'll modify the CustListProxy class to call the SVRCM program to retrieve data from the CUSTMAST file.

One reason I want to do this is to show you how, as your development progresses, you continue to evolve your workbench to suit your needs. In this case, you need to modify a Java class. However, you have no access to the Java source through the iEdit perspective. But you can easily remedy that by adding a view to your perspective.

Since this is a navigation view that you would typically use to select a member for editing, you want to be able to bring it up and then have it go away, leaving the bulk of your workbench for the editor. This is a perfect use for a fast view, so that's what you'll do.

First, add the view. You do this through the Window menu of the main menu bar. You haven't spent much time with this menu, but it has a lot of powerful features. In this case, use the option Show View/Other… from the Window menu, as shown in Figure 15-33.

❑ **15.3(a) From the main menu, select Window/Show View/Other....**

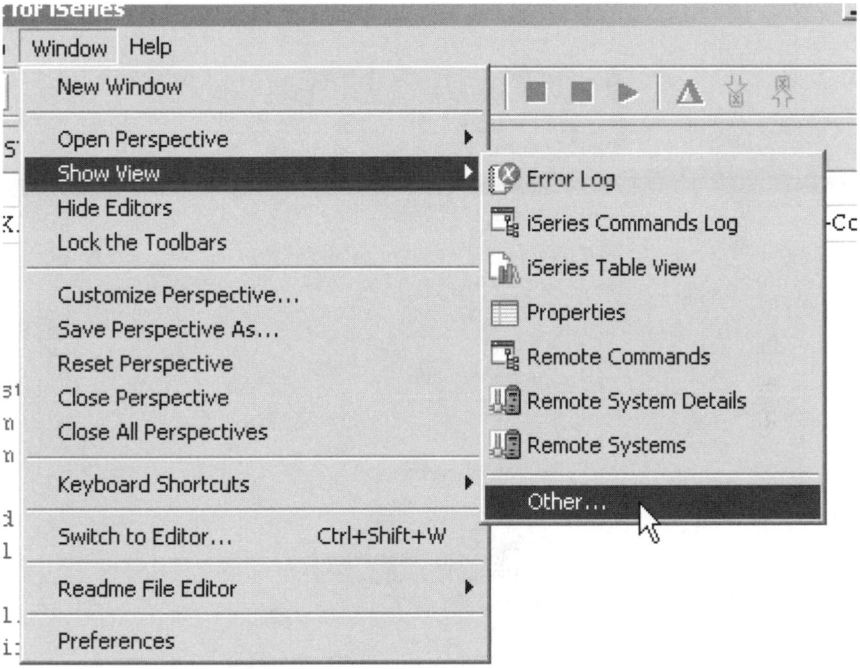

Figure 15-33: From the main menu, select Window/Show View/Other....

This brings up a list of view categories. The view you want, Package Explorer, is located in the Java category. Expand the Java category, select Package Explorer, and press OK, as shown in Figure 15-34.

❑ **15.3(b) Expand the Java category, select Package Explorer, and press OK.**

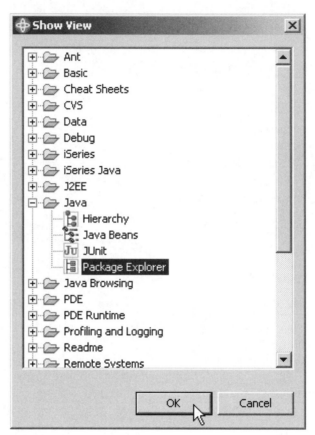

Figure 15-34: Expand the Java category, select Package Explorer, and press OK.

The Package Explorer view will be added to your perspective. However, it will show up not as a fast view, but as a normal view. In this case, it will show up in the bottom pane of your workbench. To make it a fast view, you need to right click on the title bar and select Fast View from the pop-up menu, as shown in Figure 15-35.

❑ **15.3(c) Right-click on the new view's title bar and select Fast View.**

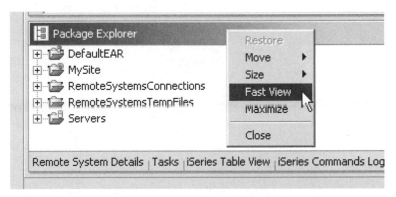

Figure 15-35: To make a fast view, right-click on the title bar and select Fast View.

The view will disappear, and you'll see a new icon among your fast views (in the perspective bar on the left). You want to use that view now, so click on it.

❑ **15.3(d) Click on the Package Explorer fast view.**

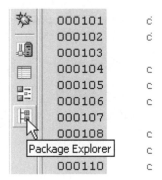

Figure 15-36: Click on the Package Explorer fast view to make it visible.

You'll see your entire workbench laid out by project. Now, you need to navigate down to the source code you want to change. The fast view remembers its state, so you don't have to do this drilldown procedure every time you open it. Start by expanding the MySite project.

❏ **15.3(e) Expand the MySite project.**

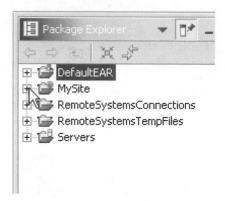

Figure 15-37: Expand the MySite project.

Then expand JavaSource and the package com.mycomp.app, and finally double-click on CustListProxy.java, as shown in Figure 15-38.

❏ **15.3(f) Expand JavaSource.**

❏ **15.3(g) Expand com.mycomp.app.**

❏ **15.3(h) Double-click on CustListProxy.java.**

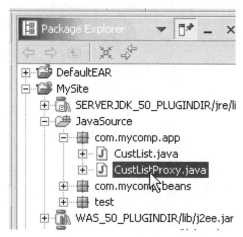

Figure 15-38: Expand JavaSource and com.mycomp.app. Then, double-click on CustListProxy.java.

Listing 15-4: This is the updated CustListProxy.java.

```
package com.mycomp.app;

import com.mycomp.beans.*;
import com.ibm.as400.access.*;

import java.io.*;
import javax.servlet.*;
import javax.servlet.http.*;

public class CustListProxy {

        private HttpServlet servlet;
        private HttpSession session;
        private HttpServletRequest req;
        private HttpServletResponse res;

        // Communication variables
        private AS400 host;
        private CommandCall addlible;
        private ProgramCall server;
        private String path;
        private ProgramParameter[] parms;

        // Translation variables
        private AS400Structure dscust;

        // The constructor does a little more now. It not only stores
        // the initialization variables, it also sets up the conversion
        // structure and connects to the host. One other thing: it
        // also throws an exception now.
        public CustListProxy(HttpServlet servlet, HttpSession session)
                throws ServletException
        {
                this.servlet = servlet;
                this.session = session;

                // Create data structure converter
                dscust = new AS400Structure(
                        new AS400DataType[] {
                                new AS400Text(6),
                                new AS400Text(30),
                                new AS400Text(30),
                                new AS400Text(30),
                                new AS400Text(25),
                                new AS400Text(3),
                                new AS400Text(9),
                                new AS400Text(15),
                                new AS400Text(15),
                                new AS400Text(64),
                        });

                // Set up host communication objects
                host = new AS400("WDSCHOST", "WDSCUSER", "WDSCUSER");
```

```
            addlible = new CommandCall(host, "ADDLIBLE WDSCLIB");
            path = "/QSYS.LIB/WDSCLIB.LIB/SVRCM.PGM";
            parms = new ProgramParameter[] {
                    new ProgramParameter(dscust.getByteLength()),
                    new ProgramParameter(1)
            };
            server = new ProgramCall(host, path, parms);

            // Add WDSCLIB to the server job library list
            try {
                    addlible.run();
            } catch (Exception e) {
                    throw new ServletException("Initialization error:\n" + e);
            }

    }

    // doGet and doPost both do the same thing:
    //    Save request information
    //    Invoke doRequest
    protected void doGet(HttpServletRequest req, HttpServletResponse res)
    throws ServletException, IOException {
            this.req = req;
            this.res = res;
            doRequest();
    }

    protected void doPost(HttpServletRequest req, HttpServletResponse res)
    throws ServletException, IOException {
            this.req = req;
            this.res = res;
            doRequest();
    }

    // The only change here is to invoke getCustomers to get live data
    // rather than create a dummy CustomerList. The live data goes into
    // the session, and then I still forward the request to the JSP.
    private void doRequest() throws ServletException, IOException {
            CustomerList cl = getCustomers();
            session.setAttribute("customers", cl);
            servlet.getServletContext().
                    getRequestDispatcher("CustList.jsp").
                            forward(req, res);
    }

    // And here's all the work. All I do is create an empty CustomerList,
    // then start calling the server program. As long as the result code
    // is an EBCDIC '0' (0xF0) then I parse the data structure and use it
    // to create a new Customer, which is then added to the list.
    // Once I receive an EOF code (anything other than 0xF0), I return the
    // list to the caller.
    private CustomerList getCustomers() throws ServletException
    {
            CustomerList cl = new CustomerList();
            try {
                    server.run();
```

```
                        while (parms[1].getOutputData()[0] == (byte) 0xF0)
                        {
                                Object[] co =
                                        (Object[])
dscust.toObject(parms[0].getOutputData()));
                                cl.addCustomer(
                                        new Customer(
                                                (String) co[0], (String) co[1],
(String) co[2],
                                                (String) co[3], (String) co[4],
(String) co[5],
                                                (String) co[6], (String) co[7],
(String) co[8],
                                                (String) co[9]
                                ));
                                server.run();
                        }
                } catch (Exception e) {
                        throw new ServletException("Runtime error:\n" + e);
                }
                return cl;
        }
}
```

At this point, you can enter in the new code in Listing 15-4 (or, of course, copy it in from the CD). The file is Step15-3.txt in the Imports folder. This version of CustListProxy.java has quite a bit more code than the original, but that's because the original version really didn't do anything. This version actually creates a connection to the host, sets up the environment, and then calls the RPG program to retrieve the data. It also translates the data structure received from the program into strings and uses those to create Customer objects. In fact, considering all that this program does, it's really quite short.

You may wonder why I didn't just use JDBC. Of my reasons, the most important is that, with this architecture, the servlet needs no knowledge of the database or where the files reside. And while in this case the data structure happens to be the same layout as the physical file, there's no reason this has to stay this way. The file layout can change, fields can be added, and *the servlet does not need to change.* This is the crucial factor in a message-based design.

In any case, it's now time to finish the process. First, save the code.

❑ **15.3(i) Right-click in the editor and select Save.**

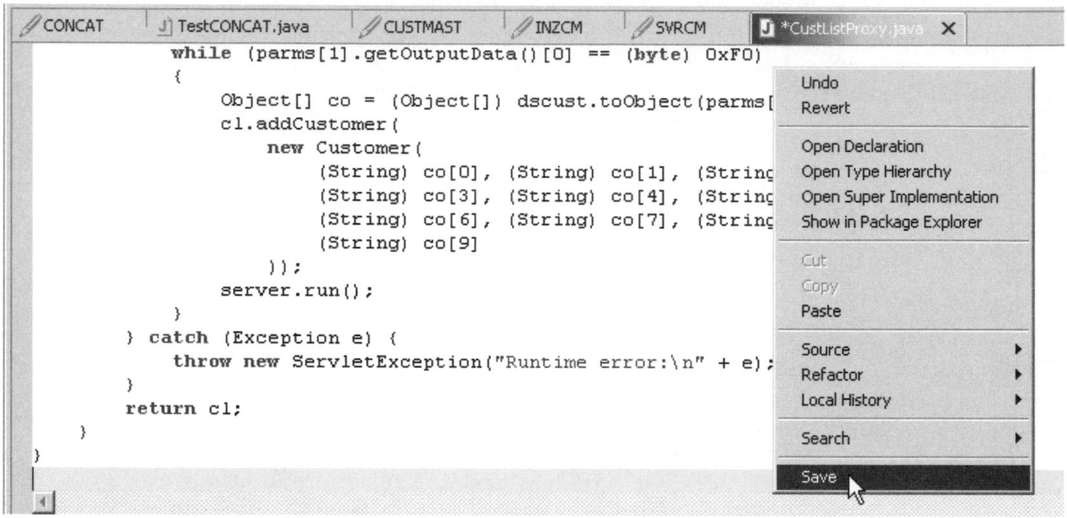

```
┌──────────┬─────────────────┬──────────┬─────────┬────────┬─────────────────────────┐
│ CONCAT   │ TestCONCAT.java │ CUSTMAST │ INZCM   │ SVRCM  │ *CustListProxy.java   ✕ │
└──────────┴─────────────────┴──────────┴─────────┴────────┴─────────────────────────┘
        while (parms[1].getOutputData()[0] == (byte) 0xF0)
        {
                                                              ┌───────────────────────────┐
            Object[] co = (Object[]) dscust.toObject(parms[   │ Undo                      │
            cl.addCustomer(                                   │ Revert                    │
                new Customer(                                 ├───────────────────────────┤
                    (String) co[0], (String) co[1], (Strinç   │ Open Declaration          │
                    (String) co[3], (String) co[4], (Strinç   │ Open Type Hierarchy       │
                    (String) co[6], (String) co[7], (Strinç   │ Open Super Implementation │
                    (String) co[9]                            │ Show in Package Explorer  │
                ));                                           ├───────────────────────────┤
            server.run();                                     │ Cut                       │
        }                                                     │ Copy                      │
    } catch (Exception e) {                                   │ Paste                     │
        throw new ServletException("Runtime error:\n" + e);   ├───────────────────────────┤
    }                                                         │ Source                  ▶ │
    return cl;                                                │ Refactor                ▶ │
}                                                             │ Local History           ▶ │
}                                                             ├───────────────────────────┤
                                                              │ Search                  ▶ │
                                                              ├───────────────────────────┤
                                                              │ Save                      │
                                                              └───────────────────────────┘
```

Figure 15-39: Right-click in the editor to bring up the pop-up menu and select Save.

Here's where a good IDE is worth its weight in gold. WDSC will save the new source code and compile it. And even though this class is syntactically correct, because the constructor now throws an exception, CustList.java must be changed. WDSC goes further than many IDEs, providing the error in the Tasks view at the bottom of the screen, as shown in Figure 15-40. This error is also a link; double-click on it as shown and the source will be opened and positioned to the error, as shown in Figure 15-41.

❑ **15.3(j) Double-click on the error.**

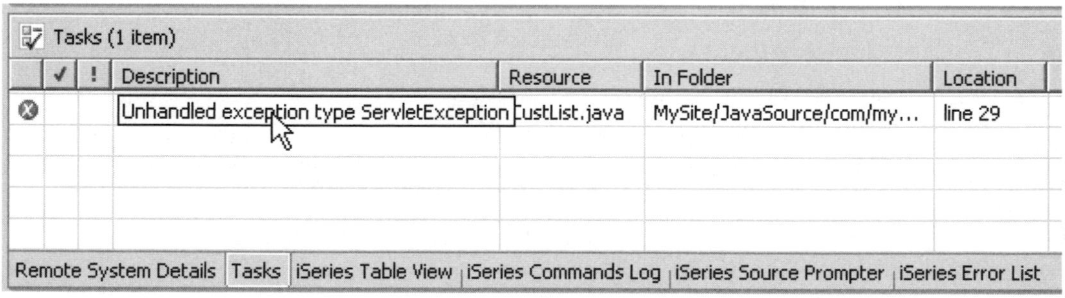

☒ Tasks (1 item)					
✓	!	Description	Resource	In Folder	Location
⊗		Unhandled exception type ServletException	CustList.java	MySite/JavaSource/com/my...	line 29

Remote System Details | Tasks | iSeries Table View | iSeries Commands Log | iSeries Source Prompter | iSeries Error List

Figure 15-40: Double-click on this new error and you will be taken to the code in question.

```
private CustListProxy getProxy(HttpServletRequest req)
{
    HttpSession session = req.getSession(true);
    CustListProxy proxy = (CustListProxy) session.getAttribute(PROXY);
    if (proxy == null)
    {
        proxy = new CustListProxy(this, session);
        session.setAttribute(PROXY, proxy);
    }
    return proxy;
}
```

Figure 15-41: CustList.java is positioned to the error caused by changes in CustListProxy.java

To fix this error, simply make getProxy throw the ServletException as well. If an error occurs, it will show up in the browser window. Figure 15-42 shows the changed line. Make this change and save the code.

Hint: If you click on the error in the left-hand column of the editor, a list of suggestions of how to fix the error will appear, one of which is "add throws clause." Double-clicking on that option will add the throws clause you are instructed to add manually in Step 15.3(k).

❑ **15.3(k) Add the throws clause as shown and save the source.**

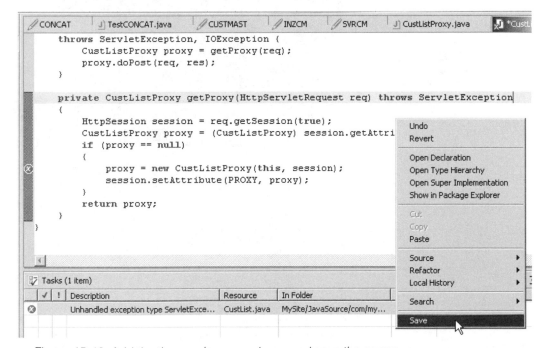

Figure 15-42: Add the throws clause as shown and save the source.

At this point, all errors are resolved and you can finally test the code. The Package Explorer also allows you to launch the application, so click on the Package Explorer fast view icon as shown in Figure 15-43.

❑ **15.3(l) Click on the Package Explorer fast view icon.**

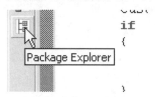

Figure 15-43: You can also launch the application from the Package Explorer, so open it.

This next part should be very familiar. Expand the WebContent folder if necessary. Then, right-click on index.html and select Run on Server… (you could also launch in Debug mode if you needed to).

❑ **15.3(m) Right-click on index.html and select Run on Server….**

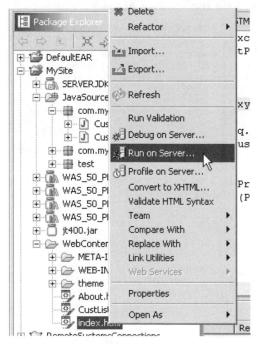

Figure 15-44: Right-click on index.html and select Run on Server….

The standard Server Selection dialog will come up. Just press Finish and wait for the server to start and the index page to come up.

❑ **15.3(n) Press Finish on the Server Selection dialog.**

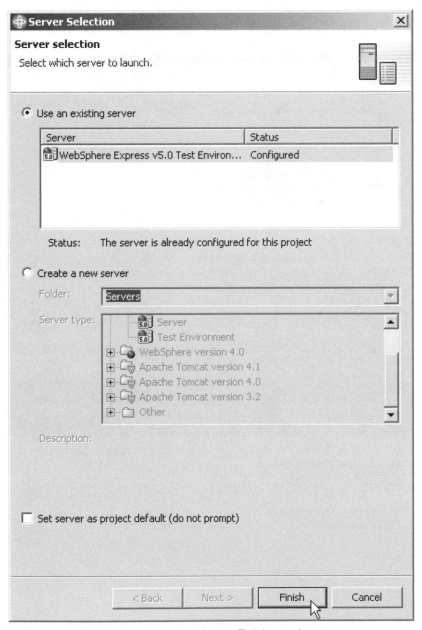

Figure 15-45: On this dialog, just press Finish, as always.

Eventually, you will see the index page as shown in Figure 15-46. Click on Customers to see the final product of your labors to this point.

❑ **15.3(o) Click on Customers.**

Figure 15-46: Click on Customers.

And behold! The data is actually coming from the host!

Figure 15-47: The final product!

You can tell that your modifications have taken effect because of one change I made specifically (I changed the email address for the last line to be thekid@cincinatti.com rather than cincinnati@thekid.com) and one change that was inadvertent (I capitalized the letter "H" in "THe" in the first line). And despite that typo, it works! A true message-based client/server application, written entirely using WDSC!

Not bad, eh?

InStep 15.3.a—Code review

> ### GOAL
> In this step, you'll see how the code for both the server program and the servlet proxy is written and why it was written that way.

I'm going to go into the code for the RPG server program and the servlet that calls it in some detail, as well as provide some direction as to how to make these programs a bit more useful in the future. You can skip this part entirely if you're just itching to get the application done. Step 16 really does quite a bit along the lines of making things pretty and getting your application ready for the Web.

However, if you want some insight into the client/server architecture, you probably want to take the time to read this.

First, take a look at the RPG server program.

```
fcustmast  if   e          k disk
d dscust        e ds                  extname(custmast)
d eof           s             1

c      *entry       plist
c                   parm                        dscust
c                   parm                        eof

c                   read     custmast
c                   eval     eof = %eof(custmast)
c                   if       eof = '1'
c      *start       setll    custmast
c                   endif

c                   return
```

Listing 15-5: This is the Customer Master server program.

As you can see, there's very little to this one. But that's the nature of this particular program and this particular file. All this server does is return all the records in the file. Note that care is taken to reset the file to the beginning when EOF is reached. You should try to guess what would happen if that SETLL was not performed.

Remove it and try the application and see what happens. Then see what happens the second time you call the server.

In a larger, more robust system, the server would have two major feature enhancements. The first would be the ability to specify filters and orders. That is, you could filter by, say, a state code and then order by name alphabetically. Especially for servers that return lists, it's very possible that you might find embedded SQL useful. The data structure parameter would become an input parameter and would house the selection and ordering criteria. The second enhancement would be the ability to return multiple record types. This is more important in situations where you need to fetch header and detail records. In those cases, your data structure may have to be a union; that is, you may need to return more than one type of data structure, so make it as large as the largest record to be returned.

On to the servlet. Or really, the servlet proxy, since the servlet barely changes (if you'll recall, the only change to CustList was the addition of a throws clause in the getProxy method). I've already discussed the servlet proxy in some detail back in InStep 9.4.a, so in this step, I'll only discuss the modifications. After each shaded section of code, I'll discuss the change.

```
package com.mycomp.app;

import com.mycomp.beans.*;
import com.ibm.as400.access.*;
```

In order to use JTOpen, I will need to include it.

```
import java.io.*;
import javax.servlet.*;
import javax.servlet.http.*;

public class CustListProxy {

        private HttpServlet servlet;
        private HttpSession session;
        private HttpServletRequest req;
        private HttpServletResponse res;

        // Communication variables
        private AS400 host;
        private CommandCall addlible;
```

```
        private ProgramCall server;
        private String path;
        private ProgramParameter[] parms;
```

The communication variables are almost all from JTOpen and are used to either invoke a command or call a program on the host.

```
        // Translation variables
        private AS400Structure dscust;
```

This is a bit of a new concept, an AS400Structure. But as you'll see in a moment, it's really no more than an internally described data structure. We use them to convert EBCDIC data structures into Java objects.

```
        // The constructor does a little more now. It not only stores
        // the initialization variables, it also sets up the conversion
        // structure and connects to the host. One other thing: It
        // also throws an exception now.
        public CustListProxy(HttpServlet servlet, HttpSession session)
                throws ServletException
```

This throws clause is what forces the change in CustList. Since an error can now occur in the initialization of a proxy, the servlet has to handle the error.

```
    {
            this.servlet = servlet;
            this.session = session;

            // Create data structure converter
            dscust = new AS400Structure(
                    new AS400DataType[] {
                            new AS400Text(6),
                            new AS400Text(30),
                            new AS400Text(30),
                            new AS400Text(30),
                            new AS400Text(25),
                            new AS400Text(3),
```

```
                        new AS400Text(9),
                        new AS400Text(15),
                        new AS400Text(15),
                        new AS400Text(64),
            });
```

This is the internally described data structure. Basically, it breaks up the 227-byte data structure into 10 strings, with the lengths shown. These match up quite nicely with the 10 fields in the CUSTMAST file.

Note that the first field is numeric in the file. But since it's ZONED decimal, not PACKED decimal, it can be treated as an alpha field. This is a bit of "clever" coding on my part (and those who know me know I *hate* clever coding), but it really made things easier. Also, this structure didn't have to be the same as the file. We could have created another structure that had only a few fields or had an extra calculated field, such as outstanding A/R balance. The layout of this data structure does *not* depend on the physical layout of the data.

```
        // Set up host communication objects
        host = new AS400("WDSCHOST", "WDSCUSER", "WDSCUSER");
        addlible = new CommandCall(host, "ADDLIBLE WDSCLIB");
        path = "/QSYS.LIB/WDSCLIB.LIB/SVRCM.PGM";
        parms = new ProgramParameter[] {
                new ProgramParameter(dscust.getByteLength()),
                new ProgramParameter(1)
        };
        server = new ProgramCall(host, path, parms);
```

This is standard JTOpen setup. Create the system object, create the command that will add the library list, and create the call to the server program with two parameters (data structure and EOF flag).

```
        // Add WDSCLIB to the server job library list
        try {
                addlible.run();
        } catch (Exception e) {
                throw new ServletException("Initialization error:\n" + e);
        }
```

Finally, invoke the ADDLIBLE command to get WDSCLIB in the library list so that it can find the CUSTMAST file. If you didn't do this, you'd have to do it in the server program's initialization routine. Where you choose to do it is up to you.

```
        }

        // doGet and doPost both do the same thing:
        //    Save request information
        //    Invoke doRequest
        protected void doGet(HttpServletRequest req, HttpServletResponse res)
        throws ServletException, IOException {
                this.req = req;
                this.res = res;
                doRequest();
        }

        protected void doPost(HttpServletRequest req, HttpServletResponse res)
        throws ServletException, IOException {
                this.req = req;
                this.res = res;
                doRequest();
        }

        // The only change here is to invoke getCustomers to get live data
        // rather than create a dummy CustomerList. The live data goes into
        // the session, and then I still forward the request to the JSP.
        private void doRequest() throws ServletException, IOException {
                CustomerList cl = getCustomers();
```

We removed the call to the make method and replaced it with the call to the local getCustomers method.

```
                session.setAttribute("customers", cl);
                servlet.getServletContext().
                        getRequestDispatcher("CustList.jsp").
                                forward(req, res);
        }

        // And here's all the work. All I do is create an empty CustomerList,
        // then start calling the server program. As long as the result code
        // is an EBCDIC '0' (0xF0), then I parse the data structure and use it
        // to create a new Customer, which is then added to the list.
        // Once I receive an EOF code (anything other than 0xF0), I return the
        // list to the caller.
```

```
        private CustomerList getCustomers() throws ServletException
        {
                CustomerList cl = new CustomerList();
                try {
                        server.run();
                        while (parms[1].getOutputData()[0] == (byte) 0xF0)
                        {
                                Object[] co =
                                    (Object[]) dscust.toObject(parms[0].getOutput
                                        Data());
                                cl.addCustomer(
                                    new Customer(
                                            (String) co[0], (String) co[1],
                                                (String) co[2],
                                            (String) co[3], (String) co[4],
                                                (String) co[5],
                                            (String) co[6], (String) co[7],
                                                (String) co[8],
                                            (String) co[9]
                                            ));
                                server.run();
                        }
                } catch (Exception e) {
                        throw new ServletException("Runtime error:\n" + e);
                }
                return cl;
        }
```

This is the most complex bit of the code. First, I create a CustomerList object. Then, inside of a big try/catch, I start calling the server program. I check the first byte of the second parameter. I don't even bother translating this, because I know it's supposed to be either an EBCDIC '0' or an EBCDIC '1'. I test for '0' (0xF0), which indicates a record is found (not EOF).

At that point, I convert the data structure, which is in the first parameter. This will create an array of strings. I use that to build a new Customer object and add it to the list. After I receive an EOF, I return the CustomerList to the caller.

```
}
```

Listing 15-5: And this is the last line of the updated CustListProxy.

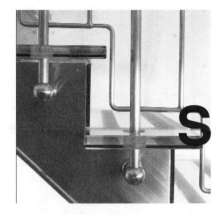

Step 16

Adding a little style

Your application is finished. Now what you want to do is add a little style to it. In this step, you'll do some of the style work that would typically be done to make an application more Web-ready. Note that this work will be done without modifying a single host program.

This is the primary difference between JSP Model II and the various RPG-CGI approaches. With RPG-CGI, at some point you have an RPG program that formats the HTML to be output. Because of this, all UI changes eventually mean changes on the host—either the programs themselves or, in the case of template-driven tools, the templates that format the HTML.

With JSP Model II, all modifications are done in the Web objects. And as you'll see, with a proper design, most of the work is done in the style sheets, rather than the JSPs. In this case, the biggest change to the JSP is to support alternating background colors on the rows in the list.

Also, JSP Model II provides platform independence for the Web serving tier. Since the Web application server does not have to reside on the same box as the business logic, you have a lot more flexibility in your deployment options.

Step 16.1—Style and substance

> ## GOAL
> Make some changes, both at the JSP level and the style sheet level, that will enhance the look and the function of the application.

If you started this step from the Checkpoint, you'll see Figure 16-1. This is the Action canceled screen, which was discussed starting back in Step 1.

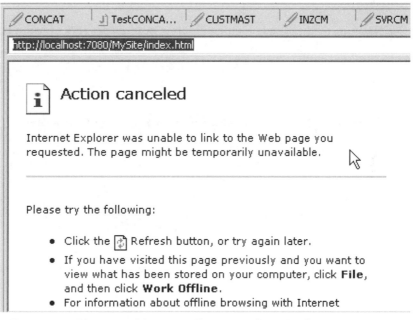

Figure 16-1: You'll see this screen if you start from the Checkpoint.

For this step, the first thing I'd like you to do is just close all the open files. Things have gotten a little cluttered during the preceding steps, and it's time to clean up a bit. Use the File/Close All option from the main menu as shown in Figure 16-2.

❑ **16.1(a) From the main menu, select File/Close All.**

Figure 16-2: Close all files using File/Close All from the main menu.

Now on to the fixes. Thanks to your new Package Explorer fast view, you can access all the Web objects from the iEdit perspective. First, open the Package Explorer by clicking on its fast view icon as shown in Figure 16-3.

❑ **16.1(b) Click on the Package Explorer fast view icon.**

Figure 16-3: Open the Package Explorer.

Search for Master.css and then double-click on it to open it. You'll probably have to expand Web Content and then theme before you see Master.css.

❑ **16.1(c) Expand Web Content and theme; double-click on Master.css.**

Figure 16-4: Double-click.

Listing 16-1: Here's the new style sheet with additions identified by gray shading.

```
BODY
{
    BACKGROUND-COLOR: #FFFFFF;
    COLOR: #333366;
    FONT-FAMILY: 'Times New Roman'
}
H1
{
    COLOR: #6666CC;
    FONT-FAMILY: 'Times New Roman';
    TEXT-TRANSFORM: capitalize
}
H2
{
    COLOR: #6666CC;
    FONT-FAMILY: 'Times New Roman';
    TEXT-TRANSFORM: capitalize
}
H3
{
    COLOR: #6666CC;
    FONT-FAMILY: 'Times New Roman';
    TEXT-TRANSFORM: capitalize
}
H4
{
    COLOR: #6666CC;
    FONT-FAMILY: 'Times New Roman';
    TEXT-TRANSFORM: capitalize
}
```

```
H5
{
    COLOR: #6666CC;
    FONT-FAMILY: 'Times New Roman';
    TEXT-TRANSFORM: capitalize
}
H6
{
    COLOR: #6666CC;
    FONT-FAMILY: 'Times New Roman';
    TEXT-TRANSFORM: capitalize
}
TH {
 color: #6060cc
}
.custlist TABLE {
        border-style: none;
        border-spacing: 0;
        border-collapse: collapse;
        margin: 0;
}
.custlist TH {
        color: blue;
        background-color: white;
        font-family: Verdana;
        font-size: 10pt;
        border-style : solid;
        border-width : 2px;
        border-color : blue;
        padding-left: 6px;
        padding-right: 6px;
}
.alt {
        background-color: #80ffff;
}
.custlist TD {
        font-family: Verdana;
        font-size: 9pt;
        padding-left: 6px;
        padding-right: 6px;
}
.custlist A {
        width: 100%;
        color: blue;
        font-size: 9pt;
        font-weight: bold;
        font-family: Verdana, sans-serif;
        text-decoration: none;
        border-style : solid;
        border-width : 2px;
        border-color : #ccccff #000050 #000050 #ccccff;
        padding: 2px;
}
```

```
.custlist A:visited {
        color: blue;
}

.custlist A:hover{
        color: white;
        background-color: blue;
        border-color : #000050 #ccccff #ccccff #000050;
        padding-left: 0px;
        padding-right: 4px;
        padding-top: 1px;
        padding-bottom: 3px;
        text-decoration: none;
        position: relative; top: 1px; left: 1px;
}
```

You can enter the code or copy it in from the CD-ROM. The code for this style sheet can be found in file Step16-1-a.txt in the Imports folder on the accompanying CD-ROM. Once the code is entered, save it as usual by right-clicking in the editor pane and selecting Save.

❑ **16.1(d) Enter the code from Listing 16-1, right-click, and select Save.**

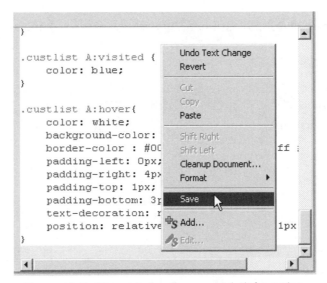

Figure 16-5: After entering the new style information, right-click in the editor and select Save.

Next, you need to edit the JSP. So, back to the Package Explorer.

❑ **16.1(e) Click on the Package Explorer fast view icon.**

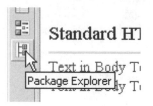

Figure 16-6: Click on the Package Explorer fast view icon.

Find your JSP, CustList.jsp, and double-click on it to open it in the editor.

❑ **16.1(f) Double-click on CustList.jsp to edit it.**

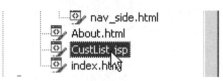

Figure 16-7: Double-click on CustList.jsp to edit it.

Listing 16-2: Here's the new CustList.jsp, with additions and changes highlighted.

```
<jsp:useBean class="com.mycomp.beans.CustomerList"
id="customers" scope="session"></jsp:useBean>
<br>
<table class=custlist cellspacing=0>
<tr><th colspan=3>Customer List</th></tr>
<tr><th>Number</th><th>Name</th><th>Email</th></tr>
<%boolean altrow = false;
  while (customers.hasNext()) {
  com.mycomp.beans.Customer c = customers.nextCustomer();
   String rowclass = altrow ? " class=alt" : "";
   altrow = !altrow; %>
<tr<%=rowclass%>>
<td align=center><%=c.getNumber()%></td>
<td><%=c.getName()%></td>
<td><a href="mailto:<%=c.getEmail()%>"><%=c.getEmail()%></a></td>
</tr>
<%}%>
</table>
```

As with the style sheet, you can enter this code manually or copy it in from the CD-ROM. The updated JSP can be found in file Step16-1-b.txt in the Imports folder on the accompanying CD-ROM. Enter the code then save it.

❑ **16.1(g) Enter the code from Listing 16-2, right-click, and select Save.**

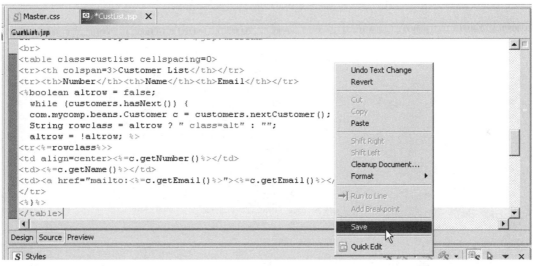

Figure 16-8: After entering the new JSP code, right-click in the editor and select Save.

That's it for changes! It's time to run what will be, for better or worse, the final look and feel for the program. As you have done throughout this Step, start with the Package Explorer.

❑ **16.1(h) Click on the Package Explorer fast view icon.**

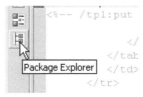

Figure 16-9: Open the Package Explorer one more time.

Now you can run the application. You've done this before, many times. Find index.html, and right-click on it. From the resulting pop-up menu, select Run on Server... as shown in Figure 16-10.

❑ **16.1(i) Right-click on index.html and select Run on Server....**

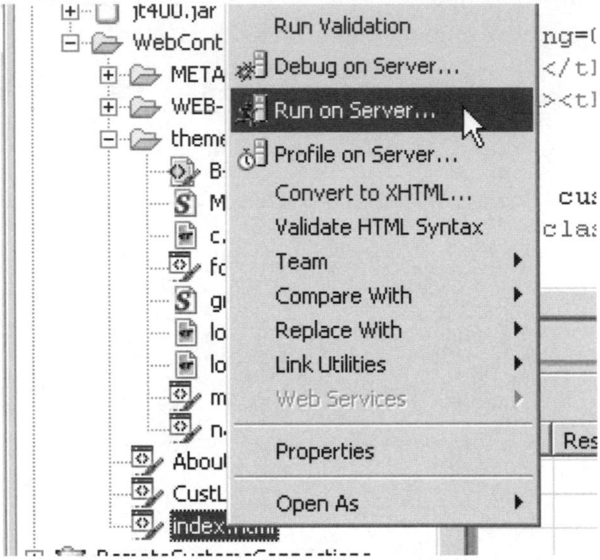

Figure 16-10: Right-click on index.html and select Run on Server…

The Server Selection dialog will come up; just press Finish. If you started this chapter from a Checkpoint, it may take a little time for the application to start up. If you've been working through the steps, the startup delay should be negligible.

❑ **16.1(j) Press Finish.**

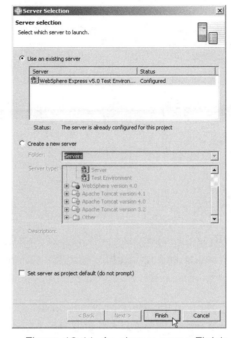

Figure 16-11: As always, press Finish.

You will now see your index page. This page will not have changed at all. However, click on Customers as shown in Figure 16-12.

❑ **16.1(k) Click on Customers.**

Figure 16-12: Select the Customers option.

And you'll see the new page as shown in Figure 16-13.

❑ **16.1(l) Click on one of the email links.**

Figure 16-13: The new screen!

Note that the headings are all now encased in a bright blue border. The rows alternate between white and light blue. And the email column actually has buttons…buttons that look as if you're supposed to press one.

So press one! And, depending on what email client you use, you should see something like the window shown in Figure 16-14.

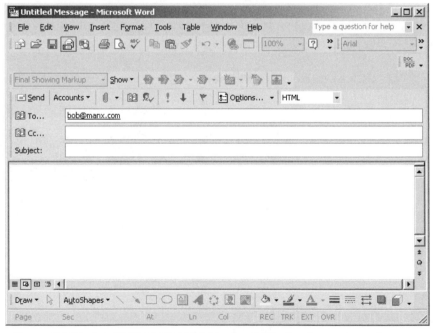

Figure 16-14: A mail client should pop up, attempting to send email.

Crazy, eh? With just a little bit of work, the style sheet manages to do a great job of changing the look and feel. And just a couple of simple tweaks in the JSP adds not only the alternating row colors, but also links that are based on data read from the host.

Not bad for a few dozen lines of code.

InStep 16.1.a—Code review

GOAL

Here, you'll take a look at the minor modifications I did to the CSS and the JSP that caused those major changes in the look and feel of the user interface.

Normally, I'd tell you that you can skip this part of the code if you want to get on to the good stuff, but frankly, the only good stuff left is deployment to the host. And while that's good stuff, it's not as cool as this part, in my opinion.

However, if you're in a hurry to create an EAR file that you can run on the Web server of your choice, then skip ahead to Step 17. But if you want to know how I did the magic I did in this step, please read on.

I'm going to do this in reverse order. First, I'll explain the changes to the JSP. I explained the JSP in some detail back in InStep 9.4.a, so I'll just address the changes here. The changes are highlighted, and I'll add my comments after each change.

```
<jsp:useBean class="com.mycomp.beans.CustomerList"
id="customers" scope="session"></jsp:useBean>
<br>
<table class=custlist cellspacing=0>
```

The <BR> is to help line the table up with the navigation links; that's all. The class=custlist is the real kicker; it allows all the rest of the formatting to occur. This single attribute allows me to treat every cell in the table separately from the rest of the document. The way CSS works is really quite brilliant. Oh, and the cellspacing=0 is because IE doesn't always handle CSS correctly. This is one area in which Mozilla really is a better browser.

```
<tr><th colspan=3>Customer List</th></tr>
<tr><th>Number</th><th>Name</th><th>Email</th></tr>
<%boolean altrow = false;
```

This is one of my favorite tricks. This is the old "greenbar" technique, alternating bars of color in a table. Start out by initializing a Boolean value to false.

```
    while (customers.hasNext()) {
    com.mycomp.beans.Customer c = customers.nextCustomer();
     String rowclass = altrow ? " class=alt" : "";
     altrow = !altrow; %>
<tr <%=rowclass%>>
```

OK, finish the alternating rows. If we are on the alternating row, set the rowclass string to " class=alt" (note the leading blank, by the way). Next, toggle the altrow variable. Those lines are in the code section of the loop. Now, in the HTML section, output the rowclass as part of the row tag. With this logic, alternating rows will start with either <tr> or <tr class=alt>.

(Special tip for those of you who chose to read this section: You can have more than two colors. Use an int, and initialize it to zero. Set the class based on the int. Add one to the int, and if it's too large, set it back to zero, like so: $j = (j + 1)$ % MAXJ.)

```
<td align=center><%=c.getNumber()%></td>
<td><%=c.getName()%></td>
 <td><a href="mailto:<%=c.getEmail()%>"><%=c.getEmail()%></a></td>
```

This was the other enhancement. I added a clickable email value. I particularly like this little technique, because it requires so little code in the JSP; the bulk of the really eye-catching work is done in the style sheet. The only work here was to add an anchor tag with an href of mailto: and the email address. Normally, that would just create a simple underlined hyperlink. However, as you've seen, I like my hyperlinks to be a little more lively. I'll get to that as I review the style sheet.

```
</tr>
<%}%>
</table>
```

Listing 16-3: The new CustList.jsp, with additions and changes highlighted.

```
.custlist TABLE {
        border-style: none;
        border-spacing: 0;
        border-collapse: collapse;
        margin: 0;
}
```

Here's a table style. The most important thing to recognize is that this will affect only tables that have the class custlist. And you'll see that nearly every style I've added uses the .custlist selector. Earlier, I mentioned that adding a single attribute to a table allows me to treat the table and all its cells differently than the rest of the document. Not only the table, but also the rows, heading cells, and data cells will all have a class of custlist. *Very* cool.

OK, for the table. First I got rid of the border, and then I tried everything to close the gaps between cells, and as it turns out, it was all for naught because there is a bug in IE (and thus I had to add the cellspacing=0 attribute I told you about earlier). These tags will work on other browsers, though.

```
.custlist TH {
        color: blue;
        background-color: white;
        font-family: Verdana;
        font-size: 10pt;
        border-style : solid;
        border-width : 2px;
        border-color : blue;
        padding-left: 6px;
        padding-right: 6px;
}
```

This is much more straightforward. Every heading in the table will be blue on white, with a two-pixel blue border. The font will be 10-point Verdana, and the words will have at least six pixels of padding on the left and right. By default, heading cells are usually centered, so I didn't specify that here.

```
.alt {
      background-color: #80ffff;
}
```

This is all that is required for the alternating rows. Set a different background color. You would need more than one if you are alternating more than two colors.

```
.custlist TD {
      font-family: Verdana;
      font-size: 9pt;
      padding-left: 6px;
      padding-right: 6px;
}
```

I make the font for the data in the cells a tiny bit smaller, but I still pad it to the right and left. (I need that padding because I've butted the cells right up against each other in the table style.)

```
.custlist A {
      width: 100%;
      color: blue;
      font-size: 9pt;
      font-weight: bold;
      font-family: Verdana, sans-serif;
      text-decoration: none;
      border-style : solid;
      border-width : 2px;
      border-color : #ccccff #000050 #000050 #ccccff;
      padding: 2px;
}
```

This is where I have a lot of fun. Anchor tags within the box will have these attributes. First, a standard anchor will be blue 9-point Verdana text inside a two-pixel box. The box will stretch across 100% of the cell and will have light blue upper and left borders and dark blue lower and right borders.

```
.custlist A:visited {
      color: blue;
}
```

Typically, a different color is assigned to a hyperlink you've already visited. This style cancels that behavior so that the hyperlinks are the same color whether you've visited them or not. The only time a link's appearance changes is when your cursor hovers over it.

```
.custlist A:hover{
        color: white;
        background-color: blue;
        border-color : #000050 #ccccff #ccccff #000050;
        padding-left: 0px;
        padding-right: 4px;
        padding-top: 1px;
        padding-bottom: 3px;
        text-decoration: none;
        position: relative; top: 1px; left: 1px;
}
```

Listing 16-4: These styles were added to Master.css to support the customer list page.

And finally, this is the hover style. A few things change. The color goes to white on blue, and the border colors swap. The change in border colors is what gives you the "pressed in" illusion. Typically, I also try to move the text a little bit using a combination of relative positioning and padding, but that's the sort of thing you can spend days trying to get perfect. For now, the settings are good enough.

Step 17

Deployment

You've written the code. You've tested the connections. You've tweaked the style sheets and you are ready to roll. The only issue now is deployment. And while I can't give you the step-by-step instructions on how to install the application in your particular environment, I can at least help you wrap it up in a nice package.

Specifically, you'll package the program in both an EAR file and a WAR file. Once your application is packaged, you can then decide how to deploy it.

Step 17.1—Rename the application

GOAL

Go into the application description and
rename the application.

When you originally created the application, I didn't bother you with any details like application name, so you ended up with an enterprise application by the name of DefaultEAR. While this isn't an issue during development, it's not exactly the most descriptive name when deploying to a server. In this Step, I'll show you how to change that default name.

All work here will be done through the Package Explorer. I suppose you could also switch to the Web perspective, but personally, I've gotten used to using a single perspective with fast views for infrequent tasks.

❑ **17.1(a) Click on the Package Explorer fast view icon.**

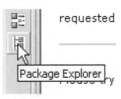

*Figure 17-1:
Expand the
Package Explorer
by clicking on its
fast view icon.*

Renaming is sometimes hidden in the Eclipse IDE. That's because it often does a lot more than just rename the current object; it also tends to go and fix any references to that object. This is called "refactoring," so the rename option is often tucked away (along with the move option) under a submenu called Refactor. That's exactly the case here.

❑ **17.1(b) Right-click on DefaultEAR and select Refactor/Rename. . . .**

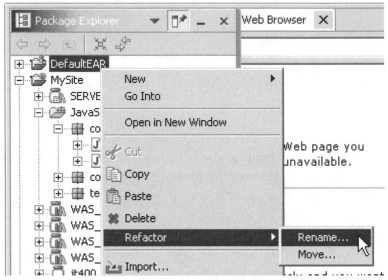

Figure 17-2: To get to the Rename option, first select Refactor.

I know this change isn't particularly enlightening, but the example here of changing the name to MyEAR at least gives you the idea of how the task is accomplished.

❑ **17.1(c) Enter MyEAR into the new name field and press OK.**

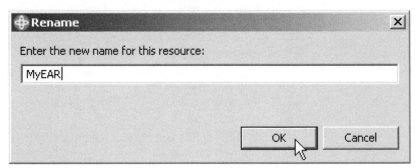

Figure 17-3: Type in the new name (MyEAR) and press OK.

The EAR file will be renamed. However, buried deep inside the EAR is the display name of the application, and it is still DefaultEAR. Unfortunately, Refactor/Rename doesn't fix this particular attribute, so you have to do it manually. Expand MyEAR and then expand the META-INF folder underneath it to uncover the application.xml file. Double-click on it to bring up the Application Deployment Descriptor editor shown in Figure 17-5.

❑ **17.1(d) Expand MyEAR and then expand META-INF.**

❑ **17.1(e) Double-click on application.xml.**

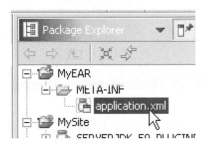

Figure 17-4: MyEar doesn't have much in it besides the Application Deployment Descriptor.

The Application Deployment Descriptor has many attributes. There are four tabs along the bottom of the editor. The attribute we want to change is in the first tab at the top of the page. Enter MyEAR into the Display name field, and save the descriptor.

> **Note:** This is one of the few editors in all of WDSC where a right-click doesn't pop up a menu with a Save option. However, you can use either File/Save from the main menu or Ctrl+S to save the file.

❑ **17.1(f) Enter MyEAR into the Display name field and press Ctrl+S.**

| S Master.css | CustList.jsp | Web Browser | *Application Deployment Descriptor ✕ |

MyEAR

▼ **General Information**

Display name: MyEAR
Description:

▼ **Modules**

Web MySite.war   Details...

▼ **Security Roles**

Details...

▼ **Icons**

Small: Browse...

Large: Browse...

▼ **WebSphere Extensions**

The following are extension properties for the WebSphere Application

Overview | Module | Security | Source

Figure 17-5: Enter MyEAR in the Display name and press Ctrl+S to save.

Step 17.2—Export the project

GOAL
Now you will export the project in both EAR and WAR formats.

This is the last step in the J2EE development cycle. The only other thing left to do is actually install this into a Web application server. By learning both the EAR file export and the WAR file export techniques, you'll have the broadest variety of deployment options available.

OK, first things first: Get to the Package Explorer if you're not already there.

❑ **17.2(a) Click on the Package Explorer fast view icon.**

Figure 17-6: Click on the Package Explorer fast view icon.

Now you can export.

> **Note:** There are two levels here: Web applications and enterprise applications. MySite is a Web application, while MyEAR is an enterprise application. An enterprise application is made up of one or more Web applications. You can either export a Web application as a WAR file or export the entire enterprise application as an EAR file. If you look in a WAR file, you'll see all of the objects you'd expect to see: servlets, JSPs, JAR files, and so on. If you look in an EAR file, you will see the application deployment descriptor and one or more WAR files.

I'd like you to first export the enterprise application.

❑ **17.2(b) Right-click on MyEAR and select Export. . . .**

Figure 17-7: Right-click on MyEAR and select Export. . .

This will bring up the Export wizard. It wants to know what your export "destination" is, which I guess is another way of saying, "How do you want to export this?" In this case, you want to export as an EAR, so select EAR file and then press Next.

❏ **17.2(c) Select EAR file and press Next.**

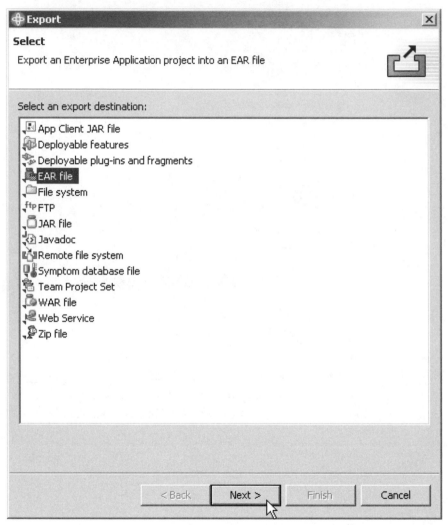

Figure 17-8: First, save as an EAR. Select EAR file and then press Next.

This will then bring up the EAR Export wizard. Type in the fully qualified name of the EAR file you wish to create. In my case, I thought I'd store the files in C:\temp (not particularly original, but it works). The file is MyEAR.ear, so type C:\temp\MyEAR.ear into the Destination field and press Finish. If you wish to use a different folder, make sure it exists and then modify your destination accordingly. And if you plan to deploy this on the iSeries, you might want to deploy the file directly to a folder on the IFS using a mapped drive.

❑ **17.2(d) Enter C:\temp\MyEAR.ear into the Destination field and press Finish.**

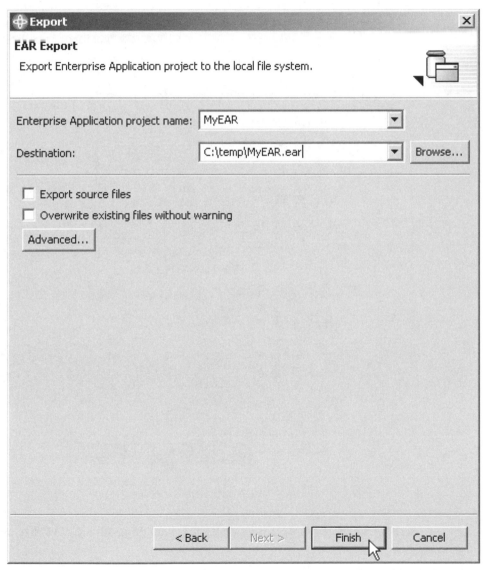

Figure 17-9: Type in the fully qualified name of the target EAR file and press Finish.

That's it. WDSC will chug along a little while and create an EAR file. While some Web application servers prefer EAR files, some only support WAR files. If instead you need a WAR file, the following steps will do the trick

> **Note:** In the following steps, please recognize that you are exporting MySite, *not* MyEAR. MySite is a Web application and thus is exported as a WAR file, whereas MyEAR is an enterprise application and so is exported as an EAR file.

Right-click on MySite (not MyEAR!) as shown in Figure 17-10 and select Export.

❑ **17.2(e) Right-click on MySite and select Export.**

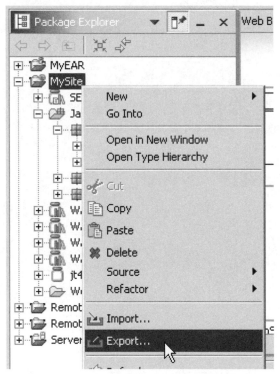

Figure 17-10: Now you're exporting MySite.

The Select export dialog comes up again. This time, select WAR file and press Next.

❑ **17.2(f) Select WAR file and press Next.**

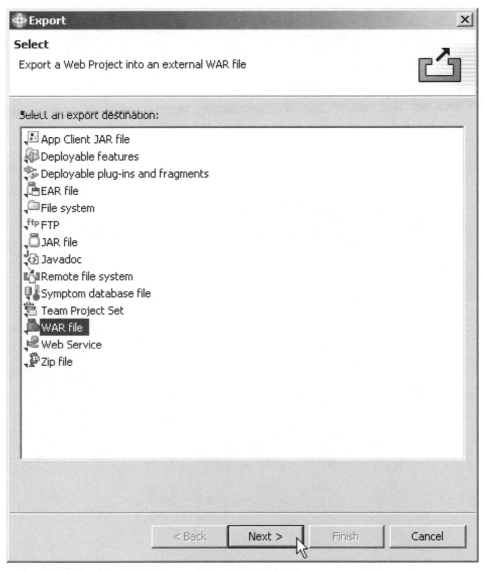

Figure 17-11: Select WAR file and press Next.

The last step is just about the same as in the previous task. Just enter in the fully qualified name of the WAR file you wish to create, and then press Finish. The folder must exist, and if you want to eventually import it into a Web server on the iSeries, you might want to export the application to a folder there as well.

❏ **17.2(g) Enter C:\temp\MySite.war into the Destination field and press Finish.**

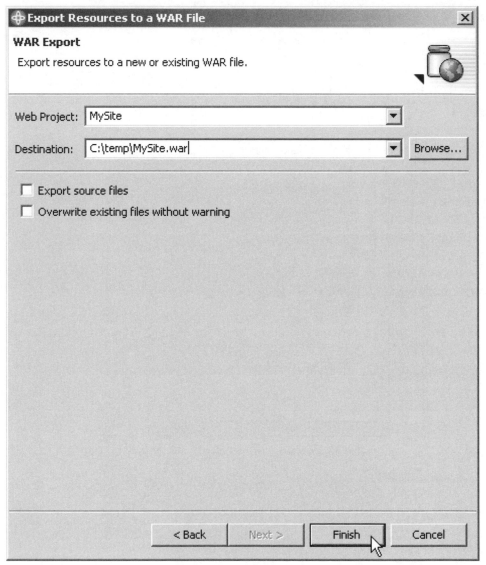

Figure 17-12: Enter the fully qualified WAR file target name and press Finish.

And that's all there is to it. You've now exported your project both as a WAR file and as an EAR file.

Step 17.3—Deploy RPG programs

GOAL

In this step, I'll introduce the issues surrounding deployment of RPG programs.

While the J2EE folks did a pretty good job of putting together a deployment mechanism for simple Web applications, the WAR/EAR file mechanism is less suitable for distributed technology applications like the one you just created.

There's no concept of external objects for a Web application. For example, if you have 20 WAR files and each uses the JTOpen JAR file, that means you'll need 20 copies of it. Of course, that gets around the issues of release-to-release compatibility; each version of the application locks in its own version of the JAR files. However, that means that in many cases, you can't combine technologies in one application because of JAR file incompatibilities. In the early days of the XML parser, that sort of thing was rampant in the Java world.

But even if you were to make your way through that particular minefield, the J2EE deployment model still has no room for anything like an iSeries save file or an RPG program. Instead, all RPG deployment will have to be done separately. Rather than attempt to install your RPG components using the J2EE deployment model, I recommend that you include automated deployment of your J2EE application in your standard iSeries installation procedures.

Different Web application servers have different deployment methodologies. You'll need to learn the specific deployment techniques of your Web application server in order to merge them with your standard RPG deployment procedures. In the end, it may simply be two different processes; this is especially true if you are implementing a true multi-tier environment with a Web server on a non-iSeries platform or even just on a different iSeries than your business logic.

SideStep 1

Upgrading WDSC

GOAL

This is the first SideStep. SideSteps are special chapters designed to help you perform additional tasks that aren't directly related to the task at hand. In this case, you're going to upgrade your WDSC to the latest version.

You should always be at the latest version. If are already at the latest version, you don't need to do it again, but at the time of this writing, a brand new upgrade (5.1.0.3) was just released, so chances are you may need an upgrade. You should always keep your iSeries at the latest PTF versions, and you should keep your WDSC up to the latest release. PTFs are part of your standard iSeries operations. In case you want to review your procedures, all the information you need is at the IBM eServer iSeries Support page:

http://www-1.ibm.com/servers/eserver/support/iseries/planning/maintenance.html

Keeping your WDSC up-to-date is explained in this step. If you just installed WDSC from CD, then you definitely need to perform this step multiple times. One of the bad things about the WDSC upgrade process is that there is no "cumulative" upgrade. You need to upgrade through all the releases one at a time. If there are four upgrades, you'll need to do the upgrade four times.

In this step, I'll walk you through the 5.1.0.2 upgrade. It's one of the more involved upgrades, because it upgrades both the WDSC workbench as well as the CODE/400 program, and it requires a reboot (by comparison, the 5.1.0.3 upgrade required only one download and no reboot).

First, start WDSC. You can start it with any workspace.

> **Note:** The updates will not be applied to any other workspaces until you open them. Suppose you have three workspaces: A, B, and C. Let's say you start WDSC with workspace A, and you upgrade WDSC. Workspaces B and C will not get upgraded until you open them with the upgraded WDSC.

❏ **S1(a) Start WDSC.**

After starting WDSC, from the main menu select Help/Software Updates/Update Manager as shown in Figure S1-1.

❏ **S1(b) Select Help/Software Updates/Update Manager from the main menu.**

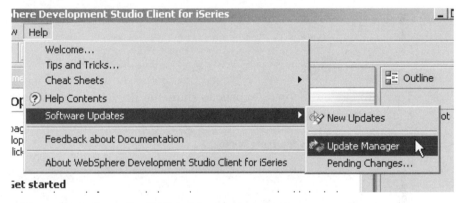

Figure S1-1: Open the Update Manager as shown.

In the update perspective, you'll see a Feature Updates view in the lower left pane. There are three options: Sites to Visit, Available Updates, and My Computer. Select Available Updates.

❏ S1(c) Select Available Updates.

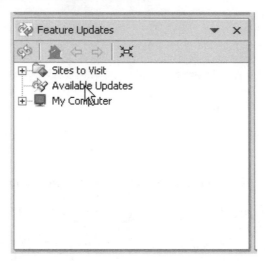

Figure S1-2: Select Available Updates.

This will cause the top right pane to show the Preview view. At that point, you can click on the Search Now button, as shown in Figure S1-3.

❏ S1(d) Click on Search Now.

Figure S1-3: The Preview view appears in the upper left pane; click on Search Now.

Doing this causes the workbench to contact the IBM Web site and start looking for updates. This can be a long-running process; at best, it takes 30 seconds or so, and it can even take several minutes. Figure S1-4 and S1-5 show how the progress bar indicates the approximate amount completed.

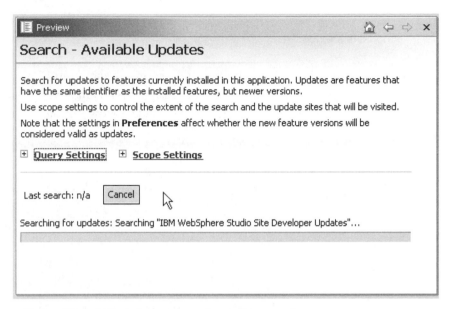

Figure S1-4: At first, the progress bar will be empty.

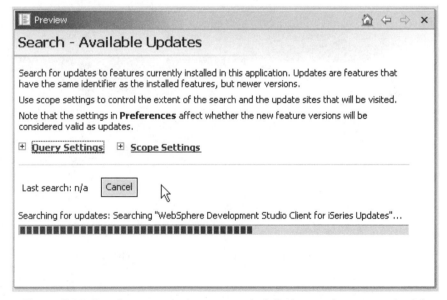

Figure S1-5: But the progress bar proceeds (albeit sometimes very slowly).

When the process is done, the lower right pane will show the Feature Search Results. One or more features may be available. In this case, there is only one.

Note: If there are no updates available, your installation is up-to-date and no updates are needed.

If one or more features do appear, click on one as shown in Figure S1-6. The upper right pane will then change as shown in Figure S1-7, indicating that you can actually install the new version. Click on the Update Now button to begin the process.

❑ **S1(e) Click on an available feature.**

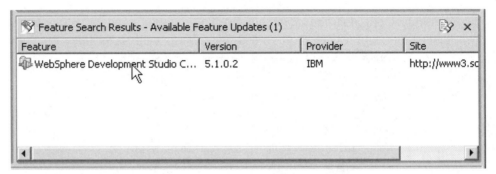

Figure S1-6: Click on a feature to select it.

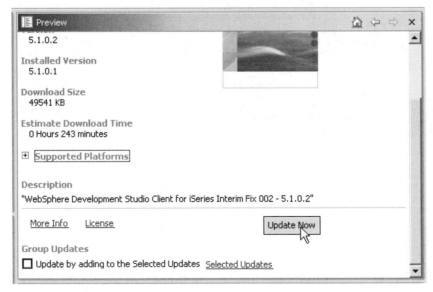

Figure S1-7: Click on Update Now to begin the upgrade.

A Feature Install dialog such as the one in S1-8 will appear. Press Next.

❏ **S1(f) Press Next.**

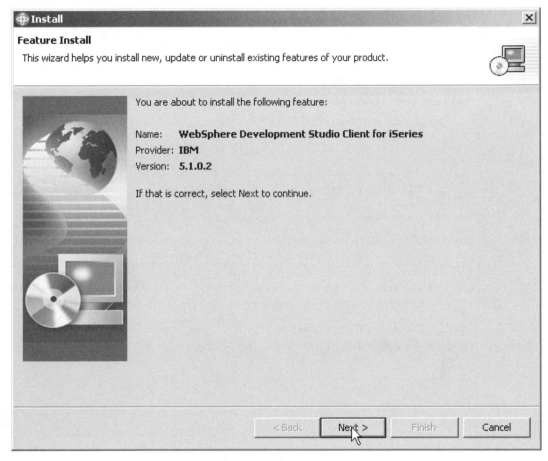

Figure S1-8: Press Next to continue the installation.

The Feature License screen will come next. You'll have to click on the I Accept radio button. I recommend reading this license if you've never done so (or if you've been having trouble sleeping). Press Next.

❑ **S1(g) Click on I Accept; press Next.**

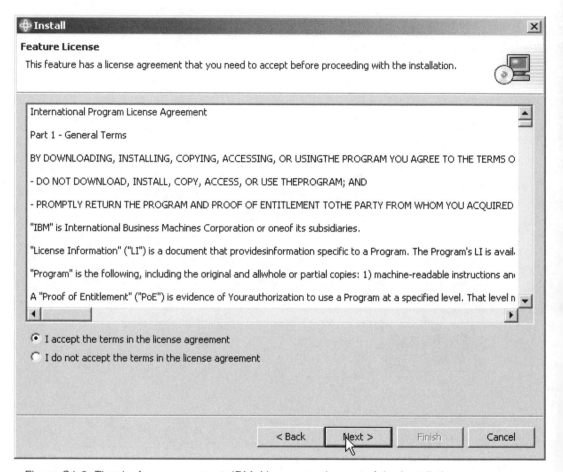

Figure S1-9: Thanks for your support, IBM. Now, on to the rest of the installation.

A screen comes up with optional features.

> **Warning:** Do not change the selection on the optional features screen.

Press Next.

❑ **S1(h) Don't touch the selections; just press Next.**

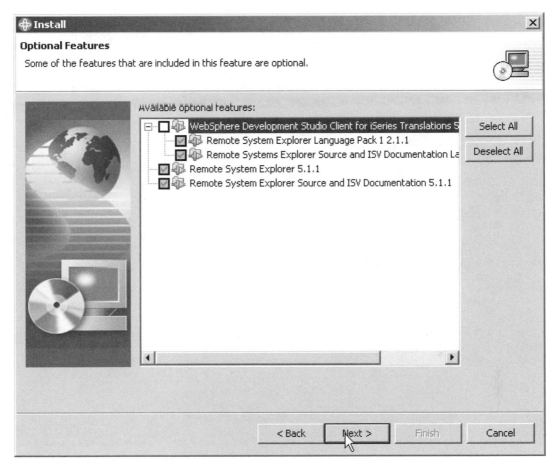

Figure S1-10: Don't change the selections on this screen, or the dreaded unpredicted results will occur. Press Next.

The Install Location page comes up now. Unless you have some absolutely good reason to not continue, leave the screen the way it is and press Finish.

❑ S1(i) Press Finish.

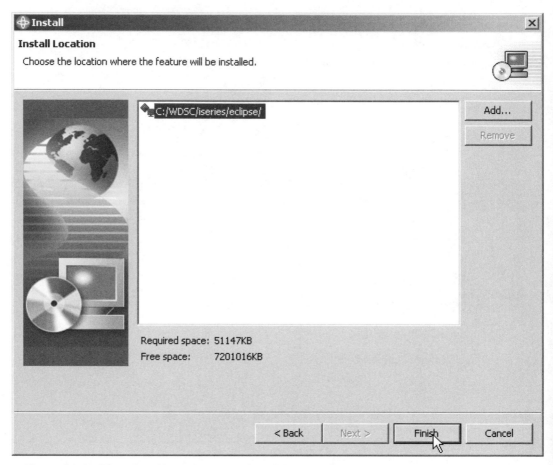

Figure S1-11: The wizard has chosen an install location for you. Accept it.

The Feature Verification screen comes up as shown in Figure S1-12. The feature is not digitally signed (I have no idea why not), so you get the error. Just press Install as shown and continue on.

❑ S1(j) Press Install.

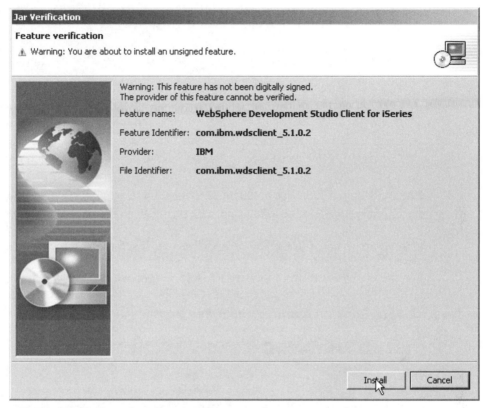

Figure S1-12: Press Install to start the upgrade.

A progress bar will appear, identifying the current file being downloaded and the total progress so far, as shown in Figure S1-13.

Free space: 7201016KB

Downloading: plugins/com.ibm.etools.iseries.core_5.1.0.2.jar (270K bytes)

< Back   Next >   Finish   Cancel

Figure S1-13: Here's the installation progress bar.

When finished, the Install/Update dialog will appear with the news that the workbench needs to be restarted. Click on Yes to finish the installation.

❑ **S1(k) Press Yes.**

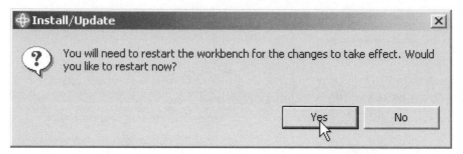

Figure S1-14: This panel is often the last thing you see in the upgrade process.

But that's only if there are no changes to the CODE or VARPG pieces of the product. For example, version 5.1.0.3 has no such changes, so the update ends here.

If there are updates to CODE or VARPG, you'll see more screens, as shown.

For the CODE portion of the update, select Approve and press Next.

❑ **S1(l) Click on Approve and press Next.**

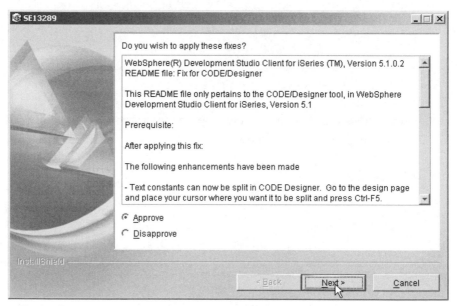

Figure S1-15: Accept the changes to be downloaded.

When the summary screen appears, press Next.

❏ **S1(m) Press Next.**

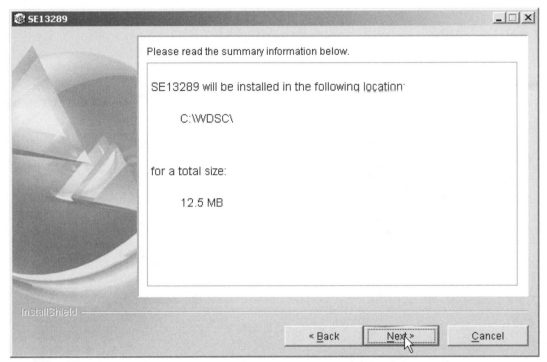

Figure S1-16: This screen shows how much needs to be added and where.

The machine will process the update and then present the following screen (in Figure S1-17). Press Next.

❑ **S1(n) Press Next.**

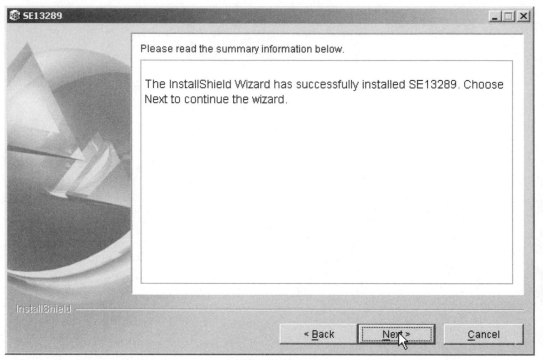

Figure S1-17: Press Next after successful installation.

❑ **S1(o) Click on Yes, restart my computer and press Finish.**

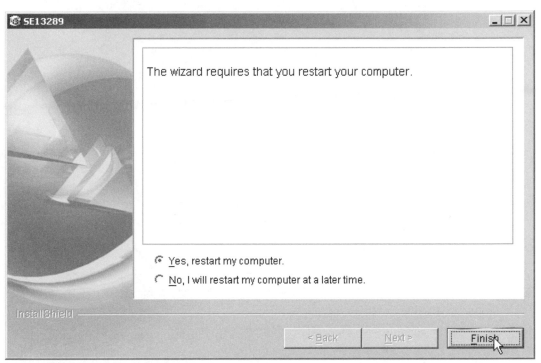

Figure S1-18: This is the last screen you see before your PC reboots.

SideStep 2

Checkpoints

GOAL

Checkpoints are a unique feature of the *Step by Step* books. A Checkpointed book has places where you can restart the book, even if it's a hands-on laboratory. This step explains the Checkpoint restart procedure and identifies the Checkpoints in the book.

WDSC: Step by Step is all about using WDSC. One of the nice things about WDSC is the fact that it supports multiple workspaces, and each workspace is a self-contained folder hierarchy. Essentially, if you copy the top folder of a workspace and everything underneath, you have a new workspace. So, at least from the workstation side of things, restarting at a Checkpoint is as simple as copying a folder and its subfolders off of the CD-ROM and onto your hard drive.

Once you get to the later steps, you also need some software up on the iSeries. This is done via the tried-and-true method of the iSeries savefile. Throughout the book, you'll be using a library on the host called WDSCLIB. If you decide to restart from a Checkpoint, you just copy the appropriate savefile up onto your iSeries (FTP is the typical approach) and then restore the library WDSCLIB from the savefile.

Warning: Restoring a library is a destructive step. Prior to the restore, you may want to rename any WDSCLIB you are currently working with.

✓ **Here is your step checklist:**

This is a straightforward procedure. Let's for the moment assume that you are following the suggestions laid out in Step 1, and therefore you have a folder called C:\WDSCSBS, which you are using for your workspaces.

Step	workspace		Step	workspace	savefile
2.1	ch0201		10.1	ch1001	
2.2	ch0202		10.2		
2.3	ch0203		10.3		
2.4	ch0204		11.1		
2.5	ch0205		11.2	ch1102	
2.6	ch0206		11.3	ch1103	
2.7	ch0207		11.4	ch1104	
2.8	ch0208		11.5	ch1105	
3.1	ch0301		11.6	ch1106	
3.2			11.7	ch1107	ch1107
3.3			12.1	ch1201	ch1201
4.1	ch0401		12.2	ch1202	ch1202
4.2			12.3	ch1203	ch1203
4.3			13.1		
4.4			13.2		
4.5	ch0405		13.3		
4.6			13.4		
5.1	ch0501		13.5		
6.1	ch0601		14.1	ch1401	ch1203
7.1	ch0701		14.2	ch1402	ch1203
7.2			15.1	ch1501	ch1203
8.1	ch0801		15.2	ch1502	ch1502
8.2	ch0802		15.3	ch1503	ch1503
8.3	ch0803		16.1	ch1601	ch1503
9.1			17.1	ch1701	ch1503
9.2			17.2	ch1702	ch1503
9.3	ch0903		17.3		
9.4	ch0904				
9.5	ch0905				
9.6	ch0906				

Figure S2-1: This reference table identifies your chapters/Checkpoints.

The first thing to do is to identify which is the closest Checkpoint. Different steps have different Checkpoint capabilities. For example, Step 2 allows you to restart at just about any substep, while Step 3 is pretty much a "sit down and work through it" step and has only one Checkpoint. If the topic you want to start with does not have a Checkpoint, it will be grayed out in Figure S2-1, and you'll have to restart from the immediately previous Checkpoint.

Also, any Step from Step 11.7 on requires the appropriate level of WDSCLIB on the host. Note that not every WDSC Checkpoint has its own savefile; for example, Steps 14.1 and 14.2 both use the same savefile as Step 12.3. That's because nothing changed on the host.

So let's start: Identify the workspace and savefile Checkpoints. Just to give you the idea, I'll walk you through a couple of examples: Steps 2.3, 3.2, and 16.1.

To start at Step 2.3, use workspace ch0203. There is no savefile.

You cannot start at Step 3.2. You'll have to go back to Step 3.1. To start at Step 3.1, use workspace ch0301. There is no savefile.

To start at Step 16.1, use workspace ch1601 and savefile ch1503.

❑ **S2(a) Identify which step you will actually be starting from.**

❑ **S2(b) Identify the workspace and optional savefile you will reload.**

At this point, you need to copy your files. Copying the workspace folder is probably easiest done using Windows Explorer and just dragging and dropping the folder from the CD to the hard drive:

❑ **S2(c) Drag the workspace folder from D:\Workspaces to C:\WDSCSBS.**

> **Note:** This assumes your CD-ROM is in the D: drive and your workspaces are on the C: drive in folder WDSCSBS.

If you also have a savefile, execute the following steps:

❑ **S2(d) FTP the savefile from D:\Savefiles to a savefile on your iSeries.**

❑ **S2(e) Rename your current WDSCLIB library.**

❑ **S2(f) Restore WDSCLIB from the newly uploaded savefile.**

Now you can start WDSC. However, you still have one more choice to make. Do you want to leave your workspace with the Checkpoint name (such as ch0203), or do you want to rename it? That's entirely up to you. But whether you leave it the way it is or rename it, be sure to specify that workspace when you start WDSC.

> **Release Note:** Significant changes occurred to the workspace structure in V5.1.2. You can use the workspaces here for Checkpoint purposes, but if you do, you'll get a message saying "Completing Install" and then you'll see a completely different workbench than what you would expect. To eliminate that problem, I have included a separate Zip file that contains all of the workspaces updated for V5.1.2. For more information on this and other V5.1.2-specific issues, see SideStep 5.

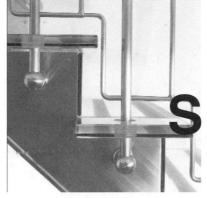

SideStep 3

Add a new Express server

GOAL

If you have access to an iSeries that has WebSphere Express installed but you've never played with it, this step will show you how to create a brand new Express Web server for testing.

In all but the simplest environments, you'll need a little information, primarily which ports you intend to run on. Also, if your machine has multiple IP addresses, you'll need to know which address you want the server to respond to. In this example, I am going to set up a server to run from the default ports.

Release Note: This example is for V5R1 of the operating system, the first release that supported browser-based administration. Later releases are similar in the setup phase.

Warning: If you create a Web server and it conflicts with an already existing server, unpredicted results will occur. The servers may not start, and if they do, they may not respond properly.

✓ **Here is your step checklist:**

This is a straightforward procedure. Let's assume that you are following the suggestions laid out in Step 1, and therefore you have a folder called C:\WDSCSBS, which you are using for your workspaces. Your HTTP admin server must be started. If you're not sure about that, you may need a little more help, but I'll give you the command here:

```
STRTCPSVR SERVER(*HTTP) HTTPSVR(*ADMIN)
```

This makes the admin server available on port 2001. Since you managed to map your IP address to the value WDSCHOST way back in Step 1, you should be able to enter the address http://WDSCHOST:2001, as shown in Figure S3-1.

Click on the second entry, IBM WebSphere Application Server - Express for iSeries, as shown.

❑ **S3(a) Browse to http://WDSCHOST:2001.**

❑ **S3(b) Click on the second entry.**

Figure S3-1: Start up the administration server interface and click on second entry.

This brings up the Express management screen. Click on Setup.

❏ **S3(c) Click on Setup.**

Figure S3-2: Click on Setup.

This brings up a menu with several options. You want to create a new server.

❏ **S3(d) Click on Create New Express Server.**

Figure S3-3: Create New Express Server.

Just click through the next panel.

❏ **S3(e) Click Next.**

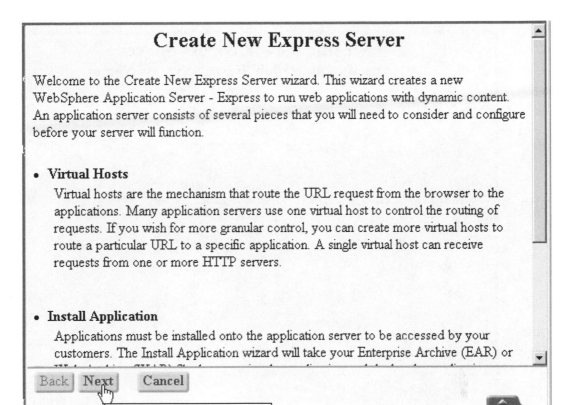

Create New Express Server

Welcome to the Create New Express Server wizard. This wizard creates a new WebSphere Application Server - Express to run web applications with dynamic content. An application server consists of several pieces that you will need to consider and configure before your server will function.

- **Virtual Hosts**

  Virtual hosts are the mechanism that route the URL request from the browser to the applications. Many application servers use one virtual host to control the routing of requests. If you wish for more granular control, you can create more virtual hosts to route a particular URL to a specific application. A single virtual host can receive requests from one or more HTTP servers.

- **Install Application**

  Applications must be installed onto the application server to be accessed by your customers. The Install Application wizard will take your Enterprise Archive (EAR) or

Back   Next   Cancel

Figure S3-4: Click Next.

Here's your first decision. You need something to distinguish your server from any others that might be added. I suggest the name WDSCSBS for *WDSC: Step by Step*.

❏ **S3(f) Enter WDSCSBS in the Application server name field and click Next.**

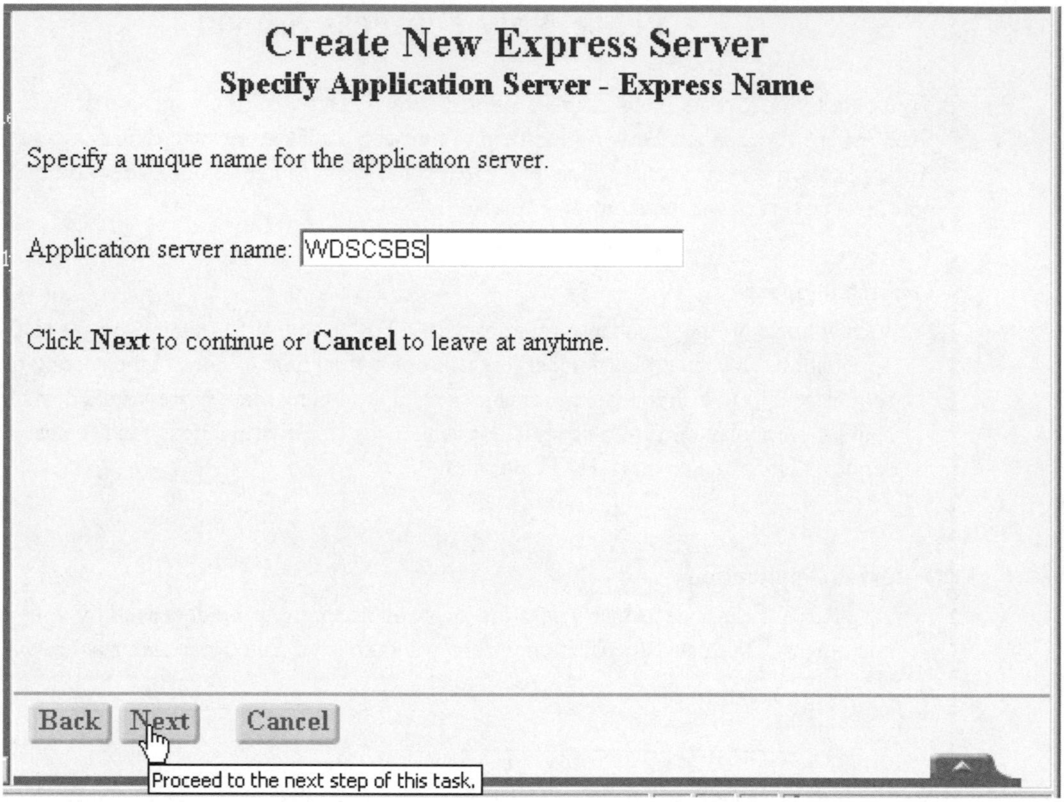

Create New Express Server
Specify Application Server - Express Name

Specify a unique name for the application server.

Application server name: WDSCSBS

Click **Next** to continue or **Cancel** to leave at anytime.

| Back | Next | Cancel |

Proceed to the next step of this task.

Figure S3-5: Enter your application server name.

Now, the system will ask which HTTP server to use. You can use an existing one or create a new one. To avoid conflicts, I suggest creating a new one with the same name as the application server.

❑ **S3(g) Select Create a new HTTP server and click Next.**

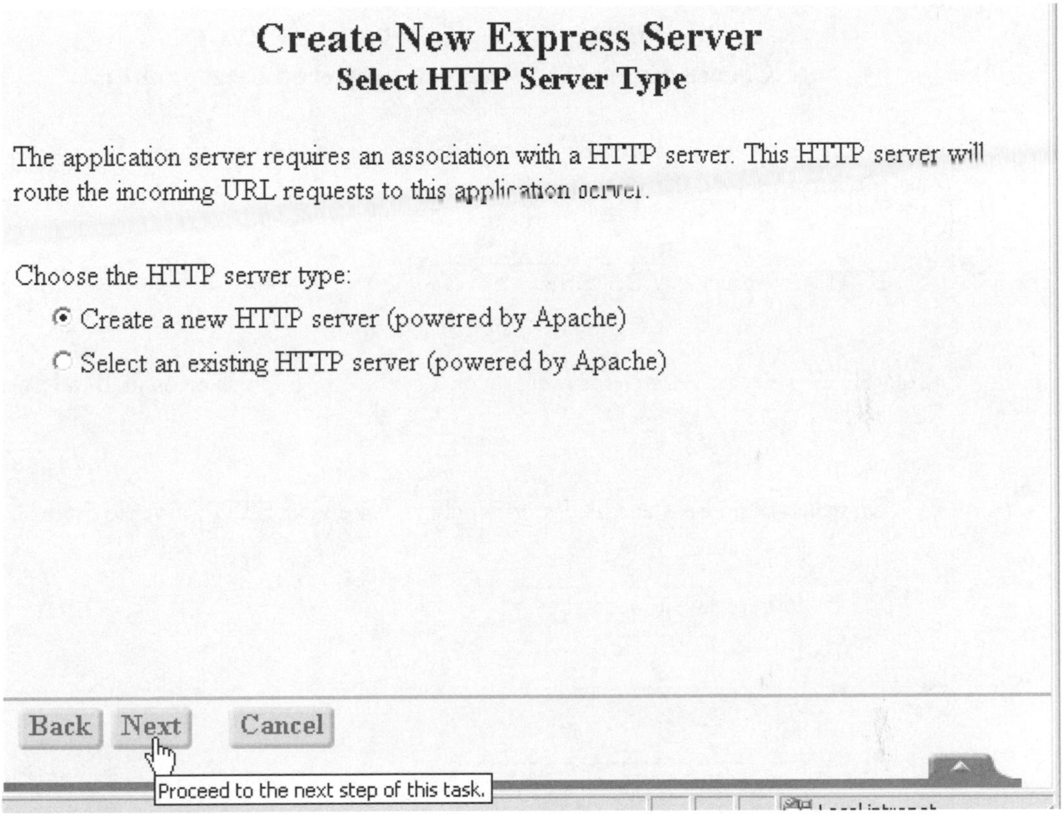

Create New Express Server
Select HTTP Server Type

The application server requires an association with a HTTP server. This HTTP server will route the incoming URL requests to this application server.

Choose the HTTP server type:

    ⊙ Create a new HTTP server (powered by Apache)

    ○ Select an existing HTTP server (powered by Apache)

Back Next   Cancel

Proceed to the next step of this task.

Figure S3-6: For testing, I suggest your own HTTP server, named the same.

The next panel contains the big decision: which IP address and ports to use. The default for the wizard is to use all IP addresses, and port 80 for the HTTP server. Typically, I use ports 3000-3011 for the Web application server. That's fine as long as nobody else is using them. I also like to use port 80 for the browser, provided nobody else is using it. The benefit of this choice is that you don't have to enter the port number on your browser; HTTP browsers default to port 80.

> **Warning:** If your iSeries is already running an HTTP server, there's a good chance it is using port 80; you should check with your system administrator to be sure you're not conflicting with existing servers.

❏ **S3(h) Leave the defaults and click Next.**

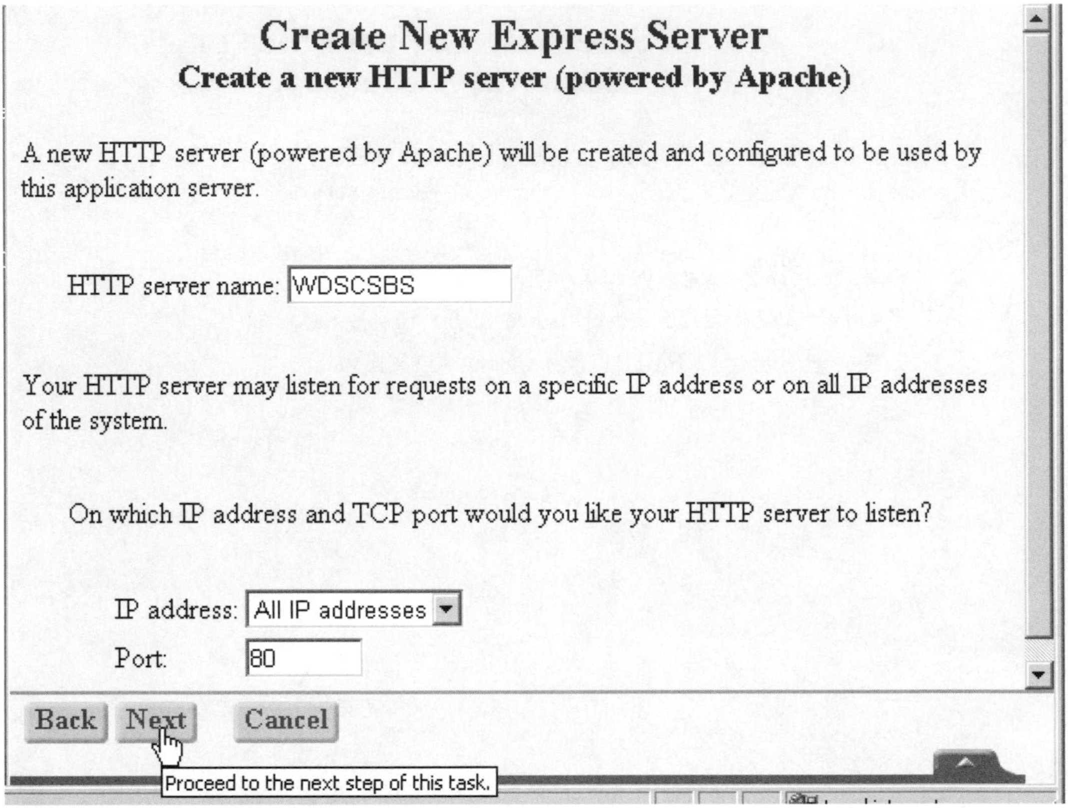

Create New Express Server
Create a new HTTP server (powered by Apache)

A new HTTP server (powered by Apache) will be created and configured to be used by this application server.

HTTP server name: WDSCSBS

Your HTTP server may listen for requests on a specific IP address or on all IP addresses of the system.

On which IP address and TCP port would you like your HTTP server to listen?

IP address: All IP addresses ▼
Port: 80

[Back] [Next] [Cancel]

Proceed to the next step of this task.

Figure S3-7: You can leave the defaults here. It will use port 80 on all IP addresses.

Next, specify the internal ports. As I noted earlier, start with 3000.

❑ **S3(i) Enter Port 3000 and press Next.**

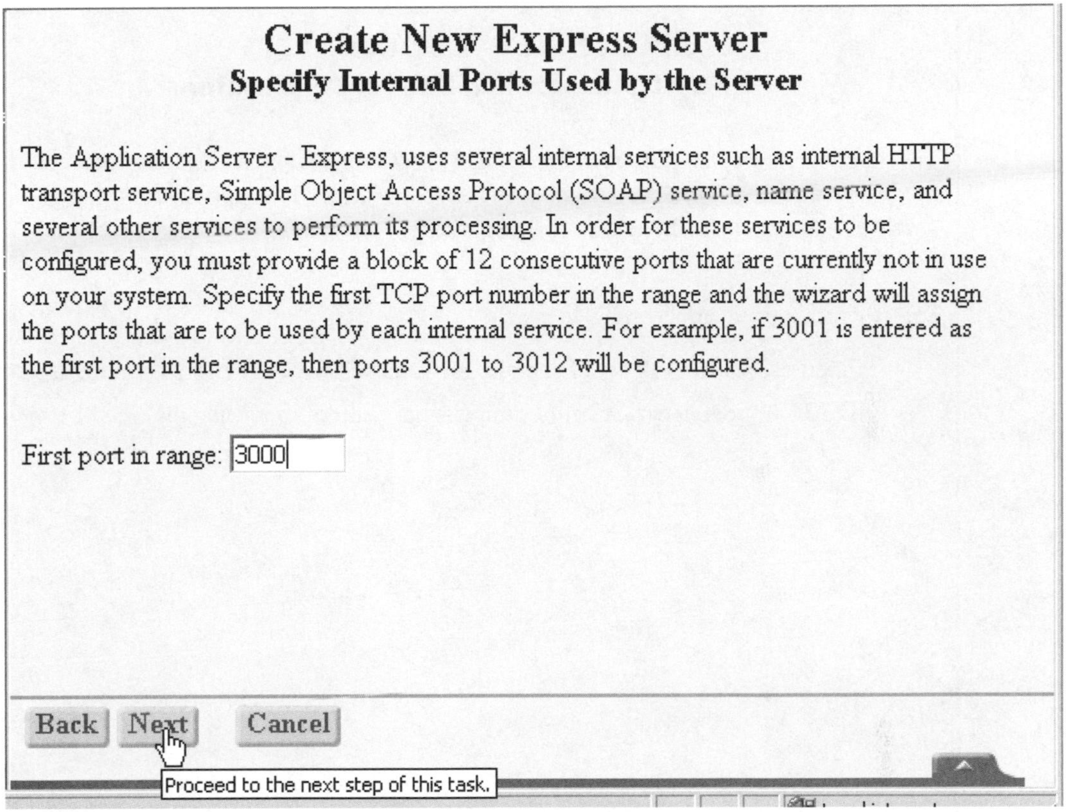

Create New Express Server
Specify Internal Ports Used by the Server

The Application Server - Express, uses several internal services such as internal HTTP transport service, Simple Object Access Protocol (SOAP) service, name service, and several other services to perform its processing. In order for these services to be configured, you must provide a block of 12 consecutive ports that are currently not in use on your system. Specify the first TCP port number in the range and the wizard will assign the ports that are to be used by each internal service. For example, if 3001 is entered as the first port in the range, then ports 3001 to 3012 will be configured.

First port in range: 3000

Back   Next   Cancel

Proceed to the next step of this task.

Figure S3-8: Select a block of unused ports for the internal use of the server.

You won't be using any samples or examples. Make sure both boxes are unchecked.

❑ **S3(j) Make sure both boxes are unchecked and click Next.**

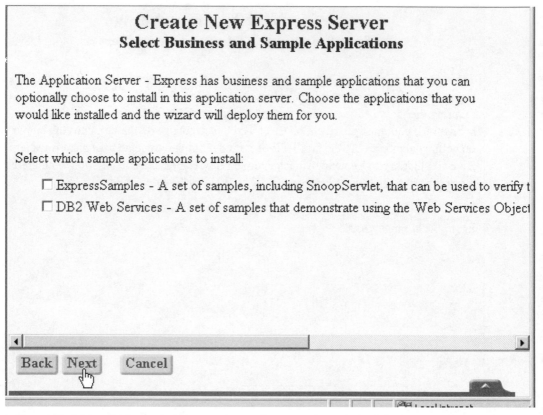

Figure S3-9: You don't need either set of samples, so make sure both boxes are unchecked.

On to the home stretch. The next panel (Figure S3-10) will recap what you've entered so far. If you're satisfied with that, click Finish.

❑ **S3(k) Click Finish.**

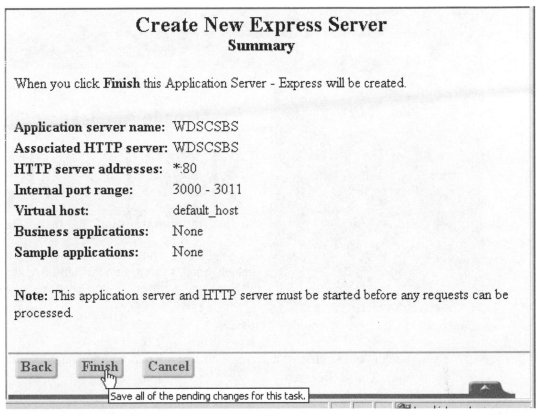

Figure S3-10: Click Finish to start the creation process.

Until the server is actually created, you'll see a page similar to the one in Figure S3-11. The bright yellow ball labeled "Creating" will be in place until the server is actually created.

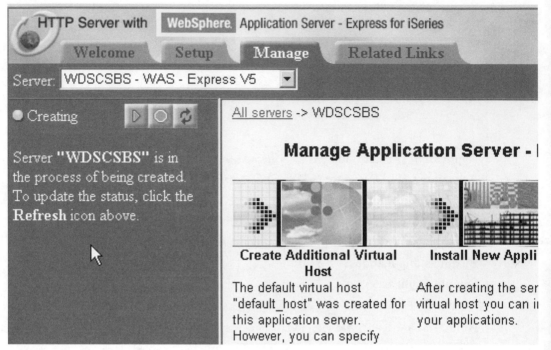

Figure S3-11: The server is now being created.

Even though you've created a server, you still have to add the actual Web application. That's SideStep 4.

SideStep 4

Install the MySite application

GOAL

Assuming you already have a working instance of WebSphere Express, this SideStep will walk you through installing the MySite application.

Note: This SideStep assumes that the EAR file has already been exported to the IFS. Specifically, it should be in a folder called \QIBM\UserData\WarsNEars. The exported file should be called MySite.EAR. In Step 17, you exported the EAR file to the hard drive (C:\temp). Sometime after that but prior to this step, you must get the EAR file to your IFS. Typically, you would do this with FTP or a mapped drive, depending on your system setup.

Release Note: This example is for V5R1 of the operating system, the first release that supported browser-based administration. Later releases are similar in the setup phase.

✓ **Here is your step checklist:**

There are two assumptions for this step:

1. You created a Web server as outlined in SideStep 3.

2. You uploaded your EAR file to /QIBM/UserData/WarsNEars/MyEAR.ear.

Note: The /QIBM/UserData folder should already exist in the IFS. You will have to create your own WarsNEars folder.

```
MKDIR DIR('/QIBM/UserData/WarsNEars')
```

The first step is to start the administration interface. Since you've mapped WDSCHOST on your PC, you should be able to access the admin server at http://WDSCHOST:2001. Next, you want to manage the WDSCSBS server (or whichever server it is you want to add the application to).

❑ **S4(a) Using the admin interface, manage WDSCSBS.**

❑ **S4(b) Hide Details as shown.**

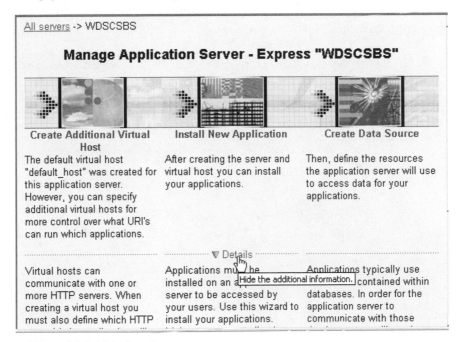

Figure S4-1: Hide Details.

❑ **S4(c) Select "Install New Application."**

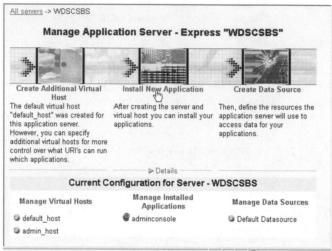

Figure S4-2: Install the new application.

The next panel will prompt you for the location of the EAR file. There is actually a nice little Browse window that you can use to explore your IFS, or you can just type in the name. Since in this case you know exactly where the EAR file is, type it in and click Next.

❑ **S4(d) Type in /QIBM/UserData/WarsNEars/MyEAR.ear and click Next.**

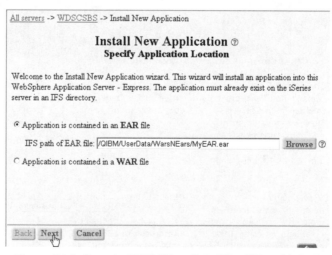

Figure S4-3: Type in /QIBM/UserData/WarsNEars/MyEAR. ear and click Next.

A deployment options screen will come up as shown in Figure S4-4. I normally take the defaults on this page, just hitting Next to go on.

❑ **S4(e) Click Next.**

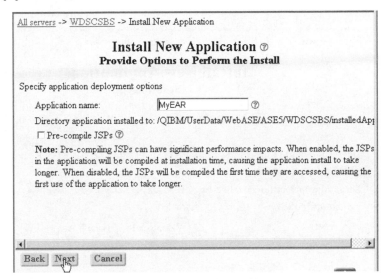

Figure S4-4: Leave the defaults and click Next.

The same for the virtual hosts page.

❑ **S4(f) Click Next again.**

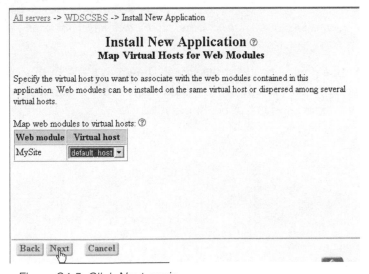

Figure S4-5: Click Next again.

The verification screen will come up as shown in Figure S4-6. Review to make sure everything looks OK, and then press Finish.

❏ **S4(g) Click Finish.**

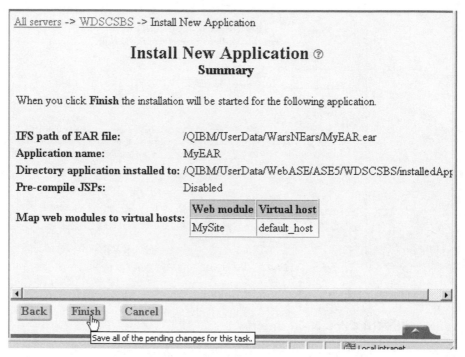

Figure S4-6: If everything looks good, press Finish to install the application.

At this point, you'll see the screen shown in S4-7. In this case, the application server is not started (which would make sense if you just created it in SideStep 3). The application is just being installed.

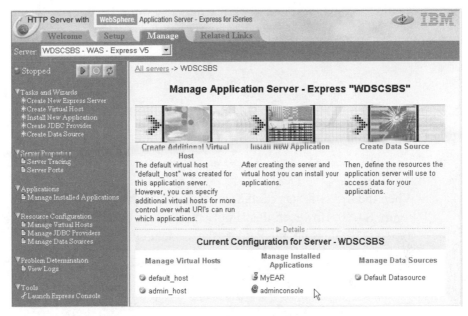

Figure S4-7: The MyEAR application is being installed.

Once the installation is complete, you can start the server, as shown in Figure S4-8.

❏ S4(h) Start the server.

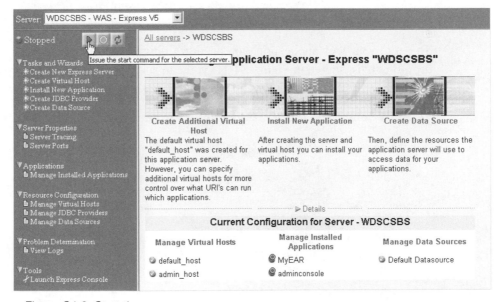

Figure S4-8: Start the server.

As the server starts, the page will look like Figure S4-9.

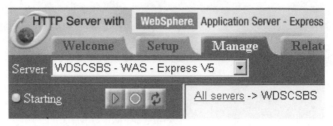

Figure S4-9: The server is starting up.

When the server is started, the screen should look like the one shown in
Figure S4-10. However, this simply means that the Web application server is
started. That does no good unless the associated HTTP server is started as well.

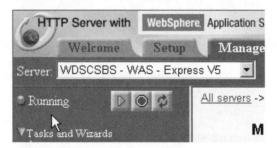

*Figure S4-10: The Web application server is
up and running, but there's no way to get to it!*

To get to your Web application, you need to fire up the HTTP server. Using the Server
drop-down list shown in Figure S4-11, you can select the WDSCSBS Apache server;
this is the HTTP server that was automatically created during this process.

❑ **S4(i) Select the WDSCSBS Apache server.**

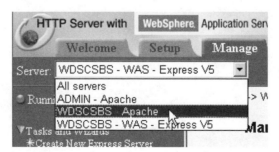

*Figure S4-11: Select the associated HTTP
server, WDSCSBS.*

You'll see that it is stopped. Start it by clicking on the Start icon as shown in Figure S4-12.

❑ **S4(j) Start the Apache server by clicking on the Start icon.**

Figure S4-12: Click on the Start icon to start the server.

Soon you'll see that the HTTP server has started (usually much more quickly than the application server), as shown in Figure S4-13.

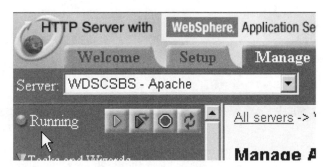

Figure S4-13: And now the HTTP sever is up and running as well.

So, based on what you've done until this point, you can now bring up a new browser and type in the following URL:

http://WDSCHOST/MySite

You'll see the screen shown in Figure S4-14.

❑ **S4(k) Start a new browser; go to http://WDSCHOST/MySite.**

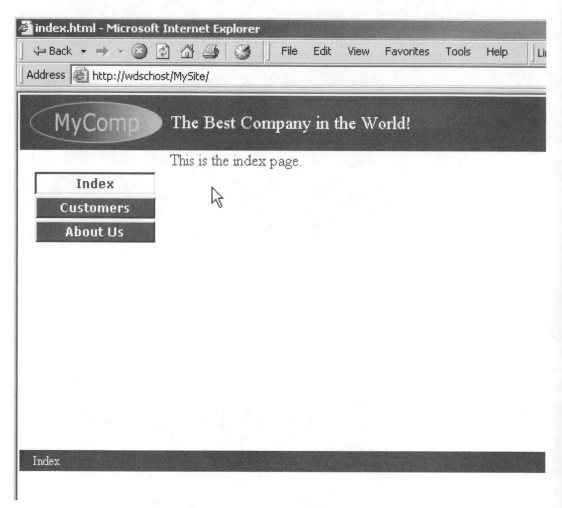

Figure S4-14: The application is served from an iSeries running WebSphere Express.

Congratulations! You have used WDSC to design, develop, and deploy a Web application to the iSeries and run it. And now that you've done one from start to finish, you should have no problem doing more.

Good luck!

SideStep 5

WDSC Version 5.1.2

GOAL

While this book was being written, a new version of WDSC was released. This step explains what I've done to incorporate the new features of that release into this book. There is no Step checklist for this step.

Version 5.1.2 of WDSC is a big release. It is so large that you cannot download the updates; you must get a separate refresh from your Business Partner. IBM has a specific Web page just for reordering WDSC:

http://www-306.ibm.com/software/awdtools/wds400/about/howToOrder.html

However, due to the fact that it was a "point/point" release (5.1.2, rather than 5.2 or even 6.0) and point/point releases typically focus on bug fixes or performance, everybody was caught off guard by the depth and breadth of changes. The good news is that most of the changes were new, advanced features: the addition of the new Enterprise Generation Language (EGL) and support for JavaServer Faces (JSF). Both of these are cutting-edge application development tools. But *WDSC: Step by Step* is an introductory text that's designed to show you how to create a simple application using the basic Web design tools available in WDSC. It doesn't cover the advanced tools (other examples include WebFacing and Struts) because these are architecture-specific; you will typically use one or the other. The techniques presented in this book are generic and apply no matter what design you choose. Because of this focus on generic techniques, the two newest features, EGL and JSF, fall outside the purview of this book.

Not everything is completely transparent to the book, however. Version 5.1.2 includes a number of changes to the user interface. Some of these changes have to do with adding new options for the new features, others revamp some of the wizards so that they're more intuitive, and still others have no immediately apparent goal but were done nonetheless. In most cases, these changes are negligible, such as adding a few new options to a menu. In those simple cases, I've simply notated the change in the text of the book. For more than 90% of the changes, you will have no problem following the text exactly.

However, in a couple of specific areas, the change to the user interface is extensive enough that I felt it necessary to provide detailed information. I considered several approaches. In talking to users, it became clear that not everyone is immediately upgrading to the new version, so people will be using both the 5.1.0.3 version and the newer 5.1.2 version for the foreseeable future. That ruled out a complete rewrite to 5.1.2. And providing alternate screen shots for every tiny difference would have pumped up the page count to an unacceptable number.

So in the end, since the vast majority of screens are nearly unchanged, I decided to provide an addendum for any differences. For example, the initial workbench has a completely new view added that is only useful when creating JSF pages. For the purposes of this book, this new view unnecessarily clutters the workbench and should be removed. Once you do that, the workbench once again looks just like the 5.1.0.3 workbench this book was built upon. The best way to handle this is to provide you with extra screenshots showing how to remedy the situation, so there is a special V5.1.2 folder on the CD-ROM. In that folder is a PDF file containing screen shots for those areas where the user interface has changed, and I've explained what steps can be taken to make the book easier to use.

One other area was significantly impacted. *WDSC: Step by Step* provides work-spaces (called Checkpoints) that allow you to start the book at nearly any point in the text. All workspaces were saved at Version 5.1.0.3 of the tool. Evidently, the changes between 5.1.0.3 and 5.1.2 are so extensive that when starting Version 5.1.2 of the workbench with a 5.1.0.3 workspace, the workspace must be completely converted—in fact, a small window pops up that says "Completing install." After this conversion, the workbench loses its place and shows a default perspective, which defeats the purpose of the Checkpoints in the first place. So I went through the book and separately saved every Checkpoint as Version 5.1.2. These Version 5.1.2 Checkpoints are also included on the CD-ROM. Unfortunately, they were too large to fit, so they've been compressed into Zip files, but there are instructions in the folder on how to use those compressed Checkpoint files.

With this approach, I managed to provide a book that works with both 5.1.0.3 and 5.1.2 without ballooning up to 900 pages. I hope you appreciate the effort, no matter which release you are on.

Index

X

Z